PREDICT
AN

M000304354

PREDICTIVE ASTROLOGY

an insight

DINESH S. MATHUR

MOTILAL BANARSIDASS PUBLISHERS
PRIVATE LIMITED ● DELHI

3rd Reprint: Delhi, 2012
First Edition: Delhi, 1999

© MOTILAL BANARSIDASS PUBLISHERS PRIVATE LIMITED
All Rights Reserved

ISBN: 978-81-208-1388-5 (Cloth)
ISBN: 978-81-208-1627-5 (Paper)

MOTILAL BANARSIDASS

41 U.A. Bungalow Road, Jawahar Nagar, Delhi 110 007
8 Mahalaxmi Chamber, 22 Bhulabhai Desai Road, Mumbai 400 026
203 Royapettah High Road, Mylapore, Chennai 600 004
236, 9th Main III Block, Jayanagar, Bangalore 560 011
Sanas Plaza, 1302 Baji Rao Road, Pune 411 002
8 Camac Street, Kolkata 700 017
Ashok Rajpath, Patna 800 004
Chowk, Varanasi 221 001

Printed in India

By Jainendra Prakash Jain At Shri Jainendra Press,
A-45 Naraina, Phase-i, New Delhi 110 028
And Published By Narendra Prakash Jain For
Motilal Banarsidass Publishers Private Limited,
Bungalow Road, Delhi 110 007

Dedicated to the memory of my parents,
Mrs. Rajrani Mathur, and
Mr. Durgesh Shanker Mathur

Preface

An attempt has been made in this work to clarify the concepts with regard to the Signs, Planets, and Houses in simple and readable language. These are the building blocks of the foundation on which an edifice of sound analytical knowledge of predictive astrology may rest. What each of these factors represents, what its characteristics are and what the postulates and rules are relating to each of them have been clearly enunciated. Further the results and effects of inter-action of these factors have also been brought out in sufficient detail. To keep the bulk of the work within limits, generally definitions and commonly known or found facts have been dispensed with. Thus, this is not a primer. It is meant for a person who, having found the subject interesting and obtained its elementary knowledge, wishes to delve deeper in it in a systematic manner.

There has been excessive emphasis on Yogas (planetary placements and combinations) in predictive astrology, so much so that, generally, the basics are lost sight of. The importance of various yogas ought not to be belittled, but astrological prediction is not mere application of yogas to the birth chart. In the present day world, when astrology has assumed a place of common interest and even a lay man likes to study the subject, to expect a modern man to learn by heart the thousands and thousands of yogas with which the astrological literature of yore is replete, is to expect too much. He is also a little bewildered as such an approach does not appeal to his rational mind.

For a sound knowledge and understanding of the subject, we

must know the fundamentals and the manner in which they can be analysed. In this book the reader is taken through the subject in a scientific manner. He will realise that there is reason in predictive astrology, and that it is not merely the product of intuitive surmisings. My effort has been to emphasise this reason and system.

In the last Chapter, the maladjustment that exists between the Vimshottari Dasa System and Gregorian calendar has been pointed out. The Dasa System has been adapted to the calendar in vogue. It obviates the possibility of timings fixed with the use of this System to fail. Suitable tables have been appended to save the reader much arithmetical labour for, to my knowledge this information is not available elsewhere in usable detail.

The strength of a planet is of foremost importance in Hindu predictive astrology. The method of calculating the shadbala (six-fold) strength of a planet is not only highly tedious but is beyond the capability of a common reader. We have, in this book, through a simple method, attempted to reach an approximation to the six-fold strength of a planet without any mathematical exercise. This has further been related to the Vinshopaka strength of the planet. These two together will give a very fair idea of the prowess of the planet to give results.

Long hours spent at the word-processor producing this book could not make my wife Lalita, and the children, Radhika and Rahul, impatient. I really marvel at their forbearance. My friends have always encouraged me to put down my thoughts on paper. This book is a result of that encouragement.

25th February, 1998   *Dinesh S. Mathur*
Bhopal

CONTENTS

has on the native, his affairs in general and his
blood relations by its placement in each house
and sign-the Sun, the Moon, Mars, Mercury,
Jupiter, Venus, and Saturn so analysed in
detail.

The description of each Node-its relationship
with other planets-its karaka qualities-matters
represented by it-its nature-Kalasarpa Yoga-
detailed rules and postulates-description of
the effect of association of each Node with
other planets-the effect of placement of each
Node in each house and sign-Rahu and Ketu
so analysed in detail.

Rules for judging various aspects of life from
houses-interpretation and use of the navansha
chart-rules for determining such owners of
houses that will cause ill health-Vipareet Raj
Yoga-general rules to determine the nature of
and strength of a house-rules for timing of an
event-the effect of the owner of a maraka
(death dealing) house on the karaka planet for
an aspect of life-matters signified by each
house-specific rules and postulates for each
house-rules for determining relationship of
the native with a relative of his-rules to determine the number and gender of children, and
pregnancies destroyed-rules for interpreting the
effect of each sign in a house-description of the
effect of each sign in a house-rules for interpreting the effect of each owner of a house in
various houses-description of the effect of each
owner of a house in various houses-First to
Sixth houses so analysed in detail.

Chapter One

SIGNS

The zodiac is divided into twelve signs, each extending over thirty degrees. They are as follows:

Sign number	Sign	Owner	Sign number	Sign	Owner
1	Aries	Mars	7	Libra	Venus
2	Taurus	Venus	8	Scorpio	Mars
3	Gemini	Mercury	9	Sagittarius	Jupiter
4	Cancer	Moon	10	Capricorn	Saturn
5	Leo	Sun	11	Aquarius	Saturn
6	Virgo	Mercury	12	Pisces	Jupiter

The signs serially represent the following:

Aries	A ram	Taurus	A bull
Gemini	A couple	Cancer	A crab
Leo	A lion	Virgo	A virgin
Libra	A pair of balances	Scorpio	A scorpion
Sagittarius	An archer	Capricorn	A crocodile
Aquarius	A waterman	Pisces	Fishes

Whenever a sign number is referred to, it means the serial number of the sign. Thus the sign number for Aries is 1, for Sagittarius 9 etc. Sign numbers are referred to below repeatedly, as many a time it is easier to remember the qualities and classification of signs by their numbers than by their names.

2.   GENDER: The odd numbered signs are male signs, even numbered are female. Thus Aries, being the first sign and odd numbered, is male; Taurus, the second and even numbered, is female etc.

3.   If the ascendant, the Moon in particular and generally most of the powerful planets are in female signs, the native will be passive, and accommodating, and will have fine qualities of the head and heart. If the ascendant, the Moon in particular and generally most of the powerful planets are in male signs in a female nativity, the woman will be manly.

4.   If the fifth house has a female sign, its owner is a female planet and the owner is placed in a female sign, the native will generally have female children. Deductions can be made for other houses like the third and the eleventh also on the same lines.

5.   QUALITY: The signs are consecutively movable, fixed and common from the first sign Aries. Thus the first sign Aries is movable (also called cardinal), the second Taurus is fixed and the third Gemini is common (also called mutable). They can be grouped according to the Quality in the following manner:

Quality	Sign numbers
Movable (or Cardinal)	1, 4, 7, 10
Fixed	2, 5, 8, 11
Common (or Mutable)	3, 6, 9, 12

These groupings are also called the Quadruplicities.

For the purposes of analysis, many a time the first half of a common sign is taken as having the characteristics of a fixed sign, and the last 15 degrees as those of a movable sign.

6. (i)   MOVABLE signs are rajasik (active, passionate, and agitated).

(ii) They are self confident, forceful, outgoing, energetic, quick, dynamic and active. The native will under their influence, will exhibit much ambition and enterprise if most of the planets are in movable signs. He will have leadership qualities, will be aggressive and assertive, and will be independent minded. He will lack in sensitivity and may ride rough shod over others, thus hurting many people on his way to the top. He may be reckless and destructive.

(iii) There will be several changes in his life, each leading to greater success and enhancement in status. The native will have the potential to rise to the highest level in his chosen field. He will have a public career. He will be a man of action.

(iv) He may over-extend his energies and exhaust himself. The head, kidneys, stomach and joints relate to this quality. The diseases run their courses quickly.

(v) When this quality is dominant in the horoscope, the native will have an independent business and do well at it. He may also be a pioneer in a field. He may take up a new and untried venture or may adopt methods which are innovative.

7. Any project that is begun when a movable sign is rising will come to its close quickly.

8. Movable signs primarily refer to the head, and gaseous state. They are the closest to Mars.

9. (i) FIXED signs are tamasik (dull and inactive).

(ii) They are the opposite of the movable signs. They are sedentary, stable, neutral and stationary. They accumulate and build up. If majority of the planets are in these signs, the native will be lazy, inactive, miserly, dogmatic, conservative, and not given to enterprise and change. He will be patient, prefer status quo and will not be responsive to new ideas and trends. He will however be capable of serious and deep research. He will have good memory. He will be firm, stubborn and not open to others' points of view. He will have unwavering faith in himself, will be self reliant and autocratic. He will prefer solitude, and may be insensitive and self centred.

(iii) The native will have good stamina. The diseases will be chronic and will generally relate to the heart, spine, lungs and the generative system.

(iv) The native will earn through accumulated wealth, banking, investments and influence.

(v) He will serve the government, a well established institution or a firm. He may be a medical practitioner.

10. The fixed signs primarily relate to the organ heart, solid states and can be said to correspond to Saturn closely.

11. If it is desired that one should stay in a house or at a post for long, the occupation of the house or taking over of the charge of the post should be done when a fixed sign is rising.

12. (i) COMMON signs are sattvik (pure, serene and harmonious).

(ii) If the majority of planets are in common signs, the native will be versatile, flexible, dreamy, easily discouraged, indecisive, restless, sometimes superficial and cunning, and fickle. He will lead a mental life and will be introverted. He will be intellectually inclined and will have preference for studying various subjects due to overweening curiosity in his nature. He will have a philosophical mind and will be intuitive. He may not be worldly. He will not have the ability to be self reliant but he will genuinely be emotional and sentiments exhibited by him will have the ring of truth. His efforts, many a time, will not be recognised and rewarded. He may not seize an opportunity that comes his way. Though methodical, he will not be thorough. He will be unreliable but sympathetic and though he will be meritorious, he may not achieve fame. He will be a likable person. He would prefer a subordinate position.

(iii) He will be physically agile and active but will lack stamina. Common signs relate to lungs, bowels and extremities. The native will suffer from nervous disorders and will be prone to allergies. The diseases can become chronic owing to indifference shown by the native towards their treatment.

(iv) The native will do well in a subordinate position or when he works for somebody. He may also join a uniformed service, work in places where public commodities are handled and be a speaker, teacher, editor or a traveller.

(v) Venus in a common sign is likely to give more than one wife.

13. These signs are the closest to Mercury and liquefied state.

14. If planets are evenly distributed in signs of the three qualities, it indicates that the personality is not tilted in favour of any one particular trait. However it will have pulls in different directions.

15. ELEMENTS: The signs consecutively represent the elements fire, earth, air and water from the first. Thus Aries represents fire, Taurus earth, Gemini air and Cancer water; again, Leo represents fire, Virgo earth etc. Signs can be grouped according to the elements in the following manner:

Element	*Sign numbers*
Fire	1, 5, 9
Earth	2, 6, 10
Air	3, 7, 11
Water	4, 8, 12

Each group above is called a Triplicity. Reference may also be made to the opening remarks in the Chapter on Planets.

The signs can also be classified purely on the basis of water content in them. Thus Cancer, Capricorn and Pisces have full water content; Taurus, Sagittarius and Aquarius have half water content; Aries, Libra and Scorpio have quarter water content; and Gemini, Leo and Virgo have no water content.

Thus from the above two categorisations we can say that Cancer and Pisces are purely and fully watery.

16. That element will generally be predominant in a personality which has the most number of planets in it, or the most powerful planets are placed in that element in a horoscope.

17. (i) The FIERY element is separating in nature.

(ii) It is courageous, energetic and active. It is assertive, enthusiastic and independent. It is dynamic, proud and enterprising. It is a leader. It is argumentative and self confident. It is mentally sharp and quick. It is impatient of others and headstrong. It is the lower mind, unlike the Airy which is the higher one.

(iii) It is prone to fevers, inflammation and short duration acute disorders.

(iv) It is intellectually inclined to the study of engineering, and chooses professions that involve dealing with metals, electricity or fire. Thus hazardous jobs or jobs dealing with fire in the process of production, soldiers, uniformed services, mechanics, engineers, smiths, etc. come within its purview. Planets in these signs tend to give more of their results.

(v) The Fiery element corresponds to the mental body and the intellect.

18. (i) The EARTHY element represents aggregation. It is stable.

(ii) It is involved with the material and the physical world. Wealth, power, status and position are attractive to this element. It is careful, thrifty, systematic, scientific, reserved, suspicious, practical, obstinate, slow, and tenacious.

(iii) It is partial to surgeons, trading, business, mining, agriculture, gardening, timber and grain trade, restaurants, supply of edible goods and cloth, construction jobs, and jobs involving much time and effort.

(iv) Welfare of the physical body and physical culture are within its field. It suffers from chronic and rheumatic disorders.

(v) The Earthy element corresponds to the physical body.

19. (i) The AIRY element represents harmony.

(ii) It has lower vitality but a very high mental vigour. It is humane, refined, well behaved, sympathetic, and gentle. It is artistic, imaginative, cultured and balanced. It is cheerful and interested in music and arts. It is inquisitive and tactful. It does not force but convinces. It is well informed and a reader.

(iii) Under its influence the physical body will be plump and the complexion clear. There will be over-exertion leading to exhaustion and nervous breakdown.

(iv) Scientists, mathematicians, reporters, artists, literary personalities, accountants, lawyers, teachers etc. come within its purview. The job must involve use of the brain rather than the brawn.

(v) The Airy element corresponds to reason, the superconscious and the higher nature of man.

20. (i) The WATERY element relates to the psychic.

(ii) It is timid, accommodative, receptive and inactive. It is sentimental, contemplative, intuitive, mediumistic, impressionable and sensitive. It is changeable. It is interested in the occult. It is introverted and shy.

(iii) The constitution will be weak and resistance to disease will be limited. Anaemia, tumours, cancerous growths, digestive disorders, diseases in the upper respiratory tract and gastro-urinary systems relate to this element.

(iv) All jobs that relate to or involve dealing with liquids and changes fall within the purview of this element. Occupations that deal with emotions (drama, theatre etc.), fine fabrics and chemicals also fall within the ambit of this element.

(v) The Watery element corresponds to feelings and the emotional personality.

21. DIRECTIONS: The signs represent directions in the following manner:

Direction	Sign number
East	1, 5, 9
South	2, 6, 10
West	3, 7, 11
North	4, 8, 12

It will thus be noticed that each triplicity defined above corresponds to a particular direction.

These are as follows:

(a) Fire-East

(b) Earth-South

(c) Air-West

(d) Water-North.

22. If a sign is strong and located in the ninth or eleventh house, it will indicate fortune or gain for the native from the direction indicated by the sign. If the sign is weak, any undertaking by the native in that direction will only cause losses and trouble to him. Similarly, if a journey is to be undertaken, if the ascendant has a sign at the time of journey that indicates the direction in which the native wishes to travel and the sign is powerful, or if a beneficial Moon is in such a sign, the journey will be productive of desired results.

23. CLASSIFICATIONS of signs :

(i)   Animal-Common signs.
        Mineral-Movable signs.
        Vegetable-Fixed signs.

(ii)   Bestial- 1, 2, 5, first half of 9 and 10. These signs are strong in the tenth house.

(iii)   Blind (at midnight)- 1, 2 and 5.
        Blind (at midday)- 3, 4, and 6.

(iv)   Class- (a) Priestly 4, 8, 12
                (b) Warrior 1, 5, 9
                (c) Trading 2, 6, 10
                (d) Serving 3, 7, 11

(v)   Deaf (in the forenoon)- 7 and 8.
        Deaf (in the afternoon)- 9 and 10.

(vi)   Diurnal (strong during the day)- 5 , 6 , 7 , 8 , 11 and 12.
        Nocturnal (strong during the night)-1, 2, 3, 4, 9, and 10.

(vii)   Double (multiplicity)-3, 9 (since it is half human and half horse) and 12 (two fishes together).

(viii) Dry- 1, 5, 7, and 9.
        Dependent on water- 2, 3, 6, and 11.
        Watery- 4, 8, 10, and 12.

(ix)   Fruitful- 2, 4, 7, 8, 9, 10, 11 and 12.

Sterile (barren)- 1, 3, 5, and 6.

(x) Human- 3, 6, 7, last half of 9 and 11. These signs are strong in the first house and during the day.

(xi) Length-Short- 1, 2, 11, 12
Medium- 3, 4, 9, 10
Long- 5, 6, 7, 8

(xii) Mute- 4, 8, and 12.

(xiii) Reptile (crawling)- 4, 8, second half of 10 and 12. These signs are strong in the seventh house.

(xiv) Rising-Head first- 3, 5, 6, 7, 8, and 11. These are beneficial signs, and, beneficial planets when placed in they become more beneficial. Planets placed in these signs give their results early in their major, sub, or inter-periods.
Back first- 1, 2, 4, 9 and 10. These signs make malefic planets worse if they are located in them. Planets placed in these signs give their results towards the end of their major, sub, or inter-periods.
Both ways-12. It has the characteristics of both the above. Planets in this sign will give their results in the middle of their major, sub, or inter-periods.

(xv) Violent- 1, 8 and 10.

(xvi) Vocal- 3, 7 and 11. All the airy signs are vocal signs.

24. Depending upon the house, the sign in there will indicate the class of person the native will gain from, get inimical to, etc. For example if the sixth house has Virgo the native is likely to have enemies in the trading class {paragraph 23/(iv)(c) above}.

25. Fruitful signs in the fifth and eleventh houses, and the owners of the fifth and eleventh houses also in fruitful signs, indicate that the native will have children. Sterile signs in the first, fifth and the eleventh houses indicate that the native will be childless.

26. If the relevant house (for eyesight the second or twelfth; for hearing the third or eleventh) has the sign which is blind or deaf, as the case may be, at any given time in the day, and the house also has malefic influence, the native will suffer from the concerned disability.

27. Depending upon whether a planet denoting gain is situated in an animal, mineral or vegetable sign, the gain will be of, or from the material or person indicated by the sign.

28. If a house has a short sign and the owner of the house is also in a short sign, the part of the body indicated by that house will be small.

29. Mercury in a mute sign afflicted by Saturn will cause stammering. Saturn in the first house in a mute sign causes defective speech. Mars so placed will cause indistinct speech. Ketu in a mute sign in the second house will cause defective speech or even dumbness.

30. Unafflicted Mercury or Venus in a vocal sign in the second house will make the native eloquent or musically gifted. Jupiter or Mars so placed, will make the native a powerful demagogue.

31. If the native does not have most of his planets in human signs, he will not be social and humane.

ARIES

(i) This sign is described as a ram which is combative, obstinate, impulsive, hardy, active and lascivious. It is rajasik in nature.

(ii) (a) For physical and mental characteristics of a sign a reference may usefully be made to the details given for each sign in the first house in Chapter Four.

(b) When the diseases and professions related to a sign are enumerated, it generally does not mean that a person having a particular sign in the ascendant will suffer from some of those diseases or will pursue one or few of those professions. It more particularly means that if that sign is in the sixth house the native will be susceptible to the diseases or troubles that the sign in the sixth house indicates, or if the sign is placed in the tenth house, the native is likely to pursue that profession. To make the point clearer let us take Aries in the first house. The native in this case is likely to suffer from diseases that Aries indicates, but he is likely to also suffer from such diseases that Virgo indicates since that is the sign that tenants the sixth house. The native is likely to again not only take to a profession that Aries points to, but also to a profession that is indicated by Capricorn which will be in the tenth house.

(iii) A person under its influence will be ambitious, courageous, inventive, confident, impatient, ready to face a challenge and active. He will keep an eye on an opening and make use of it but basically he will be an open person. He will have a quick temper, and will be aggressive. He will have an independent personality and will be restless for a change. He will be a leader and a good organiser. He will be perceptive, blunt, sensuous, argumentative, and self-opinionated. The urge to forge ahead of others, do well in life materially and be famous will be so strong that the native will be unscrupulous. He will however not concentrate on one thing at a time. He is likely to be involved in impractical schemes and escapades. There is a distinct lack of discretion. He may not be religious. He will like to have friends and company. The native will have inventive, and scientific abilities. He can excel at research and development of innovative concepts.

(iv) The native will lose money owing to indiscreet and ill thought out investments and schemes.

(v) The female of this sign will be proud of her ancestry and family. She will be jealous, and intolerant of inattention. She will be house proud and will like to keep a neat and hospitable establishment. The native will prefer a beautiful, intelligent and good spouse. He will love his family and be proud of it.

(vi) The native will be physically energetic. He will be of medium stature with a ruddy complexion, long neck and face that tapers to the chin. He will be resistant to disease and will have good health. He will be prone to get injured and involved in accidents. He will be fond of short duration sports. More details relating to the physical characteristics of the sign can be found in paragraph 38 under FIRST HOUSE in Chapter Four.

(vii) This sign represents the head, bones of skull and the forehead except the bone of the nose. Between 13 degrees 20 minutes to the end of the sign it also has a bearing on the eyes and vision. Likely diseases are of the head, severe pains, high fevers, small pox and similar inflammatory eruptions, ulcers, sun stroke, burns, indigestion, inflammations and wounds.

(viii) If the owner of the second, sixth or the tenth house is in this sign in the nativity or navansha chart, or if this sign happens to fall in one of these houses and Mars is powerful in the chart, the vocations preferred by the native will be those where dealing with metals, fire, poisons or danger and risks are involved. The jobs indicated by this sign also involve quick and skilled movements. Thus uniformed forces, surgeons, butchers, dentists, wrestlers, boxers, armourers, cooks, thieves, tailors, carpenters, chemists, dealers in sports goods, factory workers, etc. are indicated.

(ix) Mines, hills and undulating grounds, plateaux, unfrequented spots and hide-outs of thieves, ceiling, and sheep fold are the places that relate to this sign.

(x) (a) A drekkan is defined in paragraph 27 (iii) of the Chapter on Planets. When the first drekkan is rising in the ascendant, the influence of the owner of the sign will be unalloyed and the sign will manifest itself in its purest form; which is how it is recorded in the paragraphs above. How far the drekkans are going to alter and amend this picture, is recorded for each sign in paragraph (x) subparagraphs (b) (c), and (d) on each sign.

(b) When the first drekkan is rising in the ascendant, the first, fifth and the ninth houses will be to the fore, i.e., the affairs of these three houses will be prominent in the life of the native, and location of Mars in any of these houses will be conducive to much fame and wealth. The native may gain through marriage, industry or property. The 18th, 28th and 36th years of life will be important.

(c) If the second drekkan is rising, the strength and

position of the Sun and the fifth house should be taken into account as the honour of the native will depend on it. If the Sun is powerful and the fifth house is strong the affairs governed by the fifth house will prosper and will be clearly visible in the native's life. The native will be more emotional. The 20th, 24th, 29th, and 36th years of life will be important.

(d) If the third drekkan is rising in the ascendant, the Martian influence will be mellowed by that of Jupiter and the ninth house will be to the fore. The native will not be so impulsive etc. A strong Jupiter and the ninth house will make the native religious and elements of higher nature will be evident in him. A weak Jupiter can make the native rebellious, go against the established authority and get involved in litigation. He will be lucky in financial matters but may suffer losses caused by enemies. The 31st, 34th, 36th, 42nd and 45th years will be important.

TAURUS

(i) This sign is described as a bull that is determined, energetic, tenacious, and fierce. This is an intuitive sign.

(ii) Please refer to paragraph (ii) under ARIES above for an important clarification.

(iii) The native will be even tempered but once the ire is roused it will be terrible and difficult to control. He will not forgive easily. The native will be convinced that in all circumstances he is correct. He will be persevering, strong willed, cheerful, productive, kind, patient, charming and fond of finer arts and luxuries. He will be liked by his kinsmen and colleagues. He will also be passionate, jealous, straightforward, conservative and possessive. He will have certain prejudices and will have strong likes and dislikes. He can communicate well and will easily mix with people of different backgrounds. He will be keen on amassing wealth and will be well off but many a time will also be wasteful. He will be a person who has an eye and memory for details, and therefore, will be precise and a good planner. He will be very careful in his speech and behaviour. He can be lethargic, comfort loving and may have a vast appetite for good food, preferably sweet. He will think over an issue long before deciding a line of action, but once a decision is taken and an objective has been set, he will work single minded for achieving it.

(iv)   He will have speculative and gambling tendencies.

(v)   The native will be a steady and faithful partner in all situations. He will like to have a good home. He will prefer to stay at his place of birth. The female of the sign will like to be hospitable and lavish in her entertainments. She will expect a similar treatment in return and if not so treated, will be offended. She will appear to be reserved. She will look after the house carefully. She will also be a dutiful mother. The native will take time in deciding to get married but will be devoted, attentive and protective to the spouse. He will prefer an attractive wife. The native will appear to be a strict parent but that will only be for the good of the children in the long run.

(vi)   The native will be of medium build, broad shouldered, stocky, muscular with thick neck, bright eyes, dark hair and a clear and fair complexion. The female will be beautiful, and buxom. More details relating to the physical characteristics of the sign can be found in paragraph 38 under FIRST HOUSE in Chapter Four.

(vii) This sign relates to the face, nose, throat, mouth, teeth, neck and eyes (especially till the first 23 degrees 20 minutes of the sign). Over-indulgence can be a cause for ill health. The native will have tremendous capacity to bear pain and physical distress silently. He will recover from disease slowly and will have a tendency to contract chronic diseases. Diseases of the throat, eye, teeth, etc. are commonly indicated. The native may be wounded by animals.

(viii) Agriculture, horticulture, real estate, share market, trading in luxury goods, institutions for women, fine arts, banks and financial institutions, taxation, animal husbandry, automobiles, plying of vehicles commercially, etc. are the areas of work. He will like to work with his hands.

(ix)   Cattle shed, village, threshing ground, grazing ground on the edge of the forest, and cellars relate to this sign.

(x)   (a) If the first drekkan is rising, the sixth and the tenth houses will be to the fore. He will be very extravagant, will suffer losses due to litigation and may end up in heavy debt. The 31st, 42nd and 51st years of life will be important.

(b) When the second drekkan is rising, Mercury will merge its influence with that of Venus. It will give the native more intuition and will also make him more practical in business and day to day life. He will be interested in matters pertaining to disease and nursing, hygiene and physical body. The sixth house will be to the fore. He may also be more critical of others, self centred and possessive. He will have the ability to appreciate art and will have musical talent. The tendency to spend heavily will not be visible and the native will be able to accumulate wealth. The 17th, 21st, 24th, 33rd and 50th years of life will be important.

(c) The third drekkan, when rising will make Saturn another factor to influence the native along with Venus. It makes him very cautious, industrious and conventional. The native will have more of intellect and reason and less of intuition. A powerful Saturn will raise the native to a high position. He will hold responsible positions and will attain to fame and recognition. The tenth house will be to the fore. He will be a poor manager of his wealth. He will either lose it or waste it. The native may, at the close of his life, be in penury. The 42nd, 51st and 57th years of life will be important.

(d) Attention is invited to paragraph (x)(a) under ARIES where analysis of a house being to the fore is given at some length.

GEMINI

(i)   This sign is described as a couple; the woman is holding a harp, the man a mace. The key words are duality or multiplicity, intellect and education.

(ii)   Please refer to paragraph (ii) under ARIES above for an important clarification.

(iii) This is an intellectual sign. The native will be engaged in reading, writing and correspondence. It rules the mind and communication. This sign has the rare ability to understand people and correctly divine their innermost hidden thoughts. The native will be talkative. He does not mind starting an argument or debate for its own sake. The native will be intelligent, quick witted, and adaptable, but he is not suited to command and manage. Decision taking is not easy for him. He will have mechanical ability. He will be interested in several things at the same time, and will therefore dissipate his attention and mental energy. He will find it difficult to concentrate. Since he looks for success or at least progress in a manner satisfactory to him, he gets discouraged easily if the progress is not according to his expectation. The native will be hasty, cheerful and desirous of travel and change. His personality will be a mix of contradictory traits, and because of this it is difficult to understand a Geminian. If the mind is turned inwards, the native has the ability to progress far in the spiritual field.

(iv)   The native will have ups and downs in his finances. He is likely to have a side business or occupation too. If the sign or Mercury has adverse influence, the native is likely to have tendency to mishandle or misappropriate money.

(v)   The native will change his residence several times. He will like his house to be well appointed and will entertain frequently. He will have friends and it will be easy for him to make friends. He may not be totally happy with his friends and may also break his friendship with some. He will like a spouse who is intelligent, likes travelling and change, and appreciates his intellectual bent of mind. He will find it difficult to tolerate a nagging and overbearing wife. The female of the sign will not be a mere housewife. The native will love his children dearly and the sentiment will be reciprocated by them. Many a time he will be like a friend to them.

(vi) The native will be tall or at least above average height with long arms, light complexion and of slim build. Mercury represents a complexion that is light with a shade of grass green. More details relating to the physical characteristics of the sign can be found in paragraph 38 under FIRST HOUSE in Chapter Four.

(vii) This sign relates to arms, shoulders, larynx, vocal chord, ears, and upper respiratory tract. He will worry easily and will be of nervous temperament. Inflammation and catarrh in the upper respiratory tract, nervous break-down due to worry or excessive mental exertion, and troubles in the shoulder or arm are indicated. The native may also suffer from severe colic.

(viii) Jobs that are intellectual in nature, require quick thinking, eloquence and convincing others, are scientific, require knowledge of state of art or latest developments in the concerned field are covered by this sign. Offices that have come in existence recently, or involve reading or writing will be close to native's heart. Thus diplomats, salesmen, brokers, computer experts, journalists, mathematicians, railwaymen, travellers, authors, teachers etc. are produced by this sign. A powerful Mercury will ensure that the native will have talent for mathematics or astrology. The native may not have public recognition but will have a place in intellectual circles of the field in which he is working.

(ix) Schools, places of learning, debating halls, clubs, gambling dens, bedrooms, indoors, etc. are represented by this sign.

(x) (a) If the first drekkan is rising, the third house will be of importance. The finances of the native will fluctuate. He will gain or lose mostly through women. His financial status will improve only after he has crossed the age of thirty. The 16th, 23rd and 30th years of life will be important.

(b) The second drekkan is ruled by Venus. If this drekkan is rising, the native will not only appreciate art but will also have real artistic ability. He may also be musically inclined. There will be a fine mix of the head and the heart. The seventh house will be to the fore. Partnership, if any, will be life long and very productive. The native is fit for business. The restlessness characteristic of Gemini will be reduced and the tenor of life will be more peaceful. The 29th, 32nd, and 45th years of life will be important.

(c) The third drekkan is ruled by Saturn along with Mercury. The native will have a powerful influence of a guardian or friends. The eleventh house will be to the fore. He will have success in public life if Saturn is unafflicted and powerful. The native will have the ability to concentrate his mind and apply it to deeper studies. The native will stand to lose if he invests in speculation or gets involved in litigation, most probably around the age of 45 years. The 33rd, 35th, 41st, 47th, 60th and 62nd years of life will be important.

(d) Attention is invited to paragraph (x)(a) under ARIES where analysis of a house being to the fore is given at some length.

CANCER

(i) This sign is described as a crab. This is a demagogic sign. It is satwik in nature.

(ii) Please refer to paragraph (ii) under ARIES above for an important clarification.

(iii) The native will see numerous ups and downs in his life. He will be imaginative, emotional, sensitive and romantic. He will be sociable, moody, adaptable, introverted, impressionable and talkative. He may be impatient, sympathetic and nervous. He cannot be forced into something. He may be indolent sometimes. In a situation where an attempt is made to force him into something, he resists and does not yield. He will gain by moving and carrying the public with him but at the same time will value his privacy. He will be courageous in moral and mental matters and timid in physical. His temper will be changeable and the anger will come and go. He will like appreciation and kindness but cannot bear neglect or being ignored. He will have the ability to work hard and will be exacting. He will have psychic ability. Many a time he will miss the available opportunity since he will think over the matter but not act. He will be loyal and appreciate this quality in others. He will be a determined person insofar as achieving a goal set by him for himself is concerned. He will, in his later years, hark back to his early years of trial and tribulations. He will be interested in things of the past, in history and in antiquities. He will have a good memory.

(iv) He will be honest, intolerant of dishonesty and careful with his money. He will not spend on ostentation nor make a show of his wealth. His income will be in small amounts at a time, never in large sums. In some cases the native may find it difficult to acquire wealth. It may be lost through children, love affairs, speculation, relatives or pleasurable pursuits. The second part of life will be more prominent and important than the first.

(v) He will be fond of his family, comforts and home. He may even have his place of work at home. The female of this sign will be discreet and independent. She will be true in her love and devotion to her husband. She is easily satisfied and will be a good mother. The native will be very hospitable, and affectionate towards his relatives. He will like to marry a person who will look after the home well and further his prosperity. The native will look after his children well and provide them with comforts, education and facilities to the best of his ability. He will be a good parent. The children will also respect and love him.

(vi) The native will have a short build with a round face and fair or pale-red complexion. The constitution will not be strong, especially in childhood. He will be slim. The upper part of the body will be larger than the lower. The abdomen may grow in proportions as the age advances. This sign is conducive to the birth of a dwarf. More details relating to the physical characteristics of the sign can be found in paragraph 38 under FIRST HOUSE in Chapter Four.

(vii) This sign rules the breasts, chest, ribs, respiratory system and lungs and ailments relating to these parts of the body. The native is likely to get injured, face violent attacks by his enemies and animals and may suffer falls. The native will suffer due to his worrying nature. He may have brain disorder. He will also disturb his system by over-indulgence in drinks.

(viii) He will be a dealer in water produces or watery goods. He may also deal with liquids (water, alcohol, milk, soft drinks etc.). He may have a sea faring job. He can also be a preacher or a public figure or deal with history and related subjects. The female of the sign can work in nursing or management side of hospitals.

(ix) Water bodies, canals, rivers, washing places, dairies, liquor shops, sewers etc. relate to this sign.

(x) (a) If the first drekkan is rising, the fourth, the eighth and the twelfth houses will be to the fore. The native will not be able to handle his money and will lose it through relatives, children, affairs of the heart or speculation. The 49th and 52nd years of life will be important.

(b) The second drekkan of the sign is ruled by Mars alongwith the Moon. The native will have control over his feelings but will be more ambitious, have will to power, will be determined, and will be proud. The eighth house will be to the fore. He will have his feelings hurt or offended leading to sorrow. He will contract some diseases. He will develop a keen interest in the occult. His transactions will be more in secret than in the open. He may be subjected to blackmail. The 34th, 44th, 53rd and 60th years of life will be important.

(c) If the third drekkan is rising, the influence of Jupiter will work with that of the Moon. The twelfth house will be to the fore. The native will be extraordinarily hospitable and sympathetic. He will all the time strive for acquisition of knowledge and will to some extent be intuitive. Depending upon the strength and condition of the Moon, the native may be very sensitive, obsessive, and worrying sort and even imbalanced (if the Moon is afflicted and weak) or intellectually sound and kind (if the Moon is strong and free from adverse influence). The native will have some contact with hospitals or asylums and may even have to live in them through ill health or other circumstances beyond his control. The close of life may be spent in dire circumstances. The 33rd, 36th, 45th and 48th years of life will be important.

(d) Attention is invited to paragraph (x)(a) under ARIES where analysis of a house being to the fore is given at some length.

LEO

(i) This sign is described as a lion. The key words are predominance and the self. It is satwik in nature.

(ii) Please refer to paragraph (ii) under ARIES above for an important clarification.

(iii) The native will be noble, dignified, energetic, forgiving, generous, tolerant and helpful. He will rely on his acquaintances and will inspire confidence and respect among his colleagues and subordinates. He will be proud, reserved and wise. He will have a big ego and will like being praised but will genuinely be a great organiser. He will be a brilliant leader who would revel in pomp. He will be interested in sports, pleasurable pursuits, his children and speculation. He is determined in the face of difficulties and is generally firm in his views. He has faith in his abilities. He is frank and just. He hates pettiness to which he does not stoop down even in the worst of situations. Though he is generous, he hates people who importunate for favours. There is a tendency to pay little attention to views of others and be impatient with them. He may be hasty. Thrift is not his hallmark.

(iv) The native will by nature be at the head of an enterprise. He would be interested in policy decisions, leaving the day to day running of the organisation to his subordinates. The native will come about wealth and power in the first half of his life, in fact, declining in power and prosperity as the age advances.

(v)   He will expect his family members to be obedient to him and accede to his wishes. He will be hurt if his family members show low mindedness in their lives. He will look after their honour well. He will go to any extent to keep the good name of the family aloft. He will be hospitable and the standard of entertainment and living will be, many a time well above his financial status. He will be romantic, sensuous and devoted but will not be demonstrative of his feelings in public. He will be attractive to the opposite sex. He will expect his partner to be obedient, hospitable, large hearted and understanding. The female of this sign will manage the house well, will be self sacrificing but will expect that everybody accepts what she says. The native will have a few children. He will love his children and will be proud of them. However the children will resent restrictions and may try to be independent of filial control at an early age.

(vi) The native will be a large person, with big bones and well built broad shoulders. The head will also be big and round and the forehead broad. The complexion will be ruddy or fair. The personality will be imposing. More details relating to the physical characteristics of the sign can be found in paragraph 38 under FIRST HOUSE in Chapter Four.

(vii) The heart, spine, back, bones, spleen, and stomach relate to this sign. The constitution will be strong and the native generally does not fall ill. Though recovery from illnesses is rapid, the native will be very anxious of his health and well being when he falls ill. Usually the illnesses that beset the native will be of the parts described above. Fever is another ailment that is connected to this sign. The native may be severely wounded by wild animals.

(viii) The native may join a high service in government which offers security of service and fixed income, or he may take up scientific pursuit. He may head large commercial or other organisations. He may earn through entertainment, sport, medicine or speculation. He will like to be self employed and will not like subordination.

(ix)   Hills, caves, dense forests, deserts, palaces, forts, govern-
       ment buildings, offices of top functionaries or managers,
       place of meditation or yoga practice etc. are indicated by
       this sign.

(x)   (a) If the first drekkan is rising, the fifth house will be
          to the fore. The condition and strength of the Sun will
          also be of utmost importance. The native will do well
          to take to business or trading in cloth or commodities,
          for he is likely to face serious ups and downs in
          service. The 21st, 26th, 31st and 33rd years of life will
          be important.

      (b) In the second drekkan, the influence of the Sun is
          tempered by Jupiter. The native may go to the extremes
          and may not tolerate any kind of authority imposed
          on him, if the Sun is not in a good condition. The will
          may not be as strong as in the first drekkan. The
          native may be more philosophical and demonstrative.
          A good Sun will alleviate these characteristics, giving
          a more positive development. A weak Jupiter will
          make the native arrogant and pompous. The ninth
          house will be to the fore. The native is likely to
          undertake long journeys and may develop power to
          foretell. He is likely to come about wealth through
          investments after the age of 50 years. The 31st, 36th,
          45th, and 53rd years of life will be important.

      (c) If the third drekkan rises, the influence of Mars will
          also be visible and the first house will be to the fore.
          The head and the heart will join together making the
          native not only more determined and impulsive but
          he will also be more self centred and ruthless. He is
          likely to do well in shipping or contracts. The 20th,
          25th and 30th years of life will be important.

      (d) Attention is invited to paragraph (x)(a) under ARIES
          where analysis of a house being to the fore is given
          at some length.

VIRGO

(i)   This sign is described as a young virgin in a boat holding ears of grain and fire. The key words are change and intellect. The nature is tamasik.

(ii) Please refer to paragraph (ii) under ARIES above for an important clarification.

(iii) The native will be shy, self-conscious and always desiring change. He will be very conscientious and able to face heavy odds. He will be methodical, practical, orderly, sensible and thorough. He will be an intellectual, especially interested in languages, science, medicine, cleanliness, nursing and nutrition. He can speak well. His knowledge is oriented to practical application. He will deal with matters in hand quickly but will be very dilatory in his speech, to the extent of going into irrelevant descriptive details. He will be reserved, critical of others, usually misunderstood and will have a fault finding tendency. He will continue to moan over his fate, feel insecure and will indulge in self pity. He may not have self confidence and ability to apply himself steadily. He may sometimes find it difficult to take decisions . If Mercury is weak, he will have a defeatist outlook.

(iv) The native will be thrifty, excessively careful and prudent. He will have an urge to amass wealth. He will be poorly remunerated for his efforts and his investments will yield inadequate returns. The financial status will be fluctuating.

(v) The native will keep changing residences and his surroundings. He will be choosy with regard to his friends and will keep changing them. He will also be choosy with regard to the person with whom he will get married. This will delay marriage. He will insist upon an intelligent spouse. However he will look after his family well. The female of the sign will like her house to be orderly. She will be thrifty. She may avoid sex.

(vi) The native will look younger than his years. He will be on the taller side in his build with ruddy or dark complexion. He will worry over his health and will be impatient to get well when ill. Digestive, nervous and excretory systems relate to this sign. The diseases are difficult to cure and will be chronic. He can also suffer from overexertion. More details relating to the physical characteristics of the sign can be found in paragraph 38 under FIRST HOUSE in Chapter Four.

(vii) The native will be athletic and like physical exercise. The native will be shy of opposite sex in the early years but later will develop a more than average sexual appetite though it will be carefully kept hidden. It represents intestines, waist, kidneys, abdomen, and bowels. Hypochondria and nervous disturbance of bowels are common. The native is likely to contract diseases related to the parts indicated by this sign. He may be injured due to a fall.

(viii) He can be a good doctor if the Sun aspects, or is associated with, the owner of the second, sixth or the tenth house in this sign. He can also be a good teacher, craftsman, artist, linguist, actor, chemist, mathematician, accountant, author etc. He will be good at jobs that involve detailed work.

(ix) Land with ears of grain, granaries, store room, place of artisans, etc. relate to this sign.

(x) (a) When the first drekkan is rising the sixth house will be to the fore. It will be common for the native to suffer losses, especially in his early life and he cannot gain in speculation. The 18th, 24th and 30th years of life will be important.

(b) The second drekkan when rising will modify the characteristics of the sign as the influence of Saturn will mingle with that of Mercury. The native will be very practical, persevering and fit for major business ventures. He will be wealthy but miserly. The transit of Jupiter through the third, sixth and the eleventh houses from the ascendant will be of importance with regard to his finances. He will excel in political or demagogic field and may have some responsibility or honour conferred on him. He will exhibit artistic or musical inclination. The tenth house will be to the fore. However Saturn should not afflict Mercury as it will make the native very unfortunate. The 36th, 42nd, and 49th years of life will be important.

(c) When the third drekkan is rising, the native will be successful in his ventures and wealthy as alongwith Mercury, Venus will also be operating. The native will be successful financially, more in his early career than later in life. He will have a tendency to gamble and speculate and he may squander his money away in this manner. The native will however be very firm minded. The native may turn out to be a good artist. If Venus conjoins Mercury the native will come about a lot of wealth and prosperity. The second house will be to the fore. The 32nd, 35th, 40th and 44th years of life will be important.

(d) Attention is invited to paragraph (x)(a) under ARIES where analysis of a house being to the fore is given at some length.

LIBRA

(i)   This sign is described as a man holding a pair of scales in his hand. The key words for this sign are balance and harmony. It is rajasik in nature.

(ii)   Please refer to paragraph (ii) under ARIES above for an important clarification.

(iii) The native will be level headed, gentle, popular, refined with good taste, sympathetic, peaceable, and modest. He will be imaginative, warm, impressionable, amiable and intuitive. He can control his mind and concentrate effectively. He will not lose his temper for long. He will like comforts and will enjoy luxuries of life. He will be interested in fine arts. He will not be decisive but his judgement will be correct. The native will not be selfish and will be ready to forego his benefit for the welfare of others. Being the seventh sign from Aries, Libra is in many ways opposite of it. Taurus is also seventh from Scorpio. Thus the two signs of Venus are opposed to the signs owned by Mars. Thus Mars and Venus are the greatest enemies.

(iv)   The native will get along well with his partner and business in partnership will suit him. He is likely to be extravagant and charitable.

(v) He will be close to his family and enjoy being with his wife and children. He will like female company. He will be a good conversationalist. He will like his home to be elegantly furnished and neat. He will be a steady friend and enjoy being with friends. He will be socially a success. He will like a wife who would live according to his tastes but in case this does not work out, he will try to adjust and will not think of divorce or dissatisfaction.

(vi) The native will be tall, proportionately built and good looking. He will be slender with a good complexion and dark hair. He will have a round face with regular features. He is prone to baldness in middle years of his life. The female of the sign will be beautiful and attractive. More details relating to the physical characteristics of the sign can be found in paragraph 38 under FIRST HOUSE in Chapter Four.

(vii) The part of human body below the navel upto the genitals relates to this sign. This sign also is responsible for a good skin. The native is prone to suffer from disturbances in these parts of the body.

(viii) The native will be engaged in teaching, fine arts, diplomacy, arbitration, therapy, consultancy, marketing etc.

(ix) Shops in the town where luxury and valuable goods are sold, outhouses and sides of hills are represented by this sign.

(x) (a) The first drekkan when rising makes the seventh house very important in the nativity. Marriage or partnership will play a crucial role in the life of the native. The native will be successful in a political, legal or business career. The 24th, 31st, 33rd and 40th years of life will be important.

      (b) If the second drekkan is rising the influence of Venus will be modified by that of Saturn. The native will be more sympathetic, social and intuitive. He will be much under influence of his friends. The eleventh house will be to the fore. The native will not hesitate to adopt unscrupulous methods to earn wealth and may have to face charges of misappropriation of money. If the third house and Mercury are powerful

he can be a successful writer. The 36th, 42nd, 44th
and 51st years of life will be important.

(c) If the third drekkan rises the native will have to
struggle in life and make a place for himself in society
by his own efforts. He will take a keen interest in
intellectual matters and travelling, from which he
may gain. The influence of Mercury will join that of
Venus and the third house will be to the fore. The
career best suited for the native will be fine arts,
teaching, catering or hoteliering. The early years of
his career will be lack lustre. Later he will have
sudden gains and promotions. The 18th, 23rd, 25th,
27th, and 32nd years of life will be important.

(d) Attention is invited to paragraph (x)(a) under ARIES
where analysis of a house being to the fore is given
at some length.

SCORPIO

(i)   This sign is described as a scorpion. The key words are
head and not the heart, hard and sustained work, extremism and sensuality.

(ii)   Please refer to paragraph (ii) under ARIES above for an
important clarification.

(iii)   The native will be determined, self confident, exacting,
direct, hard working, assertive and willing to accept
challenges. He will set high goals and standards for himself
which he will set about attaining tirelessly. He will be
intense, introverted, intelligent, intuitive, independent and
imaginative. He will have the ability to express emotions
powerfully and thus can be a successful debater, orator,
artist or a poet. He may sometimes show keen interest in
the occult, and in nature and its mysteries. He may have
the tendency to procrastinate due to his overconfidence
in his abilities. He will revel in excitement and recklessness.
He can be highly sensual and may be involved in intrigues
and enmity with women. He may also overindulge in
alcoholic stimulants as a relaxant after hard work and
may get addicted to it in the process. He will not be
garrulous but talk only when required and to the point.

He respects the privacy of others as he loves his own. He may be rude in his speech, irritable and may be critical of others. He will be secretive and will not divulge his thoughts, emotions and strength. He will be well informed and clever. At times he will be unforgiving. He can be a firebrand and may work against the tranquility and order of society. In the extreme he can be brutish, lacking feelings, deceitful, violent and bloodthirsty.

(iv) He will have good business acumen, and executive ability and be successful in trading. He will be lucky in money matters and will gain in speculation. He will earn well but will be extravagant. The native may be dishonest in his business dealings.

(v)   The native will expect total obedience from his family. He will like to have all the comforts and pleasures of life. He will enjoy life. He is a good friend but a bad and relentless enemy. He will not have long standing friendships as he will expect a lot from his friends. However the friends will be in powerful and influential positions. The native will expect love and approbation from the spouse and even a small critical observation from the spouse will put him off. The native will have a good wife unless the second, seventh or the eleventh house receives adverse influence. The native will have a big family.

(vi) The native will be of medium height with a firm, muscular and stocky body. He will be robust and physically powerful. The face will be broad, hair curly and the complexion swarthy. He will like outdoor sports. More details relating to the physical characteristics of the sign can be found in paragraph 38 under FIRST HOUSE in Chapter Four.

(vii) The scrotum, rectum, and the anus relate to this sign. The native may disturb or ruin his health by his own excesses. He will have unusual vitality and recuperative powers. Diseases of the reproductive and eliminatory systems relate to this sign.

(viii) He can be a good chemist, physician, surgeon or a dentist. He can also do well at jobs that involve hard and detailed work, research or investigation, use of cutting instruments, or machines mainly used for processing different liquids.

(ix) Ruins, dilapidated buildings, old wells and crevices and drainage system of old dwelling places where reptiles and insects breed, moist places, abattoirs, operation theatres, cremation grounds, lavatories, muddy spots, chemical laboratories etc. refer to this sign.

(x) (a) If the first drekkan of the sign is rising the eighth house will be to the fore and the influence of Mars will be unadulterated. The native has the potential to earn substantial wealth through business enterprises. He will have fascination for stocks and shares but will not be successful at speculation. He will have to face enmity at a sizable scale leading to massive litigation. The 14th, 22nd and 23rd years of life will be important.

(b) If the second drekkan is rising the influence of Mars will be tempered with that of Jupiter and the twelfth house will be to the fore. The bad qualities of Scorpio will predominate and the native will not be fortunate, unless Jupiter is powerful in the chart. He will be troubled by enemies especially by female enemies. He will face some very dangerous situations in life and will have to bear loss and sorrow. He will be closely linked with hospitals etc. and may be ailing throughout his life. He may also be confined or his liberty severely restricted. The role of Jupiter for this drekkan is of importance. If Jupiter is powerful the evil indications may be mitigated. In such a case the native will have intense spiritual or philosophic development and may have psychic experiences. The 24th, 29th, 31st, 36th and 42nd years of life will be important.

(c) If the third drekkan rises, the influence of the Moon will also have to be taken into account and the fourth house will be to the fore. A powerful Moon will make the native inclined to be emotional and keen on attachments. Therefore to an extent the selfish and brutish side of the sign will be mellowed. The native will be given to study and practice of the occult, magic or the bizarre. If the Moon and the fourth house are weak, the native will have a difficult time with his mother and senior female members of his family. The 41st, 44th, 49th and 52nd years of life will be important.

(d) Attention is invited to paragraph (x)(a) under ARIES where analysis of a house being to the fore is given at some length.

SAGITTARIUS

(i) The sign is described as a centaur-half man and half horse-carrying a drawn bow with an arrow on it in his hands pointed at the sky. Optimism, truth, justice and high principles are the key words. It is satwik in nature.

(ii) Please refer to paragraph (ii) under ARIES above for an important clarification.

(iii) The native will be frank, sometimes to the verge of tactlessness, bold and ambitious. He will have an optimistic view of life, and will face adversity with courage. He will not be deterred from acting by the fact that sometimes his acts will be unpopular. He will take his decisions after carefully weighing the various aspects of an issue. This will sometimes delay action that is to be taken. He may be lethargic in his efforts. He will be broad minded, independent, generous and methodical. He will be interested in acquiring knowledge and may go in for higher studies especially in law, philosophy or religion. He will like change and going on long journeys. His sense of justice will be of a high order. He will prefer company of foreigners and like living abroad. He will be religious and God-fearing. He will be changeable in his opinions and will harbour suspicions in his mind. He can have a tendency to exaggerate matters, be self righteous and conventional and talk indiscreetly. He may not keep his word. The sign being dual, the native will generally exhibit both aspects of a characteristic.

(iv) He will be lucky and will not have to work hard for

achievements. He will gain from father and family. Speculation will not be paying for him.

(v)   He will like pets, company of the opposite sex and friends
      who will be life long ones. He is likely to marry a
      'foreigner. He may attend parties regularly and may
      indulge in rich food and liquor to excess. He will like
      outdoors and nature. There may be a tendency to avoid
      close relatives. He may spend more time in social circles
      than at home leading to the neglect of the family. The
      female of the sign will be a dutiful wife and accommo-
      dating in nature.

(vi) The native will generally be on the taller side, well formed
      and good looking. He will have a high forehead, clear eyes
      and a frank expression. The hair will be light in colour.
      He will have a ruddy complexion. More details relating
      to the physical characteristics of the sign can be found in
      paragraph 38 under FIRST HOUSE in Chapter Four.

(vii) The hips, thighs and parts of body located in that region
      are represented by this sign. The diseases indicated by
      this sign are the disorders of nerves located in this region,
      rheumatism, troubles in the hips, thighs, and spinal parts
      lying here. The native may also face troubles due to his
      tendency to overindulge in food and drink. The native
      will suffer injuries from projectiles, trees or wood. He will
      also face danger from water.

(viii) The native can be a teacher, physician, preacher, or a
      pleader and can successfully do research.

(ix) This sign relates to the stables, top most storey of a house,
      magazine, court, college, and a temple.

(x)   (a) The ninth house is to the fore when the first drekkan
          of the sign is rising. The native will not be successful
          in partnership. He will have more than one source of
          income. The 32nd, 37th, 38th, 46th and 55th years of
          life will be important.

      (b) If the second drekkan is rising, the effect of Jupiter
          will be diluted by that of Mars and the first house will
          be to the fore. The native will be obstinate and
          impulsive and will squander his energies in going to

the extremes which he may regret later. He will be liable to accidents, and brain and nervous disorders. He may keep changing his vocation. There will be several ups and downs if in service. The 20th, 29th, and 39th years of life will be important.

(c) If the drekkan rising is the third one, the influence of Jupiter will manifest alongwith that of the Sun and the fifth house will be to the fore. The native will be very intuitive and will have the ability to look into the future and foretell. He will be demonstratively affectionate but is likely to have several love affairs. The native should be careful in speculation if the Sun is weak. He may be a physician. The native will be prosperous and will gain by marriage. He is likely to get legacies suddenly which later in time are likely to cause trouble for him. A well placed and strong Jupiter will avert bad results. The 17th, 26th, 29th, 35th and 38th years of life will be important.

(d) Attention is invited to paragraph (x)(a) under ARIES where analysis of a house being to the fore is given at some length.

CAPRICORN

(i) This sign is described as a goat in western astrology and in the Indian tradition it is taken to be a crocodile with the face and neck of a deer. Hard work, practicality and prudence are the key words. It is a tamasik sign.

(ii) Please refer to paragraph (ii) under ARIES above for an important clarification.

(iii) The native will be reasonable, persevering, confident, business like, patient, down to earth, thrifty and prudent. He will be disciplined, hard working, will see any job that he takes up to its logical conclusion and a good planner and organiser. He will be a trust worthy leader. He will have an urge to do well in the world. He will be conservative, consolidating, reserved, self reliant, careful in approach and speech. He will be polite but not naive. He will like fine arts and entertainment. He can develop a selfish trait, pessimism and may have a tendency to over exert himself. He can also be ruthless and calculating. He will have inclination for science, technology and mathematics.

(iv)   He can do well at speculation but due to his careful and thrifty nature the Capricornian will keep away from such investments where chance plays a major role. He will be careful with his money.

(v)   He will not prefer to marry early or have a large family. He will love his family but will not display his emotions. The family may labour under a false notion that the native is cold towards them. He will like his privacy and will prefer domestic quietitude. He will work quietly for the welfare and well being of his children. The female of the sign may dominate and run the household like a clock work. He will have a large circle of acquaintances but he will not befriend anybody in a hurry. He will be a loyal friend. He will have an eye for items of artistic or aesthetic value.

(vi)   The native will be small in build and slender with a long and thin face and sunken eyes. The complexion will be pale. He will look weak and emaciated. The build will be poor and the native may be a hunch-back if there are other supportive signs. The constitution will improve with age. More details relating to the physical characteristics of the sign can be found in paragraph 38 under FIRST HOUSE in Chapter Four.

(vii) This sign relates to the knees and skin. The sign produces diseases of the knees, knee caps, skin and allergic manifestations on the skin. The native may also have troubles arising out of over work and nervous disorders. Colic and nervous break downs are also indicated by this sign.

(viii) The sign produces successful businessmen, agriculturists, horticulturists, scientists, chemists, divers, and indicates professions for which firmness, sagacity, steadiness and application are needed.

(ix)   Mortuaries, graves, secluded spots, safe vaults, dungeons, watery places, forests and grasslands are indicated by this sign.

(x) (a) If the first drekkan is rising the tenth house will be to the fore. The native will earn well on his own merit and also through speculation. The 40th, 45th, and 50th years of life will be important.

(b) The second drekkan when rising will show mixed results of Saturn and Venus. The second house will be to the fore. The native will not be very ambitious. He will be very hard working and persistent in his effort. He will also be more conservative. The urge to amass wealth and property will be stronger. The 35th, 42nd, 45th and 50th years of life will be important.

(c) The third drekkan when rising brings the sixth house to the fore and the influence of Mercury will also be present alongwith that of Saturn. The native will not be sure of himself and will not be self reliant. He will be better educated and a better member of the society than natives born in the other two drekkans. He will however not do so well in life. He will be adaptable. The health is likely to suffer due to worry. He is likely to lose through his friends. He will have to face disappointments in life. Success will come to him after his 40th year. The 36th, 41st, 46th, 49th and 55th years of life will be important.

(d) Attention is invited to paragraph (x)(a) under ARIES where analysis of a house being to the fore is given at some length.

AQUARIUS

(i) This sign is described as a man carrying a water pot on his shoulder. The key words are community, humanitarianism, freedom and independence of thought. It is a tamasik sign.

(ii) Please refer to paragraph (ii) under ARIES above for an important clarification.

(iii) The native will be intelligent and observant, have a good memory, have the ability to be a good judge of men, and will form his judgement after deliberation. He will be sympathetic, supporter of the oppressed, outspoken and of a broad outlook. He will have new and independent ideas and will be receptive to such ideas. He will be scientific in his thinking. He will be a man of principles and persevering. He will be inventive and will have the capacity to do detailed and in depth studies. He is a man of strong likes and dislikes. He will be social and involved in group activities. He will bring about harmony but will fight against injustice. He will boldly be prepared to go against the established ways of behaviour or accepted norms of society, if he feels that in doing so he is morally in the right, though it may be legally incorrect. Many a time due to his spirit of rebellion and independence, he associates with such people or espouses such causes which he has been advised to avoid. He is not after honour. He is very firm in his views though he is prepared to correct himself if he is convinced that he is in the wrong. He practises what he preaches. The personality does not have any charisma, therefore the native may not succeed as a political leader. His will be a powerful personality in the religious field if he so chooses. His attitude will be dignified.

(iv)   The native will earn money through his innovative thinking. He will not hanker after wealth though he realises its importance in life and therefore will not shun it.

(v)   The native will entertain and be entertained frequently. He will be cheerful and lively in company. He will have a number of good and steady friends. The native will be a loyal friend and will be helpful to his acquaintances. He will prefer an educated and intelligent spouse. He will not express his love and feelings. The female of the sign will like a tidy house and will prefer to have the most modern household gadgets. She will however not hesitate to separate from her husband or partner if he does not measure upto her expectations. The native will treat his children more as equals and friends and therefore will be loved by them.

(vi)   The stature will be middle, and the build stocky and powerful. The complexion will be brown and the face long. Teeth may be defective. He will be good looking. The female of the sign will be beautiful. More details relating to the physical characteristics of the sign can be found in paragraph 38 under FIRST HOUSE in Chapter Four.

(vii) This sign relates to the shins, calves, and ankles. This sign causes susceptibility to colds, and infections. The native may suffer from coughs and fever. Troubles are caused in the parts of body enumerated and due to over-exertion. Rheumatism and arthritis are also indicated with advancing years.

(viii) The native will join a profession that involves contact with a large number of people and working in groups. This could mean social service, working with a group of researchers, heading pressure groups or even advertising. The native can succeed at dealing with land and property, civil appointments, and at creative arts like painting, clay modelling, sculpture etc.

(ix) Caves, ledges, rivulets flowing through undulating terrain, grounds containing springs, recently excavated trenches, places for storage of water or pots relate to this sign.

(x) (a) If the first drekkan is rising in the ascendant, the eleventh house will be to the fore. The native will always be well off provided Jupiter is powerful. The 35th, 46th and 57th years of life will be important.

(b) If the second drekkan is rising in the ascendant, the influence of Mercury will be superimposed on that of Saturn and the third house will be to the fore. A powerful Mercury will ensure that the native will take interest in intellectual pursuits and will be involved in literary work. His work may also bring him in close contact with people who are active in the fields of journalism, writing, etc. The native may himself travel a lot in connection with his work. Otherwise the native will be active in the field of business. He may succeed at speculation to some extent. The 26th, 27th, 37th, 38th, and 51st years of life will be important.

(c) When the third drekkan rises in the ascendant, the native will be under the influence of Venus alongwith that of Saturn. The seventh house will be to the fore. The quality and characteristics of the sign will be improved and refined. There will be a clear inclination towards the mystical side of life. Though love or marriage will be prominent in the life of the native he will prefer to remain a celibate. The native will prosper in partnership and his mother may have plenty of immovable property. The native will face financial stringency in his early life. He will do well in real estate business. The 33rd, 40th, 44th, 49th and 53rd years of life will be important.

(d) Attention is invited to paragraph (x)(a) under ARIES where analysis of a house being to the fore is given at some length.

PISCES

(i)   This sign is described as two fishes, each has its mouth touching the tail of the other. Impressionability, impracticality and sentimentality are the key words. It is of satwik nature.

(ii) Please refer to paragraph (ii) under ARIES above for an important clarification.

(iii) The native will be romantic, imaginative, idealistic, restless and philosophical. He will be sympathetic, generous, compassionate, helpful and humane. He will love animal life. Thrift will not be his strong point. He will be polite, tolerant, timid, accommodating and forgiving. He will be indolent and ease loving. He will lack in self confidence and will not be able to judge men correctly. He cannot assert himself. He finds it difficult to take decisions quickly. There will be certain lack of clarity in thinking and expression. He will not like to hurt anybody. There will be contradictions in his nature and sometimes he will be misunderstood and misused. He may be worried, gloomy or moody at times. The native will be sociable and friendly. He can get along with a large variety of persons. He may be impractical and a visionary. He will be emotional and impressionable. He will keep changing his opinions and thoughts and will modify his views according to the liking of others. He may be suspicious of others. Detailed and rigorous work is outside the capability of a Piscean. He will be interested in the spiritual and mystical sides of life and will if other factors assist, attain emancipation from the cycle of birth and death. He will always be keen on going abroad and if circumstances permit, will settle there. He may have musical talent and will prefer to have ceremonious demonstration of emotions or faith.

(iv) The native will be very generous or will be persuaded to lend money in good faith. The income will many a time fall short of expenditure. He would like to put his money in steady and paying investments so that he remains financially independent in his old age.

(v) The native will look for company so that he could give vent to his woes or indulge in expression of self pity drawing sympathetic reaction from his audience. He will like his wife to be beautiful, accomplished and well educated. He will ensure good education for his children. He will love his family and will like a tranquil domestic life. He cannot bear petty mindedness on the part of his wife or children. The native will have a weakness for the opposite sex and may be sensual. There may be moral degradation. He will be a loyal and kind friend.

(vi) The native will be short and of thick build. The complexion will be pale and dull and the eyes will have a dreamy and sleepy look. His feet will be large and the constitution will be poor and sickly. More details relating to the physical characteristics of the sign can be found in paragraph 38 under FIRST HOUSE in Chapter Four.

(vii) This sign rules the feet and toes. The diseases will therefore relate to these parts of the body or due to retention of fluids in the body. He may face danger from water. The native will be liable to take to drugs or intoxicants, or he may overeat as a reaction to his psychological inadequacies.

(viii) The native will be indecisive as to which profession he should adopt. He may either have more than one job at the same time or may have some hobbies to be pursued

in his spare time and earn through them. He will prefer
a job where his helpful nature, interest in fine arts and
compassion can come into play. So jobs in a hospital,
asylum, as a therapist, teacher, or social worker will suit
him admirably. He may also take to water related or
water based jobs. His sensitivity will make him well liked
among his subordinates. He will certainly not like to take
orders and the best arrangement will be where he can
have a capable partner to look after the management of
the company.

(ix) Fishery, water body, oil field, hospital, asylum, sanatori-
um, and monastery relate to this sign.

(x) (a) The twelfth house will be to the fore if the first
drekkan is rising in the ascendant. The native will
have number of opportunities to earn wealth. He will
have a tendency to become more and more careful
with money as he advances in age. He can be a
successful physician. He will also do well at speculation. The 24th, 29th, 34th, 38th, 41st and 49th years
of life will be important.

(b) The fourth house will be to the fore and the influence
of the Moon will combine with that of Jupiter if the
second drekkan is rising. The native will become
more compassionate, sensitive and eager to help. It
will make the native more ambitious and useful and
may awaken the latent urge to power in him. However domestic felicity will be lacking. His mother will
play an important role in his life. The native will also
be highly susceptible to charm of the opposite sex
and may get entangled in avoidable complications.
He will have an insatiable appetite for wealth. The
43rd, 47th, and 55th years of life will be important.

(c) The rising of the third drekkan in the ascendant will
signify that the native bears the influence of Mars
with that of Jupiter, and that the eighth house will be
to the fore. The native will be jealous, and material-
istic. He will be worrying, reckless, hard hearted and
unsympathetic. He will face several deaths in his life
time and face sorrow time and again. The native is

likely to suffer loss from thefts. There is a possibility of success in speculation and also at public life. The 25th, 27th, 28th, 32nd and 37th years of life will be important.

(d) Attention is invited to paragraph (x) (a) under ARIES.

Chapter Two

<u>PLANETS</u>

A planet gives the results in its periods, i. e, major, sub or inter-period, of the houses to which it is related in many ways. Planets get related to the houses by ownership, aspect, occupation, etc. The planets also give results relating to their significations. The nature of a planet and that of the period will determine the nature of the results. The strength of the planet will determine the quantum of the result that the planet may give. It has been mentioned in classical literature that when a planet that is expected to give favourable results is devoid of strength, the results take place only in dream. It is not only important to study the signification that a planet stands for, but also its relationship with other planets, its strength and the method to assess it, its nature and the way to determine it, its dignity, etc. The physical description and general characteristics of each planet too ought to be clearly understood. The planets, signs and houses are very closely related, and the art of successful prediction depends upon correct interpretation of planets in signs and houses.

2. The influences received by the Moon and ascendant, in the birth chart and navansha chart, the characteristics displayed by the most powerful planets in the chart etc. determine the person-ality of the native. If a planet strongly influences factors repre-senting any part of the body, or a faculty of the mind, it moulds

that part or the faculty according to the characteristics that it stands for. If such a planet is adverse for that horoscope, it may even cause the native to display traits which are just the reverse of good qualities that the planet represented.

3. We list all the planets (including Rahu, but not Ketu) according to their longitudes in signs, degrees, minutes and seconds in a nativity. For Rahu, the distance covered by it from the end of the sign in which it is placed should be taken into account. Thus, in the illustration below we should deduct the longitude of Rahu from 30 degrees before finalising the karakas. We ignore the signs. If the degrees are the same for two planets, minutes are taken into account. In the rare case when the minutes are also the same, we take seconds into consideration. The planet with maximum degrees (or as clarified above, with more minutes or seconds) in any sign is called the Atmakaraka. It is the significator of the self. The planet next to it in degrees is the Amatyakaraka which is the significator of the mind and also of the person to whom we are the closest. Next in order come the Bhratrikaraka-significator of brothers, the Matrukaraka-significator of mother, the Pitrukaraka-significator of father, the Putrakaraka-significator of children, the Jnatikaraka-significator of relatives, and the Strikaraka-significator of wife. It is obvious that for each horoscope the karakas determined in this manner will be different. We call these the chart specific karakas.

We will take an illustration to explain the method for determining these karakas. Let the longitudes of the planets in a chart be as follows:

Planet	Longitude			
	Signs	*Deg*	*Min*	*Seconds*
Sun	10	2	34	21
Moon	4	23	21	6
Mars	6	3	7	47
Mercury	10	3	6	6
Jupiter	8	19	27	5
Venus	9	26	44	9
Saturn	7	23	21	10
Rahu	4	13	12	8

Note: The longitude of Rahu (having ignored the signs) should be deducted from 30 degrees when we start determining the karakas. Thus the degrees, minutes and seconds for Rahu, in the above illustration, that are to be taken into account shall be 16, 47 and 52 respectively.

Ignoring the signs, we notice that Venus has the maximum number of degrees in a sign. So, Venus is the Atmakaraka. Thereafter, the Moon and Saturn have the same number of degrees. To determine the Amatyakaraka, we therefore consider the minutes. We find that both the planets have the same number of minutes. We then take seconds into consideration. Here we find that Saturn has more seconds than the Moon. Therefore, Saturn is the Amatyakaraka. We can determine other karakas described above also in this manner.

The Atmakaraka is as important as the owner of the ascendant in determination of the status of the native in life, and his prosperity.

The navansha sign in which the Atmakaraka is placed is called the karakamsha. Most of the statements made for the ascendant also hold true for karakamsha. Planets placed in the karakamsha show results similar to their placement in the ascendant. Planets placed in second to twelfth house from the karakamsha show results similar to their placement in the second to twelfth house from the ascendant.

A powerful and well placed Atmakaraka or the Amatyakaraka will be an excellent indication for a brilliant future for the native. The Amatyakaraka is next only to the Atmakaraka in conferring status and prosperity on the native. The Atmakaraka is stated to be capable of making the native a ruler. The Amatyakaraka can take him close to the seat of power, but cannot make him a ruler.

A sambandha between the Atmakaraka or its dispositor, and the Amatyakaraka is excellent for the wealth and high position of the native. A sambandha is described in the succeeding pages.

A sambandha between the Amatyakaraka or its dispositor, and the owner of the tenth house is also highly beneficial in this regard.

4. According to Parashar there are constant significators (karakas) also for relatives and other matters in life. These are as follows for relatives:

Planet	*Relative*
(i) Sun	Father
(ii) Moon	Mother
(iii) Mars	Younger brother and sister
(iv) Mercury	Maternal relatives
(v) Jupiter	Children
	Husband
	Elder brother and sister
	Paternal relatives
(vi) Venus	Wife

Parashar in his Brihat Parashar Hora Sastra, Chapter 32, paragraphs 31 to 34 has said that each house is the main significator for certain matters and a planet has also been indicated by him as karaka for each such group of matters. These are as follows:

Planet	Matter	House
Sun	Soul, constitution and self	I
Moon	Mother	IV
Mars	Younger brothers and sisters, courage	III
	Wife's brother	V, IX
	Enemies	VI
Mercury	Honour	X
Jupiter	Family, wealth	II
	Children	V
	Religion, fortune	IX
	Elder brothers and sisters	XI
Venus	Wife and married life	VII
Saturn	Longevity	VIII
	Expenditure and separation	XII

Parashar in his Brihat Parashar Hora Sastra, Chapter 7, paragraphs 39 to 43 has also said that matters that are to be derived from certain houses in the chart, should also be examined from a planet in the following manner:

IX from the Sun	Matters relating to father.
X from the Sun	All matters that are to be examined from the X house from the ascendant.
XI from the Sun	All matters that are to be examined from the XI house from the ascendant.
I from the Moon	All matters that are to be examined from the I house from the ascendant.
II from the Moon	All matters that are to be examined from the II house from the ascendant.
IV from the Moon	All matters that are to be examined from the IV house from the ascendant.
IX from the Moon	All matters that are to be examined from the IX house from the ascendant.
XI from the Moon	All matters that are to be examined from the XI house from the ascendant.
III from Mars	All matters that are to be examined from the III house from the ascendant.
VI from Mercury	All matters that are to be examined from the VI house from the ascendant.
V from Jupiter	All matters that are to be examined from the V house from the ascendant.
VII from Venus	All matters that are to be examined from the VII house from the ascendant.
VIII from Saturn	All matters that are to be examined from the VIII house from the ascendant.
XII from Saturn	All matters that are to be examined from the XII house from the ascendant.

The word karaka is used throughout this book in the Parashari constant karaka sense unless it is otherwise clarified.

5. Both the kinds of karakas can be used in two different ways. First, we can predict about the father, or any close relative of the native by making use of the karakas; and second, we can confirm our prediction with respect to a matter in the life of a native by their use. We take an illustration to clarify this. A native wishes the astrologer to predict about his father by studying the native's horoscope. This can be done by making use of the karaka. The

exact manner of doing it is presently clarified. The same native also wishes to know from the astrologer if he will have a son. Here too the astrologer ought to make use of the karaka to be sure of his analysis.

We can determine a matter with regard to a relative by making use of the karakas in the following manner:

(a) From the ascendant, we take the house that stands for a relative as the first house for that relative. For example, we take the seventh house from the ascendant as the first house for the wife. We can find various matters relating to her life by analysing the twelve houses from the seventh house.

(b) From the karakamsha, we take the house that stands for a relative as the first house for that relative. For example, we take the seventh house from the karakamsha as the first house for the wife. We can find various matters relating to her life by analysing the twelve houses from this seventh house.

(c) A relative is represented by a house counted from the ascendant in the chart of the native. We take the same number of house from the karaka for the relative. We take this house as the first house for the relative and analyse the twelve houses for the relative. For example, taking the seventh house from the house that has Venus in it as the first house for the wife, we can find various matters relating to her life by analysing the twelve houses.

(d) A relative is represented by a house counted from the ascendant in the chart of the native. We take the same number of house from the chart specific karaka for the relative. We take this house as the first house for the relative and analyse the twelve houses for the relative. For example, taking the seventh house from the house that has the strikaraka in it as the first house for the wife, we can find various matters relating to her life by analysing the twelve houses.

When the query is with regard to a matter in the life of the native, it can be answered in a confirmed manner by studying the relevant house determined in the three different ways mentioned above, i.e., (a), (b), and (c), and also the karaka. We do not use (d) since the chart specific karakas only refer to relatives and not matters in the life of a native.

For, example if the query relates to acquisition of a vehicle, we ought to consider Venus, the karaka for vehicle; the fourth house from the ascendant that represents, inter-alia, vehicles; the fourth house counted from the karaka; and, also the fourth house counted from the karakamsha.

6. Planets placed in exaltation, own or friendly signs and in angles from each other become mutually highly beneficial planets. If such planets are placed in angles from the ascendant the combination becomes all the more powerful. This is further accentuated if one of the planets is in the tenth house. This is a rajyoga. Such planets, even if by nature antagonistic to each other, will work for each other. Their association, aspect on each other or any other type of sambandha will not be taken to be adverse. Their results would be experienced during the mutual major-period and sub-period of the planets. However, as stated above the planets have to be placed in exaltation, own or friendly signs, otherwise the results will not be forthcoming.

7. The results set out for each planet in different signs are modified according to the nature and strength of the dispositor. If Saturn is placed in Aries and Mars is exalted in Capricorn, results that Saturn is likely to give will not be so bad as in the case when Mars is in its sign of debilitation or in an inimical one.

8. A planet is taken to be COMBUST when it is very close to the Sun. A beneficial planet when combust is incapable of giving good results. It may give some adverse results. Its karaka properties will suffer. A combust malefic planet is likely to give worse than normal results. Following are the degrees within which planets become combust when they come near the Sun:

(i)	Mars	17
(ii)	Mercury	13
(iii)	Jupiter	11
(iv)	Venus	9
(v)	Saturn	15

Generally the combustion of Mercury is not taken seriously since it is never farther than 28 degrees from the Sun.

9. A planet is said to be VARGOTTAMA if it is in the same sign in the navansha chart as the sign in which it is placed in the birth chart. (See NOTE at the end of Chapter Five for an easy

method to find the navansha sign in which a planet is placed).
If the planet is in a movable sign it will be vargottama if it is in
the first ninth part of the sign, i.e., it is within 0 degrees 0 minutes
and 3 degrees 20 minutes in the sign. For fixed signs the planet
will be vargottama if it is in the middle ninth part of the sign,
i.e., between 13 deg 20 min and 16 deg 40 min, and for common
signs it will be vargottama if it is in the last ninth part of the sign,
i.e., between 26 deg 40 min and 30 deg 0 min. This is tabulated
as follows:

(i)	Aries	0 deg 0 min-3 deg 20 min
(ii	Taurus	13 deg 20 min-16 deg 40 min
(iii)	Gemini	26 deg 40 min-30 deg 0 min
(iv)	Cancer	0 deg 0 min-3 deg 20 min
(v)	Leo	13 deg 20 min-16 deg 40 min
(vi)	Virgo	26 deg 40 min-30 deg 0 min
(vii)	Libra	0 deg 0 min-3 deg 20 min
(viii)	Scorpio	13 deg 20 min-16 deg 40 min
(ix)	Sagittarius	26 deg 40 min-30 deg 0 min
(x)	Capricorn	0 deg 0 min-3 deg 20 min
(xi)	Aquarius	13 deg 20 min-16 deg 40 min
(xii)	Pisces	26 deg 40 min-30 deg 0 min

10. A vargottama planet is as powerful as a planet in its own
sign.

11. Following are the rules for determining the NATURE of a
planet for a particular ascendant. The nature determined in this
manner is used for the determination of the nature of the sub-
period and inter-period in a major-period:

(i)   The owner of a triangular house-the first (for the purpose
        of ascertaining the nature of a planet the first house,
        which is both an angular and a triangular house, is taken
        as the latter), the fifth or the ninth house-is a beneficial
        planet.

(ii)   The owner of an angular house will be neutral. Its nature
        will depend upon the ownership of the other house it
        owns. In case of a luminary, it will be neutral. A naturally
        malefic planet, like Mars or Saturn, owning an angular

house will not give adverse results. A naturally beneficial
planet, like Venus or some Jupiter, owning an angular
house will not give favourable results, unless it also owns
the first house, or some other good house. The Moon and
Mercury are by themselves naturally beneficial planets.
But if the Moon is waning and is within 72 degrees of
the Sun, it will be a malefic planet. A waxing Moon close
to the Sun will also be weak. Mercury, if influenced by
a naturally malefic planet will be a malefic planet. In the
following categorisation we have assumed the beneficial
nature of these two planets.

(iii) A planet owning either the third, sixth, or eleventh house
will be a bad planet. A planet owning two of the above
three houses, will be a very bad planet.

(iv) A planet owning the eighth house will be a malefic
planet, unless it also owns the first house, and is placed
in a house owned by it. If the planet owning the eighth
house is a luminary, it will be a neutral planet.

(v) If a planet owns the second or twelfth house and another
house, the nature of the planet will be determined
according to the other house owned by the planet, since
for the purpose of ascertaining the nature, the second
and the twelfth houses are taken to be neutral.

(vi) A planet owning the second house will have the ability
to terminate the life of the native when the longevity has
come to an end. Such a planet is called a maraka planet.
A naturally beneficial planet that owns the seventh house
will be a maraka. This does not hold true for a naturally
malefic planet.

(vii) A maraka planet owning a triangle will first give good
results in its period, and may later end the life of the
native. Such a maraka may be termed a good maraka.

(viii) A planet owning an angle and a triangle (including the
first house) will be an excellent planet for the chart and
shall be capable of giving the very best results in its
periods.

(ix) A planet that owns two houses, one of which is a good
house and the other an adverse house as above, shall be
classified as a good-but-impure planet. It must be kept
in mind that in this case if the mooltrikona sign of the

planet falls in an adverse house, the planet will have more malefic tendency in it. If on the other hand, the mooltrikona sign falls in a good house, the planet will have more beneficial tendency.

(x)   The fifth and ninth houses are the primary houses that give wealth. The seventh and tenth houses are givers of happiness.

(xi) The houses of a category shall gain in strength with their distance from the ascendant. Thus among the triangular houses, the ninth house is more powerful than the fifth, and the fifth is more powerful than the first. Similarly, the eleventh house is more adverse than the sixth, and the sixth is stronger than the third, etc.

(xii) A planet owning a more powerful house will be able to overcome the influence of a planet owning a less powerful house. Thus a good combination formed by a planet owning the fifth house can be disturbed by the owner of the eleventh house, but not by that of the third house.

(xiii) When the owners of an angle and a triangle join, aspect each other or form a sambandha between themselves in any laid down manner, the combination shall be highly beneficial for the native.

(xiv) A neutral planet in sambandha with a planet will take on the nature of the planet with which it is in sambandha.

(xv) (a) A Node of the Moon will give results of the houses the planet with which it is in association owns. The Node will also give results of the house it occupies. The nature of the Node will be influenced by the nature of the planet with which it is associated. If there is no association, the nature will be determined by the sign and asterism occupied by Node.

     (b) When the Node occupies a house it becomes the most powerful factor in giving the results of that house. Therefore, occupation of an adverse house by the Node will make it an adverse planet for the chart.

     (c) The Node becomes an excellent planet when it occupies an angle and is associated with the owner of a triangle, or, it is placed in a triangle and is associated with the owner of an angle.

(xvi) With the above fundamental rules the nature of planets for each ascendant is laid down in the table below. Planet marked with an asterisk shall be good only if it occupies its own house:

Asc	Exc	Good	Neutral	Bad	V. Bad
Aries	-	Sun, Jup Mars*	Moon Venus	Mars Sat	Merc
Taurus	Sat	Merc	Sun Mars	Moon Venus	Jup
Gemini	Merc	Venus	Jup Moon	Sun	Mars
Cancer	Mars	Moon	Sun	Merc Venus	Sat
Leo	Mars	Sun	Moon	Merc Venus Sat	
Virgo	Merc	Venus	Sun Jup	Moon	Mars
Libra	Sat	Merc Venus*	Mars Moon	Sun Venus	Jup
Scorpio		Moon Jup	Sun Venus	Mars Sat	Merc
Sagitt	Jup	Sun Mars	Moon Merc	Sat	Venus
Capri	Venus	Sat	Sun Moon	Mars Jup	
Aqua	Venus	Sat	Sun	Moon Mars Jup	
Pisces	Jup	Moon Mars	Merc	Sun Sat	Venus

The list of planets which are good-but-impure or maraka for various ascendants is as follows:

Asc	Good-but-impure	Maraka
Aries	-	Venus
Taurus	-	Merc
Gemini	Sat	Moon, Jup
Cancer	Jup	Sun
Leo	Jup	Merc
Virgo	Sat	Jup, Venus
Libra	-	Mars
Scorpio	-	Jup, Venus
Sagittarius	-	Merc, Sat
Capricorn	Merc	Moon, Sat
Aquarius	Merc	Jup
Pisces	-	Mars, Merc

12. A planet is said to be lajjit (abashed) if it is associated with (at least one of) the Sun, Mars, Saturn, Rahu or Ketu in the fifth house. In the major-period or sub-periods of such a lajjit planet the native has to wander aimlessly, his wife and children fall ill and suffer, he is separated from his family, and the native gets confused and worried.

13. A planet in a watery sign having the aspect of an inimical planet and no beneficial aspect is called trishit. Such a planet in its major-period or sub-periods causes financial harm and disease to the native. If it is located in the tenth house it causes loss to the native through the wrath of the government.

14. Following are the rules for assessing the STRENGTH of a planet without calculating the shadbalas (six fold strength). Each point of strength is to be set off against a point of weakness. The net result-plus or minus-would indicate the strength of the planet. The more plus points the planet is left with, the stronger would it be. The same in reverse applies for the weakness.

This can be expressed and evaluated mathematically. If a planet has four plus points and two minus points, it scores four out of six. Its strength therefore will be 4 * 100/6=66.66% . If it has two plus points and four minus points, it scores two out of six. Its strength will be 2 * 100/6=33. 33 % . If it only has minus points, its strength will be zero. Reference is also invited to paragraph 7 of Chapter Six.

   (i)   Strength (or Plus):

      (a) The planet is exalted in the birth chart or navansha.

      (b) It is placed in its own sign in the birth chart or navansha.

      (c) It is placed in its mooltrikona sign in the birth chart or navansha.

      (d) It is placed in a friend's house in the birth chart or navansha.

      (e) It is placed in a triangular house.

      (f) It is placed in an angular house.

      (g) The planet is a beneficial one for that particular ascendant.

      (h) The planet is associated with or aspected by a planet that is a beneficial one for that ascendant.

      (i) The planet is vargottama.

      (j) The planet is retrograde.

      (k) The planet has directional strength (The Sun and Mars in the tenth, the Moon and Venus in the fourth, Jupiter and Mercury in the first and Saturn in the seventh house have directional strength).

      (l) The Moon gets stronger as it moves away from the Sun. A waxing Moon is more powerful than a waning Moon. For the Moon this strength is of foremost importance. The Sun is more powerful when it is in signs from Capricorn to Gemini. Then it is called to be in its Uttarayana (Northern Hemisphere). However for computing the strength of the Sun this factor is of minor significance.

    (m) The planet is hemmed in by beneficial planets for the chart (i.e., has beneficial planets in both the adjoining houses to the house in which it is situated).

      (n) The planet has aspect of beneficial planets for the chart on the adjoining house on either side of the house in which it is placed.

(o) The planet is close to the cusp of the house or is between 12 deg and 18 deg in a sign.

(ii)   Weakness (or Minus):

(a) The planet is debilitated in birth chart or navansha.

(b) The planet is in enemy's sign in the birth chart or navansha.

(c) The planet is in the sixth, eighth or the twelfth house.

(d) It is associated with or aspected by a planet that is a malefic planet for that ascendant.

(e) The planet is a malefic planet for that ascendant.

(f) The planet is combust.

(g) The planet is hemmed in by malefic planets for the chart (has malefic planets in both the adjoining houses to the house in which it is situated).

(h) The planet has aspect of malefic planets for the chart on the adjoining house on either side of the house in which it is placed.

(i) The planet is in the last degree of a movable or fixed sign. If this is true for a common sign, the planet will be in vargottama and strong therefore.

(j) The planet is devoid of directional strength.

15. It is not bad to have Venus in the twelfth house, Mercury in the eighth or Jupiter in the sixth. However Venus in the twelfth should not be in the sign or navansha of Saturn.

16. It must be remembered that a planet in a sign gives many results that are the same as those that were to be had if the planet was in the same number of house from the ascendant. Thus the first house corresponds to the first sign Aries, the second house to Taurus etc. A planet in the tenth house, therefore, is likely to give results similar to its placement in Capricorn, and vice-versa.

17. The Sun and Mars are dry and represent fire; the Moon and Venus are wet and represent water; Mercury is wet and represents earth; Jupiter is wet and represents ether; and Saturn is dry and represents air.

18. Powerful planets in EARTH signs infuse a sense of practicality and order in the native and make him engage in work related to the earth, the physical matter, finance, the body and the material world in general. The native may also display

coarser influence in his personality. An earth sign in the ascendant, and an earth planet there, or the owner of the ascendant in an earth sign, will make the native short but strongly built.

The planets in WATER signs make the native more emotional and intuitive. He may be devotional. Relationships assume great importance in the life of the native. The circle of acquaintances, friends and associates is much larger for such people. If the ascendant has a watery sign and a watery planet is placed in it or the owner of the ascendant is placed in a watery sign, the native will be fat.

If planets are located in FIRE signs it indicates that native has the ambition, grit and determination to forge ahead in life. He will seek power and revel in it. The native would like to be popular but in a dominant manner. He does not mind sacrificing relationships, if need be, for attaining his goals. If the ascendant has a fiery sign and the owner of the ascendant is also placed in such a sign, the native will be very strong but not stocky in build.

If powerful planets are in AIR signs the native would be versatile, and adaptable. The native would be of mental or intellectual type. He would live in the realm of thought. He can be philosophical or humane. An airy sign in the ascendant with Saturn there will make the native very intelligent and sharp witted.

19. The ELEMENT of the signs and those of the planets tenanting them should be analysed to come to a conclusion. For example if there are several planets in the EARTH sign but the nature of these powerful planets is fiery, the two influences would combine and we will have a person who has lot of energy and drive to achieve things in the material world. If the planets located in a sign are of a nature opposed to the element of the sign, there would be modification of the natures of both. If the planets are weak, the sign will overpower the nature of the planets to a large extent.

20. If most of the planets are in more than one element (i.e. in say fire and water, or, earth and air etc.) then there would be a certain tussle in the personality of the native between the traits indicated by these signs. For example, if the two elements are fire and air, the native will aspire to achieve results but the energy would dissipate itself.

21. The Sun or Mars is strong in a fire sign, Venus in earth ánd air signs, Jupiter in air and water signs and Saturn in air and earth signs.

22. If the nature of the planet and of the element of the sign in which it is placed are similar the planet becomes strong. For example the Sun or Mars is strong in a fire sign.

23. A luminary (the Sun or Moon), if hemmed in between malefic planets, gets the power to kill.

24. Malefic planets gain in strength if they are associated with the Moon.

25. If a planet is powerful in a sign it can retain its nature even under adverse aspects. The aspect is also an indication whether the native would act on his own or he will be aided or hindered in his task by other factors. The planets that are beneficial for the chart shall, by their aspect help a matter, those that are adverse will hinder. For example if the owner of the tenth house is unaspected, it means that the native will not be helped or harmed in his profession by anybody.

26. Of the two malefic planets, Saturn and Mars, the latter afflicts the Moon more whereas Saturn is considered a bigger malefic planet for the Sun than for the Moon.

27. Following are the SHADVARGAS (Six fold divisions of a sign):

(i)   Rasi, The whole sign
(ii)   Hora, Half of the sign
(iii)   Drekkan, One third of the sign
(iv)   Navansha, One ninth of the sign
(v)   Dwadasansa, One twelfth of the sign
(vi)   Trinsansa, One thirtieth of the sign.

A planet is said to be in its own vargas if it occupies its own sign in each of the above six divisions. This is very auspicious. Even when a planet is a malefic for the ascendant, if it is in favourable shadvargas, i.e., in its own vargas, or in varsa of exaltation or mooltrikona, or vargas of its friends, its major or sub-period whenever current, will not be as troublesome as it would have been otherwise. Beneficial planets so placed will give still better results. The strength of planets according to their placement in various shadvargas is calculated as Vinshopaka Strength and it can be accurately expressed in mathematical terms. The method of calculating the Vinshopaka Strength is given in paragraphs 4 to 7 of Chapter Six.

28. The planet that is the closest to the cusp of the tenth house indicates the profession that the native is likely to adopt and income that is likely to be derived from it.

29. When the dispositor of a debilitated planet is also debilitated, the major or sub-period of such a dispositor is likely to yield excellent results.

30. Combination of the Moon with Saturn is considered excellent from the point of view of prosperity, for Aries, Libra and Scorpio ascendants.

31. If the Sun and Saturn are comparatively more powerful than the Moon and Venus, the father of the native will survive the native's mother.

32. Lucky Days:
(a) The day when the Sun or the Moon transits through the house in which Jupiter or Venus is located, or through a house that is triangular to it, will be lucky for the native.
(b) If the Sun and the Moon have aspects of beneficial planets for the chart in the horoscope and the Sun transits through a house that is triangular to the house where the Moon is located on a particular day, that day will certainly be lucky for the native.
(c) If the Sun, the Moon, Jupiter or Venus, unafflicted in a horoscope, passes over the cusp of the first, second or the tenth house on a particular day, that will be a good day for the native.
(d) If the owner of the ascendant is strong and is a naturally beneficial planet, the day the Sun or the Moon forms an aspect with this planet, that particular day will be good for the native. If the owner of the ascendant is a naturally malefic planet this will not be so.

33. Two planets are said to be in special relationship (SAMBANDHA) if:

   (i)   they are placed in each other's sign, for example, Jupiter in Aries and Mars in Sagittarius; or,

   (ii) they aspect each other fully, for example Jupiter in Libra and Venus in Aries; or,

   (iii) if a planet is aspected by the other planet which is the owner of the sign the first planet occupies. For example, the Sun in Aries is aspected by Mars in Capricorn; or,

   (iv) if a planet aspects the owner of the sign in which it is located. For example Saturn in Gemini aspects Mercury in Pisces; or,

   (v)   the two planets are in the same sign, for example, Venus and Mercury in Taurus.

34. An examination of the horoscope will tell as to which planets are powerful in the horoscope of the native. The native will have those matters in a good measure in his life for which the powerful planets are the karakas (significators). The matters signified by planets that are weak will not be available to the native to a satisfactory extent.

35. If a malefic planet (including the owner of the sixth, eighth or the twelfth house) is located in a sign, the part of the body indicated by that sign will bear a mark, wound or scar. A beneficial planet so placed will make that part of the body fully developed. If the house indicating that part of the body is also similarly afflicted, the native may have serious trouble there.

36. A planet in a house, which is twelfth from the house of which the planet is a karaka, will not be able to give good results for that house for which it is a karaka. Thus Mars in the second house will be ineffective to give results with regard to its karaka properties, etc.

37. A sufficiently powerful beneficial planet aspected by malefic planets may not give its full good results. A badly placed or debilitated malefic planet aspected by beneficial planets will not give adverse results. It will become neutral.

38. Powerful malefic planets do not give bad results but an afflicted and weak malefic planet will give very adverse results.

39. It is generally observed that planets give results relating to their mooltrikona sign at the beginning of their major-period or sub-periods and of the other sign later. Similarly, a planet situated in an even sign will give results of that house at the beginning of its major-period or sub-periods, if the sign occupied is odd, the result will be felt towards the end of the major-period or sub-periods.

40. The sub-period of one planet in the major-period of another in the sets of following planets will generally be troublesome:
   (i) Mars and Rahu
   (ii) Mars and Saturn
   (iii) Sun and Saturn
   (iv) Moon and Mercury
   (v) Venus and Jupiter.

41. The Sun and Mars each give their results immediately on entering a sign, i.e., while in the first third part of the sign (if the sign is taken to been divided in three equal parts of 10 degrees each); the results of Jupiter or Venus will be felt during the middle third part of the sign, and Saturn or the Moon will give its results when in the end of the sign, i.e., in the last third part of the sign. Mercury and Rahu give their results irrespective of their positions in the sign. This can also be broadly applied to major-period or sub-periods of the planets. If a planet is expected to give certain result, it will be felt during the first part, the second part or the third part of its major-period or sub-period as the case may be.

42. A planet owning the fifth, seventh or the eleventh house and some other house, and located in one of these three houses only which it owns, will give results pertaining to that house only occupied by it during its major-period or sub-periods and not of the other house owned by it. To illustrate the point let us take Saturn in the seventh house in Capricorn. During its major-period or sub-periods it will only give results pertaining to the seventh house and not of the eighth house where its mooltrikona sign will fall.

43. A planet which becomes STATIONARY after or before it gets retrograde is powerful and shows noticeable results, both in transit and during its major-period or sub-periods.

44. The ASPECTS of various planets are full on the seventh sign from the sign in which they are placed. There are special aspects, in addition to the seventh sign aspect, of Mars (on the fourth and eighth signs), Jupiter (on the fifth and ninth signs), Saturn (on the third and tenth signs), Rahu (on the fifth and ninth signs) and Ketu (on the fifth and ninth signs). Partial aspects are not being discussed here. The effect of aspect of a planet on other planets is given under details for each planet. Following basic principles should be kept in mind when interpreting effect of aspects of planets:

(i)   The aspect of a planet on another planet will set up a relationship between the houses that the two planets occupy, and between the house occupied by the aspecting planet and the houses owned by the aspected planet.

(ii)   The aspect of a planet on a house sets up a relationship between the planet and houses owned and occupied by it, and the aspected house.

(iii)   The karaka qualities of each planet involved in the aspect will also operate. In case of mutual aspect, the karaka qualities will combine to give resultant effects.

(iv)   The aspecting planet will pass on its influence according to its nature for a particular ascendant. It will modify the influence of the aspected planet accordingly. The aspect of a friend of the owner of the ascendant on another planet will be beneficial.

(v)   The aspecting planet will also carry with its aspect the effect of any planet that is in conjunction with it or aspects it, and the sign in which it is placed.

(vi)   When there is mutual aspect between two planets, one of which is a beneficial planet and the other a malefic in nature, the beneficial planet will stand degraded to some extent due to the influence of the malefic planet, and the malefic planet will be improved. Such influence on each of the planets will be perceptible in their respective major-periods or sub-periods.

(vii)   The extent of influence, referred to above, will depend on the strength of the planet aspecting and also the strength of the planet receiving the aspect. The effect of the aspect of a weak malefic planet on a powerful beneficial planet will not be as much as that of a powerful malefic planet on a weak beneficial planet.

(viii) Mutual aspect between two planets has an effect similar to their conjunction in a sign.

(ix) The good or bad results of mutual aspect will appear during the major-period of one planet and the sub-period of the other, or in the major-period or sub-periods of the more powerful of the two planets.

(x) Aspects to the ascendant and the tenth house should always be carefully worked out and understood, as these are of great importance in analysing the (from the first house) personality, longevity, well being, (from the tenth house) honour and profession of the native. Aspects of naturally beneficial planets which are also beneficial for the chart, on the tenth house will ensure that the native will take to a profession or find a livelihood easily, will have good returns from it and the source of his earning will be good. The aspect of malefic planets will have just the reverse effect. If a Saturn or Mars that is beneficial for the ascendant, aspects the tenth house, it will give the native plenty of power and authority but if there is no other beneficial influence, the native is likely to meet with a fall from the position sometime.

(xi) The aspect of a powerful planet that is a beneficial planet for the ascendant, on a badly placed or adverse planet or on an afflicted house will reduce the adverse results that were to follow from such adverse planet or house. If the aspecting planet is a friend/intimate friend of the aspected planet, the results shall improve further.

45. A planet, in its major-period or sub-periods, will also give the results of the planet in the constellation of which it is placed. Thus a planet that is expected to give excellent results, will fail to do so fully in its major-period or sub-periods, if it is in the constellation of a planet which is adverse for the ascendant.

46. Sambandha between planets which are inimical to each other is considered bad. But of these planets if one is a male planet and the other a female planet, the adverse results will be much less.

SUN

1. The Sun has a masculine and majestic personality, curly but scanty hair, small feet, long hands, broad shoulders and is not

very tall. It has honey coloured eyes, a well developed bone structure and has a squarish appearance. It has a very sharp mind. It is active. It is satwik in nature. It wears orange or saffron coloured clothes. It does not stay at one place for long. It is of clean habits. Its vehicle is a horse with seven heads. It is wise, truthful, kind, and firm. It respects the guru and gods.

2. Its RELATIONSHIP with the other planets is as follows:

Friendly with	Moon
	Mars
	Jupiter
Neutral to	Mercury
Inimical to	Venus
	Saturn

3. It is the KARAKA for the following:

Soul, self, separation, bones, illustrious appearance, king, steady temperament, represents 50 years of age and also age between 23 and 41 years, father, strength, valour, health, eyes, general well being, and devotion to Lord Shiva.

4. It REPRESENTS the following:

(i)   Honey coloured eyes, scanty hair, throat, brain, fever, right eye, spleen, spine, belly, mouth, heart, vitality, the native looks upwards, consciousness, individuality, resistance to disease, typhoid, meningitis and bitter taste.

(ii) Authority, aristocrats, high government officers, government buildings, boss, administrative head, captain, leader, royalty, royal favour, respect for elders, son, reputation, permanent service, independent business financed by the father, career, hard work, and capacity to command.

(iii) Will, good fortune, ambition, faith, generosity, hope, happiness, loyalty, optimism, expansion, splendour, deliberate act, prestige, scruples, arrogance, bluff, subtle, pure, fundamental, long standing anger, success in worldly affairs, jealousy, pomposity, anger, domineering attitude, prominence, and determination.

(iv) Copper, ruby, gold, dhatu (inanimate objects like minerals and metals), wool, positive, heat, summer, dry, fire, temple, Shiva temple, forest, wood, thorny plants, months of June and July, dark red, orange colour, square shaped, numbers 1 and 4, east, mountains, sharpness, bank of a river, chemicals, thick cloth, wheat, medicine, fortress, child of a coward, noon, quadrupeds, lion, horse, boar, Saurastra, and Kalinga (Orissa).

(v)   Rudra, mantras, Yoga, Brahma, truth, purity of the mind, and self realisation.

(vi) The Sun represents a half year. It rises with hind part first. It presides over Danda (Punishment).

(vii) Magistrates, masters, medical practitioners, doctors, physician, kshatriya (warrior caste), and goldsmiths.

5. Sun causes heat and burning in the body, sun stroke, and diseases in the heart, skin, eyes and parts of the body below the navel. It also causes fevers particularly of undetermined origin.

6. If the Sun is in an even sign and even navansha, the native will not have good relations with his father.

7. The Sun is powerful in the tenth house.

8. The strength of the Sun in any horoscope shows the strength of the soul that the native is endowed with and is therefore the indicator of divinity in a man.

9. The Sun represents the spiritual authority. The Sun and Jupiter together determine the nature of the guru (preceptor) and spiritual direction that the native is likely to take.

10. The presence of the Sun in any house illuminates that house and accentuates the affairs of that house.

11.   (i) If the Sun is favourable for the horoscope and aspects the Moon, the native will be fortunate and successful throughout his life.

(ii) If a favourable Sun is associated with or is in aspect with Jupiter or Venus, the native will have strokes of good fortune every second year, especially in his 12th, 24th, 30th, and 60th years.

12. An unfavourable Sun aspected by a malefic planet in the horoscope will cause misfortune for the native in his 45th year.

13. The results indicated by a planet will materialize in its major-period or sub period when the Sun transits a sign of exaltation or mooltrikona of the planet, or one owned by it.

14. If the Sun is aspected by Jupiter in a horoscope, the native will be on good terms with the government and will be favoured by the government. The extent of such favour will be determined by the nature of Jupiter for that particular nativity and its strength. Here aspect includes association.

15. The reverse would be the case if Saturn is connected with the Sun as in paragraph 14 above. The native will be persecuted and troubled by the government if Saturn aspects the Sun. If Saturn is adverse for the horoscope, the troubles will be magnified several fold. Here aspect includes association.

16. By nature the Sun is a malefic planet.

17. The aspect of the Sun on other planets, and vice-versa (See paragraph 44 under the opening remarks at the beginning of this Chapter for guidelines for analysing the influence of an aspect.):

(i)   On the Moon—On the positive side (if the aspecting planet is a beneficial planet for the ascendant), the native will be self reliant and independent. He will be active, successful and popular. He will enjoy good health and will have a strong constitution. The native is likely to have happiness from children and father. The native will be wealthy. The two houses in which the aspect takes place become dominant in the horoscope, and show noticeable results. The material welfare will be great. The native will be highly prosperous, esteemed, wealthy, happy with his children and marriage and will generally be well above the level of comfort and prosperity in which he was born. On the negative side (if the aspecting planet is a malefic for the ascendant), the reverse of what has been recorded above will come to pass. He will be vacillating, unable to grasp the opportunity that comes his way, troubled by heavy expenditure, mentally disturbed and ailing. He may not be generous and large hearted. He will be easily influenced by females. He may make fake items but will be skilful. There may be a conflict in the personality of the native between the head and the heart.

(ii)   On Mars—On the positive side (if the aspecting planet is a beneficial planet for the ascendant), the native will be impressive, bold, assertive, industrious, prosperous, determined, healthy, long-lived and energetic. He may be in the army or in a force or profession which wields weapons. The life of the native will have predominance of activity to be decided by the sign in which Mars is placed. For example in an earth sign, the native will be good at games and body building; in airy, he will be intelligent and mentally alert, etc. The aspect between these two planets will make the native a leader and an achiever. He will gain from his parents and will be blessed with sons.

On the negative side (if the aspecting planet is a malefic for the ascendant), he will have none of the above good effects. He will be untruthful, passionate, impulsive, lacking in intelligence and one who keeps bad company. He will not have favour from his superiors and may fall out with his son or parent. He may have to recompense for the bad deeds of his father. He is likely to face accidents, fever, sun-stroke, surgical interventions, enmities and assaults. There will be danger from fire arms and fire. His family life will be bad.

(iii) On Mercury—Astronomically no aspect can form as the planet is never more than 28 degrees away from the Sun. According to Hindu system only conjunction can be formed. The result of which is being given.

The mind will be energetic, firm and conservative. However if a new idea comes up it will be examined in the perspective of the established mental make up and accepted or rejected within that ambit. The mind will not respond to lowly persuasions. It will be able to appreciate sublime concepts. There will not be any apprehension of fading away of mental power with age. The native will be mentally sound and energetic till his end. He may not have fear of mental instability. He will be scholarly, respected for his mental status and wealthy. He will have ability for mathematics, astrology or astronomy. He will be successful in trading. There may be travels. These good results will be diluted if the Sun is an adverse planet for the horoscope.

(iv) On Jupiter—On the positive side (if the aspecting planet is a beneficial planet for the ascendant), the native may have respect for religion. He may be honest and sympathetic. He may have good relations with his father. The father and native's children may also be well off and prosperous. He may be on the right side of the government. He may go on long journeys on official work or under orders of his superior. The native will be energetic, sincere, responsible and reliable. He may also be involved, or inclined to, charity, nursing or hospital work. He may have a large circle of friends. He may be scholarly and may be in the teaching profession. He may be reputed. In the horoscope of a female, her husband will be highly placed and prosperous.

On the negative side (if the aspecting planet is a malefic for the ascendant), the native may suffer from problem of overweight, derangement of liver or spleen or trouble in the heart. The areas where good results were expected, as described above, will show reverse results. He may be a hypocrite in religious matters or a religious zealot. He may have trouble or loss from judiciary. He may contract a disease which he has been trying to cure as a doctor in a medical institution. However, the negative results will not be serious unless other malefic planets, such as Mars or Saturn, also contribute their mite.

(v)   On Venus—Astronomically no aspect can form as the planet is never more than 48 degrees away from the Sun. According to Hindu system only conjunction can be formed. The result of which is being given.

The native will be successful, popular and musically inclined. He will have taste for and knowledge of fine arts. He will earn through the opposite sex. He will have a happy marriage and good children. He will be a warm hearted person. His marriage may emerge out of a love affair. He will marry even if there are indications to the contrary in the horoscope. He will be wealthy and hold a high position. He will have good residence and vehicles. He may have defective eyesight. The good results will be diluted if the Sun is an adverse planet for the horoscope.

(vi) On Saturn—On the positive side (if the aspecting planet is a beneficial planet for the ascendant), the native will have a strong personality and will be the master of himself. He will be honest, persevering and patient. He will be a good leader, organiser and administrator. He does not shirk from taking up responsibility. He will carry on regardless of approbation or otherwise. He will be successful in his endeavours. He will have the good will of his superiors and the government. He will attain a high position. He will remain in the company of persons above him in standing. Persons older than him in age will help him in his affairs. He may have limited number of children. He may get patrimony. He will have a healthy and affluent old age. He will be long lived.

On the negative side (if the aspecting planet is a malefic for the ascendant), the native may have to face obstacles in his path, his affairs may get delayed, he may face humiliations and losses in business; and his father or son may pass away, may lose his wealth or there may be serious disagreement with the native. There will be many sorrows and disappointments in his life. He will suffer from colds and rheumatic troubles. He will suffer from the machinations of his enemies and may not be able to achieve his goals. His bosses may get annoyed with him or he may incur the wrath of the government. The native will be unsympathetic and callous. He may tend to develop some heart ailment.

18. Effect of the Sun in various HOUSES:

First

This is a good position and will confer good health if there is no detracting factor. The native will have good relations with the government. He will be respectful and obedient to his father. His spouse will be from a high family. He will be on good terms with the people in power. He will be morally upright and will have a religious or ethically correct attitude to life. He will be frank and magnanimous. Such a Sun will be highly beneficial for the younger sister/brother of the native. The younger sister/brother will be well placed, wealthy and will have friends at high places. It will also make the native's mother inclined to religion and she will go on pilgrimages. His children will do well at the highest levels of studies. They may also go abroad in this connection. If the Sun is adversely placed in the first house it will make a person aggressive, impetuous, lazy, unforgiving, ambitious, proud, of impressive appearance, and impatient. He will be full of vitality, bald, tall, lean, and may suffer from ailments in the head and eye but on the whole will enjoy good health. The health may remain indifferent during the childhood. He is likely to gain from cattle. The native will have restricted number of children.

Second

The Sun in the second house, if adverse, makes the person struggle for money and may have to face confiscation of wealth and property by the Government. Such a Sun will make the younger sister/brother of the native not well disposed towards his father. His father will be in service, not rich, and weak in constitution. The younger sister/brother may either have physical deformity or trouble in his eyesight. The sibling may also not be morally upright and may be deprived of children. If the Sun is favourable, well placed and powerful it can make the native very wealthy. He may gain from government and by trading or dealing in copper, gold and other metals. He may have diseases of the mouth and face. He will find it difficult to learn things and he cannot express himself well. His relations with his immediate family may be unsatisfactory. If the Sun is well placed here it will confer favour of the superiors, inheritance, and good eye-sight. Such a Sun will bring wealth to the mother of the native and very high position and riches to his children. The children will be of good conduct. His wife will face a critical time in her middle years. A good Sun with powerful second house will be favourable signs for her to expect a legacy.

Third

This location of the Sun makes the relationship with younger brothers/sisters and other relatives strained. Some of his younger brothers, sisters, neighbours or colleagues may reach high positions in life. It can also lead to early death of a sibling. The native would however be fortunate, high minded, good looking, learned, successful in litigation, intelligent, valorous, and in an authoritative position. He may travel a lot in connection with his business. He will have success in the field of publishing and editing. He will have the satisfaction of having good servants. He will have a tendency to associate with rough or undesirable persons. His mother will either be interested in the occult or may devote her time to charities, hospitals or asylums. His father will be successful at litigation and may do well in life.

Fourth

The native would be an employee of the Government. An adverse Sun in the fourth house leads to difficulties in relationship with the mother and native's boss. He will not generally be happy in life especially at the close of it, would not have peace of mind and would do away with his property if the Sun occupying this house is weak. Such a Sun is not good for the wealth of native's father and that of his younger sister/brother. He may suffer from high blood pressure and heart trouble. There would be several changes of residence. A powerful Sun will bring success to the native abroad. He will realise his ambitions. He will have immovable property and will be highly educated. The native would have honour towards the end of his life. This position is good for the native's wife. She may be of a good and pious conduct or be highly placed in life depending upon the influence that the Sun receives and on the sign in which it is placed. It will give results of its placement in the first house according to its strength and nature for the ascendant to native's mother. This position of the Sun in the fourth house is not good for native's children. They may have stomach, eye or heart trouble or they may lead an inconspicuous life.

Fifth

The Sun, if weak and afflicted, in the fifth house leads to strained relationship with the children or their premature death. Though the native would be very intelligent, he would be given to love affairs which can bring dishonour to him. He will make risky and unproductive investments. He will be of anxious disposition. The native is likely to suffer from heart and stomach diseases, particularly so if the house and Leo are also afflicted and weak. The Sun in a navansha owned by a malefic planet and the owner of the fifth house weak and badly placed, will severely curtail the longevity of native's father. A powerful Sun will bring the native into contact with highly placed persons who will be friendly with him. The native is likely to be scholarly and have a few elder brothers. An elder brother of the native will reach a high position in life. The native's younger sister/brother will do well in life.

Sixth

This indicates that the native would take up service at which he would perform well, help others and have a successful career. He is likely to take up medicine or chemistry as his special branch of study. The native will be troubled by his enemies but will successfully overcome them. Though the native will have good vitality, he would generally be concerned over his health. Financially he would be well off. The health of the wife of the native will not be good. There would be danger to the native from quadrupeds. His mother's family will have problems. The mother may develop strained relations with her younger sister/brother during the major-period or sub-periods of the Sun. The native will have a heightened sexual appetite. This is considered a good location for the Sun. The native will be susceptible to fevers and eye trouble early in life. A weak and afflicted Sun may cause the native to suffer humiliations at the hands of his enemies and he may lose in litigation. It will give results of its placement in the second house to his children. A benign and powerful Sun shall be excellent for the progress of native's father in service. The father may be in service of a foreigner. Such a Sun may make the elder sister/brother of the native learned in occult matters.

Seventh

The sexual urge would be strong in the native and there would be certain amount of restlessness in him. A weak Sun will be indicative that problems with regard to his marriage may arise later in life and the wife of the native may not keep good health. She will be dignified and proud. Even a slightly tainted Sun here can be troublesome for marital felicity and harmony for the native. The native can suffer from humiliations and insults due to women. He may antagonise the Government. His younger sister/brother may have troubles from his children, or he may not have children at all. The native may go abroad. He may have problems with regard to his business and partnership. He will have intestinal trouble and colic. A good Sun will make the native successful after marriage, popular and gain through partners. The native will be able to resolve matters by arbitration and will thus avoid litigation. This is a good position of the Sun for the children and father of the native. It will give results of its placement in the third and eleventh houses respectively to them.

Eighth

This position is an indicator that the native would suffer from eye trouble, particularly in the right eye. The native will be susceptible to fevers. He will hardly have friends and his relationship with his father would be tense. His health however will be good though the span of life may not be more than medium. It can lead to separation from the family, loss of wealth, miseries and heavy expenditure. The native is likely to have a tendency to sexual promiscuity especially with foreigners. The native will get inheritance or money by way of legacy through his wife. In the horoscope of a female this shows widowhood. The native may die committing an act of heroism. He will face critical time in his middle age. The native may die of fever, or fire. A well disposed Sun may make the native scholarly or to have deep interest in the occult.

Ninth

This position ensures success and gain through long journeys but, like the previous one, also indicates poor relations with the father and religious preceptor. The father may pass away early in life. Native's relations with his younger sister/brother may also get strained during the major-period or sub-periods of the Sun. When the Sun is well placed and has beneficial influence, the native would be interested in law, religion, and philosophy. He may have close connection with colleges or law firms. He will tend to do well in life after 21 years of age. He would earn respect in his field, be wealthy, fair minded and comfort loving. He will successfully pursue higher studies. He will also travel abroad. His children may have cause to worry on account of their children.

Tenth

The Sun, when favourable, in the tenth house makes the person intelligent, learned, famous, wealthy, and self-confident. He would earn his livelihood by doing mental work. He would be a leader of men and will be successful in his career. Such a Sun will give success, respect, repute and fame to him. The native will earn well through his profession and he will hold responsible positions, may be in government as well. He may be concerned over matters relating to his mother. His relations with his father will be satisfactory and the father will be long lived. He may live away from his relatives. He may have an ungovernable or worried mind throughout his life. He may live at a place away from the place of birth. The native will find his 22nd and 70th years as particularly fortunate. It will give results of its placement in the second house to the father. It is an excellent placement for the children of the native. The eldest child may become a doctor. If the Sun is the owner of third house, and Mars is weak in the horoscope, the native may not have younger sister/brother. If Mars is afflicted in the combination just described, some of the younger sister/brother may die at an early age. The elder brother or sister of the native may not be rich. It will give results of its placement in the fourth house to his wife, and in the second house to his father.

Eleventh

This position is excellent for material welfare of the native. The Sun here is an indication of successful investments and good income from them. It also ensures realisation of ambitions. The native is likely to acquire wealth. This position is harmful to the eldest child. It is likely to cause mental disquiet to the native on account of his children. It promises success without much effort, good reputation and position. The native may not be friendly with politicians. His wife will be good looking. His friends will be highly placed and the native will gain through their help and support. He will have favours from his superiors and will be in the good books of the government. It will give results of its placement in the first house to the elder sister/brother, in the fifth house to his wife, and, in the ninth house to the younger sister/ brother of the native. This position is not good for the health of his mother. Sun in the eleventh house is excellent for the welfare of his maternal uncle.

Twelfth

The native may live abroad and may not be rich. This is not a good position for relations with the father. The native has to work hard for achieving his ambitions and suffers at the hands of the Government. He will have a lot to do with hospitals, asylums, charitable institutions, prisons and philanthropic work. He will successfully pursue a career in medicine, chemistry or occult sciences. The early years in his life would be obscure. He may be given to incessant practice of Yoga. He may lack in self confidence. A powerful and beneficial Sun here will be excellent for the advancement of his younger sister/brother in his career and in the world. An afflicted Sun is bad for the health of native's children.

19. Effect of the Sun in various SIGNS [As a rule:

(i)   if the planet is vargottama, exalted, in mooltrikona or in a friend's sign in the birth or navansha chart, strong, beneficial for the chart and has good Vinshopaka strength, the good results will be exaggerated and the adverse will be reduced.

(ii) If the planet is in the sign of an intimate friend (having taken into account the temporary relationship as well, for which see paragraph 3 of Chapter Six) in the birth or navansha chart, the foregoing observation will be further accentuated.

(iii) On the other hand if the planet is debilitated in the birth or navansha chart, or in an enemy's or great enemy's sign in one of these charts, weak and does not have sufficient Vinshopaka strength, the good effects will be reduced and the evil will be dominant.

(iv) However if the planet is debilitated and vargottama (which means that the planet is debilitated in the ascendant chart and also in the navansha chart) but has above average resultant Vinshopaka strength (see paragraphs 2, 4, 5, 6 and 7 of Chapter Six), or there is annulment of debilitation (see paragraph 8 of Chapter Six), the effects of debilitation will be considerably reduced.

(v)   Another point to be borne in mind is that the interpre-
      tation of the location of a planet in a sign ought to be
      done in the light of the ascendant. The Sun in Aries for
      Aries ascendant will not give the same results as the Sun
      in Aries for Taurus ascendant. For the former the Sun
      will indicate a rajyoga and make the native, inter alia,
      wealthy, but for the latter the Sun will be in the twelfth
      house and may make the native spend heavily.

(vi) The aspects should also be taken into account. Rules have
      been laid down in paragraph 44 in the opening remarks
      above for this purpose. They may be referred to.

(vii) The houses occupied by the Sun and Moon are also taken
      almost at par with the ascendant.

(viii) It need not be stressed again that the nature of the planet
      for the ascendant, association with other planets, its
      placement in the eighth navansha, strength of the planet
      in the sign, the strength of the dispositor of the concerned
      planet and its karakatva (matters for which the planet is
      the significator) must be taken into account before reading
      the results for the location of the planet in the sign.].

Aries (*Maximum exaltation at 10 deg*)

The native is likely to be wealthy, wise, very intelligent, an
able doctor, an arms trader or manufacturer and will excel
himself in his field. The native will be long lived. He will be a
leader of men, ambitious, aggressive and self confident, but his
health will be poor. The native will have a good bone structure.
He will have to travel a lot and may be interested in exploration.
He will get help from highly placed persons. This is a good
position for realisation of political ambitions. The native will not
be averse to religion. His attitude to life will be positive. This
location is excellent for Cancer (a very superior rajyoga), Leo
(affluence and power), Libra (wife from an aristocratic family
and rajyoga through her) and Sagittarius (patrimony and high
position) ascendants. For Aquarius ascendant it makes the wife
religious and fortunate since the owner of the seventh house gets
exalted in the ninth house from it. The native may also be
fortunate after his marriage. The aspect of Saturn on the Sun,
except for ascendants owned by Venus, may not be good.

Taurus

The native may earn well from manufacture of clothes, perfumes and similar luxury items. He may get wealth from his father, speculation, shares and similar sources. He may be very careful with his money. He will be a skilled artisan and a connoisseur of music. He will not be close to his wife. He is capable of very hard work and is likely to be handsome, lean, and wise. He will be prone to suffer from diseases of eyes, face and the mouth. He will have musical talent and will face danger from water. It is good for Cancer (being in the eleventh house in a feminine sign it indicates gain through females), Leo (high position), and Aquarius ascendants. The aspect of the Moon on the Sun will make the native come in touch with a number of females, either by way of sexual liaisons or in the discharge of his duties. The aspect of Saturn on the Sun will not give good results.

Gemini

The native will be a mathematician, good writer, learned, fortunate, and intelligent and will be able to communicate well. His education will be of a high order and his mind will be capable of working in several areas at the same time. He will like change and may travel about. He will be financially well off. His father may marry more than once. He will be well behaved and fond of his children. For Leo ascendant the Sun in this sign is very good for the father; for Scorpio, the Sun may shorten the life of the native; for Sagittarius, the native will have a well behaved spouse, and the native may become fortunate after his marriage; for Capricorn, the native will come out successful in litigations; and for Aquarius, the number of children will be severely restricted. The aspect of the Moon or Mars on the Sun, except for ascendants owned by Venus, will not give good results.

Cancer

He will be in the service of others and will have to work hard. His financial status will be average and will wax and wane. He would be good looking, and fickleminded but of anxious disposition and of poor stamina. He will oppose his father and elders of his family. He will be close to his mother and family. He will be easy going. He will be honourable. The native is likely to earn through shipping, water related jobs, or public, including stage performances meant for the public. He may get property and wealth from his parents. The native is likely to live near water from time to time. If the Moon is weak, the wife will either be simple looking or the married life will be unsatisfactory. He will like intoxicants. If the ascendant is Scorpio or Sagittarius, it reduces the longevity of his father. The aspect of Mars or Saturn on the Sun will not give good results.

Leo *(Mooltrikona from 0 to 20 deg)*

The native will be famous, of good stamina, courageous, aggressive, ambitious and powerful. He will be capable to man responsible positions and take on important leadership assignments. He will be careful of his dignity. This position tends to produce persons who have to appear before the public, such as those who are the rulers, instructors, managers or directors. He will be rich, generous, ambitious, intelligent, talkative and will occupy a good position in life. But aspect of Saturn on the Sun will reduce these qualities to a large extent. He would like non-vegetarian dishes and going to forests and mountains. He will overcome his enemies. The father will be fortunate and long lived. The Sun will not give good results in this sign for Virgo ascendant. Such a situation of the Sun will however be conducive to a prosperous stay abroad.

Virgo

The native will have opportunities to travel. He will have the ability to write well and will show skill in arts. He will also be mathematically inclined. He will have feminine traits. He will be good at repair of vehicles. He is likely to work in a subordinate capacity. He may have trouble from servants or subordinates. This trouble will be there in a still greater measure if the Moon or Mars aspects the Sun here. Aspect of Jupiter will yield the best results. The native may be a doctor or a scientist. He may find it difficult to assert himself or make up his mind. The Sun for Virgo ascendant will be a factor for heavy expenditure. If the ascendant is Sagittarius, placement of the Sun in Virgo will be a major rajyoga.

Libra (*Maximum debilitation at 10 deg*)

He will be fickleminded, indulge in excesses, may have liaison with other women and will not be confident of himself. The tendency to seek other women will be accentuated if the Moon aspects the Sun. He will be unfortunate, dishonourable, will face frustration and may have to leave his native place due to difficulties faced by him. He will be persecuted by the government. The aspect of Saturn will make things worse. If the Sun is in the ascendant it gives very adverse results-the man loses his children and has to face abject poverty. A debilitated Sun in the horoscope at 10 deg in Libra is capable of countermanding all other good indications in the chart. The aspect of Jupiter will improve matters.

Scorpio

He will be irascible, obstinate, energetic and untruthful. He may join an armed or uniformed service, particularly so if the Sun has the aspect of Mars here. He will lack in intelligence and suffer from weapons, fire and poison. The foregoing will not come to pass in case the Moon aspects the Sun here. He will be unfortunate with regard to parents. This position is particularly not good for the father of the native, who may die early or the relations between him and the native may be soured. The native is not likely to rise in life. His married life will be bad and he may lose his wife early. He will be involved with low class women. He may meet with accidents. The native will be long lived and rich in case the ascendant is Capricorn. Similar results will be given by the Sun if it is aspected by Jupiter. In such a case the native may be a judge.

Sagittarius

The native will be fond of reading the scriptures, interested in medicine, and religious activity. He will prize his independence and will be rich. He will have good relations with persons in power, he will be helpful, skilful in use of weapons, peaceful, honourable, and will have a good physique. However, if Mars aspects the Sun, he keeps getting annoyed with his family members. He may be an original thinker and may become famous for a discovery that he would make. He would be inclined to travel and change his residences. The Sun in Sagittarius for Aries, Leo, Libra, Sagittarius and Aquarius ascendants will be particularly good. For Taurus ascendant the Sun in this sign is an indicator that the native's father may reach a high position during the periods of the Sun. For Pisces ascendant this placement will give fame and high position. Aspect by the Moon or Jupiter will further improve matters.

Capricorn

The native will be unforgiving, of moderate means, interested in low class women, timid, hold an insignificant job, and greedy. He will lose due to conflict with his relatives. If the Moon aspects the Sun, the loss would be due to females. He is likely to be lonely and isolated and may not have any persons loyal or intimate to him. He will be conservative, pessimistic and reserved and may be lacking in energy. Aspect of Mars on the Sun will improve the mentality just referred to in the previous sentence but it may cause trouble from the enemies and make the native susceptible to injuries. Aspect of Jupiter or Saturn will improve matters considerably insofar as material well being is concerned. He will have a good appetite. The Sun will give moderately good results in this sign for Aries and Taurus ascendants.

Aquarius

He may have heart trouble. He will be physically strong but for Cancer ascendant, this placement of the Sun may cause death of the native in its major-period or sub-periods. He would be miserly and will not have much wealth. For Aries ascendant, the Sun in its major-period or sub-periods may give highly placed friends or a male child and confer lot of wealth on the native. Aspect of Jupiter or Saturn will improve matters considerably insofar as material well being is concerned. He has a responsible attitude to his duties and can therefore be relied upon. He will not be a firm friend, but he will be popular and sociable. He will like to be his own master. His life may have influence or participation of masses in it. He will be unhappy with his children.

Pisces

The native will earn through products related to water. He would be fond of female company, be wealthy, a good speaker, friendly, reputed, happy and learned. He would have a tendency to amass wealth. If the ascendant is Taurus, the native will be successful in making plenty of money. He will be honourable if the ascendant is Gemini. He will defeat his enemies and will be successful in litigation. He will have a good wife, children and servants. He would be able to communicate well but will be untruthful. He may have disease in his private parts. Aspect by the Moon or Jupiter will improve matters.

MOON

1. The Moon is feminine, fair, with handsome eyes and melodious voice. It is svelte, tall, youthful, with curly and short hair, and is intuitive and beautiful in appearance. It is learned, friendly, kind, fickleminded and likes to wear clean white clothes. It is satwik and specially partial to aged women. It is a queen. Its vehicle is a deer. It gets hurt easily. It is passive and impressionable. It is quick moving.

2. Its RELATIONSHIP with other planets is as follows:

Friendly with	Sun
	Mercury
Neutral to	Mars
	Jupiter
	Venus
	Saturn
Inimical to	None

3. It is the KARAKA for the following:
Mental state, mother, breasts, temperament, mind, chest, and lungs.

4. It REPRESENTS the following:
(i)   Intellect, meritorious deeds (punya) in the past lives, fickleness, tolerance, infancy (from birth to 4 years of

age) and also 24 years of age, orthodoxy, insanity, pleasant banter, learning, laziness, sleep, equanimity, devotion to Goddess Durga, faith, love, openness, peace,
happiness, fame, mediumship, occult studies, hypnosis,
telepathy, clairvoyance, artistic accomplishments and a
pleasure loving person.

(ii)   Phlegm, sleep disorders, lethargy, carbuncle, fever with
chills, danger from horned or marine animals, blood
disorders, lack of appetite, trouble from women, jaun-
dice, epilepsy, enlargement of spleen, cold and fever,
childbirth, conception, anaemia, embryo, tuberculosis,
blood-pressure, neurological disorders, left eye, esopha-
gus, ovary, uterus, and diseases in the shoulder.

(iii)   Strength, beauty or lustre of the face, fair complexion,
attractiveness, if the Moon is afflicted it gives sickness in
infancy and old age, and makes the native unfortunate.

(iv)   Flower, fruits, milk, water, affluence, north-west, sweet
substances, home, place of residence, fragrance, brahmin,
soft cloth, new unused cloth, crystal, ornaments, comfort,
silver, well, tank, journey, noon, pearl, masses, white
colour, belt, salt, favour, radiance, poets, powerful at
night, journey to distant lands, fish, marine life, pilgrimages, wanderings, eatables, beads, rainy season, change-
ability, sense of taste, canopy and other royal insignia.

(v)   Queen, women, female, sailor, hawker, traveller, nurse,
midwife, and such other professions that deal directly
with the people at large.

(vi)   Moon represents the Yavana desh (North West Frontier
Province, now a part of Pakistan), Europe, Dama (getting
one's work done by temptation), governs Moola (plants,
creepers, grass, trees etc.), rises head first, represents
crawling insects, looks squarely ahead.

5. If the fourth house, its owner and the Moon are influenced
by Saturn the native is dispassionate. If these are under the
influence of Rahu the native is fearful.

6. The native suffers from epilepsy if the waning Moon is in
the eighth house under the influence of Rahu, the fourth house
is likewise affected by Rahu and there is no beneficial influence.

7. If the Moon is in the sixth or the eighth house, not connected with Rahu but under malefic influence, the native suffers from blood pressure problems.

8. If the Moon is located adversely in the twelfth house it harms the left eye.

9. If the Moon is very weak in a horoscope and so is the ascendant, the infant is likely to die in its infancy.

10. The native will have mass appeal if the Moon is powerful and is related to the fourth house and its owner.

11. (i) The native will suffer from tuberculosis if the fourth house, its owner and the Moon are related to Saturn and Rahu and there is no mitigating beneficial influence.

(ii) The Sun and the Moon, when they exchange signs in the birth or navansha chart or join together in Leo, also cause chest ailments.

12. The longevity of that relative of the native represented by the house from which the Moon is placed in the sixth house will be harmed by it. Thus if the Moon is in the sixth house from the fourth, i.e. if the Moon is in the ninth house, the longevity of native's mother will be badly effected.

13. In continuation of the preceding paragraph, the longevity of the first born is seriously endangered if the Moon is located in the tenth house (being in the sixth house from the fifth house).

14. If the Moon is strong in a horoscope and has beneficial aspect, the native will by nature be sympathetic, will be sensitive, will have emotional maturity and the capacity to influence the society beneficially.

15. The nature of child birth, whether easy or difficult, for the mother of the native at the time of his birth can be judged from the Moon. If the Moon is associated with or under the influence of malefic planets, the native's mother had much trouble at the time of his birth. If it is under the influence of Mars or Ketu also, surgery was performed at the time of his birth.

16. A powerful Moon is also, like the Sun capable of giving power and pre-eminence but whereas the Sun will also make the

person strong willed, the Moon would make him a leader or administrator responsive to the needs of the people.

17. Whereas the Sun overcomes and influences any planet with which it is associated, the Moon accepts any planetary influence that is brought to bear on it. The Sun is therefore the indicator of native's spirit of independence; the Moon is that of dependence.

18. The Sun is the indicator of native's prestige, the Moon of popularity.

19. The importance of an unblemished and good Moon cannot be overemphasised with regard to the longevity of the infant. (i) If the Moon is in the drekkans of Mercury, Venus or Jupiter, or of a planet which is a beneficial planet for the ascendant or, (ii) if the dispositor of the Moon is powerful, it can safely be predicted that there is no BALARISTA and the infant will live to a good age. The exceptions to these rules are as follows:
  (a)   The Moon is in the first, sixth, eighth, or the twelfth house and is weak and afflicted.
  (b)   The Moon is in the eighth house from the ascendant and the eighth house from the Moon contains a malefic planet. This subject has been treated in detail under the Eighth House in Chapter Five.

20. If the Moon is in aspect to a beneficial Jupiter or Venus, the native will enjoy strokes of good fortune every fourth or sixth year.

21. If the Moon is between the ascendant and the cusp of the fourth house, or between the cusps of the seventh and the tenth houses it is considered to be in low tide. Elsewhere it is in high tide. The Moon in low tide is considered weak.

22. The Moon is powerful in the fourth house and gives results there provided it is waxing. A waning Moon there will be powerless to give results.

23. The Moon damages the eighth house from the house it occupies.

24. By nature the Moon when waxing is a beneficial planet. It is a malefic planet when waning (within 72 degrees of the Sun).

25. The aspect of the Moon on other planets, and vice-versa (See paragraph 44 under the opening remarks at the beginning of this Chapter for guidelines for analysing the influence of an aspect):

(i) On the Sun—See under SUN above.

(ii) On Mars—On the positive side (if the aspecting planet is a beneficial planet for the ascendant), the native will be magnanimous, enterprising and ambitious. He will benefit from his mother or from her side of the family. He will be lucky in property matters and get very rich by the close of life. He will retain his mental and physical faculties in good order till an advanced age. He will be hard working, energetic, active and healthy with a robust physique. The circulatory and muscular systems will be finely developed and functioning. He may be successful in armed forces or jobs connected with water. He will love sports and do well at them. Journeys will be pleasant and successful.

On the negative side (if the aspecting planet is a malefic planet for the ascendant), he will be rash, reckless and irritable. He may not have the good indications written above, or in a still worse situation, he may have the reverse results of the above good ones. He may have bad reputation. He will be attracted to women, leading to disreputable entanglements. He may be accident-prone and may have adverse results in litigation. When the fifth or seventh house is involved, the native may suffer loss of a child or wife. He may have diseases of blood, lungs, head or the mind, and in a female chart this may indicate trouble in the breasts. There will be danger from robbers, surgery, water or fire. The native will suffer losses due to his own rash acts.

(iii) On Mercury- On the positive side (if the aspecting planet is a beneficial planet for the ascendant), the native will be pliable and changeable. The native will be ever willing to try out new ideas. He will be happy, imaginative and intuitive. He may have special aptitude for languages. He will have good memory and eloquence. He may have poetic abilities and a pleasant temperament.

On the negative side (if the aspecting planet is a malefic planet for the ascendant), he may always be anxious, indecisive and mentally imbalanced. There may be an inclination to pilfer things even when not needed, tell lies and indulge in back biting. He may have weakness for female company. He may lose due to incautious signing of documents.

(iv) On Jupiter-On the positive side (if the aspecting planet is a beneficial planet for the ascendant), the native will be rich, well behaved, and religious. He will be imaginative and intuitive. He will have a productive mind. He will be honest and just. He will have very good relations with his mother and gain through watery pursuits. His children will be a source of happiness to him. He will respect his superiors in position and age. He will have good relations with the government and his bosses. He will be healthy, well known, successful, popular and friendly. He will come across inheritance. He will gain through law and litigation.

On the negative side (if the aspecting planet is a malefic planet for the ascendant), he will be extravagant, excessive in his living style and reckless with his money. He will suffer losses in games of chance or speculation. He will be given to pomp and show. He may have to face baseless charges.

(v) On Venus- On the positive side (if the aspecting planet is a beneficial planet for the ascendant), the native will have a happy marriage. He will have good-looking and loving children and he will be pleasure loving. He will like to lead a luxurious and comfortable life. He will have an attractive personality and will have interest in fine arts and music. He will gain through mother or females in general. He will be socially active and popular. He may be wealthy and have vehicles. He will be clever in trading. In sum, he will be blessed with all material benefits, and he will enjoy them.

On the negative side (if the aspecting planet is a malefic planet for the ascendant), the native will have a roving eye and may not be a steadfast partner in married life. He may have several affairs outside marriage. Females will keep appearing in his life, on whom he will spend lavishly. He may face humiliations on account of his liaisons. His style of life will be excessive leading to health problems.

(vi) On Saturn-On the positive side (if the aspecting planet is a beneficial planet for the ascendant), the native is likely to be close to his parents, may look after them well and may benefit from them. He will be a tradition respecting person, and will like to abide by the social norms. He will be self reliant, tactful and methodical. He is likely to reach a high position in life and win popular approbation. He will also be relied upon by his superiors and entrusted with responsibility. He may be interested in agriculture and water resources, and may earn through these professions. The native will be a cautious and careful person and act with due thought. He will be hard working, conscientious and a person given to minute examination of the matter at hand, but he will neither be slow nor dilatory. There will be noticeable age difference between married partners.

On the negative side (if the aspecting planet is a malefic planet for the ascendant), during the major-period or sub-periods of the more adverse of the two planets involved in this aspect the relations with the parents, especially with the mother, may deteriorate, a parent may fall seriously sick or pass away. There may be trouble from the Government or the native's superior.

26. Effect of the Moon in various HOUSES:

First

The native may be bold, handsome, sociable, cheerful, and fond of travelling. He will travel abroad, will be interested in metaphysical matters and will be highly placed. He will be desirous of change, will like walking and be attached to his wife. His wife would have got married at a comparatively early age. She will be happy with her marriage. He will be passionate and sentimental but of changeable nature. He will have a strong constitution. He would be in contact with the masses in his life. He would be easy going, wealthy and long-lived. This position however adversely affects intelligence or the sense of hearing, sight or speech if the planet is located in a sign other than Aries, Taurus or Cancer, is waning and weak. If the Moon is waxing the native will have fair complexion and a pleasing personality but will have desire for money and worldly goods. The Moon in Cancer in the first house can cause death by drowning, oedema or cold and problems from liquids. The native's father will be happy with his children and if there is no other influence to the contrary, the native is likely to have more sisters than brothers.

Second

The native will belong to a good and large family, will have profits in his business and be wealthy. Females will be helpful to him in earning wealth. He may also earn by employing a number of persons. He would have good education. His finances will wax and wane like the Moon. He will be sensual. He would be generous and soft spoken but the speech may have some flaw. He will have a pleasant face. He will suffer from eye trouble. He will enjoy good food and will be reputed. He would be learned and generous but there may be break in his early education. His younger sister/ brother may work in a hospital or prison, or may be deeply interested in the occult. His mother will be well liked. His children will travel abroad and may change their vocation several times.

Third

The native will be thrifty, artistic, inquisitive, and can communicate his ideas well. He will keep changing his hobbies from time to time. He will have more younger sisters than brothers and his relations with his younger brothers/sisters would be satisfactory. There will be change in his surroundings from time to time. He would be changeable, courageous, cheerful and fond of travelling and his publicity. If the Moon is badly influenced or is waning, the native may begin to lose his wealth after 25 years of age. His elder sister/brother is likely to have female children. His father will change his business partners several times and travel a lot. His wife will travel abroad, be charitable and may execute works of philanthropic or public interest.

Fourth

He will have cordial relations with his mother and family. He would be generous and if the Moon is powerful and well aspected, the native will be cheerful and his mind will be at peace. If the Moon is weak and afflicted, the native or his mother may suffer constantly from diseases. He would have comforts, immovable property, good conveyances and friends. He would be sensual. He would live near water. If the sign in the fourth house is watery, the native will earn from marine products or generally by dealing with water or liquids. He will be popular and towards the end of his life will , if the Moon is powerful, have the adulation of the masses. He will change his residence several times. This is not considered a good position for the Moon, though it has the highest directional strength here, since it is the karaka for this house. A good Moon here is an indication that the native will have a peaceful end. The native's wife may be well known and popular. His children may be engaged in a hospital, asylum, nursing home or a prison. His elder sister/ brother may have diseases of the chest or lungs or he may be mentally troubled.

Fifth

The native would be of romantic nature and will be fond of amusements and pleasures. His children would be a source of great satisfaction and happiness to him. He would be intelligent and will love entertainment, arts and sports. He will rise to a high position in life. The native will have a number of female issues and one of the children will have a very close bearing on the future course of native's life. He will have interest in speculation, the occult and spiritual side of life. A well placed and powerful Moon under beneficial influence will make the native's mother religious and involved in charitable work. He will gain through his wife.

Sixth

The native will be in service of others and will change jobs several times. His relations with his mother and colleagues at work will be difficult. He will suffer from eye and stomach troubles and humiliations. He would be of poor intelligence. He will be able to check his enemies if the Moon is well placed and powerful here. A full Moon here is a good augury for long life. He will have an unsatisfactory childhood. He will time and again face demands for repayment of loans from his creditors. If the Moon is waning and under malefic influence, the native is likely to suffer from oedema or trouble in the lungs. A weak Moon will be bad for the health of younger sister/brother and the mother. His children will be very wealthy provided the Moon is powerful. Such a Moon will raise the father to a high position who would also be inclined to do philanthropic work.

Seventh

The native will be happily married and if there are other indications in the horoscope that confirm it, he may get married more than once. He may marry early. He and his wife would be good looking and passionate. He may earn well through successful business partnership, may be from abroad. The wife would be dominant. The native and wife would like travelling. An afflicted and weak Moon may bring about early death of the wife. His children will travel around and may change their hobbies and interests from time to time. It will give results of its placement in the fifth house to his younger sister/brother, and in the ninth house to his elder sister/brother.

Eighth

The native will suffer from eye trouble and poor health. His relations with his mother would be unsatisfactory. The mother will face danger. The longevity of his wife or mother is curtailed. He will be fickleminded and not confident of himself. This position generally tends to curtail life but if the birth is during the day and the Moon is waning but aspected by beneficial planets, or if the birth is during the night and the Moon is waxing and aspected by beneficial planets, the danger of death during infancy is removed. A waxing Moon here gives money through marriage. The death of the native can be of a public nature. If the Moon is waning and under malefic influence, the native is likely to suffer from oedema or trouble in the lungs. The native will die of drowning or imbalance of watery element in the body.

Ninth

The native will be popular, prosperous, religious, generous, devoted to his father and will be happy with his children. He will have a successful career and may be respected by all. He will tend to do well in life after 23 years of age. His undertakings will fructify. He will travel abroad and live there for some periods. He will be imaginative, and inquisitive about metaphysical matters. He will like doing charitable works for public good like making hospitals, and digging wells. It will give results of its placement in the first house to his father, and in fifth house to the children of the native.

Tenth

The native will have a high moral standard, be successful and popular. He will be helpful to others and will have cordial relationship with his mother. He will get along well with women. He may not be happy with regard to his children. He will change his vocation several times. He will travel abroad and will be well-known. If the Moon is not powerful it will make the native pursue a vocation where he serves large number of people for example ferryman, hawker etc. A powerful Moon will also make the native come in contact with a large number of people but he will be occupying a high and responsible position, perhaps in government. The native will find his 24th and 43rd years particularly fortunate. Good longevity is ensured if the Moon is powerful.

Eleventh

The native will realise his ambitions. He will be wealthy, honest and happy with his children and servants. This is a lucky position. He will not be constant in his friendship though his circle of acquaintances and friends will be wide. He will be sociable and will be able to mix in society easily. He will be successful at politics. He will have a number of female children. The native will possess expensive vehicles and will gain in trade. He may be in government service. It will give results of its placement in the first house to the elder sister/brother of the native.

Twelfth

He would be lazy and emotionally disturbed. He may be infirm in a limb or of poor eye-sight. He will be interested in mystical and romantic subjects. The native is likely to travel overseas frequently. This position increases the number of enemies. He may be involved with hospitals, monastery or prisons. He may be holding a nursing job. The native will experience restrictions. He will not be firm minded and can easily be led away. He will be worried and may face heavy expenses. It will give results of its placement in the sixth house to his wife.

26. Effect of the Moon in various SIGNS (See opening remarks in paragraph 19 under SUN):

Aries

The native will be haughty, independent, sensual, head of an enterprise, fickleminded, courageous, and fond of travelling. He will be rich but will spend whatever money he would earn. A full Moon will give excellent results with regard to wealth if it is in the ascendant or in the second house in this sign. He would keep bad company. He will have a ruddy complexion. He would have bad nails, knees, and hair. There would be marks of wounds and boils on his body and he would be afraid of water. He may suffer from troubles in the head and fevers. The wife and mother would be dominating and he would not pull along well with his brothers. If the Moon is located in this sign hemmed in by two malefic planets, the native will die of burns or injuries inflicted by weapons. He will be afraid of water. The Moon in this sign in the ascendant is good. If the Sun aspects the Moon, the native will have quick temper and he will be keen to join the army or police. Aspect of Jupiter or Venus will be welcome as it will make the native rich and highly placed.

Taurus (Exalted at 3 deg/Mooltrikona from 4 to 30 deg)

The native is quiet, patient, generous, handsome, broad chested with thick neck, has curly hair, has a well developed aesthetic sense, and prefers female company. He will be conservative and may resist change. He may successfully acquire property and friends. He may involve himself in his family business. He may be prosperous. He may talk well and may be an interesting conversationalist. He will be happier in the middle and end of his life. For Aries ascendant, a powerful Moon will give riches but some sickness as well. The aspect of Mars is bad for the morals of the native. When Jupiter aspects the Moon the native will be wealthy. He will be learned and good if Mercury aspects it. The aspect of Saturn will make the native have an uncertain financial status.

Gemini

The native has a developed intellect. He will be very fond of books and reading. He is learned, humorous, witty and can express himself well. He is fond of female company, handsome, and likes to travel. He may have a prominent nose. He will think of the welfare of all, will do good deeds, will be popular among women, and will be respected for his gentlemanliness. A powerful Moon in this sign with Virgo ascendant will make the native very rich and highly placed. The aspect of Jupiter on a Moon placed well in Gemini will make the native very learned. The aspect of Venus is excellent for wealth.

Cancer

The native will be under the influence of his mother. He will be generally susceptible to female influence. He would be wealthy, owning property, highly placed, fond of flowers, travelling and waterbodies. He will have interest in astrology and the occult. His family life will be happy. He will have a good house. His career may have periodic ups and downs. He may live abroad. It is not good from the point of view of longevity for Gemini ascendant, especially so when Mars influences it. If, with such a combination, Mars and the Moon have their major-period and sub-period current in the childhood of the native, he may not survive it. When the ascendant is Scorpio, combination of the Sun with Moon in Cancer will take the native high in life and make him prosperous. Even aspect of the Sun on Moon will produce excellent results. The aspect of Jupiter or Venus will likewise produce very favourable results, but the aspect of Venus on the Moon in Cancer may make the native lustful and he may not have a good moral character.

Leo

Though the native will be attached to his mother and will respect her, the cause of most of his troubles will be women and his married life may not be satisfactory. He would be a man of principles and would have a dignified air about him but he would be of anxious and vindictive temperament. He would be generous in nature. He would have a broad chest and face. He would suffer from teeth and stomach trouble. This position of the Moon for Aries ascendant is not good. The native will, with great difficulty, be able to have a daughter. If the ascendant is Leo, the native will have some defect in his eyesight. Aspect of the Sun on the Moon will make him a highly placed person. When Mars aspects the Moon in Leo, the native is likely to be a prosperous and senior army officer.

Virgo

He would be truthful, handsome, learned, eloquent, persevering, patient, helpful, wealthy, teacher of Vedas and compassionate. He would have more daughters than sons. He would be partial to female company. The native will be fortunate. If the Moon is located in this sign hemmed in by two malefic planets, the native will die of blood disorders. The native, with Taurus ascendant and the Moon placed in Virgo, will have a daughter who will be very rich later in life. This placement of a full and powerful Moon in the ascendant will make the native very wealthy and handsome. Aspect of Jupiter or Venus will further improve matters.

Libra

The native will have property, be generous, active, a trader in cattle, very wealthy, religious, interested in philosophy, intelligent and fond of travelling. He may be tall and slim and may have a prominent nose. He may have liaison with more than one woman. The Moon in Libra for Aries ascendant may not give good results. Here, the native will be ailing and may succumb to diseases in the major-period or sub-periods of the Moon. For Taurus ascendant , such a Moon will cause the native to get involved in litigation and debts. A powerful Moon in Libra will be excellent for Gemini, Virgo or Libra ascendant, provided Venus is powerful and the Moon is not associated with the Sun.

Scorpio (Debilitated at 3 deg)

The native may fall ill repeatedly in his childhood. He may be greedy, miserly, and fickleminded and may not be able to express himself satisfactorily. He may have to live away from the family. He would be capable and clever at his work. He may have to suffer displeasure of the government in the form of financial penalties. The native would be overbearing, of thievish disposition and will not get along well with his relatives. He will gamble away his money. He may have a painful death. He may join service. If the Moon is located in this sign hemmed in by two malefic planets, the native will die of burns or injuries inflicted by weapons. A full Moon in Scorpio will be very good as far as marital felicity is concerned for Taurus ascendant. A weak Moon in Scorpio is also good for Aquarius ascendant. Aspect of Mars on the Moon will make the native rich and powerful.

Sagittarius

The native can communicate his ideas well. He may have an oval face and an elongated neck. He would be strong, learned and generous. He may be short statured or he may have normal height but abnormal weight if Jupiter is powerful in the horoscope. He will live near water. He will be well built, courageous and eloquent. He will be rich but miserly. The native will succeed at speculation well if the ascendant is Gemini but his married life may cause sorrow to him. For this ascendant the native may have trouble in his teeth. Cancer in the ascendant and the Moon weakly placed in Sagittarius is a bad combination. The native may be of bad conduct and may indulge in giving and taking of loans, gambling, womanising and he may be in the habit of taking alcohol. A waning Moon in Sagittarius may bring about separation from spouse for Capricorn ascendant, and give ailing children to a native having Aquarius ascendant. If strong, it shall be excellent for Pisces ascendant. The aspect of the Sun, Venus or Jupiter will yield good results. The aspect of Mars on the Moon in Sagittarius will make the native a wealthy and well placed senior army officer. The aspect of even Saturn will make the native morally upright and a good speaker.

Capricorn

He can be unforgiving. He would be a slow worker. He would like travelling but he is basically a family man. He would be tall and lean in appearance. He may have musical talent. He will be highly sensual, truthful, unexcitable and ruthless. He will look for company of young women. He will be susceptible to cold. If the Moon is located in this sign hemmed in by two malefic planets, the native may die of burns, hanging or fall from a height. The Aries and Libra ascendants with the Moon in Capricorn are good for power and pelf. The aspect of Mars, Jupiter or Venus on the Moon is good.

Aquarius

He has finely developed aesthetic sense but would have a bad temper. He would not be religious and may like intoxicants. He would be lazy, inimical to good persons and will be poor. His build would be large. If the Moon is located in this sign hemmed in by two malefic planets, the native will die of burns, hanging or fall from a height. The native will earn well if the planet is favourable for the ascendant. A powerful Moon in Aquarius will yield good results for Gemini and Scorpio ascendants. The aspect of Jupiter on the Moon will be auspicious.

Pisces

The Moon is generally good in this sign. The native would be generous, fond of young women, well educated, balanced, handsome and wealthy. He can be successful in the field of fine arts. He will have an unpredictable temper, taste for good music, and an interest in things foreign. He may get or inherit wealth suddenly or may come upon buried treasure. He will be fond of journeys overseas and may profit from them. The Moon in this sign for Aries, Leo, Libra and Aquarius ascendants may yield poor results. The aspect of the Sun on Moon will make the native join the army. He will have a martial frame of mind. The aspect of Mercury or Jupiter will be excellent for affluence and learning.

MARS

1. Mars is masculine, short in stature, and has a thin waist. It has reddish brown eyes, and is powerfully built. Its hair are short and shining, and it is red and shining in appearance. It is courageous, a skilful speaker, tamasik, intelligent, liberal, slim, of changeable disposition, is wrathful, adventurous and capable of causing hurts. It dresses in red. It is the son of the Earth. Its vehicle is a ram. It is active. It is the god of war.

2. Its RELATIONSHIP with other planets is as follows:

Friendly with	Sun
	Moon
	Jupiter
Neutral to	Venus
	Saturn
Inimical to	Mercury

It is noticed that the signs owned by Mars and Venus are seventh and also twelfth from each other. Mars therefore dissipates Venus and stands on many matters opposed to what Venus signifies. There is opposition between the two planets in the above sense.

3. It is the KARAKA for·the following:

Physical and mental strength, things produced out of the earth, immovable property but not agricultural land, younger brother/sister, enemy, enmity, courage, kinsmen, weapons, boils, soldier, injury, self-praise, bone marrow and energy.

4. It REPRESENTS the following:

(i) Ruthlessness, enthusiasm, generosity, boldness, misdeeds, self-confidence, will, independence, determination, argument, leadership, conflict, the tendency to look upwards, drive, wit, organising ability, ability to get the work done, foolhardiness , unruliness, misunderstandings and telling lies.

(ii) Head, muscle, testicles, sexual vitality, blood, acute fever, inflammations, burns, bleeding, miscarriage, smallpox, sunstroke, measles, surgical operations, wounds, epidemics, excessive thirst, injury due to fire, poison or weapon; dry and rough skin, fracture of bone, loss by thieves, and diseases in upper part of the body.

(iii)   Battles, enemies, crime, accident, violence, litigation, hearth-fire, fire, electricity, logic, debates, science, iron, south, cutlery, athletic performance, engineering, Dhatu (inanimate objects like minerals and metals), quadruped, slightly burnt cloth, warrior class, Lord Hanuman, Lord Subramanya, summer, coral, deep-red, savage beasts, birds of prey, acids, tiger, wolf, battle fields, slaughter house, machinery, and smithy.

(iv)   Interest in other's women, territory from Krishna river to Ceylon. Like the Sun it represents Danda (Punishment). Mars governs the age of 28 years and also between 42 and 56 years.

(v)   Surgeons, warriors, lawyers, debators, cooks, butchers and barbers.

5. It is powerful in the tenth and infructuous in the second house.

6. The difference between Venus and Mars is obvious insofar as emotional side of human nature is concerned. Venus is emotionally sensitive whereas Mars is emotionally excitable. Therefore Venus generates emotional impressions but Mars projects passions. Affection and refinement thus fall within the domain of Venus. Mars governs violence.

7. Mars is male. Venus is female. When the two join, aspect each other, or Mars influences Venus in any manner, in the birth chart or the navansha chart, it leads to heightened sexuality in the native. This gets exacerbated if the association takes place in a fixed sign.

8. If Mars and Ketu influence the factors indicating the self in a horoscope, the native suffers from accidents, violence and injuries.

9. When Mars and Jupiter together influence the self of an individual, they lead him to put in hard work for the good of the society. A good samaritan is born. Contrary is the result when Saturn joins Mars. In this case the native is selfish and perverted, and will have criminal tendencies.

10. Mars is a malefic planet by nature. It rises hind part first.

11. Placement of Mars in the first, second, fourth, seventh, eighth, or the twelfth house causes early death of the spouse, separation, divorce, or marital discord or incompatibility.

12. Mars or a malefic planet in general in the eighth house in a female horoscope, is known to cause widowhood.

13. If Mars is afflicted in a horoscope it will cause serious problems for the native every 3 years and 9 months.

14. If Mars is an adverse planet for the horoscope and is in aspect with either the Sun or Moon, the native will be in serious difficulties at the age of 52. 5 years. If such a Sun or Moon is also afflicted by Saturn, death of the native may occur.

15. The aspect of Mars on other planets and vice-versa (See paragraph 44 under the opening remarks at the beginning of this Chapter for guidelines for analysing the influence of an aspect.):

(i)   On the Sun-See under SUN.

(ii)   On the Moon-See under MOON.

(iii)   On Mercury- On the positive side (if the aspecting planet is good for the ascendant), the native will have a sharp and vigorous mind. He may be successful as an engineer, surgeon or a mathematician. He will be precise, correct and dexterous. He will be witty, humorous, resourceful, prompt and lively.
        On the negative side (if the aspecting planet is bad for the ascendant), the native will display prejudice, passion and anger. He will be oblivious of discretion and reason. He may take recourse to untruths. He may be critical, deceitful, self-centred and arrogant. He may marry a widow or a characterless woman, and may not be wealthy.

(iv)   On Jupiter-On the positive side (if the aspecting planet is good for the ascendant), the native will have a positive approach to life. He will be independent minded, persuasive, candid, learned and noble. He will be financially successful. He will have innovative methods of dealing with issues confronting him. He will be just and a champion of the weak and oppressed. He will like travelling and will benefit from it. He will be upright and straightforward. He will be able to motivate others to a higher degree of efficiency.

On the negative side (if the aspecting planet is bad for the ascendant), he may have to face trouble due to religion. He may face religious persecution or may suffer damage due to occult practices. He may be the victim of other's dishonesty or he may harm others by such practice. He may die away from home, may be killed due to enmity, or die in confinement, a monastery or a hospital. He may be extravagant.

(v) On Venus- On the positive side (if the aspecting planet is good for the ascendant), the aspect energises the talents that the native will be given by Venus, and which would have remained dormant in the personality otherwise. He will be fond of sports. He will be bold and able. He will be reputed, wealthy and will spend well. He may earn through the stage, art, decoration, women, music etc. He will be popular and friendly. He may gain through women. He will marry early and will have a good married life. His can be a case of love at first sight. His attachments may be beneficial.

On the negative side (if the aspecting planet is bad for the ascendant), he will be extravagant, passionate, lascivious, and may run after women. He may spend on sex, finery, jewellery, pomp, show and fellowship. When other malefic planets also put in their influence, he may even have perverted sex drive. The wife may not be long lived. There may be danger to his life through females. He will have a weak will and will be unable to check his wayward ways. If the aspect takes place in a watery sign, the native may get addicted to alcohol. He may like to gamble and have liaison with several women. He may have trouble with money related to the dead.

(vi) On Saturn- On the positive side (if the aspecting planet is good for the ascendant), his personality will be masterful. He will be ambitious, brave to the extent of being contemptuous of danger, and energetic. He will be of tenacious attitude to work. His mind may be subtle. He will have leadership abilities and may attain fame.

On the negative side (if the aspecting planet is bad for

the ascendant), he will be fanatically attached to his ideas and faith, and he will be the right material of which militants are made. He will be overbearing and may get notoriety. There may be serious threat to his honour. There may be accidents, injuries or a violent death. The native will suffer at the hands of the government or his enemies. He may have losses due to thefts or disputes with labour. His parents may get estranged from him or may pass away early. If he attains a high position, there is a danger of fall from it. He will have bad relations with his bosses and he will suffer for his hot-headedness. He may be unfeeling and callous.

16. Effect of Mars in various HOUSES:

First

The native would be adventure loving, independent, assertive, moody and physically powerful. In case Mars is an adverse planet for the horoscope, he may be liable to suffer from troubles in the head or be involved in accidents. He may be bothered by his enemies. He may not be truthful. His mother may be rash and may have quick temper, she may be an active person and may be authoritative. His married life may not be cordial. He may have the habit of pilfering things, or his possessions may be stolen. He will be young looking and may have ruddy complexion, a scar on the temples or head and may suffer from piles. He may not be long-lived. He will be liable to get fever. He may join a service where he may have to bear arms or may join an engineering profession. His younger sisters/brothers may be well off in life but they will have some problem with regard to their children. His elder sister/brother may have a satisfactory life but the elder sister/brother will not have good relations with some of his younger sisters/brothers. His father will be troubled on account of his children. Mars influenced by a Node here will make the native's mother abort.

Second

He would be irritable, poorly educated, and will have to work hard for success in life. It will not be so if Mars is placed in its own sign or in the sign of its exaltation. He may speak harshly or his speech will appear disagreeable to others. He will like the company of wicked people. This position is dangerous to the longevity of spouse. Mars is restricted in giving full results in this location. The native may suffer from troubles in the eyes, piles, fistula etc. He will live away from his place of birth. The native's children and his father will be rash and of quick temper. The children will be very energetic and powerfully placed in life. An adverse Mars is bad for the longevity of the first child. Some child of the native, who had reached a high position in life may suffer a severe fall from that position. This may also cause dissensions in the family. The native may spend his wealth over loose women and in meeting his expenses arising out of his dissolute habits. He may be irreligious and unfortunate. His younger sister/ brother may find that his secret enemies have grown powerful and active during the major-period or sub-periods of Mars. The younger sister/brother may also be in danger of being confined or getting injured in an attack by animals or robbers. His mother may be deceived or misguided by her friends. His wife may either be extravagant or meet with a violent end.

Third

The native will be courageous, healthy, wise, and intelligent. He will have poor relations with his younger brothers/sisters, can communicate well and will love adventure. When Mars is adverse and weak, the native has to guard against ear trouble, injuries to his arms, accidents in short journeys and loss through correspondence. The native may be prone to fits of violent temper. The native may have to face trouble through colleagues and neighbours. An adverse Mars when in sambandha with Ketu or another malefic planet is also likely to make his elder sister miscarry. The native will have aptitude for Chemical or Mechanical Engineering. He may join a service where he may have to bear arms. The native's father will be rash and of quick temper who may lose his wealth in disputes. However, the father will in all probability overcome his enemies and come out successful in litigation. This is not considered a good position for Mars as it is the karaka for this house.

Fourth

He cannot pull along with his mother and will be an introvert, but will have a good career and home. If Mars is debilitated here and is associated with Ketu, the native will lose his mother shortly after his birth. He will suffer losses pertaining to family property. His life towards its close will be troublesome. He is likely to get involved in litigation over property. The mind is likely to be in turmoil or be violent, more so if the Moon and the owner of the fourth house are also influenced by Mars, the owner of the sixth house or Ketu. There may be serious tensions in married life and the native may be at loggerheads with his elder sister/brother. The native's father will have difficult family life and he may lose his wealth in disputes. The native is not likely to obtain an educational degree. He will face obstructions, and lack of help from parents. He is likely to face popular opposition.

Fifth

He will suffer losses due to excesses and speculation, and be tense, aggressive and impetuous. He will be intelligent. His first child will have quick temper and be prone to accidents and injuries. There will be threat to the life of the first child and the children will be disobedient. If Mars is in debilitation or in an enemy's sign here it gets power to kill the native. This location indicates that the native's children will be born with surgical assistance. The native may suffer from stomach troubles, piles, fistula etc. The native will be attractive to the opposite sex and looking to the nature of Mars, there is possibility of scandals involving the native. He may be rash in speculation which may cause him losses. He will enjoy vigorous exercises. When Mars influences Mercury from this house, his mother may speak harshly which may be the cause of tension in the family.

Sixth

He will earn well and will fulfill his desires by working hard. He will be angry and passionate. The native will have difficulties with his servants. He will be able to suppress his enemies. He may suffer losses in rearing of poultry and animals. The native's father will be rash and will have bad temper. In a female nativity it indicates accidents, difficult and life threatening labour and miscarriages. Mars here may cause boils or wounds. Mars in its own house here is likely to make the native join service. An afflicted and weak Mars is likely to be bad for the younger sister/brother of native's mother. It is also not good for the younger sister/brother of the native. They may suffer from illnesses during the sub-periods of Mars in the major-period of owner of the second, eighth or the tenth house. It will give results of its placement in the second house to his children. A powerful and good Mars here is excellent for his father. Such a Mars will raise the father to a very high position in life.

Seventh

He will be restless, irritable and argumentative. He will have to work hard for success in life. He is not likely to have friendly relations with women, his relations with his wife will be difficult and there may be separation from spouse. He will have a strongly sexual nature. He will suffer losses in litigation. The wife will be unhealthy and short lived. If the planet is close to the cusp of this house it is likely to make the fixing up of the marriage of the native very difficult. Several proposals will not materialise. He is likely to face popular opposition. He may suffer losses through litigation. His younger sister/brother will have his source of worry and trouble in his children, or he may have recurrent colic pain in his stomach. The native's second child may not live, or may suffer seriously from illnesses. His elder sister/brother may have strained relations with his father.

Eighth

He will be of weak constitution but will have strong sex desire. The native may suffer from piles, fistula etc. Mars here may cause boils or wounds. An adverse Mars with a Node or aspected by one, may make the native get involved in an accident. He will not be wealthy. His death can be violent. He will suffer losses due to theft and fire. His wife will be extravagant. His income may dry up. The native's father will face danger to his life. The married life of native's parents must also have been poor. The native is likely to die of wounds or due to poison or injury by weapon. The younger brother will have bad temper. Mars here for Aries ascendant is considered good.

Ninth

The native will face difficulties due to his father. The parents and younger brother will be rash and short tempered. He is likely to face legal problems. Long and overseas journeys can be dangerous. He will not have many friends but he will be ambitious and will have urge to forge ahead in life. He will tend to do well in life after 27 years of age. He will be successful. If the Moon is either weak or afflicted and Mars is a seriously adverse planet, the mother may not live long. Such a Mars when it influences the Sun may cause heart ailment to his father. The native may be of bad conduct and may face a threat of imprisonment. If Rahu influences the twelfth house, the threat of imprisonment will be very real.

Tenth

He will be ambitious, persevering and successful but will be self centred. The native will face slander and unfounded allegations and will face the possibility of falling from his high position. An unaspected Mars close to the cusp of this house and unassisted, makes the native argumentative, rash, sharp of mind and shrewd. If the planet is powerful and unblemished, the native will have much power, riches and authority. The native can be a Mechanical or Electrical engineer or an employee of the armed or uniformed service, well versed in the science of mantras, a physical culturist, or a surgeon. His best years will be 28th and 58th. Mars in Leo in this house gives great progress in life and profession. A bad Mars will bring about loss of younger sister/brother through violent means. Such a Mars alongwith an afflicted Moon is bad for the longevity of mother, and the native's and his wife's mental equilibrium. If in place of the Moon, Jupiter is afflicted, he may lose his eldest child. A bad Mars is liable to cause trouble through servants, enemies, litigation or maternal uncle to the native's children.

Eleventh

He will realise his ambitions with the help of his friends but he will face opposition and dispute also from them. The friends will be few and if there is a watery sign here, they will turn inimical later. If an adverse Saturn influences Mars here the native stands in danger of severe accident or injury. If Jupiter is adverse and it is influenced by an unfavourable Mars, the native will face trouble from judiciary and losses through friends. He will be wealthy and influential. If other factors support this result, the native is likely to earn his livelihood through thefts, or his income may be from stolen goods. His enemies will be suppressed and he may be successful in litigation. He may have to face problems connected with the birth of or affairs of his children. He may speak rudely and may be fond of non vegetarian food. His elder sister/brother will be irritable but energetic.

Twelfth

He will be indebted, and lonely and will have strained relations with his younger brothers/sisters. He will have strong sex urge. He will suffer from secret enemies. He can be injured by robbers and quadrupeds. There is danger of the native getting imprisoned, especially so if Rahu also influences the twelfth house or its owner. He may have eye trouble. His mother may have fistula or piles. He is likely to lose his mother around the age of 27 years and may face a serious financial reverse in his 45th year. He is not likely to have an upright moral character and will have liaisons with several women. The marriage will show signs of failure. He may be violently opposed to his wife. She may also be given to consumption of alcohol. Mars in Libra or Pisces is bad for financial status of the native. It will make the younger sister/brother and father of the native angry and irritable and the native or his eldest child may have to undergo surgery. A powerful and beneficial Mars here will raise his younger sister/brother to a very high and powerful position in life. It will give results of its placement in the second house to his elder sister/brother.

17. Effect of Mars in various SIGNS (See opening remarks in paragraph 19 under SUN) :

Aries *(Mooltrikona from 0 to 12 deg)*

The native will occupy a position of authority or will be associated with the affairs of the government. He would be full of energy, sensual and fond of travelling. The native will be courageous, truthful and have martial qualities. He will be rich and gain from the government. This sign location is excellent for Mars, since this sign not only is the mooltrikona and own sign of Mars, but the element of the sign is also the same as that of this planet. Mars is not comfortable in its other sign Scorpio as the element is watery there. This location of Mars for Cancer, and Sagittarius ascendants is excellent. Mars in Aries for Cancer ascendant will give wealth and make the native do well in a uniformed service. Mars in Aries for Sagittarius ascendant will also give wealth but is likely to keep the native worried due to his children. The aspect of the Sun or Jupiter on Mars will be excellent for both the ascendants.

Taurus

The native would be lazy, fond of female company, sensual, shy and interested in beautiful things. He will be well dressed but not rich. He will lack self confidence. He will be talkative, cunning and unstable in life. He will not have domestic happiness. He will have trouble from enemies or his children. He may do badly at litigation. The native may face dishonour due to his love affairs or liaisons with women. This location of Mars for Cancer and Leo ascendants is excellent. The native will amass wealth; if the ascendant is Cancer, this will be done unscrupulously. Mars will give the native power, wealth and high position if the ascendant is Leo. The aspect of Jupiter on Mars for both the ascendants will be good. The aspect of Saturn on Mars will be beneficial if the ascendant is Libra, Capricorn or Aquarius.

Gemini

The native would have some talent for music. He will be handsome, without fear and of a helpful nature. He will have good vitality and stamina and will be capable of taking a lot of strain. He will be rich, have a number of friends and sons and will be fond of travelling. He will engage himself in a variety of occupations. He will have a sharp intellect and an urge to apply himself to educational pursuits. He may get into trouble due to his subordinates. He may have a weakness for women and there may be more than one marriage or liaison. There may also be changes in jobs or vocations. When Mars major or sub-period runs for a native having Pisces ascendant, he will have both learning and wealth. The aspects of the Sun, Moon or Jupiter on Mars will be beneficial. The aspect of the Moon will make the native have influence of women in his life.

Cancer *(Debilitated at 28 deg)*

He will travel and live abroad. He will suffer from enemies, a powerful woman or stomach troubles. He will be intelligent but self-centred. The native is likely to get a scholarship in his childhood, but his childhood may not be happy. His wealth and health will wax and wane. He may not have much happiness from his mother. The native will be domesticated. He will always be worried and may face sorrows. Its placement in the third drekkan of Cancer will be the best when the native will be inoffensive, sober, peaceful and quiet. Such a Mars will be very bad for ascendants owned by Mercury. Much will depend on the strength of the Moon and the aspects on Mars. The aspect of Jupiter on Mars will be the best.

Leo

The native will be physically strong. He will be courageous, impatient with others, hard working and fond of visiting forests and hunting. He will not be rich. His married life will be unsatisfactory. His wife may predecease him. He will be fond of his children. He will face trouble from subordinates. He will benefit from his connection with the government and may attain a responsible position. He may work till his death. There will not be formal retirement for him. Wealth will come to him late in life. Mars will give religiousness if it is in the second drekkan of the sign. Mars in this sign will give wealth if the ascendant is Cancer or Leo, but for Cancer it will also cause an unhappy family life, and for Leo little comforts. Scorpio ascendant is also good for wealth, but the native will have serious reverses in his health and education. The aspect of Jupiter on Mars will be excellent. The aspect of Venus will be good for marital well being but it will also make the person lascivious.

Virgo

The native will be timid, avoid enmity, learned, cultured, rich and respected. He will speak pleasantly and will have a number of children. He will have happiness from wife and property. He may go abroad or away from his place of birth, to work. Alternatively he may deal in international trade or goods produced abroad. He may be knowledgeable of stocks and shares and may gain from speculation. Mars shall give the best results in the second drekkan of the sign. When the ascendant is Sagittarius, the native may write books and will earn fame therefrom. He will also be wealthy and will have property. However Saturn or Venus should also be powerful. The aspects of the Sun, Moon or Jupiter on Mars will be beneficial. The aspect of the Moon will make the native have influence of women in his life.

Libra

The native will be sensual, timid, fortunate and fond of female company. He will be handsome, talkative and given to consumption of intoxicants. This location of Mars makes the native lose his wife early. The native will have to face heavy expenditure and trouble from wife. He will have several friends and will be successful in partnerships. The native will have good and refined children if Mars is placed in the second drekkan of the sign. This placement of Mars in Libra is good for Cancer and Capricorn ascendants, though he may be sensual in case of the former. The aspect of Jupiter, Venus or Saturn will be excellent.

Scorpio

The native will do well at business or as head of an institution. He will be wealthy, happy with his wife and children, and have the support of the government. His integrity will be in doubt. He will be aggressive, intrepid, be able to suppress his enemies and will be vindictive. He will suffer from fire, injuries and poison. He may get involved in litigation or intrigues. He may work as the leader in a plot. This placement is conducive to confinement of the native. He may go abroad, particularly so if the planet is in the third drekkaṇ. His end may be violent. Mars in this sign will be good for Cancer, Leo, Capricorn and Aquarius ascendants. The aspect of the Sun or Jupiter on Mars will be beneficial.

Sagittarius

The native will become eminent in his chosen field. He may work for the government. He would be courageous. The native will suffer losses due to his temper, and harsh and impulsive speech. He may be rash and may have to face dishonour or slanderous charges. He will have to work hard to gain success in life. He may be fond of the outdoors and sports. His wife will be obedient and loving. He will have to face trouble from his enemies. He will have a better life after marriage. He may be interested in weapons and may try to be a marksman. This planet, when placed in the third drekkan of the sign, will make the native law abiding and morally upright. This location of Mars for Aries, Leo, and Pisces ascendants is excellent. The aspect of the Sun will be excellent.

Capricorn (Exalted at 28 deg)

The native will belong to a good family. He would be active in society, hard working, a leader and rich. He will be a reliable person and can be entrusted with responsibilities. He will be bold and will have success over his enemies. He will occupy a high position and will be helpful to his relatives. The native may join a uniformed or armed service and may rise to the highest position therein. He may possess immovable property and may have highly placed younger sister/brother. Mars in the second drekkan of the sign will bring benefits from speculation, and in the third, it will make the native a shrewd businessman or a person having good scientific knowledge. It will be bad for Gemini ascendant. For Virgo ascendant, it will be in the fifth house, where it may cause loss of or trouble through the children. When the ascendant is Aries, an exalted owner of the ascendant in the tenth house will ensure a high status and fame for the native. For Cancer, a powerful Mars, being the owner of the fifth and tenth houses and therefore a very beneficial planet for this ascendant, located in the seventh house in Capricorn, will no doubt give results of a powerful rajyoga, but will not be good for the longevity of the spouse. The aspect of Jupiter or Saturn on Mars will be excellent.

Aquarius

The native will be dishonest, poor, and unhappy. He may indulge in gambling and horse racing. His appearance will be displeasing and he may look older than his age. He will be unhappy on account of a wayward son and poor health. He will be cruel, an alcoholic and malicious. A good and well placed Mars in this sign may turn the native into a scientist, especially if the planet is placed in the second drekkan of the sign. He may work energetically in group activities for public welfare. When the ascendant is Leo, a powerful Mars, being the owner of the fourth and ninth houses and therefore a very beneficial planet for this ascendant, located in the seventh house in Aquarius, will no doubt give results of a powerful rajyoga and will give benefits to the native through his spouse and marriage, but it may make the native's spouse sensuous and irritable. This description of the spouse may not be true if the drekkan in which the planet is placed is the third one. The aspect of Jupiter or Saturn on Mars will tone down the adverse results. When Mars in this sign aspects Jupiter placed in Virgo, the native is likely to be childless.

Pisces

The native will rise to a high position in life, will be courageous, reputed, ill-tempered and will live away from his birth place. The native may go abroad and live there if the drekkan in which the planet is placed is the third. His children will not do well in life, or one or two may pass away early. He may get married late in life, may have liaisons outside marriage or he may be jilted in love. If the ascendant is also Pisces and the major-period of Mars is not the first major-period after birth, the native will have all the wealth and position that he may desire. If the major-period is the first after birth, there is a danger of balarista. The native may die in infancy. The aspect of the Sun on Mars will be excellent for reputation and fame. The aspect of Venus on Mars will also be good but there will always be the apprehension that the native may be sensuous and wayward.

MERCURY

1. Mercury has grass green complexion, is pure, a yogi, rajasik, and of skilful speech. It is of happy disposition. It puts on green clothes. It is witty and likes jokes and laughter. Its vehicle is a lion with the trunk of an elephant. It is the son of the Moon. It is adaptable.

2. Its RELATIONSHIP with other planets is as follows:

Friendly with	Sun
	Venus
Neutral to	Mars
	Jupiter
	Saturn
Inimical to	Moon

3. It is the KARAKA for the following:
Learning, eloquence, skill, maternal uncle, studiousness, Lord Vishnu, childhood, education, trade and commerce, truthfulness, mathematics, friends , consciousness, astrology, humour, speech and places of entertainment.

4. It REPRESENTS the following:
(i) Arts and crafts, earth, prince, trader, female eunuch, leafy trees, charms, birds, boy, partly wet cloth, playgrounds, October and November, race-courses, clubs, emerald, alloy of metals, mixture of things, grass green colour, north, Bheda (tact and diplomacy), paper money and broker.
(ii) Intellect, vocation, intelligence, writing, attention to details, training, discrimination (Buddhi), publishing, command over languages and adaptability.
(iii) Skin, brain, intestines, bronchial tubes, larynx and impotence. Sense of smell. The tendency to look sideways like a shy damsel.
(iv) School teachers, brokers, editors, reporters, authors, printers, orators, mathematicians, accountants, insurance

agents, sanitary inspectors, merchants, messengers, con-
jurers, and jokers.

(v)   Mercury represents hypochondria, disturbance in thinking process, worry, apprehension of the likelihood of
something untoward happening, bad speech, diseases in
the eye, throat, nose and skin.

5. Mercury is by nature neutral and whenever it comes under
the influence of another planet, it takes on its nature and influence.

6. Jupiter governs the realm of abstract thinking. Mercury
relates to more concrete side of it. It represents mental energy.
It governs quick grasp of thought, writing, education, rapid
exchange of information, publishing, journalism and calculation.

7. Since Mercury relates to pre-adolescent period of life after
infancy, any affliction to it can lead to illnesses during this period,
or an unhappy childhood.

8. Since Mercury is the significator of trade and since money
is an essential part of trade, Mercury represents acquisition,
accumulation and expenditure of money.

9. A weak Mercury can make a man naive, irrational, given
to fantasizing, confused, immature and even insane. Under the
influence of a powerful Saturn it can lose its inherent intelligence
and may make the native dull.

10. It is powerful in the first house and infructuous in the
fourth. It rises head first.

11. It is by nature a beneficial planet and if it is not under the
influence of a malefic planet, or placed in an adverse sign or sign
of a naturally malefic planet, it will give results like a naturally
beneficial planet.

12. An at least averagely strong Mercury influenced by Venus
in any manner in the birth chart may give musical ability.

13. The aspect of Mercury on other planets and vice-versa (See
paragraph 44 under the opening remarks at the beginning of this
Chapter for guidelines for analysing the influence of an aspect.):

(i)   On the Sun-See under SUN.
(ii)   On the Moon-See under MOON.
(iii) On Mars-See under MARS.

(iv) On Jupiter- On the positive side (if the aspecting planet is good for the ascendant), he will be interested in humanities as a subject. He will also be interested in the study and welfare of the man. He will be eloquent and will like meeting people. His attitude will be philanthropic. The intellect will be capable of soaring to the highest levels of thought and mental speculations. He will always be keen to learn. He will gain respect and repute due to his learning and a fine intellectual personality. He will travel, go abroad and be wealthy. He will be happy and will have a positive attitude to life. He may be a legal luminary.

On the negative side (if the aspecting planet is bad for the ascendant), he may be worried, suffer through litigation and may have losses in business. He may commit forgery or fraud, or may suffer as a result of it. His speech will be his handicap, which may, many a time put him in trouble.

(v) On Venus- Astronomically no aspect can form. According to Hindu system only conjunction can be formed. The result of which is being given.

The native will be rich, optimistic, talented, soft spoken and interested in music and poetry. He will be imaginative and refined. He will have an equable temper and be friendly. He will have an attractive personality. He will spend heavily on marriages, and entertainment of guests. He may encounter trouble through females which may cause him anguish.

(vi) On Saturn- On the positive side (if the aspecting planet is good for the ascendant), his mind will be profound and wide ranging. He will be a sound and sober person with good judgement. He will be inclined to exactitude, be practical and will be a capable person who can head a large organisation. He can think consecutively and his vision will be broad. He will have good memory and concentration of mind. The instability of Mercury is taken care of by Saturn under this aspect.

On the negative side (if the aspecting planet is bad for the ascendant), the mind may be slow and dull. The native may be in danger of losing his mental equilibrium. He may suffer from depression and pessimism. There may be a tendency to postpone matters. He may travel about aimlessly. He may be a person given to causing dissensions.

14. Effect of Mercury in various HOUSES:

First

He will have charm, and will be happy, calm, sharp, witty , intelligent, friendly, learned and eloquent. He may master several languages. He will be long lived, handsome, slender and tall. He will delve in several subjects in depth particularly astrology, engineering, mathematics, magic etc. He will have a well developed business acumen. If there is influence of Saturn or of a Node of the Moon on Mercury in the first house, the native may suffer from nervous disorders. Such an influence can also cause skin disorders. The native may live away from the place of his birth. His marital life may be satisfactory. The spouse may be beautiful. His younger sister/brother will be wealthy and will have happiness from his children. His mother will be prosperous and of good and religious conduct. His children may write books, be learned or in diplomatic service. They may engage in profitable international trade or in goods from abroad, or be successful brokers. His mother's younger sister/brother will be well placed, have a large family and live long. The spouse may be long lived. In a female's chart, Mercury in the first house may indicate that her husband may not be able to satisfy her sexually. The native's father may be highly and well placed in life.

Second

The native will be well-educated, learned and very wealthy. He can be a poet, a teacher, a commission agent, an owner of presses or bookshops, or a writer. He may do well at business. He will be able to express himself pleasantly and well. He will generally not tell lies. He will gain through correspondence, trade, brokerage and advertisements. He will have a large family. If the planet is weak the native will lose through thefts and fraud. When the eighth house is also powerful, there is a possibility that the native may get wealth through death of a senior member of the family. His younger sister/brother may either languish at a paltry position in life or his education may suffer; if he succeeds in getting to a good position, he is likely to lose it later. The native's mother will have a large circle of female friends and she may be well off in life. His children, particularly the first child will be highly intelligent and of good conduct. The children will do well in life. If Mercury is well and powerfully placed in the second house, the native's father may not suffer from enemies and will not get involved in litigation. Such a Mercury will also be helpful to the elder sister/brother of the native to lead a happy and contented life, and be close to the mother.

Third

The native will have a reasonably long span of life. He will have good relations with his younger brothers/sisters. He will be mentally alert and active and succeed in literary activities. He may have several hobbies. He will have trading acumen and will be prepared to take risks. He will work hard. He will travel a lot, particularly if the sign in the third house is a movable one. He will be proficient in science. The native will be religiously inclined and he will not deviate from the path of righteousness. It will give results of its placement in the first house to the younger sister/brother of the native. His mother may have beautiful eyes. His children and elder sister/brother will be highly placed and wealthy and they in their turn will have good children. His wife will be a lady of learning and good conduct. If the owner of the ninth house is not inimical to Mercury, his father will be close to his younger sister/brother.

Fourth

The native will like travelling and meeting people. He would be well educated and can talk well. He will be at a powerful position. This position indicates that the native will change his residence several times. He will have a likable and friendly mother. His domestic life will be happy. He will like to change his vehicle often. If the planet is strong here it will make the native wealthy and he may be proficient in some art. However he is not likely to get property or wealth from parents. He will be comfortable and contented. His conduct will not be dubious. The end of life will be peaceful. His mother may be of literary taste and may be an avid reader. His children may find that their efforts do not meet with commensurate success. His maternal uncle will be highly placed and rich. His spouse will be well behaved and well placed in life. His father may have a deep and abiding interest in the occult. His elder sister/brother may have no trouble from thieves or enemies, provided Mars is also benign and well placed in the horoscope. If the fourth house and the Moon have adverse influence, the mental health of the native may be jeopardised. Mercury in the fourth house is not considered capable of giving full results.

Fifth

The native will get good returns from his investments. He will have good children and he will be mild tempered, generous and always eager to learn. He will be a scholar. He may have several children. He may be sentimental and may be involved in intense love affairs. Affliction by Mars will cause dishonour due to a love affair. This position is good for amusements and entertainments. He may be an adviser, minister or an ambassador. He will be intelligent and inquisitive. He may have faith in religion and devotional practices. The mind may be speculative, and if Jupiter aspects Mercury here, the native may get rich on account of successful speculation. His income may also be from writing, publishing or amusement and clubs. His elder sister/brother may be good looking and well read. It will give results of its placement in the second house to his mother, and in the third house to his younger sister/brother. His father will be a decent and religious man.

Sixth

It must be kept in mind that the results that this placement will give will depend on (a) how Mercury is going to influence the matters that the sixth house stands for, and (b) how Mercury, representing the affairs of the houses that it owns and aspects, and also those of which it is the karaka, is going to be effected by its placement in an adverse house. If Mercury is under malefic influence and weak, the native will have multiplicity of enemies and they will keep changing; he will be restless, irascible, argumentative , worried and interested in matters related to health and medicine; he will suffer losses through litigation; trouble from servants is also indicated and he may get into debts. However an unafflicted Mercury well placed here will rid the native of the troubles mentioned above and he will be wealthy. The course of his education in his early years may not be uninterrupted. The native may be of worrying nature, especially if Mercury is aspected or influenced by Saturn, which may also cause him a nervous breakdown. If it is influenced by Rahu, Ketu or Mars, the native will act rashly, take on enmities and may head for some mental imbalance. Mercury will not be able to give out its best mental results here howsoever powerful it might be. It must be borne in mind that any kind of adverse influence on Mercury shall be bad for the native since it will affect the health of the native through his mind.

Seventh

The native will gain through his wife. He and his wife would be intelligent, well read and fond of elegant dresses. His spouse will be much younger than him in age. She may be related to him through a distant branch of the family. She will be quick witted and smart. If Mercury has adverse influence, there may be constant tension in marital life due to her sharp tongue. Losses by way of litigation related to marriage are also indicated by this location when Mercury is under adverse influence. Marriage may take place through correspondence or may be a result of travelling. The native will be intuitive. When the planet is weak or is influenced by adverse factors, the native's spouse will be an indiscreet talker and the native may not be able to sexually satisfy her. His relationships with persons coming in contact with him will be fast changing and superficial. It will give results of its placement in the fifth house to his younger sister/brother, and in the fourth to his mother. His children will do well at business, will have several interests apart from their fields of business and will travel much. When Mercury is well aspected and powerful, his maternal uncle and father will be wealthy and will talk well. His father may have a large circle of friends. His elder sister/brother will be a person of good conduct with interest in religion.

Eighth

A reference may be made to initial stipulations made under the Sixth House above with regard to effect of Mercury in that house. Mercury in the eighth house does not, per se, give adverse results. The native will deal with other's money and gain from it. He will be reputed, and enjoy good health but will have a restless mind. His education will be of an average standard. He will be interested in the occult. A powerful and well influenced Mercury may make the native reputed, long lived and a well placed magistrate. He will have a large family. He will be wealthy and may get a legacy if the eighth house is also powerful. His children will be highly educated and wealthy in case Mercury is powerful and without adverse influence. Such a Mercury is excellent for the career and conduct of his elder sister/brother. But if Mercury has adverse influence, the native will have several extra marital relationships and may suffer serious losses on account of these liaisons. He may have a tendency to have brain or nervous disorder. He may tend to worry on account of financial mismanagement caused by his business partner or wife. The native may have a difficult boyhood. It will not be good for the father. It will give results of its placement in the sixth house to his younger sister/brother and in the fifth to his mother. The native may die of intermittent fever.

Ninth

The native will be highly educated, skilful, fortunate, able to express himself effectively, wealthy and religious. He will have interest in philosophy. He will have several children. It will give results of its placement in the fifth house to his children. The native will have several younger sisters/brothers with whom he will have cordial relations. It will give results of its placement in the seventh house to them. He will travel extensively both within the country and abroad. He may be scholarly and write books, or he may be a diplomat. He may be in international trade or he may buy and sell foreign goods. He will tend to do well in life after 31 years of age. He will be studious and may have to live abroad. His father will also be learned and will have a good position and respect in life. If Mercury is not under adverse influence, the native will be happy with his father, and his mother will be long lived and healthy. He will also have an interest in dancing and playing of drums. If Venus aspects or joins Mercury here, the interest in music will be heightened. His wife will also be long lived and interested in literary activity. His elder sister/brother will be rich and of friendly disposition. When Mercury is under the influence of a malefic planet or it is placed in a sign owned by such a planet, the native may change his religion or he may not be religious at all.

Tenth

The native will be eloquent, happy, bold, handsome, respected, learned in several subjects, clear headed, able and very intelligent. He will continue to acquire knowledge throughout his life. If afflicted, it will make the native cunning, unreliable and given to deception. He will be famous or at least well known. He will be upright and straight forward. He will earn from several sources and will possess vehicles. Influence of Saturn will reduce wealth and make the native dishonest. He will have good houses but he may change his residence from time to time. He may serve the government. He will be successful in his chosen career and undertakings. The native can be a diplomat, railwayman, representative, surveyor, priest, author, broker etc. and his best years of life would be the 12th, 32nd and 42nd. He will be happy with his children and parents. His conduct will be beyond reproach. It will give results of its placement in the eighth house to his younger sister/brother, in seventh to his mother, and in the sixth to his children.

Eleventh

The native will be happy, wealthy, wise, and honest. He will have a number of children and intellectual friends, particularly if the sign in the eleventh house is owned by Mercury. He can get along amicably with all kinds of people. He may have more daughters than sons. He will do well at qualifying or departmental examinations. He can be good at mathematics or astrology. His sisters/brothers will be learned, wealthy and happy.

Twelfth

The native will lack energy, and drive. He will be miserly, and may be poorly educated since he may not have the ability to learn well. His character may not be beyond reproach and he may be put to trouble by false reports and scandals. A good Mercury will endow the native with a subtle mind capable of spiritual or metaphysical speculations. His enemies will be few and far between and his maternal uncle will do well in life. His younger sister/brother will do well in life. His mother will be religious and known for her good conduct. His children will be reputed and wealthy. His wife will be happy with her servants. If the planet has adverse influence, the native will have the ability but may not get an opportunity in life to put the ability to test or use. He may suffer from severe set back in life. He may have defect in his speech.

15. Effect of Mercury in various SIGNS (See opening remarks in paragraph 19 under SUN) :

Aries

The native will be irreligious, argumentative, obdurate, dishonest and deceitful. His mind will be active, exaggerative, sharp and quick. He will be of a changeable mind. He may have the capacity to think clearly and invent concepts. He will be fond of sex, eating, gambling and music. He will be poor though he may work hard. He may talk fast and indistinctly. The native may have to live under restrain, which may also take the form of imprisonment. The planet will give good results for Cancer, Scorpio and Sagittarius ascendants. The aspect of Mars on Mercury will make the native highly placed, courageous but untruthful and a person given to promoting dissensions. The aspect of Jupiter on or Venus associated with Mercury will give good results.

Taurus

The native will be fond of his family, sensual, generous and rich. He would like to preach. He will respect his teacher and father. He will have a number of sons and will be rich. He will be determined, practical, learned and generous. He will be a man of strong likes and dislikes. He will have a well developed sense of humour and would enjoy doing callisthenics. He will be discreet when talking and musically inclined. Mercury will give good results in this sign for Leo ascendant. The aspect of the Moon on or Venus associated with Mercury will give good results.

Gemini

The native would be intelligent, learned and a persuasive speaker. He will be independent minded and rich. He will be of an active disposition and is likely to have twins, also have a step mother or he may marry more than once. The mind will be clear, open, given to details, incisive, inventive and versatile. He may like travelling and studying new subjects. He will be handsome and may have several children. Mercury will not give particularly good results in this sign for Capricorn ascendant since the ownership of the ninth house will get vitiated as the other house owned by the planet will be the sixth where it will be placed.

Cancer

The native's business would be connected with water. He would be learned and musically inclined but not popular. He will be of bad temper, oversexed, suffer losses on account of women, live away from the place of his birth but be of active habits, intelligent and talkative. He will be held in high esteem due to the eminence of his forefathers. He will not get along well with his relatives. Mercury will not give good results in this sign for Aquarius ascendant since the native is likely to take to drinking heavily. It shall be good for Pisces ascendant. When the Moon aspects Mercury, it will make the native develop a great weakness for women. It will put a severe strain on the wealth and health of the native. The aspect of Jupiter on Mercury will give good results.

Leo

The native would not be successful as he would not be a stable personality. He will be given to telling lies, and committing misdeeds. He will not have good relations with his younger brothers/sisters or may lose some of them early in life. He will also not be happy with his wife. He may seek female company outside wedlock. This position is generally indicative of lack of wealth and trouble from enemies. A strong Mercury will give somewhat good results in this sign for Pisces ascendant. The association of the Sun with Mercury will only aggravate the adverse results that this placement of Mercury indicates. The aspect of the Moon or Jupiter on Mercury will improve results.

Virgo (*Exalted at 15 deg/Mooltrikona from 16 to 20 degrees*)

The native would have a brilliant and scientific mind. He may also have mechanical ability. He will be of equable temperament and will be liked by the opposite sex. He would have comforts of life, and a well developed sense of values. He would be generous, religious, well behaved, rich, literary, happy and well educated. He will reach a high position in life. Mercury will give comparatively unimpressive results in this sign for Scorpio and Aquarius ascendants. The aspect of Saturn on Mercury will give good results. The aspect of Jupiter will yield brilliant results. Under this aspect the native will reach a high position, and will be handsome and wealthy.

Libra

The native will be religious, attached to his family, and engaged in earning money. He will have a large business and will have the acumen to invest correctly. It also makes the native seek company of women of easy virtue. The native may marry a foreigner or a person from another region if Mercury is associated with the Sun in this sign. Mercury will give good results in this sign for Leo and Capricorn ascendants. The major-period or sub-periods of Mercury will be highly fruitful if the ascendant is Leo. The aspect of the Moon or Jupiter on Mercury will give good results. The association of Venus with Mercury will make the native handsome, popular with the opposite sex, debonair and suave.

Scorpio

The native will be greedy, unintelligent, thievish, and given to telling lies. He will not be rich and command no respect. He will have little faith in God. He will like good food and may indulge in gambling. Married life will be unsatisfactory and the native may have illicit liaisons with other women. Mercury will give good results in this sign for Cancer, Capricorn, Aquarius and Pisces ascendants. The aspect of Jupiter on or Venus associated with Mercury will give good results. The aspect of Mars on Mercury will make the native highly placed, courageous but untruthful and a person given to promoting dissensions.

Sagittarius

The native would be respected by the rulers. The location of Mercury in a sign of Jupiter, with Jupiter powerful in the horoscope or aspecting Mercury, makes the native unusually learned, wise and a good writer. This aspect also confers a high position on the native. He would be knowledgeable about science and law. When the ascendant is Leo, the native may be a confidante of a high dignitary or may be a minister or adviser. He will have the ability of expressing himself well both orally and in writing. He may be engaged in teaching. He may be highly placed, wealthy, liberal and well known. He will have an independent mind. Mercury will not give good results in this sign for Taurus, Cancer, and Scorpio ascendants. The aspect of the Moon or Jupiter on or Venus associated with Mercury will give good results.

Capricorn

The native will have a studious, and critical mentality. He would be suspicious, tactful, timid and philanthropic but financially weak and indebted. He serves others and has to work hard for his livelihood. He will be troubled by his enemies. He may lack in sexual vigour. Mercury will give good results in this sign for Taurus, Sagittarius and Pisces ascendants. If the ascendant is one of the first two, the native will be wealthy and comfortable; if it is the third, he will be very close to his mother. The aspect of Jupiter on Mercury will further enhance the good prospects for wealth. The aspect of Saturn will not be favourable.

Aquarius

The native will have an unclean appearance. He will be indebted and earn money through dubious means. He will serve others and will have to work hard. He will be tormented by his enemies and will be unhappy in life. His married life may be unsatisfactory and he may not be able to have normal sex relations. Mercury in this sign makes the mind capable of concentration and grasping abstract thoughts. The planet will give good results in this sign for Taurus, Gemini, Libra and Capricorn ascendants. When the ascendant is Aries, Mercury will be in the eleventh house in the sign of Saturn. It will give the native very good income but the means of getting the wealth may be dubious. The aspect of Jupiter on Mercury will give good results. The aspect of Saturn will not be favourable.

Pisces (*Debilitated at 15 degrees*)

The native will not be rich. He will lack self confidence. He may be nervous and irritable. He may have an open mind. He may be friendly and religious. The location of Mercury in a sign of Jupiter, with Jupiter powerful in the horoscope or aspecting Mercury, makes the native unusually learned and wise. He will be known by excellent service he renders. His conduct will be pure and beyond reproach. He will have a happy married life and will have a beautiful wife. He will be a custodian of other's money. He may live abroad or away from the place of his birth. His mind will be impressionable and adaptable. The native may be intuitive. The debilitation of Mercury is indicative of the fact that the native will suffer at the hands of enemies from time to time, and he may have to undertake short journeys frequently. He may have trouble in his throat or arms. If the ascendant is Virgo or Pisces, there will always be danger of his marriage breaking up. Mercury in this sign is also bad for Capricorn ascendant. The aspect of the Moon or Jupiter on or Venus associated with Mercury will improve results.

JUPITER

1. It has a big fat body with broad chest and large limbs. It is intelligent and well versed in religious texts. It has yellow hair

and a golden complexion. It is satwik in nature. It is modest,
forgiving and peaceful. It likes the virtuous. It is the teacher of
the gods. Its vehicle is an elephant. It is adaptable.

2. Its RELATIONSHIP with other planets is as follows:

Friendly with	Sun
	Moon
	Mars
Neutral to	Saturn
Inimical to	Mercury
	Venus

3. It is the KARAKA for the following:

Wealth, thighs, knowledge, children, minister, guru,
dharma (duty or good conduct enjoined upon the native by
religious tradition), happiness and husband (in a traditional
society. In a permissive society where a male partner is taken up
on the spur of passion and discarded when emotions subside, it
is Mars that more appropriately represents a partner), and elder
brother/sister.

4. It REPRESENTS the following:
(i)   Good qualities, good behaviour, devotion to God, high
      moral standard, greatness; respect for and faith in elders,
      guru and God; dispassion, justice, Lord Indra, grace of
      God, expansion, principles, optimism, compassion, mild-
      ness, Sama (appeal to reason), fortune, worldly wisdom,
      adaptability, sincerity, common sense, broad mindedness,
      law abiding nature, honesty, steady progress in life and
      respect.
(ii) Vedas, religious texts of yore, exalted after-death state,
      religious practices, ether, law, philosophy, religion, trea-
      sure, health, wealth, minister, religious preceptor of the
      Devas, winter, gold, banks, safe vaults, yellow, topaz,
      bipeds, Vindhya region and Sindh, education, brahmin,
      temples, courts, large and pompous buildings, charity,
      orthodoxy, learned gatherings, extravagance, finance,
      whale, dolphin and north-east direction.
(iii) Fat in the body, sense of hearing, pale complexion,
      jaundice, masculine, Jeeva (animate creatures), protuding
      abdomen, liver, feet, over-eating, hips, brown hair, the

tendency to look directly ahead, preference for sweet
dishes, age 30 years, and also between 57 and 68 years.
(iv) Priests, professors, judges, scholars, attorneys and intellectuals.
(v) Tumour in the abdomen, typhoid, ear diseases, disputes
over religious property or property of a trust, bank or
treasury.

5. By nature Jupiter is a beneficial planet. It is powerful in the
first house. It rises simultaneously with hind parts and the head.

6. If in a horoscope Jupiter is strong but not Mercury, the
native would be wise but since he would not be articulate, he
would not appear wise.

7. If in a horoscope Mercury and Jupiter are powerful and
connected, the native will pursue an intellectual vocation.

8. Jupiter, if powerful and well placed in a horoscope, is
indicative of good karmas (deeds) done by the native in previous
lives. Such a Jupiter will get unearned rewards for the native like
success at speculation, lotteries, a large inheritance or success
without much effort. It will also make the native have faith in
religious and ritualistic practices.

9. Jupiter is also fun loving but whereas Venus finds its
pleasure in mostly sex, Jupiter is happy in gatherings. It therefore
makes the native throw parties or share things with others.

10. Jupiter improves the affairs of a house by aspect. Its
occupation may not prove to be as beneficial for a house.

11. The aspect of Jupiter on other planets and vice-versa (See
paragraph 44 under the opening remarks at the beginning of this
Chapter for guidelines for analysing the influence of an aspect.):
(i) On the Sun-See under SUN.
(ii) On the Moon-See under MOÒN.
(iii) On Mars-See under MARS.
(iv) On Mercury-See under MERCURY.
(v) On Venus- On the positive side (if the aspecting planet
is a beneficial planet for the horoscope), the native will
be wealthy, respected, scholarly, jovial, broad minded
and magnanimous. He will be well liked, helpful, healthy
and at peace with himself. He will have a good wife and

the married life will be contented. He may have more than one marriage, more than one love affair or he may marry a distant relative of his. He will have good residence, vehicles and comforts. He will have happiness from children. He will have a well developed aesthetic sense. He will earn from more than one source.

On the negative side (if the aspecting planet is a malefic planet for the horoscope), the native could be so generous that he would help others to his detriment. He may suffer losses in business, or spend excessively on religious or marriage celebrations, ornaments or functions. The marital life may have tensions, but it is not likely to cause permanent damage.

(vi) On Saturn-On the positive side (if the aspecting planet is a beneficial planet for the horoscope), the native will have the respect of his superiors and elders. The native will experience superior luck. He will be wealthy and will be respected. He may hold a high post in the government and he will progress well in his career. He will have property. He will conform to the traditional but will not shirk from the new. He will have a firm character and can stand on his own. He may travel abroad or go on long journeys. He may have friends in other countries. He will have happy relationship with his father. He will have little harm or trouble from enemies.

On the negative side (if the aspecting planet is a malefic planet for the horoscope), the native is prone to have financial trouble. Generally, the reverse of good things written above can be expected. His education may suffer. He may not be straightforward or may lose due to dishonesty of others.

12. Effect of Jupiter in various HOUSES:

First

Location of Jupiter in the first house ensures long life, good health and a good constitution for the native. He will be happy with his children and father. He may be hopeful, fortunate, religious, mature, worldly-wise and handsome. He will have happy married life and the wife will be long lived. His father will

also be wealthy and mature. He will be learned and wise. He will
be over-indulgent in food and drinks. He will be rich and
generous. His younger sisters/brothers will have good children
and will be wealthy and comfortable. His mother will be of good
conduct. His children will be highly educated and fortunate. A
weak, badly placed or afflicted Jupiter will cause problems to the
native from children and may make the conduct of the native
suspect. A well placed Jupiter in the first house counters other
adverse indications in the horoscope.

Second

The native will be fortunate and financially well off. He will
be particularly wealthy if the second house has Cancer, Sagittarius or Pisces. He will hold a high and powerful position. A
powerful Jupiter, not having adverse influence may get the
native an honour early in life. He will enjoy good food, be well
educated and loquacious. The native will have good eye-sight.
He will be good to look at. He may be a poet. He may not have
trouble from enemies and may be successful in litigation. If the
eighth house is strong, the native may get a legacy. His younger
sister/brother may not do well in life. His mother will have a
large circle of friends and she may respect her elder sister/
brother. His children will be happy, rich, respected and well
educated. His wife will be long lived. His father will not have
a good physical constitution but he will be free from troubles
created by enemies. His elder sister/brother may be well established in life.

Third

The native has the ability to communicate well. His younger
brothers/sisters will do well in life. He will have cordial relations
with his neighbours. He will gain by travels and unscrupulous
means. He will be miserly though rich, and ungrateful. His
income will be of a substantial nature. He may not have happy
and informal relationship with his wife, or the wife may be
overbearing. The wife may be fortunate in worldly matters. He
will not take advantage of opportunities. He may occasionally be
humiliated. The mental ability will not be of a particularly high
order, unless Jupiter is placed in an airy sign. His mother may

be interested in charitable work connected with hospitals. His
children will have a large circle of friends through whom they
may earn well. His father will be long lived and successful. His
elder sister/brother may have trouble having children.

Fourth

The native loves his family, is successful in life and maintains
a lavish life style. He will be very rich. He will be fond of his
mother. Here the karaka for children will be in the twelfth house
from the house of children. This is not a good indication. The
native stands in danger of facing some problem with respect to
his children. He will have extensive landed property. His old age
will be easy. He will be well educated, mature, with a balanced
mind and long lived. He will reach a high position in life and his
conduct will be beyond reproach. If Jupiter is powerful, the
native may be charitable and may like to attach himself with
hospitals or homes for this purpose. He may have interest in
mysticism. His younger sister/brother may be wealthy. His
mother may be corpulent but good natured. His maternal uncle
may be a friendly person and have a good income. His wife will
be well behaved and wealthy. His father may be in service of
someone but he will be long lived. His elder sister/brother will
not be troubled by enemies or litigation.

Fifth

The native has political ambitions, earns from his investments
and is cheerful. He will have good children who would succeed
in life. Since the karaka is in the house that it signifies, there will
be some trouble from the children. He has talent for arts and
drama. He will be very intelligent and may hold a position of an
adviser, or be a writer. He will be fortunate and learned. He may
have good income. He may be peaceful and long lived. His father
may be long lived and wealthy. His wife may have a large circle
of friends. It will give results of its placement in the third house
to his younger sister/brother, and of the second house to his
mother. In a female's chart this placement of Jupiter will be
indicative of the fact that the native may get married to a
widower.

Sixth

The native has a charming personality and is efficient but lazy. He will have good servants and a number of uncles. The native will gain through enemies or in litigation. His potency to procreate may be less than average. He will have good health, the only danger to good health will be from overindulgence in good things of life. He will have good servants and will gain through them. He will have good relations with his superiors and will have their full confidence. He may rise in his career by gaining the confidence of his boss. He will have some proficiency in occult practices. He will be thrifty. It will give results of its placement in the fourth house to his younger sister/brother, in the third house to his mother, and in the second to his children. There is a possibility of some tension in married life. His elder sister/brother will be long lived. Jupiter in the sixth house, per se, does not give adverse results, but it should have enough strength to counter the effect of this adverse placement.

Seventh

The native will have a happy married life. Marriage will bring him prosperity and material gain. His wife may have her own independent income. She may be religiously inclined. The native will be successful in partnership or career. He will be of a friendly and generous disposition. He will be well liked and will be successful in litigation. There is a possibility of the native getting opportunities for having physical contact with a number of females. He may marry a divorcee or a widow. His younger sister/brother may prosper. His second child may do well in life. It will give results of its placement in the fifth house to his younger sister/brother, in the fourth house to his mother, in the third house to his children and in the second house to his maternal uncle. This location of Jupiter may not be wholly good for a female chart as it is the karaka for her husband.

Eighth

He will have good health and be long lived. But he will not be financially well off and will have difficulties with his career. He may be in service. He will maintain a facade of honesty but will secretly misappropriate funds. His wife will earn or bring a lot of wealth. She will have a good appetite. If the eighth house is powerful and Jupiter well placed here, the native may get a legacy. The native will have a peaceful or natural end. The native will stay away from his ancestral home. The native may die of unknown causes or undiagnosed disease. He may suffer from tumours, or if Saturn or Rahu influences Jupiter here, from cancer. He may spend carefully. There may be some disappointments or breaks in his education. It will give results of its placement in the sixth house to his younger sister/brother, in the fifth house to his mother, in the fourth house to his children and in the third house to his maternal uncle. His father may not be well off in life, but his elder sister/brother will certainly rise higher than the father.

Ninth

He will be long lived, well and highly placed, fortunate, balanced, having good and fortunate children, religious, interested in philosophy, well educated, and wealthy. He will tend to do well in life. His father will be well known, learned and wealthy. He may visit abroad to lecture or take part in seminars. The native may stay abroad and have association with foreigners. He may have more younger brothers than sisters, who may do well in life. If Jupiter is weak and has the influence of an adverse Mars, the native may meet with an accident abroad, or may have to be operated upon or he may suffer losses there due to theft or enemies. It will give results of its placement in the sixth house to his mother, and in the third house to his wife. His elder sister/ brother will have a large circle of friends and good and steady income.

Tenth

The native gains some expertise in law, education , philosophy or governing. His ambitions get fulfilled. His conduct will be unblemished. He is likely to have the proverbial golden touch. Whatever he begins will bring him successful returns. He gets a high position, may be in government. He will gain by long voyages. He will be closely associated with charitable institutions. The 16th, 34th, and 50th years of his life will prove to be fortunate. His mother may be on the heavier side and may have a greater and more dominant role in his life. He may have some unhappiness from his children. When an adverse Saturn influences Jupiter here, the good effects of its placement in this house will be heavily diluted. It will give results of its placement in the eighth house to his younger sister/brother, in the seventh house to his mother, in the sixth house to his children, in the fourth house to his wife and in the second house to his father.

Eleventh

He has a good set of friends who help him further his career goals. The native will realise his ambitions. He will have good income and financial success, particularly so if Jupiter is influenced by another beneficial planet. He will be wealthy and will keep good health. He will be happy with his children. He will have a happy and contented married life. The native may only be averagely educated. If Jupiter is in a movable sign here, it is an indication of progress and of the fact that the native will have managerial ability; if it is in a fixed sign, it will cause jealousy among friends; and, if it is in a common sign, the native's friends will be religious or scientific but unreliable. It is a favourable position for businessmen and the younger sister/brother of the native. His elder sister/brother may have difficulty keeping his body weight under control. His mother may be long lived.

Twelfth

The native will be introverted, lazy and cannot express himself effectively. He will be interested in the occult and will overcome his enemies. He may not be fortunate. He will get concealed assistance from his friends. He may be the subject of others charity. He may travel substantially. He may not be on good terms with his relatives. His conduct may be questionable, which, however, may improve with age. He may spend on education, or mother. He may have worries on account of children. It will give results of its placement in the tenth house to his younger sister/brother, though since the planet is not well placed, the results may not be qualitatively of a high order. The same may be said with regard to the results that his mother may expect. For

her the results will be similar to those which the planet is likely
to give for its placement in the ninth house.

13. Effect of Jupiter in various SIGNS (See opening remarks in
paragraph 19 under SUN) :

Aries

The native would be a leader of men. He may be in the army.
He will have good servants. He will be courageous but may have
to face a number of enemies and heavy expenditure. He would
be rich, generous, reputed, and happy. He will head an institution and would be a martinet. When Jupiter is favourable for the
native, it will give him a powerful and well developed brain. He
will have good children and will have happiness from them.
Jupiter will give good results in this sign for Aries, Gemini,
Cancer, Leo and Sagittarius ascendants. A native, having Aries
ascendant and Jupiter in the first house, will travel abroad during
the periods of Jupiter. The results will not be good if the planet
is placed in this sign and the ascendant is Virgo or Scorpio.
Jupiter in Aries with Mars in sambandha with it by aspecting
Aries will make the native wealthy and highly placed. The aspect
of Mercury or Saturn on Jupiter will not give good results.

Taurus

The native may have a good but heavily made constitution. He
may be rich, generous, firm, peaceful, dignified, reserved and
friendly. He may have a large circle of friends. He may have
proficiency in medical science, especially if the ascendant is Leo.
He may be handsome. He may be healthy, religious, eloquent,
and popular. He may have good children and may be attached
to his wife. Jupiter will give good results in this sign for Aries,
Cancer, Leo, and Aquarius ascendants. The aspect of any of the
planets on Jupiter will give good results, but the aspect of Mars
on Jupiter in the sign of Venus, or the aspect of Mercury placed
in the sign of Mars aspecting the planet, will make the native
wayward in his sex life. The aspect of Venus on Jupiter will make
the native handsome and rich.

Gemini

The native would lead a contented, happy and comfortable life. He will have several houses and will be fond of, and own elegant clothes. He will be respected, intelligent, and religious. The location of Jupiter in a sign of Mercury, with Mercury powerful in the horoscope or aspecting Jupiter, makes the native unusually learned and wise. He may become a minister or an adviser to a highly placed dignitary. He may be a successful writer or poet. However if the ascendant is Gemini and the first major-period in the life of the child is that of Jupiter, with the Moon waning, weak or badly placed, there is a possibility that the child may die in its infancy during this major-period. The native may marry a cousin or a relative. In a female horoscope, location of Jupiter in this sign creates the possibility that the native may marry more than once. Jupiter will give good results in this sign for Leo and Pisces ascendants. The aspect by any planet will be good but the aspect of Venus is likely to make the native lascivious. The aspect of Mercury on Jupiter will be from Sagittarius, a sign owned by Jupiter. There will therefore be an exchange also between Mercury and Jupiter and the sambandha will be very intimate. The native will under this influence be an intellectual of no mean calibre. He will, under this aspect, also have astrological insight and good wife and children.

Cancer (*Exalted at 5 degrees*)

The native will be rich and will lead a happy and comfortable life. He will have happiness from his children. He would be intelligent, powerful and learned. He will be known for speaking the truth and his good conduct. He may have popular appeal and may command respect of the masses. The mind may be inclined to the mystical. He may die peacefully. When Jupiter is favourable for the native, it will make him have a powerful and well developed chest. He may live in a big airy house. Jupiter will give good results if the ascendant is Cancer, Scorpio, or Pisces. The best results can be expected if Jupiter is placed in this sign and the ascendant is Pisces. Jupiter will not give good results in this sign for Leo and Sagittarius ascendants. For the first ascendant it may be bad for the prosperity of the native and for the second it may constitute balarista. The aspect of the Moon from Capricorn will prove to be exceedingly beneficial. The native will be very wealthy, comfortable and will have all the facilities in life. He will also be exceptionally lucky with respect to his wife and children.

Leo

The native will be a leader of men. He will have administrative ability and will like sycophancy. He may have ruling powers, reach a high position in life, and may be well known. He will be physically fit and full of stamina. He will have good wife and children. He will be religious and reputed for his good deeds. He will be a firm friend but his enmity will be long lasting. He will keep his enemies firmly under check. He will like visiting the mountains and forests. A good Jupiter will make the native large hearted and generous. Jupiter in Leo is considered to be as well placed as in its sign of exaltation. Jupiter will not give good results in this sign for Pisces ascendant. The aspect of the Sun from Aquarius will make the native rise to a high position and amass wealth. This aspect will also make the native virtuous and well behaved. The aspect of Saturn on Jupiter will give bad results.

Virgo

The native will be a religious, virtuous and courteous person who will be good at his work. He will lead a comfortable life and have many good sons and friends. He will be careful in choosing friends and in his speech. Some of the friends may be deeply interested in mysticism. He may travel abroad in connection with his profession. He can attain a high position in life. The location of Jupiter in a sign of Mercury, with Mercury powerful in the horoscope or aspecting Jupiter, makes the native unusually learned and wise. He may earn his livelihood through his learning. His virility may be suspect. If the planet is aspected by Saturn, or by an adverse Mars placed in Aquarius, he may be impotent. Jupiter will give good results in this sign for Virgo, Scorpio and Sagittarius ascendants. The aspect by any planet on Jupiter will be good but the aspect of Venus is likely to make the native lascivious. The aspect of Mercury on Jupiter will be from Pisces, a sign owned by Jupiter. There will therefore be an exchange also between Mercury and Jupiter and the sambandha will be very intimate. The native will under this influence be an intellectual of no mean calibre. He will, under this aspect, also have astrological insight and good wife and children.

Libra

The native will be engaged in the process of learning throughout his life. He will have an attractive personality, his conduct will be worth emulating, and he will long for and get all the comforts in life. He will be just, rich, modest, happy, religious and popular. He will reach a high position in life. He will be happy with his children and wife. He may succeed in partnership. He will reside at a place away from his place of birth. He may gain from strangers and may have friends abroad. He may gain through servants and inferiors. He may travel abroad in connection with his work. A good Jupiter will make the native gain through business partnerships. Jupiter will not give good results in this sign for Scorpio and Pisces ascendants. The native may have to spend heavily, may have limited wealth and he may get indebted when one of these ascendants rises with Jupiter in Libra. The aspect of any of the planets on Jupiter will give good results, but the aspect of Mars on Jupiter which is placed in the sign of Venus, or the aspect of Mercury from the sign of Mars on Jupiter, will make the native wayward in his sex life. The aspect of Venus on Jupiter will make the native handsome and rich.

Scorpio

The native will be generous, and happy with his family. He will have a small number of children. Cancer ascendant with Jupiter in Scorpio is likely to deny the native children unless Mars is powerful or aspects Jupiter. He gets involved in philanthropic activities. He will be learned, showy, vindictive and respected but will suffer from chronic diseases. He may suffer from getting involved in intrigues against his superiors. He may be connected with the government. Jupiter will give good results in this sign for Scorpio, and Pisces ascendants, though Jupiter in Scorpio in the ascendant is likely to give diseases. Jupiter in Scorpio with Mars in sambandha with it by aspecting its sign Scorpio will make the native wealthy and highly placed. The aspect of Mercury or Saturn on Jupiter will not give good results.

Sagittarius (*Mooltrikona from 0 to 10 deg*)

The native will have a position of authority. He will lead a happy and contented life. He will be rich and religious. The native will be learned, friendly, and intelligent. He will live away from his birth place. Great wealth, spiritual upliftment and desire to be alone are also indicated by Jupiter in this sign. Jupiter will give ordinary results in this sign for Cancer ascendant. An unaspected Jupiter in this sign for Leo ascendant may cause problems with regard to children. The aspect of the Sun, Mars or Saturn on Jupiter will not give good results; the Sun will make the native oppose his superiors or the government, Mars may cause him to get injured, and Saturn may be bad for wealth and honour.

Capricorn (*Debilitated at 5 deg*)

The native is likely to be discontented with his station in life. He may have to face sorrow and disappointments. He will suffer from chronic ailments, and his virility may be low. He will be unclean, poor in intelligence, irreligious, of low moral fibre and not rich. He may have to leave his homeland in search of livelihood. Jupiter will give good results in this sign for Aries ascendant. The aspect of any planet that is beneficial for the ascendant will improve matters. Mars will be particularly good as it is likely to make the native a successful professional in the army. When Saturn aspects Jupiter the native will be very learned. He may be a legal luminary. He will be very wealthy and highly placed. He will have all the comforts in life.

Aquarius

He will have a happy family life. He will be rich and will study the occult. He will have an interest in humanitarian work. The results of Jupiter being in this sign between 13 deg 20 min and 20 deg are sometimes as good as for its location in its sign of exaltation. Otherwise the rest of the results will be almost the same as described above for Jupiter's location in Capricorn.

Jupiter will give good results in this sign for Gemini and Scorpio ascendants. The aspect of any planet that is beneficial for the ascendant will improve matters. Mars will be particularly good as it is likely to make the native a successful professional in the army. When Saturn aspects Jupiter the native will be very learned. He may be a legal luminary. He will be very wealthy and highly placed. He will have all the comforts in life.

Pisces

The native is learned and is of independent views. He works quietly and hard and is respected for it. He will be rich and will reach a high position in life. He has the ability to get along with people well. He will be generous, hospitable, and fond of animals. He may undertake philanthropic or humanitarian work. He may have hereditary religious influence on him. He may have a quiet end. Jupiter will give good results in this sign for Gemini, Scorpio, Sagittarius and Pisces ascendants. The aspect of the Sun, Mars or Saturn on Jupiter will not give good results; the Sun will make the native oppose his superiors or the government, Mars may cause him to get injured, and Saturn may be bad for wealth and honour.

VENUS

1. It is very handsome to look at, has dark curly hair, and beautiful eyes. It has long hands, broad chest, prominent shoulders, big thighs and a swarthily clear complexion. It is of rajasik temperament, is very fortunate and likes to wear coloured clothes of various hues. It is intelligent, joyful and fond of sports. It is the teacher of the demons. It is of a peaceful nature. Its vehicle is a white horse. It is passive.

2. Its RELATIONSHIP with other planets is as follows:

Friendly with	Mercury
	Saturn
Neutral to	Mars
	Jupiter
Inimical to	Sun
	Moon

3. It is the KARAKA for the following:
    Kidneys, buried treasure, wealth, conveyances, clothes, music, wife, concubines, sexual pleasure and bed.

4. It REPRESENTS the following:
   (i) Ornaments, perfumes, flowers, opulence, marriage, festivals, south-east, beloved, beauty, comfort, art, dance, pleasures, guru of the demons, minister, painting, luxury, multicoloured objects, diamond, place of entertainment, restaurants, cinema house, theatre, bedroom, water, brahmin, decorated or embroidered cloth, biped, Goddess Lakshmi, youth, spring season, flowering trees and articles of luxury.

   (ii) Affection, good taste, sense of taste, one's liking, self indulgence, harmony, love, aesthetic sense, elegance, refinement, pleasure seeking, show, charisma, charm, easy going, accommodating, and cooperative.

   (iii) Semen, genitals, fair complexion, face, chin, cheeks, eyes, throat, the tendency to look side ways like a shy damsel, from 15 to 22 years of age and also 25 years of age, feminine gender.

   (iv) Jewellers, actors, musicians, perfumers, artists, and generally people dealing with entertainment, pleasure and beauty.

   (v) Anaemia, diseases of urinary or reproductive system, breaking up of friendship, and impotence or inability to have normal sex relations.

5. By nature Venus is a beneficial planet. It rises head first. It represents Jeeva (animate creature). It is powerful in the fourth house. It is not considered good in the seventh house, and is powerless in the sixth. It is inclined to Sama (appeal to reason) like Jupiter.

6. When Venus comes under the influence of Mars it gives rise to passions and manifests intense sexuality and sensuality.

7. Venus connected with Mercury or Jupiter promotes true love, beauty, learning, purity and general well being.

8. A well placed and powerful Venus in a horoscope ensures a continuous run of good fortune and a career which steadily remains successful.

9. A Venus in debilitation or afflicted by Mars or Saturn reduces the longevity of the wife , causes marital discord and generally makes the family life of the native disturbed.

10. The aspect of Venus on other planets and vice-versa (See paragraph 44 under the opening remarks at the beginning of this Chapter for guidelines for analysing the influence of an aspect):

(i)   On the Sun-See under SUN.

(ii)   On the Moon-See under MOON.

(iii) On Mars-See under MARS.

(iv) On Mercury-See under MERCURY.

(v)   On Jupiter-See under JUPITER.

(vi) On Saturn- On the positive side (if the aspecting planet is good for the ascendant), the native will be known for his upright behaviour and honesty. He will be hard working. He will have wealth and good reputation which will stand him in good stead in business. Progress in life and career will be due to his good name and hard work. The progress may be slow but it will be steady and towards the close of his working life he may succeed in reaching the pinnacle of his career. He will be thrifty. He will have a healthy bank balance. Gains may be had from father or aged persons, through marriage or due to his own efforts. He will maintain marital fidelity and will not marry more than once. There will be noticeable age difference between him and his wife.

On the negative side (if the aspecting planet is bad for the ascendant), he will display a lax moral character and will be known for it. He will find it difficult to keep his passions in check. Married life will be disturbed, there may be separation or he may lose his wife early. He will not have domestic felicity.

11. Effect of Venus in various HOUSES:

First

The native would be long lived, healthy, happy, rich and a big spender. He may be very good looking and may have a beautiful wife. He will be a man of refined tastes and fortunate. He will have ability for fine arts. He will be attractive, especially to the opposite sex, will like company and will be a happy family man.

A bad Venus will make the native gullible. If Mars is adverse or afflicted in the chart, the native may be sexually promiscuous. He may not be bold. This is considered a good location for Venus. His younger sister/brother will be wealthy, will own vehicle and have a good number of friends. His mother may like to be associated with clubs and societies for entertainment where she may hold some honorary position. His children will be well behaved and well educated. They may travel over long distances and may enjoy it. His father may be pleasure loving, successful at speculation, imaginative and a man of refined tastes. His elder sister/brother may be proficient in music, or painting or he may be a poet.

Second

The native will be handsome, polite, rich and will spend lavishly. If the planet is connected with a benign Saturn, the native will save well and have a good bank balance. He would be friendly, will talk well and be engaged in artistic pursuits through which he would earn well. He will have beautiful eyes. He will like the best quality food. He may have a large family with a number of female relatives. He may attend a good and expensive school. When the eighth house is powerful and has beneficial influence, the native may get a legacy through a female relative. His end will be peaceful. His younger sister/brother may have a secret love affair. His mother may have a comfortable and prosperous life with a number of friends. His children may get high positions in life through their contacts. His wife may have a peaceful end. His father will lead an excessive life style which may cause him derangement in health from time to time. His elder sisters/brothers will have prosperity, vehicles and comforts in the second part of life. They may be close to the mother. His wife may have some gynaecological trouble.

Third

The native would exhibit talent in arts and music. He will be bright and cheerful. His mind will be free of evil thoughts. He would have more younger sisters than brothers and will have good relations with them. He would be introverted. He will enjoy travelling and may visit places as a tourist. Venus in a sign of

Mars, or, under its influence, may make the native write passionate love letters to his beloved. His mother may be long lived and he may be close to her. His wife will have influence over her. A powerful and benign Venus will make the native fortunate. Such a Venus connected with the twelfth house as well will make the native go overseas to a developed country. It will give results of its placement in the twelfth house to his mother and in the first house to his younger sister/brother.

Fourth

The native will be rich, have a luxurious and comfortable home and a peaceful and contented close of life. He would have close ties with his family and would be specially close to his mother. He will possess fine vehicles. The native will also be on friendly terms with his boss. The aspect of the Moon on or association of the Sun with Venus here will make the native very fortunate. It is good for the wealth and happiness of the children. It makes the wife social and active in community life or in art circles. It will give results of its placement in the first house to his mother. She may be stout but good looking. It will give results of its placement in the second house to his younger sister/brother.

Fifth

The native will have good and handsome children and his first child will be especially good looking. He will have more daughters than sons. He will be wealthy. He will earn well through speculation and sound investments. He will be intelligent, and have aesthetic sense. He will be pleasure loving. He may have good imagination and, if the third house or Mercury is also involved, he may use it to write long stories or novels. If Saturn or Rahu influences Venus here, the native will not have success in love affairs and he may have to face humiliations due to such affairs. He may even be a lonely lover grieving for his long gone beloved. He may occupy a position of trust. His maternal uncle will lead a luxurious and prosperous life. It will give results of its placement in the third house to his younger sister/brother, in the second to his mother and in the first to his children.

Sixth

The native will keep good health and he would work in the field of arts. He would be friendly and a gourmet. He will have faithful servants. The native may suffer from diseases in the reproductive or urinary system, may be due to excesses that the native is prone to indulge in. The native may dislike his wife or there may be marital difficulties. A badly afflicted Venus here may indicate death of wife. He and his wife, both, may have secret love affairs and he may be licentious. He may have some enemies who may keep troubling the native. These enemies may be females. A powerful Venus will ensure that the native remains free of enemies. The native may have good longevity. This is a good position for younger sister/brother, as Venus will be in the fourth house from the third house. His mother may have musical talent. His children, especially the first child, are likely to be wealthy and eloquent. His father will head several entertainment, fine arts or speculation organisations in honorary capacity. He will get these positions due to his wide acquaintance and contacts, and not so much due to merit.

Seventh

He would get married early and the wife will be well behaved and good looking. His relations with acquaintances would be smooth and he will have a good number of friends. He may have better fortune after marriage. In male horoscope, Venus is the karaka for wife, marriage and sex. The placement of karaka in a house, the affairs of which it signifies, is not considered good. There may be some trouble in his marriage due to his sex habits. The wife may be short lived. The native will be handsome, talented and a person of refined taste. He will be popular. He would gain through his spouse and partners. This location of Venus may cause reproductive or urinary trouble for the native. His younger sister/brother may have mostly female children. The native will be wealthy and artistic. His mother will lead a comfortable and pleasant life. His second child may be good looking and rich.

Eighth

The native would have sensual nature but he would keep good health. He would be happy and wealthy and will gain through his partner in business. His end would be easy. Venus here for Libra ascendant is considered particularly good. The native may die of thirst. He may have reproductive or urinary trouble. The native may gain through death of others. There may be trouble to the native through his wife, female children or other women; or, there may be danger to his wife, daughter or mother. This indication will be more prominent in his life if the sign in the eighth house is a fixed one. His father is likely to lead a luxurious life. His younger sister/brother may be healthy. His children will be wealthy and well placed in life. His elder sister/brother will be a person with wide contacts.

Ninth

This is a good location for Venus. The native may be happily married to a foreigner. The native will have love for art, music or refined literature. He may gain through water, shipping or travel overseas. He will have happiness from children, will be prosperous, and will have numerous friends. He will tend to do well in life after 26 years of age. He will have sound higher education and, when Venus is also related to the twelfth house, will travel to developed countries. He will be sympathetic to not so fortunate human beings as he, and may be engaged in philanthropic work. He will be religious. He will have favour from the government. It will give results of its placement in the first house to his father, who may gain through his wife's relatives. His children may be in the field of art and may do well in life.

Tenth

The native may pursue an artistic career and earn well from it. He may serve under a female superior or his job may involve females. He may come in contact with a large number of females in discharge of his duties. He will have a large circle of friends and benign superiors. He will have pleasing manners and may be appointed as head of an institution on the basis of his contacts.

The years between 25 and 32 of life will be favourable. He will
be attached to his wife and children. His conduct will be good
and he may exhibit charitable disposition. He may have vehicles
through his profession. An aspect of a benign Jupiter will enhance the good effects of Venus placed in this house. An adverse
Moon on the other hand, is likely to ruin the prospects, if it casts
its influence on Venus here. It will give results of its placement
in the eighth house to his younger sister/brother. This location
is very good for the elder sister/brother of the native as Venus
will be in the twelfth house from the eleventh. A powerful Venus,
placed in the sixth house from the fifth, will be beneficial to his
children.

Eleventh

The native will have numerous female friends, will have
comforts, conveyances and wealth. He will gain through friends
and by trade. He will have obedient servants and subordinates.
He will gain by proper means. His ambitions will be fulfilled. He
can trust people with ascendants ruled by Venus, or the Moon
placed in the signs of Venus. If the Sun is favourable to the
ascendant and is associated with Venus, the gain to the native
will be through female friends. If the Moon is so associated or
aspects Venus, the native will be popular and will like meeting
people, pleasure and amusement. His elder sister/brother will be
wealthy and handsome. It will give results of its placement in the
third house to the father and in the eighth to the mother. His
children may have handsome spouses but their married life will
not be trouble free. His wife will be intelligent, artistic and fond
of good company. This placement is conducive to enhancement
of spirituality in the native. If this indication is supported by
other factors in the horoscope, the native may progress well on
the spiritual path. But, when Venus is placed in an earthy sign
or a sign owned by Mars, the native will have to overcome his
senses which shall also be strong.

Twelfth

He will be fond of sensual pleasures and wealthy. He will be
particularly wealthy if the planet has aspect of or association with
at least another beneficial planet. Such beneficial influence will

also make the native selfless and ever willing to help others. He will be easy going, and long lived and will love horses. He will indulge in pleasures secretly. He will have intuitive ability. His elder sister/brother will be eloquent and wealthy. His mother will have the good effects of Venus placed in the ninth house and his father will have wealth and vehicles. If Saturn, particularly one which is bad for the ascendant, aspects Venus or is associated with it, the native may get involved in a love affair after marriage and may get separated from his wife. Venus in Pisces when the ascendant is Gemini, Virgo or Aquarius will give excellent results. When the ascendant is Pisces and Venus is placed in the first house in exaltation, in the twelfth sign, the native will be very long lived and prosperous. Venus in the twelfth house, per se, does not give adverse results. When the ascendant is Aries, Venus will be in Pisces in the twelfth house. Such a placement of Venus will make the native susceptible to eye trouble, and heavy expenses.

12. Effect of Venus in various SIGNS (See opening remarks in paragraph 19 under SUN) :

Aries

The native will display a well developed streak of sensuality in his nature. If Venus is influenced by Mars or Saturn, or if Jupiter is also adverse or weak in the chart, he will have physical relations with other women and will visit prostitutes. He may get into trouble or face imprisonment due to women. He will not be reliable and will bring dishonour to his family. He will come in conflict with his family. There will be some defect in the eyesight. He would be extravagant and irresponsible and will lose his wealth and property due to these habits. He will make friends easily. He will like travelling abroad. Venus will give good results in this sign for Cancer and Capricorn ascendants. The aspect of Jupiter on Venus will give good results and moderate the negative traits.

Taurus

The native will be handsome and popular. He will earn well through artistic pursuits, agriculture, milch cattle, and white collar jobs. He will be learned, virtuous and obliging. He will be constant in his affections. He will have strong likes and dislikes. He will be social. This is a good position for business as the native will be known for his steadfast nature and reliability. He will not be intellectually inclined. His wife may predecease him and thereafter he may remain a widower for the remainder of his life. When Venus is aspected by Mars or Saturn, the native is likely to face trouble from women, through his loose morals or a bad marriage. Travels may bring trouble to him. His eyesight will be defective if Venus is weak and the ascendant is Taurus. Venus in this sign for Capricorn and Aquarius ascendants will be highly favourable. One will however have to be careful with regard to sub-period of Venus in the major-period of Saturn, or vice versa. The native will be long lived if the ascendant is Pisces.

Gemini

The native will be rich, learned and a high dignitary. He may have a refined mind. He will have facility with the pen and in expressing himself. He would be fond of music. He may have friends among well travelled, literary or artistic persons. He will be sensual, handsome, and religious. He may have to face sorrow at the close of life. He will have pleasant travels. He will marry again, or have more than one love affair if Venus is afflicted. He is likely to have good relations with his younger sister/brother. He may earn through writing, literary or artistic pursuits. Such a Venus will also make the native susceptible to trouble in the joints and lungs, and fall from height. When Venus has adverse influence on it and the ascendant is Aries, it may cause early death of a younger brother/sister of the native. Venus in this sign for Cancer ascendant can be troublesome for the mother of the native. For Leo ascendant, Venus may make the native excel in his career and earn well from it. The native shall be wealthy and highly placed if the ascendant is Virgo. Venus in this sign for Scorpio ascendant will be particularly bad. He may get involved in prostitution. There may be love intrigues within the family. The aspect of Mars or Saturn on Venus will not give good results. Venus will give excellent results for Aquarius ascendant provided Mercury does not have adverse influence. The association with Mercury will be good. It will make the native wealthy, peaceful, comfortable and well educated. It will enable him to reach a high position in life. The native may have liking for music or he may be a good musician himself.

Cancer

The native will lack courage. He will be arrogant and unhappy and will marry more than once, particularly if the Moon is waning. There may be trouble from women or alcohol. He will be domesticated and home loving. He may get married with the hope of making a home. Marriage may bring money. He will be careful with his money. His wife may pass away abroad. He will be prominent, handsome, and sensual. He will lead a comfortable life. He may contract chronic diseases due to his excesses. The bad results will be prominent if the planet occupies a position between 6 degrees 40 minutes and 10 degrees. Venus will not give good results in this sign for Aries and Aquarius ascendants. The native may face trouble on account of his mother if Aries is the ascendant. In case Mars is adverse in the chart and it influences Venus, the native with Aries ascendant will have lax morals and may have liaison with women outside wedlock. Venus is an excellent planet for Aquarius ascendant. Its location in the sixth house owned by an enemy will considerably reduce the munificence that one could expect from a well placed Venus. A waxing and well aspected Moon will generally curb the bad effects of Venus for any ascendant. Venus in Cancer will give good results when Capricorn is rising. The aspect of a good Moon on Venus makes the native fortunate. The aspect of Saturn on Venus will not give good results.

Leo

The native will get married to a person with whom he had come in contact and had been friendly. He will get in close contact with a number of women in discharge of his professional duties, but he will be a devoted husband. The native will be happy, rich and peaceful. He will be successful at speculation. He may gain wealth through females. He will marry in a family higher than his. His virility may be below average. He will have a few children. The good results will get diluted if the planet occupies a position between 16 degrees 40 minutes and 20 degrees in the sign. Venus in this sign with Aries ascendant is bad for children. If it is placed in this sign when Taurus is rising, the native's mother will be close to her sisters; if Gemini is rising, his younger brothers/sisters will do well in life, and if Mercury is powerful in the chart and is in contact with Venus, the native will have proficiency in music; if Cancer is rising, the native will be wealthy; if Leo is rising, the native will do very well at his career; if Virgo is rising, the native will visit abroad but shall always be bothered by heavy expenditure; if Libra is rising, the native will be long lived; if Scorpio is rising, the native may face domestic discord due to irritable nature of his wife; if Sagittarius is rising, the native will be unlucky and may not be able to make a place for himself in life, though his father would have done very well at his profession; if Capricorn is rising, the native again will be unlucky and may have trouble on account of his wife and children; if Aquarius is rising, the native will have a very happy married life and his wife and business partners will be a source of his prosperity; and, if Pisces is rising, the native may find the periods of Venus troublesome. The association of the Sun with Venus will make the native attractive to the opposite sex. The aspect of Mars, Jupiter or Saturn on Venus will give good results.

Virgo (Debilitated at 27 deg)

The native will not like his job and will be unhappy. He will feel insecure. He will be poor, and will not have comforts of life. He will prove to be successful in a subordinate position. He may suffer from diseases in urinary or reproductive system. He will have liaison with women of ill repute. He may marry more than once. There may be delay or incompatibility in marriage. He may have more daughters than sons. He will be eloquent but may cause disputes and discord through his speech. The native may have to raise loans on account of women. He may not be happy with his wife and marital happiness may be absent in his life. The above adverse results shall be mitigated if Mercury is exalted or otherwise powerful in the chart. The association of Mercury with Venus will be good. The association of Mercury with Venus will make the native wealthy, peaceful, comfortable and well educated. It will enable him to reach a prominent position in life. The native may have liking for music or he may be a musician of some standing himself. Venus in this sign for Pisces ascendant will give the native very bad results with respect to his married life. The aspect of Mars or Saturn on Venus will not give good results. It is good to have the planet between 6 deg 40 min and 10 deg, or, 13 degrees 20 minutes and 16 degrees 40 minutes, or 26 degrees 40 minutes and 30 degrees.

Libra (*Mooltrikona from 0 to 15 degrees*)

He will be handsome, very rich, courageous, and learned. He will show respect to his religion and preceptor. He will live away from his homeland. He will be popular and well known. He may have a refined mind and a taste for music, painting or poetry. His marriage will be successful and he may get money and status through it. He will have good children. There may be sorrows through death of the loved ones. If the ascendant is Aries, Venus in this sign will prove to be a major maraka for the native; if it is Taurus, the native will suffer from ill health from time to time; if it is Gemini, the native will be very happy with his children, though there may be heavy expenditure also on their account once in a while, especially during the sub-period of an adverse planet in the major-period of Venus or during the sub-period of Venus in the major-period of an adverse planet; if it is Cancer, the native will be wealthy; if it is Leo, the native, who will be long lived, may take up writing, publishing, journalism etc. as his vocation, at which he will do well; if it is Virgo, the native will be handsome, eloquent and very wealthy; if it is Libra, the native will be long lived; if it is Scorpio, the native may be rich (since Venus well placed in the twelfth house is conducive to wealth) and highly sexed; if it is Sagittarius, the native may be in money lending business, may be worried over the physical well being of his eldest child, and if Mars or Ketu influence Venus, the native may meet with a serious accident; if it is Capricorn, the native will earn name and wealth well from his profession and his children may do well in life; if it is Aquarius, the native will be fortunate and wealthy; and if it is Pisces, the native will be long lived, but he may not be happy with his wife. When Venus is aspected by Mars or Saturn, the native is likely to face trouble from women, due to his loose morals or a bad marriage.

Scorpio

The native will be bad tempered, hasty in matters of affection, wicked, irreligious, and talkative. He will have enmity with women of bad character. He may suffer from venereal diseases and indebtedness. He may get involved in litigation in which a woman would be interested, and would lose his property in the process. He will be morally degraded and may have a bad marriage. He may get married to somebody who has been married earlier. He will not be socially acceptable. Venus is shorn of its good results in this sign and is generally capable of giving only bad results. The evil results recorded above will be magnified if the planet occupies a position between 6 deg 40 minutes and 10 deg in the sign. If the ascendant is Aries, the native is likely to lose his wife early and he may be of loose moral character; if it is Taurus, the native will again be in for a troublesome married life; if it is Gemini, the native will not be wealthy; if it is Cancer, the native will be rich, well placed and intelligent; if it is Leo, the native will be known for his efficiency and a successful career; if it is Virgo, the native will gain from his younger brothers, who will also be well off; if it is Libra, the native will not be long lived; if it is Scorpio, the native will be short lived, and he may get involved in extramarital affairs; if it is Sagittarius, the native will have an adverse time during the major and sub-periods of Venus due to his enemies and heavy expenditure; if it is Capricorn, the native will have more than one daughter and also elder sisters; if it is Aquarius, the native will be learned, highly placed and fortunate; and, if it is Pisces, the native will be long lived. The aspect of Mars will not be good. The aspect of Jupiter on Venus will give good results and moderate the negative traits.

Sagittarius

He will be known for his honesty and will be financially comfortably off. He will be popular, handsome, humorous, loyal, learned and respected. He will reach a high position in life. He will be virtuous, elegant and interested in fine arts. He may get married more than once or may have a liaison outside the wedlock. He may have good children. Venus will give particularly good results in this sign for Virgo ascendant. Venus here will give learning and immovable property. If the ascendant is Aries, Venus may prove to be a maraka for the father of the native; if it is Cancer, the native is likely to suffer from diseases of the urinary or reproductive system since the planet will be the owner of the fourth and the eleventh houses (thus being an adverse planet for the ascendant) and will be placed in the sixth house. The aspect of Mars on Venus will not give good results. The aspect of Jupiter on Venus is an indication that the native will be prosperous, happily married with good children and will lead a luxurious life.

Capricorn

The native will be popular especially amongst women and will be influenced by them. He will be careful of his honour. He may be disappointed in love. He may have liaison with women of bad reputation. He will be prudent and careful in matters of affection. He will be faithful and constant in his sentiments. His marriage may be delayed, it may not be fortunate, or it may be dissolved early. This location of Venus will make the native poor in virility and in a situation when the planet is afflicted, he may be impotent. He may be prosperous in later life. Exception to this will be Virgo and Capricorn ascendants where the prosperity will be on the rise through out life. The aspect of Saturn will be beneficial. This aspect will improve the house where Venus is located and in cases of Virgo and Capricorn ascendants, it will act as the magnifier of good results.

Aquarius

The native may face failures in his undertakings. He will not be able to resist charms of other females. He may not have good relations with his children. He will be inactive and lethargic. His marriage may be delayed. This is not good for the longevity of his wife. He may be popular and socially a success. He will be prudent and careful in matters of affection. He will be faithful and constant in his sentiments. This location of Venus will make the native poor in virility and in a situation when the planet is afflicted, he may be impotent. Venus will give good results in this sign for Gemini and Aquarius ascendants. The aspect of Saturn will be beneficial.

Pisces (*Exalted at 27 deg*)

The native may work for institutions. He will be sympathetic to persons who are distressed or in need of help. He will be imaginative and intuitive. He may fall in love with someone who is not really fit for such sentiments. He may have a secret liaison or marriage. He may benefit from his marriage. He will have good education. He would be popular, happy, artistic, sensuous and a spendthrift. He will be wealthy and well placed, particularly so if the planet is placed in the second, fifth, ninth or the eleventh house. He may also have power and fame if the planet is in an angular house. He may be easy going and not particularly active. He will be elegant and have good taste. His wife will be good looking and long lived. Venus placed in this sign for Leo ascendant will give a very long life to the native. The aspect of Mars on Venus will not give good results. The aspect of Jupiter on Venus is an indication that the native will be prosperous, happily married with good children and will lead a luxurious life.

SATURN

1. It is tall and lean with big and defective teeth and coarse hair. It is lame and lazy. It is dark in complexion, has sunken eyes and prominent veins. It is old, tamasik, dirty, foolish, miserly, and contentious. It is a eunuch. It is irritable. It dresses in dark blue or black clothes. Its vehicle is an ox. It is fixed.

2. Its RELATIONSHIP with other planets is as follows:

Friendly with	Mercury
	Venus
Neutral to	Jupiter
Inimical to	Sun
	Moon
	Mars

3. It is the KARAKA for the following:
   Longevity, death, disease, misery, fear, humiliation, fall(from a high position or from a height), poverty, misdeeds, debt, sorrow and agriculture.

4. It REPRESENTS the following:

(i) Buffalo, air, lead, service, slavery, imprisonment, loss, fate, steel, property particularly agricultural land, limitation, contraction, separation, cold, dark, slow, dull, obstruction, delay, blue sapphire, severe winter, stone, rock, burial and cremation grounds, dirty places, labour, hard work, deserted places, gutters, slums, jails, long acting, chronic, Lord Brahma, skin, oil, west, sudra (the lowest caste), woollen cloth, birds, learning of foreign languages, and things buried deep underground.

(ii) Discipline, asceticism, solitude, ugliness, perversity, detachment, worry, pessimism, depression, fear, anxiety, miserliness, selfishness, crime, paranoia, concentration, eye for detail, sobriety, harsh, hard hearted, and black colour.

(iii) Nerves, teeth, paralysis, numbness, windy diseases, chronic and degenerative disease, cancer, senility, impotence in men, arthritis, obstruction in the functions of the body like retention of urine, intestinal obstruction etc., shin and part of leg between ankle and knee, dark complexion, pain, the tendency to look down while talking, colds, chills, asthma, paralysis, rheumatism, age from 69 to 108 years and also 36 years of age.

(iv) Farmers, gardeners, servants, sweepers, agriculturists, and menials.

(v) Lameness, exhaustion due to very hard work, mental confusion, trouble from servants, injury, worry.

(vi) It represents Moola (plants, creepers, grass, trees etc.). It is inclined to Bheda (tact and diplomacy). It stands for the region from the Ganga to the Himalayas.

(vii) The sense of touch.

3. Saturn by nature is a malefic planet. It rises with hind part first. It is powerful in the seventh house.

4. Jupiter stands for creation and expansion, Saturn for destruction, separation and contraction.

5. A bad or afflicted Saturn, or influence of such Saturn on the ascendant or the Moon sign can make a man look prematurely old.

6. If an adverse Saturn is connected with Mars or Ketu, it makes the native a criminal, pervert, or an evil minded person.

7. (i) Saturn is inimical to the Sun and the Moon and has an eclipse like influence on them.

(ii) A powerful Jupiter can really balance its influence.

(iii) Mercury and Venus can take away the grosser aspects of Saturn.

8. Saturn does not prove to be that baneful to the house it occupies as to the houses that it aspects.

9. The aspect of Saturn on other planets and vice-versa (See paragraph 44 under the opening remarks at the beginning of this Chapter for guidelines for analysing the influence of an aspect.):

(i)   On the Sun-See under SUN.
(ii) On the Moon-See under MOON.
(iii) On Mars-See under MARS.
(iv) On Mercury-See under MERCURY.
(v)   On Jupiter-See under JUPITER.
(vi) On Venus-See under VENUS.

10. If Saturn is adverse for the ascendant and is in aspect to or conjunction with the Sun or the Moon, misfortune visits the native every 7. 5 years.

11. Effect of Saturn in various HOUSES:

First

The native will be disciplined, thin, solemn, and hard working. He will have a difficult childhood, and will face health problems. There will be delays and obstacles in his projects. The native has to work hard and long for success. He will have a defective limb, and bad morals. If the planet is afflicted in a sign it will give weakness to the part of the body indicated by that sign. He may suffer from colds and rheumatic trouble. He may be long lived if Saturn is in the signs of Jupiter or it is powerful and benign for the ascendant. The native will be nervous and timid in his early years but will be bold as he reaches middle age. He will like to be alone and silent. He may get married late or the wife may be of comparatively advanced age. His marriage may suffer and he may not be successful in partnership. Saturn in the first house placed in its exaltation, own sign or in a sign of Jupiter will confer high status and wealth on the native. Unless the planet is under good influence or well placed, the native will suffer a fall from high position that he may reach. In Gemini, it will make the native progressive, perceptive, scientific and interested in the occult, and in Leo it will make him powerful. It is not good for the longevity of younger sisters/brothers, or they may be against the native. They may suffer from deception by friends or their ambitions may not be fulfilled. His mother will live at a place other than her place of birth later in life. His children may not be well off and may have a philosophic attitude to life. His father may have disease or trouble in his stomach if the Sun or sign Leo also has adverse influence. The father may also lose heavily in speculation.

Second

The native will face financial difficulties but will overcome the same in his later life. The native will be thrifty but if the planet is badly afflicted here it will make the native suffer from dire poverty. On the other hand a strong and benign Saturn here gives success in agriculture, public appointments, mining and labour intensive jobs. He may not be handsome. He may leave his homeland and settle away from it. He will talk little but harshly and his speech may be defective. He may have a difficult family to contend with. He may have a disease in his face or the mouth. He and his elder sister/brother may not have comforts and his mother may be a cause of trouble to them. She may be a disappointed person with life. He may be separated from his parents. His end of life will be in misery, penury or in spartan circumstances. He may die a lingering death due to a chronic disease. He may not realise his ambitions. He may be friendless. His younger sister/brother may lead a secluded life or he might be imprisoned. His eldest child may rise high in life but he may suffer a fall later. A benign Saturn here will improve the longevity of native's wife. His father will have poor constitution and may be ailing.

Third

This is considered a good location for Saturn. The native will have to wait for success in life and work hard for it. His relations with his younger brothers/sisters and other relatives will not be satisfactory. However he will be healthy, generous, lazy, and happily married. He will be bold, intelligent and long lived. Children will be born to him with difficulty. He may have some defect or disease in his arms. He may have troubles during his journeys. His father may be pessimistic but hardworking. He may not be happy with him. His mother may keep to herself and may be very religious. The native may have some interest in the mystical side of life and may make efforts to understand it. He may remain in service far longer than average. His children will be disappointed time and again in life.

Fourth

The native will keep his own company, suffer from bad health in his childhood and be unhappy. He will however be serious and disciplined. He will be separated from his mother and the closing part of life will be in unsatisfactory circumstances. The native may have a lonely end. He will not have a happy married life. A favourable Saturn will however give much landed property. His education may suffer. He may not have healthy early years of life. He may have a worrying or mentally disturbed disposition. The mind may be dispassionate. A weak Saturn may cause trouble from enemies, thieves or maternal uncle. The native may not be of good health. His career will have fluctuating success. He may find disfavour with his bosses. It will give results of its placement in the second house to his younger sister/brother. His eldest child may have to face heavy expenditure, risk of imprisonment, confinement in a hospital due to serious sickness or a mind given to morbid religious speculations. His wife may not be of good conduct. His father is likely to be long lived.

Fifth

The native would be depressed, unhappy with his children, and financially in a tight position. This is not a good position for investments, speculation and long duration contracts. It is liable to cause great sorrow due to a bereavement. It reduces the number of children and causes trouble begetting them. Saturn placed in a sign of Mercury may make the native childless.

Pleasures for him end in pain. The native will suffer from chronic disease in the stomach, or he may have heart trouble if the Sun or sign Leo also has adverse influence. He may be disappointed in love, or there may be delay and obstacles. The native will be attracted to persons senior to him in age and of serious nature. There may be an unhappy or late marriage, or, if Rahu or the Sun also influences the seventh house, there may be a separation. His elder sister/brother may lead an ordinary life. It will give results of its placement in the third house to his younger sister/brother. His mother may talk rudely and may not get along with her family. His wife may not have any friends or she may suffer losses through them. His father may travel to distant places but it may only bring him trouble.

Sixth

The native will be a capable and ambitious person, who will be successful in his endeavours. He will be rich. If the planet is weak and afflicted, he will have trouble from servants or enemies, or rheumatic or chronic diseases. If Mars afflicts Saturn here, the native may have to undergo surgery for some disease, or he may have to face violence during a robbery. These diseases may prove fatal. He may leave his birthplace and go elsewhere. He may lead a secluded or secret life. His younger sister/brother may not be happy. It will give results of its placement in the fourth house to his younger sister/brother. The native may cause trouble to his mother. His conduct may be disgraceful. He may not like the job that he is doing or he may be forced to work at something that does not interest him. His children will have the results of placement of the planet in the second house. His father may reach a high position but is likely to suffer a fall. The father may have trouble from the government or his superior. His elder sister/brother may be long lived.

Seventh

The native may marry late in life, the spouse may be older in age and the marriage may not be happy. The spouse may be short lived. He may marry a widow or a divorcee. The native may have difficulty in having sex or he may be indiscriminate in his liaisons with females. This will be further aggravated if Venus is under adverse influence in the chart. He may travel a lot. A good Saturn here may take the native abroad and may make him rise high in society there. The native may also have difficult relationship with partners or may suffer losses in partnership. He may be disciplined in his outlook. He may not be fortunate or wealthy. His education may not be continuous, or there may be some obstruction in it. However, Jupiter or Mercury should also be weak or afflicted in the horoscope for this result to materialise in full. He may have trouble from his mother. His elder sister/brother may not get along with the father. The elder sister/brother may have a philosophical turn of mind or he may be dispassionate.

Eighth

The native may face difficulties and disappointments in life. He may be argumentative or he may not be able to communicate easily. His death can be by drowning if there is a watery sign here, or it may be slow and lingering. A powerful or favourable Saturn in this house ensures long life. A well aspected Saturn here will give an abiding interest in occult subjects. The native may die of hunger. He may have trouble from servants and rheumatic, eye, stomach, or chronic diseases. He may have trouble in the rectum. He may not be rich. The number of children born to the native will be few. He will be burdened with responsibilities. He cannot expect money by way of legacies or through marriage. He may not have a happy childhood. There may be trouble in his family. He may not be handsome. He may have a difficult career. His boss may be troublesome or he may lose the position that he may attain. His conduct may not be above board. This position is very good for the material well being of his younger sister/brother. If a lunar Node afflicts Saturn here, his mother or the native herself may suffer from miscarriages. His children will have little property or comforts.

Ninth

The native may be solemn, hard working and religious. His relationship with his wider family may be bad. If the Sun is weak, badly placed or adverse, he may have bad relations with his father. He may suffer losses through foreign and long voyages and litigation. He may be lonely and without much income. His

elder sister/brother may not do well in life. His relations with
his younger sister/brother may not be cordial. He may be
troubled by his enemies or servants, but he may not lose on their
account. It will give results of its placement in the fifth house to
his children, and in the sixth to his mother. However, Saturn in
its own house here may make the results totally different. The
native may be fortunate throughout his life. Such a native will
have a serious bent of mind, deeply interested in religion and the
mystical side of life. If Saturn is adverse and is afflicted by Rahu
or Mars, the native may be stupid or mentally imbalanced. Such
a Saturn in the ninth house will also be very bad for the well
being and longevity of native's father.

Tenth

The native is highly disciplined and persevering. He is ambitious and works hard to achieve his goals. His conduct may not
be good. He may be engaged in mining, agriculture or horticulture, particularly if the sign in the tenth house belongs to Earth
category. If the sign belongs to Water category, he may be a diver
or connected through his job with the ocean bed. He is likely to
rise in life but there may be a severe fall. Owner of the eighth
house connected with Saturn and both placed in a navansha
owned by a malefic planet indicate serious trouble from a terrible
boss. His father may not be wealthy or he may have some speech
defect including a rough tongue. The native may have to face
false allegations and may lose his father early. The 36th, 42nd,
72nd and 83rd years may be fortunate. The native may always
be bothered by heavy expenses. His married life may be disturbed. This is a good location for his children. When Saturn is
well placed here, his younger sister/brother may be long lived.
His elder sister/brother may not be rich.

Eleventh

The native may be powerful, wealthy, and highly connected.
He may have sound health and intelligence. He may be long
lived. He may earn by employing labour. He may suffer from ill
health in his infancy. He may have only daughters. If Saturn is
adverse or afflicted, the native may be childless. He may be a
leader in his community. He may have friends among common

people. He may befriend persons who are older than him in age.
The friendship may be long lasting and faithful. If the planet is
adverse for the ascendant he may either not have friends or he
may face trouble from them. Saturn in a movable sign here is
indicative of the fact that the native may face obstruction and
hindrances in his ventures from his friends. Saturn here in a
common sign causes disappointments. A good Saturn will make
the native healthy and wealthy, and he may not have many
enemies or trouble from them.

Twelfth

The native is not careful with his money. He cannot pursue
his early academic career smoothly. He would be an introverted
personality. He may face imprisonment. He may have bad
eyesight. He may suffer humiliations and may not command
respect. The native may be of bad conduct secretly. He may like
to be alone and may be a silent person. He may face failures and
his expenses may be heavy. He may have trouble from his
enemies. His maternal uncle may not do well in life. If an adverse
Mars influences Saturn here, there is a chance that the native
meets with a bad end; if an adverse Mercury influences it, some
kind of mental aberration may be looked for. He will be
perseverant in his quest for the paranormal. The native may meet
with losses if the mystical is pursued. There may be deformity
in a limb. There may be secret enemies. His younger sister/
brother may be highly placed in life, but his conduct may not be
good and he may lose his high position, that he had built up by
hard work and perseverance, some time in life.

12. Effect of Saturn in various SIGNS (See opening remarks in
paragraph 19 under SUN) :

Aries (Debilitated at 20 deg)

The native may be quick tempered, sharp tongued and deceitful. He may be quarrelsome. He will not be on good terms with
his relatives and may not have a good name in the society. He
may wander about purposelessly. He may lack wealth and
intelligence and may be friendless. He may have to work hard
for earning his livelihood. If the owner of the sixth house is also

debilitated or afflicted, the native will be ailing. He may have
chronic diseases which may not respond to treatment readily. He
may not be long lived. He will not be helpful to others. The
difficulties and bad results of Saturn are likely to be worse in the
first half of life than in the second. Saturn will show the worst
results if it is placed between 23 degrees 20 minutes and 26
degrees 40 minutes in the sign. If Mars is powerful and favourable
in the chart, the evil results will be reduced to some extent. If the
ascendant is Aries, the adverse results will be of the worst kind.
If the ascendant is Taurus, the native will be really unfortunate
because Saturn is the best planet for this ascendant. It will not
only be debilitated but shall also be in the twelfth house. If the
ascendant is Virgo, the native is likely to experience an improvement in his status during the periods of Saturn, though his
children may suffer at this time. If the ascendant is Libra, the
native not only will have a difficult married life, but during the
periods of Saturn he may even divorce his wife or she may pass
away. His children may also suffer during this time. Saturn some
times does not give such adverse results in this sign for Sagittarius ascendant. If the ascendant is Capricorn, the native's father
is likely to experience an improvement in his status during the
periods of Saturn, though his eldest child may suffer at this time.
The native's mother may also suffer severely and may pass away.
If the ascendant is Pisces, the native will be wretched and
penniless. The aspect of the Sun on Saturn will give good results
to the native with regard to wealth. The aspect of Jupiter on
Saturn will also give good results. The aspect of the Moon will
aggravate the situation since the native will be inclined to have
illicit relations with women. The aspect of Mars is likely to
generate criminal tendencies in the native, though it will reduce
the evil results of Saturn in its sign of debilitation in other
respects.

Taurus

The native may not be rich and whatever wealth he may have,
he may not be able to keep it. He may not be highly placed. He
may not talk well or may not be truthful. He may marry several
times and may like to have liaisons with several women. When
Venus is under bad influence, it is an adverse planet for the chart

or it is in contact with Mars (even by sign i.e., Venus is placed in a sign of Mars), the native will have a weakness for women and sex pleasures. He will be firm minded and persistent in his approach. He may be mild tempered. If Saturn is adverse for the ascendant, the native may lose money at the share market. He may not like to travel, or may have trouble during and due to travels. If the ascendant is Aries, the native may be rich. If the ascendant is Taurus, the native will be wealthy and highly placed. If the ascendant is Gemini, the native may travel abroad or over long distances during the periods of Saturn. Saturn will give good results in this sign for Capricorn ascendant also. If the ascendant is Pisces, the native shall travel abroad. The aspect of Mars may take the native into army. The aspect of Mercury may make the native impotent. The aspect of Jupiter will make the native helpful by nature and therefore popular. The aspect of Venus from Scorpio on Saturn will form a sambandha between the two planets. Venus will bear the influence of Mars in its aspect. When Mars is favourable for the chart, the sambandha will be conducive to increase in wealth and status of the native. The worst results will be given by Saturn when it is between 10 degrees and 13 degrees 20 minutes in the sign.

Gemini

The native will have a subtle intellect. He may have some success in an intellectual project some time in life. He may have poor bank balance, but there is a possibility that he may hold an important position with a good number of persons working under him. He may get indebted. He may be cunning, shameless and unhappy. He may be confined, or get imprisoned on charges that are unsubstantiated and the cause of this action may arise due to family differences. He will live away from his relatives and his location may not be known to many of them. He may face dishonour in public. He may have an unhappy or trouble-some childhood. He may also be bothered by his younger sister/ brother. He may face difficulties due to his education or on account of short journeys. He may get married abroad or to a foreigner. He will have trouble from legal institutions and law officers. He may contract a disease through his profession. He may have some worry on account of his children. His sources of income may be more than one. Saturn in association with Mercury in Gemini for Aries ascendant may make the native earn his livelihood through writing. Such a Saturn will limit the number of children of the native. Saturn will give good results in this sign for Taurus, Aquarius and Pisces ascendants. It will make the native change his career frequently if the ascendant is Virgo and, if the ascendant is Capricorn, he will suffer from enemies and diseases. The aspect of the Moon or Mercury on Saturn will give good results. He will be virtuous and have favours from the government if Saturn is aspected by Jupiter.

Cancer

The native may not have cordial relations with his mother. He will love his wife. His early years will be spent in a state of financial limitation and ill health. His teeth may give him trouble. An adverse Saturn may bring trouble to the native through his own imagination, or through supernatural agencies. He may suffer losses in business. There may be difficulties at the close of life. His death may take place abroad or by drowning. He may not have good relations with his relatives. He will reach a prominent position in life. Saturn having contact with the owner of the twelfth house, the Sun or Rahu, or with the dispositors of one or more of these three planets, will make the native change houses a number of times. If Saturn is adverse for the chart in the previous combination and the Moon is weak in the horoscope, the sub-period or major-period of Saturn may prove bad for the native's mother. The native may not be of sharp intelligence. Saturn will be beneficial to the native in this sign if the ascendant is Taurus but he may not have children. Saturn will give good results in this sign for Virgo and Libra ascendants. For Sagittarius ascendant, Saturn in this sign may produce childlessness. If the ascendant is Capricorn, Saturn in this sign may act as a maraka. A weak Saturn or one having sambandha with adverse planets, may be a cause of poor health for a native having Aquarius in his first house. The aspect of Jupiter on Saturn will give good results. The aspect of the Moon on Saturn may cause trouble between the native and his mother.

Leo

The native may be of irritable, determined and ambitious disposition and he may work hard in life to achieve his ambitions. He may be in service. A good Saturn will confer power and authority on the native. He may have favours from his bosses. He may be good at writing. But if Saturn is adverse, he may have to face difficulties created by his subordinates. He may not have loyal and sincere servants. He may suffer losses in such business where he may have to engage a number of labourers. He may get into complications with the government due to death of one of his subordinates. His children or love affairs may be source of much worry to him. He may get married to a friend or acquaintance. He may ruin his health due to hard work and may suffer from stomach or heart trouble. Saturn will give good results in this sign for Libra, Scorpio and Sagittarius ascendants. The aspect of the Moon, Jupiter or Venus on Saturn will give good results. The aspect of the Sun on Saturn will make it come out with all the adverse results that Saturn can give. In such a case, the native will lead an insignificant existence. He will be poor, will suffer from ill health and may be given to drinking heavily.

Virgo

The native may be of serious, cautious, critical and analytical bent of mind. He will be capable of deep thought and dealing with profound matters. He will however be diffident and susceptible to melancholia. He may sometimes be prone to failures due to his pessimism. He may find his work drudgery. He may face adverse situations in service. He may be fickle in his affections, and may be wanting in politeness. He may not be virile and manly looking. He may be disinclined to get married. Besides he may visit prostitutes and be of poor moral fibre. His conduct will be questionable. He may be wealthy but lazy. The native will be successful at litigation Saturn will give good results in this sign for Taurus, Scorpio and Sagittarius ascendants. The aspect of the Moon or Mercury on Saturn will give good results. He will be virtuous and have favours from the government if Saturn is aspected by Jupiter.

Libra (*Exalted at 20 deg*)

The native may be rich and may distinguish himself in his field. He may reach a high position and may earn wealth and name abroad. He may be very learned. He will speak well. He may have weakness for women. He may enter into partnership successfully with persons elder to the native. He may be very precise in matters pertaining to justice. He will be long lived. The intensity of good results will depend upon the state of Venus. If it is weak or afflicted, the native is likely to face deep sorrow on account of the loss of a female to whom he was very closely attached, or there may be opposition from females. His marriage will be important for him in life. He may gain, or succeed in his career with the support of his marriage. For Aries ascendant, the longevity of the wife may be in doubt. Saturn will not give good results in this sign for Gemini ascendant since it may make the children sickly. When the ascendant is Cancer, the native may not be at peace, and the end of life is likely to be spent in poverty. Saturn will give great prosperity and happiness to an individual who has Libra ascendant. This statement shall be true in a much reduced manner for Sagittarius ascendant also. If the ascendant is Capricorn, the native will be a person holding high office. Saturn in this sign for Aquarius ascendant will make the native religious and wealthy. If the ascendant is Pisces, the expenses may be heavy and on items that are looked down upon in normal daily life. The aspect of the Moon or Mars on Saturn will give good results. The aspect of Mars may take the native into army. The aspect of Venus on Saturn will form a sambandha between the two planets. It will be conducive to increase in wealth and status of the native.

Scorpio

This position of Saturn is not conducive to a tranquil and respectable life. The native suffers from depression occasionally and is incapable of making friends. He may be independent and self conscious. He will be impetuous, passionate and shrewd. He may be proud, cruel and envious. He will love power and authority, and cannot brook any dissent. He may be harmed by fire, poison or enemy. He may not have any reservations in appropriating other's wealth. He will have some wealth. His expenses may be heavy. He may face public humiliation or confinement. If Mars is adverse for the horoscope and afflicted, or Saturn has adverse influence, the native may commit heinous crimes. He may not have much interest in religion. He will have the capacity to unearth hidden or unknown concepts and facts. He may travel abroad and live there. He may not be long lived and may die suddenly. He may gain through death of others. This location of Saturn is bad for married life though good for wealth when the ascendant is Taurus. When the ascendant is Libra, the native will be well off, but the wealth may be in danger of dissipating due to his extravagance, since Saturn will be in the sign of a maraka planet. It shows the best results for Aquarius ascendant, as it will raise the native to a high position, but there may be a danger of a fall from that position. The aspect of Jupiter on Saturn will give good results. The aspect of the Sun or Moon on Saturn will give good results to the native with regard to wealth. The aspect of Mars is likely to generate criminal tendencies in the native.

Sagittarius

The native may be learned, honourable, virtuous, thrifty, loyal to his master and happy. He will be capable of good concentration and deep and clear thinking on abstruse subjects. He may have interest in science or philosophy. He may be reticent and honest. He may travel substantially or may even be an explorer. He will be in the confidence of the government and people in high positions. He will be happily married and wealthy. He will gain from his investments. He will have very talented children who will further the name of the native and his family. He will be inclined to public service and philanthropy. He will be interested in the fields of labour welfare or welfare of general masses. He will be rich in old age. He will have a peaceful and honourable death. Saturn will give good results in this sign for Aries, Sagittarius and Pisces ascendants. The aspect of Mercury or Jupiter on Saturn will give good results.

Capricorn

The native may earn well and have a high position, perhaps in the army. He stands in danger of losing the high position that he had gained through his hard work. He would be intelligent, efficient and known. He may not live at his birth place. He will have sex relations with several women and may indulge in adultery. He may take financial advantage of his illicit relationship with other women. He will never be poor and be always successful in his career. He may take away the wealth of others. He may be indifferent to personal hygiene. He will be fond of his children. Saturn will give good results in this sign for Aries, Leo, and Libra ascendants. If the ascendant is Leo, the native will have major success at litigation during the major or sub-period of Saturn. The major-period or sub-periods of Saturn for Capricorn ascendant will be beneficial financially. If Saturn is in this sign while the ascendant is Aquarius, the native may settle away from his birth place, and the native may have to spend heavily on medical attention. The aspect of Jupiter or Venus on Saturn will give good results. If Mars aspects Saturn in this sign, the native is likely to be a successful army officer.

Aquarius (*Mooltrikona from 0 to 20 degrees*)

The native will be an intellectual and a refined person. He will be thoughtful and reserved, but will generally not tell the truth. He will be rich. He may join a society, company or movement. His relationships may be of lasting nature. He is successful at his profession by sheer hard work and persistence. He will have a happy married life. He may not live at his birth place. However, he may have sex relations with several women and may indulge in adultery. He may take financial advantage of his illicit relationship with other women. He may be a victim of heart trouble or a paralytic stroke in his later life. He will have a better end of life than the beginning. Saturn will give good results in this sign for Taurus, Capricorn and Aquarius ascendants. The aspect of Mars, Pisces Jupiter or Venus on Saturn will give good results.

Pisces

The native will be sober and mature. He may be highly spiritual and towards the end of his life he will be in an exalted spiritual state. He will be in the confidence of the government and people in high positions. He will be happily married and wealthy. He may also gain from secret societies, clinics, hospitals, religious institutions or asylums. He will have very talented children. He may reach a high position later in life. An adverse Saturn placed in this sign will cause sorrows and disappointments, tragic ends to romantic involvements, losses through friends, trouble from the government and displeasure of the boss. Such a Saturn will also be bad for marriage and the respect and honour of the native. Saturn will give good results in this sign for Taurus, Gemini, Libra, Sagittarius, Capricorn and Aquarius ascendants. However barring Taurus, and Capricorn ascendants, Saturn for other ascendants enumerated above shall also cause some trouble or the other. For Gemini it may cause danger to his mother from water; for Libra it is likely to cause trouble to his children; and for Sagittarius ascendant, it may cause trouble to native's mother and he may be mentally disturbed due to frequent change of residence. For Aquarius ascendant, Saturn may not allow the native to save his money. The aspect of Mercury or Jupiter on Saturn will give good results.

Chapter Three

The Lunar Nodes (Rahu and Ketu)

The Nodes, called Rahu and Ketu in Hindu astrology, are points of intersection between the path of the Moon and the apparent path of the Sun in the sky. They are not physical heavenly bodies, but their importance in predictive astrology is well established. A physical description of each of the two Nodes, anthropomorphically, is given in the following paragraphs. Detailed rules relating to the Nodes are also given. There are some rules which are common for both the Nodes. These have been recorded under RAHU and have been alluded to under KETU.

RAHU

1. It has a head without a normal body. It is fearful to look at. Its body is that of a serpent and is amorphous. It is tamasik, dark in complexion and thievish by nature. Its vehicle is a lion.

2. It is by nature a malefic planet. When it is not under the influence of another planet, it acts like Saturn. It rises hind part first.

3. Its RELATIONSHIP with other planets is as follows:

	Friendly with
	Mercury
	Venus
	Saturn

Neutral to	Jupiter
Inimical to	Sun
	Moon
	Mars

It is exalted in Taurus, its mooltrikona sign is Gemini, and it owns Aquarius vide Brihat Parasar Hora Sastra, Chapter 47, verses 34 to 36.

4. It is the KARAKA for the following: Gambling, social or political movements, outcastes, reptiles, snakes, snake-bite, widow, and swelling in the body.

5. It REPRESENTS the following:
(i)   Disease, cancer, mysterious diseases, insanity, general unhappiness, psychic disturbances, possession by discarnate supernatural beings, epidemics, alcoholism, drug induced maladies, illusion, hallucinations, dark complexion, tendency to look downwards while talking, skin diseases, pain in the body, hiccups, Rahu represents very old age and also age of 48 years.
(ii) Gomed, south west, wild tribes, foreigners, non-Hindus, Buddhists, riots, general disorders, social unrests, travels abroad, theft, old and bad women, mass trends, diplomacy, wickedness, execution, exile, aviation, paternal grandfather and maternal grandmother.
(iii) Heart trouble, leprosy, mental confusion, pain or injury in the feet and reptile bite.

6. Since the Nodes are capable of overcoming the Sun and the Moon by obstructing their light, they are stronger than any other planet in the nativity.

7. Rahu is considered to be like Saturn. It is stronger than Saturn. Saturn is the Greater Malefic. Therefore Rahu is the strongest malefic planet.

8. Whenever Rahu or Ketu has sambandha with a planet it takes on the power of the planet and magnifies it.

9. When Rahu has sambandha with the Moon and the other factors representing the mind (Mercury, the fourth house and its owner), or influences them, insanity, criminal tendency, possession by disincarnate supernatural entities, psychic and psycho-

logical disturbances, drug taking, alcoholism and neurological problems are likely to arise. Mere sambandha between badly placed Rahu and an adverse Moon without any beneficial influence is also likely to lead to these conditions.

10. Rahu has the power to obstruct and darken the Moon which represents the mind.

11. Rahu influencing the Sun can cause indecisiveness, warped imagination and illusions about the self.

12. The sambandha of Rahu with the SUN has the following effects (See paragraph 38 below.):

This is not good for the Sun if Rahu is adverse. Matters indicated by the Sun will suffer a setback. The native may have trouble from the government, highly placed persons, or he may not get along with his father or elders of the family. His health may be disturbed and general vitality wil be low. He may have heart trouble. He may find success eluding him in his ventures. His children may face difficulties.

(i) The sambandha of Rahu with the Sun in the first, third, fifth or the twelfth house is favourable, if Rahu is not adverse. The association of Rahu and the Sun in the second house may lead the native to penury.

(ii) If Rahu has sambandha with the Sun in the fourth house the native will face problems with regard to his property and children. He will have trouble from the enemies. He will migrate elsewhere.

(iii) This combination in the seventh house leads to marital discord, or loss of wealth due to women.

(iv) This combination in the eighth house shortens the longevity, provided the Sun is adverse for the chart.

(v) This combination in the ninth house gives higher knowledge and journeys abroad.

(vi) This combination in the tenth house raises the native to a high position, but it eventually makes the career a failure. The native has a chequered career.

(vii) This combination of the Sun and Rahu in the eleventh house is good.

(viii) Such sambandhas are especially bad in Aries, Libra, Scorpio and Aquarius.

(ix) The Sun having sambandha with Rahu in Leo is favourable but the native will have bad relations with his father.

13. A sambandha between Rahu and the MOON is generally not good. The native will be under an apprehension of the likelihood of something untoward happening to him (see paragraph 38 below). He may be mentally depressed. He may suffer from a circulatory or digestive disease. He may face troubles from women.

(i) We have to be careful with respect to this combination in the first or fourth house. It is very likely to cause mental aberrations in the native. When the combination takes place in the fourth house, the native may face serious health or mental problems in his 20th year of life.

(ii) This sambandha taking place in the third house leads to early death of the mother or of sister's husband.

(iii) The Moon located in the eighth house and having sambandha with Rahu is an indication of serious balarista. The 20th day after birth will be critical. If the native survives, he will be sickly in his early years.

14. The sambandha of Rahu with MARS (see paragraph 38 below):

The sambandha of Rahu with Mars brings out the violent tendencies in the latter. The native may have uncontrollable anger. It may also develop suicidal inclination in the native. However, when Mars and Rahu are favourable for the chart, the adverse results of the sambandha will only manifest in the form of anger. The native may have a heightened libido. Some important sambandha positions are stated as below:

(i) In the third house it is an indication that the native is either the eldest brother or the eldest has not survived.

(ii) Such a combination in the fourth house leads to losses unless Mars is a beneficial planet for the ascendant and Rahu is well placed.

(iii) Such a combination in the fifth house is an indicator that the native would either not have a male issue or he would lose it early in life. The same result can be expected if Rahu is in sambandha with Mars through exchange of signs or through aspect.

(iv) Such a combination in the seventh house is an indication that the native had premarital affairs or has more than one wife.

(v) Such a combination in the eighth house spoils the health of the native, and may cause his death by poison or bite of a poisonous insect.

(vi) Such a combination in the second, tenth, or the eleventh house can lead to amassing of wealth through questionable means.

15. The sambandha of Rahu with MERCURY (see paragraph 38 below): The native may have a sharp intellect and good power to communicate, when both the planets are favourable. He may also have an inclination to gamble and speculate. Some important sambandha positions are stated as below:

(i) In the fourth house gives gains, honour, high position and wealth but in Pisces the results are just the reverse,

(ii) In the fifth house it is not good for mental health of the native,

(iii) in the sixth, eighth or the twelfth house causes an undiagnosable disease, insanity or nervous disorder.

(iv) Such a combination in the seventh house will lead to a highly disturbed married life.

16. Rahu joining JUPITER in sambandha (see paragraph 38 below):

This sambandha is productive of good results many a time. The native may be very learned, wise or wealthy. He may have exceptional legal ability. Some important sambandha positions are stated as below:

(i) In the first, fourth, fifth or the ninth house in a favourable sign, it takes the native to a very high position and makes him wealthy.

(ii) This combination in the fifth house can cause the wife to miscarry, or death of children.

(iii) This combination in the eighth house gives stomach trouble and a mark near the navel of the native.

(iv) This combination anywhere in the horoscope, unless well aspected or both the planets being favourable to the chart, causes distaste for religion in the native.

17. Rahu and VENUS in sambandha (see paragraph 38 below):
This is an adverse influence on Venus unless Rahu is good for
the chart, and may distort the attitude of the native to healthy
sex, relationship with women and marriage. Some important
sambandha positions are stated as below:

(i) 'in the fourth house gives property, wealth, harmony,
comforts and cordial relations with relatives.

(ii) This sambandha is bad in the third, sixth, seventh, eighth
and twelfth houses.

18. Rahu with SATURN in sambandha (see paragraph 38
below): This is not a good combination for native's health.

(i) In the ascendant, it indicative of the fact that native's
mother had a difficult child birth. It also signifies that the
native would suffer from poor health in childhood and
would get hurt in his early years several times.

(ii) Such a sambandha in an adverse house will give tendency to commit suicide and a criminal bent of mind.

(iii) The sambandha taking place in the fourth house may
prove troublesome. There may be imbalance or disturbance of mind. It is also bad for the mother.

(iv) It is bad if placed in the ninth house. Here it gives
displeasure of the government, parents and the guru and
the native may be forced to migrate elsewhere.

(v) When the combination takes place in the tenth house, the
native may reach a high position if the two planets are
favourable for the chart but it is also indicative of the fact
that the native may suffer a fall from a high position.

19. The association of Rahu with MARS and SATURN in
sambandha (see paragraph 38 below):

(i) in the first house causes venereal and urinary diseases,

(ii) in the eighth house it gives rise to immorality, and,

(iii) anywhere in the horoscope, it not only makes the native
accident prone but also destroys the results of that house.

20. When there is an exchange of asterisms between Rahu and
Saturn and there is involvement of the eighth house in this
combination, it makes the native prone to paralytic strokes.

21. Rahu gives better results when aspected by a planet
friendly to it rather than in association with it.

22. (i) Whenever a Node is in the third, sixth, or eleventh house, and does not own it, it will be an adverse planet for the horoscope.

(ii) Whenever a Node is in the sign or constellation of an owner of the sixth, or eighth house, or is in sambandha with the owner of one of these houses, which is an adverse planet for the horoscope, it will be adverse for the chart.

(iii) (a) If the Node is placed in an angle and has sambandha with the owner of a triangle, or

(b) it is placed in a triangle and has sambandha with the owner of an angle, it becomes highly potent to do good to the native.

(iv) (a) If a Node is placed in an angle in the sign owned by an excellent or good planet, or

(b) it is placed in a triangle in the sign owned by the owner of an angle, or

(c) it is placed in the eighth house, in its own sign, it becomes capable to do good to the native.

(v) A Node placed in an angle with no other influence will be a neutral planet. Its nature will depend on the nature of the dispositor.

(vi) A Node placed in a triangle with no other influence will be a good planet. Its nature will be modified by the nature of the dispositor.

(vii) Mixed results would be felt when the Node is placed in the second or twelfth house, or the owner of the second or twelfth house has sambandha with the Node. The nature of the dispositor of the Node will be very important and the nature of the Node determined in the above manner will be noticeably altered by it. The results to be given by the Node will be felt during the major or sub-periods of the concerned Node.

23. Rahu is important for giving worldly results, Ketu for spiritual or religious ones.

24. The major or sub-periods of Rahu or Ketu may be unpleasant if either of them is in the asterism of Ketu. The results may be beneficial if the asterism involved is that of Rahu.

25. A Node will give the results of the house in which it is placed, of its dispositor, and of the planets with which it has sambandha.

26. A Node adopts the characteristics of the planet with which it is in sambandha, but at the same time passes on its bad influence to that planet. Such a planet, even if it is a beneficial planet for the horoscope, will give at least some adverse results in its major or sub-period.

27. The Nodes attain powers to kill only when they are in sambandha with an adverse Saturn, or the maraka owner of the second or seventh house. Otherwise if they are located in the second or seventh house without any malefic sambandha, they will not kill.

28. A well placed Node in a common sign, the owner of which owns a triangular house gives exceedingly good results. A well placed Node in a common sign, the owner of which owns an angular house also gives good results. However these good results will be spoilt if the owner also owns the third, sixth, eighth or the eleventh house.

29. A well placed Node in a movable sign, the owner of which owns an angular or triangular house gives good results, but the results will be mediocre when the sign is a fixed one. However these good results will be spoilt if the owner also owns the third, sixth, eighth or the eleventh house.

30. A Node placed in the third, sixth, or eleventh house in sambandha with a beneficial planet, or placed in an angular or triangular house in sambandha with a malefic planet, will in its period first give good results but the results will be adverse towards the end.

31. Adverse results should be predicted if the major-period of Rahu is the fifth or seventh from the first major-period after birth.

32. KALSARPA yoga is formed:
(i) · if Rahu is in the first six houses from the ascendant,
(ii) all the planets are between Rahu and Ketu, and
(iii) no planet is located in the same sign as Rahu.
    This yoga destroys the good indications in a horoscope.

The house where Rahu is located suffers the most. The yoga will still operate if conditions (ii) and (iii) only are fulfilled but its strength will be less.

33. The first six months of Rahu major-period after the close of Mars major-period are as a rule adverse.

34. The dispositors of the Nodes are of particular importance. If any of them is under good influence, does not own a bad house and is a beneficial planet for the ascendant, that dispositor becomes capable of giving very good results. If it forms a good yoga (combination) with other planets, the strength of the yoga increases many folds to give good results.

Such a planet, under adverse influence or of adverse nature, is capable of harming the native to a great extent.

35. If some planets form a rajyoga and Rahu is connected with this combination, the rajyoga results shall be given by Rahu.

36. Rahu favourably placed in sambandha with the owner of an angle and a triangular house, shall give high status and prosperity during its major or sub-periods.

37. If the owner of an angle and a triangular house has sambandha with the dispositor of Rahu, the native will have high status and prosperity during the major or sub-periods of Rahu.

38. The aspect or sambandha of a Node with various planets should be analysed in the following ways:
   (a) The fundamental characteristic of Rahu is to give results similar to Saturn and that of Ketu like Mars.
   (b) Due to the special affinity that the Nodes have with the luminaries (the Sun and Moon), the sambandha with or the aspect by the Nodes on the luminaries ought to be examined differently. If there is an eclipse owing to the association of the Node with a luminary, the results will be very different. An eclipse in a good house is harmful for the affairs of that house, and is good in an adverse house.
   (c) If there is sambandha between a Node and a planet, the planet will take over some bad nature of the Node, and the Node will in turn take the nature of the planet. Thus for example, a mutual aspect between a beneficial Jupiter

and Rahu will make Jupiter lose some of its good nature, and Rahu will become beneficial.

(d) It need not be re-emphsised that whenever a planet or a house is under the influence of a Node, the affairs indicated by this factor will always exhibit some suddenness or unexpected results.

(e) If the Node is in exaltation, or under the influence of such planets that are benign planets for the ascendant, it will give overall good results in its period, but the element of the unexpected and a fear of things going awry at any stage will persist.

39. A Node in a sign owned by an adverse Saturn generally does not give good results in its major or sub-periods.

40. An interesting statement has been made in Brihat Parasar Hora Sastra, Chapter 50 verse 42. It says that when Rahu is placed in Aries, Taurus, Gemini, Aquarius or Pisces; or, Ketu is placed in Scorpio, Sagittarius, Capricorn, Aquarius or Pisces, the period of the Node shall be productive of beneficial results.

41. Effect of Rahu in various HOUSES and SIGNS: The results have to be assessed after the nature of the Node has been determined and the resultant of its placement in the sign and house is quantified on the basis of rules elaborated above. The following is a general indicator for the Node being in a house or sign. When the sign number and house occupied by a Node are different, the results narrated for the two should be read together and reconciled. The results stated below stand to be modified in the light of specific rules given above.

First

Health of the native may be poor unless there is beneficial influence on the ascendant or Rahu is well placed. He is likely to suffer from headaches and diseases in the upper part of the body. He may have an unhappy marriage. His attitude to life and behaviour may be unusual. A powerful and well placed Rahu will make the native rise to a high position and be eminent and wealthy. Rahu here associated with the powerful owner of an angle and a triangular house, or aspected by the owner will form a rajyoga. The native will get more and more prosperous as he progresses in life. If the dispositor of Rahu is powerfully placed in an angle, there shall be sudden gain of wealth for the native. Rahu in the first house in Aries, Taurus or Gemini confers good health and prosperity. Such a location of Rahu will ward off all evils. Rahu is a major beneficial planet for the native here if it is placed in Aquarius or Pisces. In Gemini or Virgo it makes the native God fearing and kind, and he will have all the comforts. If Rahu is in Aries, Gemini, Leo, Libra, Sagittarius, or Aquarius the native would be slim. The native will be wealthy and prosperous if Rahu is in Leo. If the fifth or ninth house has a sign inimical to Rahu, the native may either have problems in having children or their longevity may be poor, and the native may face hindrances in life and career. The children may not be close to the native and may be irreligious. They may do well at gambling or speculation. His younger sister/brother may be long lived and wealthy but may have hearing defect. His mother may not be of good conduct. He will succeed in litigation. His elder sister/ brother may be efficient, good at work and rich. Rahu in sambandha with a powerful maraka owner of the second or seventh house here will destroy the wealth of the native and may cause his death.

Second

The native may not be able to express himself well. He may tell lies and may talk to mislead others. He would be tender hearted and will face opposition. He may not have good relations with his family. He may have diseases in the face or mouth. He may have defect in his sight if the Moon or Sun is also involved with malefic planets. When the owner of the first, fifth or ninth house is in sambandha with Rahu here, it will make the native prosperous. Rahu here in sambandha with the owner of the third, sixth, eighth or the eleventh house will reduce the longevity and may cause death during its major or sub-periods. However, a favourable Rahu placed in the second house with the owner of the eleventh will be capable of making the native get wealth suddenly. If Rahu here is connected with Saturn, the owner of the sixth or eighth house or their dispositors, the native may not be able to build up a bank balance. This will be further confirmed if the owner of the second house is also connected with this combination. He may have troubles from the banks and other financial institutions. A well placed and powerful Rahu here will confer status on the native and gains from the government. If the dispositor of Rahu is powerfully placed in an angle, there shall be sudden gain of wealth for the native. The native will have illnesses that arise suddenly or he may meet with unforeseen misadventures. If the eighth house is powerful, Rahu is a strong beneficial planet for the ascendant and connected with the eighth house in any manner, the native will gain a legacy suddenly. He may be raised to a high position by such a Rahu but his conduct may not be good. He may earn wealth through dubious means. This may also be the cause of his fall. His younger sister/brother may live in a distant land. His children may rise to high positions but they will not be of good conduct and their transactions will not be above board. Rahu here, with the owner of the house powerful and well placed, is an indication that the native is likely to gain wealth suddenly.

Third

The native will be bold and efficient. Rahu in this house in sambandha with a beneficial planet removes all other adverse indications in the horoscope and makes the native long lived, but if it is afflicted it destroys brothers and causes disease in the neck or the throat. An adverse Rahu will cause marital problems for the native as well. The native will remain in good health during the major or sub-periods of Rahu well placed here. Generally, this location of Rahu in the chart makes for difficult relationship with younger brothers/sisters. The native will be a leader of men. He will be strong willed. He may receive news suddenly and may be criticised for his opinions. He may travel about a lot. The journeys may be by air, particularly so if Saturn influences Rahu here. Rahu here associated with a powerful owner of an angle and a triangular house will form a rajyoga. Rahu in sambandha with a powerful maraka owner of the second or seventh house here will destroy wealth of the native and may cause his death. This is not a good indication for the mother of the native. She will be extravagant and she will carry on certain activities clandestinely that cannot be called good. The native's children will be long lived and prosperous unless a powerful owner of the sixth or eleventh house is influencing Rahu in any manner, when the results will be the reverse. His wife will not be religious and of good conduct, but if Rahu is in Gemini or Virgo or it is aspected or associated with the owner of the ninth house or Mercury, she will have sudden and unexpected gains. If Rahu has sambandha with or aspected by a powerful owner of the eighth or first house, it will reduce the longevity of the wife. The native's father may be a man of loose morals. His elder sister/brother may be childless or may suffer from troubles in the belly.

Fourth

Here Rahu has a tendency to make the native extremely orthodox. He would not have an open mind and his relationship with his mother will not be satisfactory. His mother will be long lived but generally unhappy. It will give results of its placement in the first house to her. However the native will have conveyances, land, house and high status. Rahu with Mars in the fourth house is an indication that the native is of violent temperament and liable to be incarcerated in his life. The event can be timed to the year for which the annual horoscope has Rahu alone in the fourth house. Rahu is a major beneficial planet for the native here if it is placed in Aries, Taurus, Gemini, Aquarius or Pisces. If it is placed in Aries, Taurus, Gemini or Virgo here, it will get benefits to the native from the government. When Rahu is only in a friend's sign, and not adversely aspected or associated, it shall be beneficial to the native. Rahu here in sambandha with a powerful planet owning an angle and a triangle will form a rajyoga. Rahu in sambandha with a powerful maraka owner of the second or seventh house will destroy wealth of the native and may cause his death. A badly placed Rahu will adversely effect the native's higher education. His mind may be constantly disturbed or he may be petty and low minded. If the fourth house, its owner and the Moon or Mercury are influenced by Rahu, the native may suffer from nervous disorders, mental aberrations, fear, epilepsy or some kind of phobia. This combination is also indicative of the fact that the native will have to deal with riots or popular upsurges. A badly placed Rahu may cause disease to the native in the major or sub-periods of the adverse owner of the second, sixth, seventh, eighth, eleventh or the twelfth house.

It will give results of its placement in the second house to the younger sister/brother of the native. His children may be extravagant and they will live away from their native land. If such a Rahu influences the owner of the eleventh house or Venus (Jupiter in the case of a female nativity) alongwith Saturn or the Sun, the eldest child of the native will either lose his spouse early due to death or their marriage may get dissolved. The native's wife may be a influential person, who may lose the influence later.

Fifth

An exalted or a debilitated Rahu here will cause trouble through children. It will give the results of its placement in the first house to the children of the native. The native will face problems in love affairs and will suffer from stomach troubles. If Leo and the Sun in the horoscope are afflicted, the native may suffer from heart trouble. If the owner of the eighth house is also involved, the native may succumb to it. If the twelfth house is so involved the native may have to be hospitalised. There may be some defect in his speech. He will have great desire to speculate or indulge in betting, lotteries or horse racing. If a beneficial dispositor of Rahu is powerfully placed in an angle, there shall be sudden gain of wealth for the native through gambling, games of chance or speculation. When the Moon is with Rahu in the fifth house, the native will have a quick temper and will be likely to lose his children or face difficulties due to them. An adverse Rahu will be bad for the elder sister/brother of the native. Such a Rahu connected with the seventh house will indicate a difficult love affair; and, connected with the twelfth shows the tendency to sexual promiscuity which may cause severe problems for the native. When the owner of the twelfth house is so connected, the native will find life difficult and be lonely and friendless. He will not be intelligent and not interested in finer things of life. Rahu in the fifth house in association or aspect with the owner of the second or the seventh house will cause death of the native in its major or sub-periods if the life span has come to an end. Rahu here with the owner of the fifth house powerful and well placed, is an indication that the native is likely to gain wealth suddenly.

Sixth

If Rahu is placed in a favourable sign, the native will have the ability to subdue his enemies, will keep good health, be wealthy and will have a high status. The native will perform well at his career and his finances will be in a good state if the nature and state of Rahu are beneficial. If Rahu is in an adverse sign, and weak or under adverse influence, the native will have a scandalous personal life. He would be misunderstood by others. Rahu placed in the sixth house is inherently bad in nature and if it is badly placed or is under adverse influence, it can prove to be very troublesome in its sub-period in the major-period of a bad planet. Even when major-period of an excellent planet, that does not have sambandha with such a Rahu, is current, the sub-period of Rahu can be troublesome. Rahu placed in the sixth house in Scorpio or Capricorn, or associated with or aspected by an adverse Saturn here will be a highly potent cause for disease. Saturn would also be a planet to cause disease in such a situation of Rahu if there is sambandha between Rahu and Saturn. Any house influenced by such a Rahu or Saturn will manifest trouble or disease in the part of the body indicated by the house or sign. Similarly, if the owner of the sixth house occupies the house with Rahu or aspects it, the native will fall sick during the major or sub-periods of Rahu. The father of the native may be highly placed and powerful but his conduct will be bad and he will be accused of breach of trust. The elder sister/brother of the native will face humiliation and criticism, and will suffer from troubles in the anus or genitals.

Seventh

This is not a good position for Rahu. The native will be self willed and will not have peace of mind. A Node malefic in nature and under adverse influence here reduces the marital happiness and makes the native or his wife prone to immoral behaviour. She is likely to suffer from disease in her reproductory system. Death of the spouse can also happen. Separation from the loved ones is indicated. The native may squander his wealth on women of loose morals to gratify his senses. A Rahu influenced by Saturn or Mercury is likely to turn a man impotent. Rahu here associated with the owner of the sixth, eighth or the twelfth house will reduce the longevity and may cause death during its major or sub-periods. The association with or aspect by the owner of the fifth or the ninth house on Rahu here will make the native long lived and prosperous. Rahu associated with or aspected by a powerful owner of the second or seventh house here will destroy. The wealth of the native and may cause his death. Rahu here associated with the powerful owner of an angle and a triangular house, or aspected by that owner will form a rajyoga. Rahu in association or aspect with an owner of a triangle here will become highly beneficial. An adverse Rahu here will make the native poor or may make him earn through immoral means. His brother/ sister will also have a tough time in life. His younger sister/ brother may have trouble from or due to his children and the elder sister/brother may be unfortunate and irreligious. His father will be well off but may suffer from ear or throat trouble. His mother will be disturbed mentally and will remain unhappy during the major or sub-periods of Rahu. It will give results of its placement in the first house to the second child of the native.

Eighth

This is not a good position for a badly placed Rahu. When Rahu is in a favourable sign, it will give good results in its sub-period in the major-period of a favourable planet. Its association with a good planet will also be beneficial. If it is favourable the native would be able to discharge his debts, and will acquire movable property. Such a Rahu will make the native wealthy after the age of 42 years. Rahu in this house with the owner of the eighth house causes fevers like typhoid. If the owner of the eighth house occupies the eighth house with Rahu or aspects it, the native will fall sick during the major or sub-periods of Rahu. Generally Rahu in this house tends to make the native face difficulties from his children, and with regard to his family and health. He may mismanage his finances. He will face humiliation and criticism. He may suffer from small pox, stomach trouble or trouble in the rectum or testicles. He will have a highly developed sex urge and may gratify it by having secret liaisons with women of ill repute. He may thus contract sexually transmitted diseases or such ailment which can neither be diagnosed nor treated. He may not live long. He will suffer from trouble caused by his enemies and there is a chance of his getting incarcerated. An adverse Rahu will bring down the native with serious sickness in his 9th year of life. His younger sister/brother will be happy and prosperous unless exceptions mentioned for the sixth house above exist. It will give results of its placement in the fourth house to the children of the native. His wife will have some speech defect or she will talk rudely or untruthfully. His father will not have a happy married life.

Ninth

A favourable Rahu here makes the native prosperous and religious. If the dispositor of Rahu is powerfully placed in an angle, there shall be sudden gain of wealth for the native. A well placed Rahu here will be good for worldly gains and material prosperity. The native may travel over long distances and may go abroad. Rahu in the ninth house in association or aspect with the owner of the second or the seventh house will cause death of the native in its major or sub-periods if the life span has come to an end. The native will not be happy with his father and may give up his religion. His conduct may not be good. This position is also not good for the welfare of the children. His wife will be efficient, self reliant, difficult and nagging. It will give results of its placement in the third house to the spouse and in the fifth to the children. If the third house has a sign friendly to Rahu, the younger sister/brother of the native will be on good terms with the native and also progress well in life during the major or sub-periods of Rahu. His mother too is likely to have a good time during this major or sub-period. For native's father, the location of Rahu will yield results similar to its location in the first house.

Tenth

The native would have a successful career but his integrity would be doubtful. The second part of life would be happier and more prosperous. He would be ruthless, famous, a leader of men and will have mass recognition. He may also have proficiency in writing, may not have reliable friends and may be close to people of other faiths and regions. The 42nd year of life will be important for the native. He may travel widely. He may have a few children but unless Rahu is free of all blemish, the native is likely to commit irregular and bad deeds. He may hanker for sexual gratification and may have affairs with several women including widows. It will give results of its placement in the second house to his father. His mother may be mentally disturbed due to affairs of his father and the native. His children may have a prosperous and comfortable life. His wife will be dominating, irritable and mentally troubled. Rahu is a major beneficial planet for the native here if it is placed in Aries, Taurus, Gemini, Aquarius or Pisces. Rahu here associated with the powerful owner of an angle and a triangular house, or aspected by the owner will form a rajyoga. Rahu associated with or aspected by a powerful owner of the second or seventh house here will destroy wealth of the native and may cause his death.

Eleventh

It is not good for children but it multiplies the number of friends. The native will be rich, bold and powerful. If the dispositor of Rahu is powerfully placed in an angle or triangle, there shall be sudden gain of wealth for the native. Similarly, Rahu here with the owner of the eleventh house, powerful and well placed, is an indication that the native is likely to gain wealth suddenly. Rahu here associated with the powerful owner of an angle and a triangular house, or aspected by that owner will form a rajyoga. Rahu associated with or aspected by a powerful owner of the second or seventh house here will destroy wealth of the native and may cause his death. Rahu in this house aspected by a beneficial planet removes all other adverse indications in the horoscope and makes the native long lived. The native may develop trouble in his ear or may be hard of hearing, especially if Jupiter is bad in the horoscope. He may travel considerably and live abroad. There may be a number of persons accompanying him on his journeys. The native will gain from persons of a different religion than his own. It will give results of its placement in the first house to elder sister/brother of the native and in the ninth house to younger sister/brother. His father may be an unreliable person with little wealth if Rahu is adverse, or badly placed in a sign here. Rahu placed in the eleventh house is inherently bad in nature and if it is badly placed or is under adverse influence, it can prove to be very troublesome in its sub-period in the major-period of a bad planet. Even when major-period of an excellent planet, that does not have sambandha with such a Rahu, is current, the sub-period of Rahu can be troublesome.

Twelfth

It increases expenditure for good or bad causes depending on the nature of Rahu. If the owner of the twelfth house occupies the house with Rahu or aspects it, the native will fall sick during the major or sub-periods of Rahu. Rahu here in Leo, or in Capricorn or Aquarius, shall impart to the Sun or Saturn respectively a much greater separating power. The native may live abroad but he will be of helpful nature. If the Sun or the Moon is either afflicted or connected with the twelfth house where Rahu is situated adversely, the native will have trouble with his eyesight. He may suffer from nervous breakdown or oedema. The native may be associated with secret societies and may spend on them. His sex life will be unsatisfactory and an adverse Rahu may make the native look for sex outside the socially permissible parameters. The native may have a troubled mind on account of his financial status and liaison with females and may contract debts and sexually transmitted diseases. Such a Rahu will also make the elder sister/brother of the native have defect in his speech, especially if Mercury is also bad in the horoscope, and be financially unsound. His younger sister/brother will be well placed but he will indulge in bad deeds and may have a sudden fall from a position of power. His children may have diseases in genitals or the rectum. His wife will have a quiet and secure life.

KETU

1. It has a serpentine head. Normal human head is cut off. It is tall and dresses in smoke coloured grey clothes and is tamasik. Its vehicle is a snake.

2. It is by nature a malefic planet. If not under the influence of any other planet it acts like Mars.

3. Its RELATIONSHIP with other planets is as follows:

Friendly with	Mars
	Venus

	Saturn
Neutral to	Mercury
	Jupiter
Inimical to	Sun
	Moon

It is exalted in Scorpio, its mooltrikona sign is Sagittarius, and it owns Scorpio, vide Brihat Parasar Hora Sastra, Chapter 47, verses 34 to 36.

4. It is the KARAKA for the following:
Witchcraft, trouble to enemies, moksha.

5. It REPRESENTS the following:
(i)   Wounds, injuries, conflicts, intrigues, back-biting, death, liberation, fire, tuberculosis, cholera, fever, pain, paternal grand mother and maternal grandfather.
(ii) Spiritual initiation and development, seer, enmity, anger, doubt, narrow mindedness, ambition, isolation, lack of self-confidence, occult, charms, and amulets.

6. Ketu has the power to obstruct and darken the SUN which represents the self. When Ketu influences the Sun by association or aspect, the native will face sudden and unexpected difficulties in his endeavours. He may have losses in speculation and heavy expenditure. He may have trouble from his children, who may fall sick from time to time. He may not have confidence in himself. He or his father may meet with accident or suffer from ill health. The native may feel tired and drained of energy. He may be impetuous and rebellious of authority. He will have difficulties from the government, his superiors or from unexpected quarters. If Ketu is good for the horoscope these would be mitigated to a large extent, and if the Sun is also a beneficial planet for the ascendant, the native may actually have excellent results from the areas identified above. For some more guidelines see paragraph 38 above under Rahu.

7. Ketu influencing the Moon, causes depressed emotional state, melancholia, pessimism, anger, violent state of the mind, alcoholism, drug taking, and an attraction for the macabre. The native is likely to have trouble from his mother or she may fall seriously sick or meet with an accident during the major or sub-periods of Ketu. Women may be inimical to the native and he may be morbidly attracted to them as symbols of sex. He may

also face difficulties with regard to his property and home. He may be subjected to popular anger. For some more guidelines see paragraph 38 above under Rahu.

8. Association of Mars with Ketu makes the person angry and violent, and makes him liable to accidents. Mars conjoined with Ketu in the fourth house causes harm to the native through his son, weapon or disease and may lead to death of native's wife and loss of wealth. However the Ketu major or sub-periods would be beneficial towards the end. Such a sambandha in the fifth house may lead to an early love affair, baldness and multiple marriages.

9. Association of Ketu with Mercury gives the same results as recorded for Rahu in paragraph 15 above.

10. The sambandha of Ketu with Jupiter anywhere in the horoscope is bad for the affairs of the house where these two planets are located unless there is a beneficial aspect on them.

11. The sambandha of Ketu with Venus is bad. It makes the native sexually a pervert.

12. The results and achievements of Ketu major or sub-periods are temporary. Towards the end of its major or sub-periods it takes away whatever it has earlier given.

13. A house, owned by a naturally beneficial planet, shall be very strong if its owner is placed in that house with Ketu.

14. Ketu favourably placed in a triangle and associated with the owner of an angle, or placed in an angle and associated with the owner of a triangular house, shall give high status and prosperity during its major or sub-periods.

15. If the owner of an angle and a triangular house has sambandha with or aspects Ketu in a common sign or its dispositor, the native will have a high status and prosperity during the major or sub-periods of Ketu. However if the owner of the sixth, eighth or the twelfth house is also involved, the result will be considerably watered down and the native's mother will face a lot of trouble during this major or sub-period.

16. Reference is invited to relevant paragraphs under RAHU.

17. Effect of Ketu in various HOUSES and SIGNS: The results have to be assessed after the nature of the Node has been determined and the resultant of its placement in the sign and house is quantified on the basis of rules elaborated above. The following is a general indicator for the Node being in a house or sign. When the sign number and house occupied by a Node are different, the results narrated for the two should be read together and reconciled. The results stated below stand to be modified in the light of specific rules given above.

First

The native will keep poor company and may be a person given to talking irresponsibly. He may be greedy and selfish and may be worried on account of his children. His marital life may be disturbed. It bestows wealth and children if located in a Saturnine sign, in its sign of exaltation or friend's sign. It indicates lack of self confidence, poor health, loss of position and a troubled life if badly placed. Ketu associated with a planet here that is the owner of an angle and a triangular house will confer power, high status and prosperity in its major or sub-periods. The native may develop psychic powers. But Ketu associated with or aspected by the maraka owner of the second or the seventh house will destroy wealth and longevity of the native in its major or sub-periods. The native may be short tempered and he may have difficulties in his married life.

Second

Eye troubles or disease in the mouth or face, poor speech, difficulty in learning, dependence on others for food, heavy expenditure, and loss of wealth due to wrath of the government are indicated by the location of a badly placed Ketu in this house. The native may not have good relations with his family members. He may talk in a rough and rude manner. However a well placed Ketu in Scorpio, Sagittarius, Capricorn, Aquarius or Pisces will be financially beneficial to the native. Ketu associated with or aspected by the owner of the fifth or the ninth house here will confer long life and prosperity to the native in its major or subperiods. If Ketu is placed here with the owner of the sixth, eighth or the twelfth house, or placed anywhere in the chart with such association or with the owner of the second or the seventh house, it may kill the native in its major or sub-periods, if the span of life has come to an end.

Third

Loss of brother, humiliation and inimical behaviour of the associates can be the result of a badly placed Ketu. The younger sister/brother may face troubles and may meet their end early. The native may suffer from trouble or pain in the arms and shoulders. He may have to travel suddenly from time to time. A bad Ketu cannot be good for the affairs of the father. Knowledge of financial management, a strong physical constitution and poor relations with younger brother/sister can be the results if Ketu is not badly placed here. When it is favourable it may bring success and happiness to the wife in an unexpected manner. If Ketu is aspected by an adverse Saturn here the native will not have younger sister/brother. When Ketu is well placed the native will be long lived, wealthy and comfortable in life. The native will be courageous. Ketu associated with a planet here that is the owner of an angle and a triangular house will confer power, high status and prosperity in its major or sub-periods. But Ketu associated with , or aspected by the maraka owner of the second or the seventh house will destroy wealth and longevity of the native in its major or sub-periods.

Fourth

Danger from water and to native's property, troubles to and from mother and friends, and journey and life abroad may be the result of Ketu that is not particularly favourable to the native. A very adverse Ketu here aspected by or associated with a powerful malefic, and the owner of the fourth house or the Moon afflicted, are capable of killing the mother early in the life of the native. The native's mind and thinking shall be polluted and bad. His father will meet with adverse financial circumstances. The native may meet his end in an accident or violent incident or due to wounds. He may have a very angry disposition. Ketu associated with a planet here that is the owner of an angle and a triangular house will confer power, high status and prosperity in its major or sub-periods. Such a Ketu will give the native a highly spiritual temperament and he will make efforts to achieve self realisation. But Ketu associated with or aspected by the maraka owner of the second or the seventh house will destroy wealth of the native in its major or sub-periods.

Fifth

Mental derangement, loss of foetus or children, children of angry temperament or susceptible to injuries, fear of the government, diseases in the stomach, injuries and unproductive wanderings can be the result of a badly placed Ketu. The native would be self-centred. The elder sister/brother of the native may get seriously hurt. The native will be unfortunate. A good Ketu will be instrumental in turning the native to devotional approach to religion and he will be well placed in life. Such a Ketu with a beneficial owner of the fifth house, or a benign and powerful Mercury, aspected by the beneficial owner of the fifth house, or associated with a powerful owner of an angle and a triangular house may make the native get a windfall through speculation or a game of chance. The native's father will be effected beneficially or otherwise depending upon the nature of Ketu.

Sixth

When Ketu is favourably placed the native would be generous, healthy and reputed, but he may not be rich. He will succeed in his religious quest. A good Ketu may make the native bold and persuade him to wield weapon for a good cause; an adverse Ketu may give violent criminal tendency. Ketu placed in the sixth house is inherently bad in nature and if it is badly placed or is under adverse influence, it can prove to be very troublesome in its sub-period in the major-period of a bad planet. Even when major-period of an excellent planet, that does not have sambandha with such a Ketu, is current, the sub-period of Ketu can be troublesome. It is not particularly good for elder sister/brother of the native. The native may not be happy in his early years. He will have no trouble from his enemies or he may not have them at all. An adverse Ketu here with the owner of the sixth house or aspected by it may make the native fall sick during its major or sub-periods. The native will be susceptible to diseases in the rectum and teeth. Theft, defeat, disease, and sufferings due to wounds may be the result of a badly placed Ketu here. Such a Ketu may cause problems through the younger sister/brother of native's mother.

Seventh

There may be separation from the wife or she might be irritable. The native will have lot of anger and will not pull along with his family. He may have to face troubles and humiliations caused particularly by the opposite sex. Diseases in the genitals may also be the result of placement of Ketu here. Ketu associated with a planet here that is the owner of an angle and a triangular house will confer power, high status and prosperity in its major or sub-periods. Ketu associated with or aspected by only the owner of the fifth or the ninth house here will also confer long life, and prosperity to the native in its major or sub-periods. If Ketu is placed here with the owner of the sixth, eighth or the twelfth house; or with the owner of the second or the seventh house, it may kill the native in its major or sub-periods, if the span of life has come to an end.

Eighth

Sorrow, separation from wife and family, loss of consciousness, poverty, distress and death are indicated by Ketu placed here. The native will be frequently involved in disputes and he may be dishonoured. Ketu here with the owner of the eighth house or aspected by it may make the native fall sick during its major or sub-periods. The likely diseases are trouble in the rectum or anus, or wounds. He may meet with accidents. He may be a thief or may have constant desire for women. Ketu placed in the eighth house is inherently bad in nature and if it is badly placed or is under adverse influence, it can prove to be very troublesome in its sub-period in the major-period of a bad planet. Even when major-period of an excellent planet, that does not have sambandha with such a Ketu, is current, the sub-period of Ketu can be troublesome. If Ketu is well aspected it may make the native long lived and wealthy. The native is likely to earn wealth abroad. A beneficial Ketu is good for the religious or mystic side of native's life. He will endeavour to unravel the mysteries of the occult and may succeed to some extent. He may have super sensory experiences and may acquire supernatural powers.

Ninth

The native may incur the wrath of his father and deity worshipped earlier. He may be irritable and rash. There may be trouble to wife and children. He may suffer from poverty, and there may be death of family elders or father during the major or sub-periods of Ketu. Ketu associated with or aspected by the maraka owner of the second or the seventh house here may bring death to the native in its major or sub-periods. If a beneficial owner of the ninth house has sambandha with Ketu, the native will be extremely wealthy and fortunate. If Jupiter is so associated, the native will be very learned and famous. If the association is with Mercury, the native will be a prolific writer. His younger sister/brother may be irritable and and may not have a smooth married life; if Ketu is badly placed in a sign here or is badly associated, the younger sister/brother may meet with accidents or get injured. It will give results of its placement in the sixth house to his mother, and in the fifth house to his children. Ketu, unless adverse here, will be good for his wife. It will give results of its placement in the first house to his father. It will be good for his elder sister/brother too here.

Tenth

Failed endeavours, loss of honour, and forced to go abroad may be the results of Ketu here for the native. But if Ketu is a beneficial planet here it makes the career successful. Ketu associated with a planet here that is the owner of an angle and a triangular house will confer power, high status and prosperity in its major or sub-periods. But Ketu associated with, or aspected by the maraka owner of the second or the seventh house will destroy wealth and longevity of the native in its major or sub-periods. He may fall out with his family and may be injured in the face. He may also have trouble in the eye leading to surgical intervention. He will get into debt or may have trouble from enemies, in litigation or from servants. Such a Ketu will also be bad for the prosperity of his father. If other factors also support, his mother may pass away during this period. If Saturn or Mars also influences Ketu, his younger sister/brother may succumb to an accident or operation, or meet a violent death.

Eleventh

When Ketu is good the native will be frugal and successful. He may suffer from ear disease. There may be trouble to his sister/brother or children. Ketu associated with or aspected by the owner of an angle and a triangular house will confer power, high status and prosperity on the native in its major or sub-periods. His children, especially the first born, may have a disturbed or short married life. If Ketu is adverse and Jupiter is afflicted in the chart, the wife of his elder brother or his elder sister may have miscarriages or the eldest child of theirs may be lost; or there may be danger to the second child of the native. It will give results of its placement in the ninth house to his younger sister/brother, in the first house to his elder sister/brother, in the eighth house to his mother, in the seventh house to his children, and in the third house to his father.

Twelfth

The native may have to face poverty, expenditure and disease during the major or sub-periods of Ketu. He will be religious. The placement of Ketu in the twelfth house is indicative of the interest the native will have in spiritual or occult matters, especially if it is with a beneficial owner of the fifth, or the ninth house. If the owner of the ninth house is placed in the twelfth with Ketu, the native may go abroad suddenly. He may succeed in getting moksha (emancipation from the cycle of birth and death). He may be introverted in nature. The native may not have trouble from the enemies and he may lead a healthy life. Ketu here with the owner of an adverse house or aspected by it may make the native fall sick during its major or sub-periods. He may have a disturbed mind owing to ill health of his mother, or troubles that arise out of property matters or vehicles, depending upon the state of the respective karaka. It will give results of its placement in the tenth house to his younger sister/brother, in the ninth house to his mother, in the eighth house to his children particularly to his first child, in the seventh house to his maternal uncle, in the sixth house to his wife and second child, in the fourth house to his father and in the second house to his elder sister/brother.

Chapter Four

HOUSES
(First to Sixth)

Each house represents certain affairs in human life. These have been clarified below. Certain important rules that are applicable to all the houses, have also been stated below. These rules shall apply to the seventh to twelfth house also which have been dealt with in the next chapter. Rules that are applicable to a specific house are given when that house has been discussed.

2. When a house in the nativity is afflicted by a planet that is determined as an adverse planet for the chart according to the rules laid down for the purpose in the Chapter on Planets, unpleasant results pertaining to that house will be felt during the major, sub or inter-period of the planet. Such affliction shall take place when the adverse planet occupies a position in the house within 4 degrees of the cusp of the house, or it aspects the cusp within a range of 4 degrees. Similar results will be felt when the Moon transits an asterism owned by this planet, and on the day of the planet when a sign owned by the planet rises in the ascendant. The same is true, mutatis mutandis, for a planet that is beneficial for the chart. More detailed information on the timing of events is given below. The timing of events is a major and intricate subject, and needs detailed analysis. This has been given in my next book.

3. For judging any aspect of life the following factors must be carefully examined before a finding is reached: .

(a) The concerned house-its strength and the sign in it.

(b) The owner of the house-its strength, location and nature for the ascendant.

(c) The karaka for the house-its location in house and sign, nature and strength.

(d) The planets associated with, aspecting or in sambandha with the owner of the house.

(e) The planets associated with, aspecting or in sambandha with the karaka.

(f) The planets aspecting and/or occupying the house-their nature for the ascendant, their ownership of different houses and their strength.

4. The houses owned by a planet will yield satisfactory results if the planet is associated with a friendly planet in the birth or navansha chart.

5. If a planet that is related to a house:

(a) is located in the second, third, or the eleventh house from that house,

(b) is a friend of the owner of the house under consideration, or

(c) is the owner of the sign in which the owner of the house will be exalted, and,

(d) is neither combust, debilitated, nor in an enemy's sign, it will yield good results with regard to that house.

6. The affairs of the houses owned by a planet will flourish if the dispositors of the planet in the birth and the navansha charts are powerful.

7. The affairs of a house will suffer more and more as the following apply in increasing numbers:

(i)   if the house is weak;

(ii)   if the karaka for that house is weak;

(iii) if the owner of the house is weak;

(iv)   if the house, its karaka and its owner are each hemmed in by malefic planets;

(v)   if the house is occupied or aspected by planets that are malefic for the chart, or there are planets in the house which are in inimical sign there;

(vi) if the owner or the karaka is associated with or aspected by planets that are malefic for the chart, or by planets that are inimical to the concerned planet;

(vii) if the house, karaka and the owner of the house do not have redeeming aspect by or association with beneficial planets for the chart;

(viii) if there are malefic planets for the chart in the fourth sixth, eighth, twelfth or triangular houses from the concerned house, karaka or the owner of the house.

8. If the owner of a house:

(i) is located in an angle or a triangular house in exaltation, own or friend's sign, or is so placed in the navansha chart, or,

(ii) is hemmed in between beneficial planets, and

(iii) its dispositor is well placed and well aspected, or exalted, it will promote the affairs of that house very well.

9. The affairs indicated by a house will manifest themselves completely if the owner of the house, the occupier of the house, the karaka for the house, the beneficial planets aspecting the house and the house itself are all powerful.

10. If there is sambandha between the owner of the house and the karaka for it and both the planets are powerful, matters represented by that house will manifest substantially. If these two planets are inimical to each other, the result indicated will be diluted.

11. If the owner of a house and the karaka for that house are in inimical signs in the birth chart and the navansha, the affairs indicated by the concerned house will not flourish.

12. If malefic planets occupy signs owned by the karaka for a house, that house cannot yield good results.

13. If a house fulfills the following conditions:

(a) It is hemmed in by malefic planets,

(b) there are malefic planets in the fourth, sixth eighth and the twelfth houses from it, or,

(c) there are malefic planets in triangular houses from it, the affairs of the house will suffer severely. If these conditions are true for the karaka for the house as well, the house will not yield much good results. In practice, however, all these conditions are not present in a horoscope. The larger the number of these conditions are fulfilled with regard to a house, the worse will be the results given by that house.

14. The karaka is of utmost importance. If the house is strong but the karaka is weak and in a situation conforming to the ones described in the preceding paragraphs, the house will not show much good results.

15. Whenever Saturn transits a house in which any planet has got zero points in its Ashtakvarga chart, the matters of which that planet is the karaka will suffer. For example, suppose the Sun gets no points in the sixth house in its Ashtakvarga chart. Matters signified by the Sun as karaka will remain in an unsatisfactory state while Saturn transits the sixth house.

16. In an annual horoscope if the first house is taken to represent the first month etc. then those houses in the horoscope which are afflicted will indicate the months in the year which are likely to be adverse. Thus if the fifth house is afflicted, the native will face an adverse time in the fifth month from the beginning of the year for the native.

17. Each aspect of life should be judged from the birth chart as well as the navansha chart. Specific divisional chart should also be referred to. The divisional chart, where available, should be studied for assessing the condition of the specific house and karaka that relate to the event or matter that the chart stands for. To recapitulate, the divisional charts refer to the following matters:

Chart I	1/2 of a sign	Wealth
Chart II	1/3 of a sign	Younger brothers/sisters
Chart III	1/4 of a sign	Property
Chart IV	1/6 of a sign	Health and diseases
Chart V	1/7 of a sign	Children
Chart VI	1/8 of a sign	Longevity
Chart VII	1/9 of a sign	Fortune, marital happiness
Chart VIII	1/10 of a sign	Fame and success in profession
Chart IX	1/12 of a sign	Parents
Chart X	1/16 of a sign	Conveyances, and long journeys

Chart XI   1/20 of a sign   Spiritual progress
Chart XII   1/24 of a sign   Education

If we are considering the event of birth of a child, the fifth house and Jupiter should be considered in the birth and navansha chart. In chart V, the fifth house and the karaka Jupiter should again be considered. When the house and the karaka are powerful and well placed in all these charts, the native can be assured of the birth of children to him. Planets related to the fifth house in these charts are likely to give the result in their periods. This is a subject which needs more detailed analysis. The timing of events is the subject of my next book which deals with this issue in much greater detail.

If the finding is concurrent on the basis of the birth and navansha charts, it should be taken as confirmed. If it differs then the following rules should be applied:

(i)   Result indicated by that owner of the same house in the two charts should be taken which is more powerful of the two. For example if we are judging matters relating to children by the fifth house, and the owner of the fifth house in the navansha chart is more powerful than the owner of this house in the birth chart, then the results indicated by the owner of the fifth house in the navansha chart should be taken..

(ii)   If both are equally strong then the result given by the navansha chart should be taken.

18. A naturally beneficial planet in the sixth, eighth or the twelfth house, in exaltation, own sign or in the sign of its friend and aspected by beneficial planets, does not give unfavourable results in its major or sub-periods.

19. A beneficial planet having a malefic planet in the sixth, eighth or the twelfth house from it will not be able to show satisfactory results.

20. When a karaka is placed in the twelfth house from the house for which it is the karaka, the affairs of the house of which it is the karaka will suffer. For example, Saturn in the seventh house, being in the twelfth house from the eighth, is not good for the longevity of the native.

21.   (i) A planet in the sixth, eighth or the twelfth house

from a house gives adverse results with regard to
that house during its major or sub-periods or transit.
If the planet is a malefic planet the adverse results
will get accentuated. Thus, for example a planet in
the seventh, ninth or the first house will be adverse
for the affairs of the second house.

(ii) Therefore, when a planet is placed in the sixth, eighth
or the twelfth house from one of these adverse
houses, it will reduce the evil effects of the house.
However, when the planet is a natural malefic, and
also a malefic planet for the ascendant, the application of this rule should be done carefully.

22. If the owner of a house is associated with, aspected by, has
sambandha or is in a triangular house from the owner of the
sixth, eighth or the twelfth house, the affairs of the house will
suffer a setback during the major or sub-periods of the owner of
the house.

23.   (i) When a beneficial planet owns two angles and is
situated in the sixth, eighth, or the twelfth house, it
will cause illnesses in its major or sub-periods.

(ii) Disease would occur in the sub-period of a maraka
planet in the major-period of a beneficial planet
which owns two angular houses.

(iii) During the sub-period of the owner of the fourth
house in the major-period of such a beneficial planet
too there would be illnesses though they will not be
serious.

24. A weak planet in the fourth house, in its sub-period during
the major-period of the owner of the second, sixth, seventh,
eighth or the twelfth house will make the health of the native
disturbed. It will not be fatal.

25. No planet damages its own house or its house of exaltation
if it is located there. A malefic planet in its own house or house
of exaltation will promote the affairs of that house.

26. The owner of the sixth, eighth or the twelfth house:

(a)   if weak on account of being combust, debilitated, in
enemy's sign etc., associated with other owners of the
adverse houses or otherwise afflicted by malefic planets,
and,

(b)   not having any beneficial influence, and,

(c)   located in any one of these three adverse houses, will give excellent material results in its major or sub-periods. This is categorised as a VIPAREET RAJAYOGA. This yoga may still prove unfavourable for the health of the native. See paragraph 13 under the SIXTH HOUSE.

27. Beneficial planets in the third, sixth and the twelfth houses make the childhood of the native happy and comfortable. Malefic planets here make the old age so. If all the three houses are not thus occupied, the results will vary proportionately, i.e., the childhood will only be moderately happy if only two out of these three houses are so occupied etc.

28. Malefic planets in the second, fifth and the seventh houses make the childhood of the native happy and comfortable. Beneficial planets in these houses make the old age of the native so.

29. The owners of the second and the twelfth houses are per se neutral. Their nature will be determined by the other house that they own, or by the sambandha that they have with a planet.

30. The owners of the third, sixth, and the eighth houses are adverse. The owner of the eleventh house is adverse for health and longevity but good for worldly affairs.

31. A house will be considered strong if:

(i)   The owner of the house is powerful.

(ii) The house is:

(a)   occupied or aspected by its owner;

(b)   occupied or aspected by planets that are beneficial for the chart. These planets should not be combust or weak; and,

(c)   is hemmed in by planets that are beneficial for the chart, or such planets aspect houses immediately on both sides of the house.

32. The house will be considered weak if:

(i)   The owner of the house is weak.

(ii) The house is:

(a)   occupied or aspected by planets that are malefic for the chart; and,

(b)   is hemmed in by planets that are malefic for the

chart, or such planets aspect houses immediately on both sides of the house.

33. Whenever condition of a part of the body is to be examined, the concerned house and the same number of sign should both be examined. For example if we wish to examine the condition of the native's head the first house and the first sign i.e., Aries should both be examined.

34. The first to sixth houses refer to the right side of the native's body and the seventh to twelfth houses to the left. If conclusions have to be drawn from native's horoscope for his wife then the first six houses will refer to her left side and the last six to her right.

35. Powerful second, fifth, seventh, ninth and eleventh houses in a horoscope ensure that the native will have all the benefits in life.

36. The major or sub-periods of a planet will also give results pertaining to the house where it would be exalted and also of the house where it has its mooltrikona sign. For example, if the major or sub-period of Mars is current then Mars will give results of the house which has Capricorn and also of the house which has Aries.

37. A planet gives results relating to the houses owned, occupied or aspected by its dispositor during its major or sub-periods or transit.

38. If we have to determine when a particular event would occur in the life of the native, we must first ascertain if that event is likely to take place at all. If the chart indicates the possibility of the event happening, then the major or sub-periods of planets during which that event is likely to take place should be determined. To narrow down the time further these rules should then be applied:

(A) The event, if it is desirable and beneficial to the native is likely to happen (the owner of the concerned house should be powerful otherwise despite the favourable transits that are being listed below the desired result will not occur):

(i) When Jupiter transits the sign of exaltation of the major or sub-period planet.

(ii) When Jupiter transits positions triangular (the fifth or ninth sign) to the place where the owner of the concerned house is located. Suppose the owner of the concerned house is Venus which is at 250 degrees 15 minutes in the seventh house. The fifth house from the seventh house where Venus is placed will be the eleventh house from the ascendant having Aries there, and the ninth house from the seventh house will be the third house from the ascendant having Leo there. Therefore this condition will be complete if Jupiter transits through the eleventh or the third house. We can incorporate more precision here. Positions triangular to this position of Venus will be 10 degrees 15 minutes in Aries and Leo respectively. The event is likely to happen when Jupiter in transit is at or near either of these two places.

(iii) When the Sun transits the sign in which the major or sub-period planet is exalted.

(iv) When the Sun transits the sign owned by the major or sub-period planet.

(B) The event, if it is undesirable and bad for the native, is likely to happen:

(i) When Saturn transits the sign of debilitation of the major or sub-period planet.

(ii) Saturn will also give adverse results pertaining to a house when it transits over owner of the sixth, eighth or the twelfth house as counted from the house under consideration. It can also give similar results when it transits through the same navansha sign in triangular positions (fifth and ninth position) from the place where the owner of the sixth, eighth or the twelfth house, as determined above, is located.

To clarify this let us take a horoscope with Sagittarius ascendant. Let us see when Saturn can give adverse results pertaining to the tenth house. The eighth house as counted from the tenth house is the fifth house from the ascendant. We will have Aries in the fifth house. The owner of the fifth house will be Mars. Let Mars be in the second house in the navansha of Pisces. Saturn will give adverse results relating to the tenth house when it transits over Mars in the second house from the ascendant. Triangular positions from the second house will have Taurus and Virgo. Whenever Saturn transits through Taurus or Virgo sign in Pisces navansha the results will be adverse. Similarly for the sixth or twelfth house from Sagittarius.

(iii)   When the Sun transits the sign in which the major or sub-period planet is debilitated.

(iv)   When the Sun transits a sign the owner of which is inimical to the major or sub-period planet.

39. The time span that will be determined by the use of rules (for happening of pleasant events) listed above can be narrowed down further by using the following rules. The event will happen when:

(i)   The owner of the first house, in transit, passes over the owner of the concerned house in the natal chart. Suppose the ascendant is Gemini, the owner of the first house is Mercury and the owner of the concerned house in the natal chart is Venus which is located in the seventh house in Sagittarius. This condition will be fulfilled if Mercury in transit passes over Venus in the seventh house.

(ii)   The owner of the first house transits a house that is the fifth or the ninth from the house where the the owner of the concerned house is situated in the natal chart. If we take the illustration given above, the fifth house from the seventh house (where Venus is placed) will be the eleventh house having Aries there, and the ninth house from the seventh house will be the third house having Leo there. Therefore this condition will be complete if Mercury transits through the eleventh or the third house. We can incorporate more precision here. Suppose Venus is at 250 degrees 15 minutes (or 8 signs 10 degrees 15 minutes). Positions triangular (the fifth or ninth house) to this position of Venus will be 10 degrees 15 minutes (or 0 sign 10 degrees 15 minutes), and 130 degrees 15 minutes (or 4 signs 10 degrees 15 minutes). The event is likely to happen when Mercury in transit is at or near either of these two places.

(iii) The owner of the first house transits the concerned house.

(iv) The owner of the concerned house, in transit, passes over the owner of the first house in the natal chart.

(v) The owner of the concerned house transits a house that is the fifth or the ninth from the house where the the owner of the first house is situated in the natal chart. More precision can be introduced here as in paragraph (ii) above.

(vi) The karaka planet for the event or affair, in transit, passes over the owner of the first house or the dispositor of the Moon.

(vii) We have so far considered situations in which either the owner of the first house is moving in transit and the owner of the concerned house is fixed in the birth chart, or, vice-versa. Now we will take up the condition where both these planets are moving in transit. The event will take place when:

(a) The two owners conjoin each other in transit, or

(b) the two owners aspect each other in transit.

40. The rules contained in the preceding major paragraph can also be applied to the Moon ascendant chart (taking the place of the Moon as the first house and drawing the chart).

41. If the period planet is weak in the birth chart and is debilitated, combust or weak otherwise in transit then it will give adverse results pertaining to the house that it is transiting when related to it. The reverse also holds true. If the major or sub-period planet is powerful in transit due to its getting exalted, being in a friend's sign, or becoming retrograde etc., it will give good results pertaining to the house it is transiting.

42. The transit of the major or sub-period planet will be:

(i) Good, if it is transiting the third, sixth, seventh, tenth or the eleventh house from the ascendant;

(ii) good, if a planet friendly to the major or sub-period planet, or a beneficial planet for the nativity, transits the first house.

43. Having determined the timing of the result from the above upto the month, the good or bad results are determined to the day by the position of the Moon in transit. The Moon shows good results in transit if it is in one of the following positions:

(i) (a) In the sign of exaltation of the major or sub- period planet.
     (b) In a sign friendly to the major or sub-period planet.
     (c) In the same sign as the one occupied by the major or sub-period planet.
     (d) In the third, fifth, sixth, seventh, ninth or eleventh sign from the sign occupied by the major or sub-period planet. Reference is invited to paragraph 3 under ELEVENTH HOUSE in Chapter Five for some more information on the subject.

44. The Sun and Mars make their effects felt in any sign as soon as they enter that sign and are within the first 10 degrees of that sign; Jupiter and Venus in the middle 10 degrees and Saturn and the Moon in the last ten degrees. Mercury and Rahu give their results throughout the sign.

45. Following is another assignment of years to houses. If a house is powerful and under benign influence, the years indicated for it will be good for the native:

Completed years of age	House
Upto 23	IX
25	X
27	XI
29	XII
32	I
35	II
38	III
44	IV
50	V
56	VI
64	VII
From 65 till the end of life	VIII

46. Movable signs in angular houses get very powerful since the nature of the signs and the houses are similar. This is helpful in raising the native to a high position in life. If fixed signs are present in the angular houses the native will succeed after persevering and hard work, and common signs here make the native quick in grasping ideas but he will be indecisive.

47. If we have to decide the direction in which the result of

the house will be experienced, the following should be considered:

(i) The direction indicated by the owner of the house,

(ii) the direction indicated by the planet occupying the house,

(iii) the direction indicated by the planet aspecting the house,

(iv) the direction indicated by the sign in which the karaka of the house is situated in the ascendant or navansha chart, and

(v) the direction indicated by the sign in which the owner of the house is situated in the ascendant or navansha chart.

The directions indicated by the signs are the usual, i.e., Aries, Leo and Sagittarius indicate East etc. (Please refer to Chapter on Signs). The most powerful among the above five will be the direction for the event to take place in or the affair to materialise in.

48. The first, fifth, and ninth houses are fiery. The second, sixth and tenth houses are earthy. The third, seventh and eleventh are airy houses and the fourth, eighth and the twelfth houses are watery.

49. It is a well known rule that, barring an exception, the location of a karaka in the house for which it is a karaka is not good. The exception is Saturn which increases the longevity of the native if it is well placed in the eighth house, of which it is a karaka.

50. A planet that is a maraka planet for the native (or for a particular relative of the native in the native's chart), will destroy the prospects for a matter for the native (or for that relative) if this maraka planet influences the karaka for that matter.

This can be explained by an illustration. Take Gemini as ascendant. Let Venus be in the eleventh house and Jupiter in the fifth. The eleventh house is the house that represents elder brother/sister. We wish to know if the elder brother/sister of the native will have children. The general karaka for children is Jupiter. The second house as counted from the eleventh house is the twelfth house of the chart having Taurus, and the seventh house again from the eleventh house, is the fifth house having Libra in it. Thus the owner of the second and the seventh houses from the eleventh house is Venus. This planet therefore is a maraka for the elder brother/sister. Jupiter is the general karaka for children. Since the maraka for the elder brother/sister is in sambandha with the karaka for the children, this relative of the native will not have children.

But does it mean that the native's chances of having children will also be destroyed by such an aspect of Venus. It must be clarified that the native's prospects of having children will in no way be jeopardised by this aspect of Venus on Jupiter. On the other hand this aspect on Jupiter will be a factor promoting the prospects and welfare of children for the native. The location of Jupiter, the karaka for children, in the fifth house alone would not have been good for the prospects of having children for the native. Venus for Gemini ascendant is a very auspicious planet. The sambandha between Jupiter and Venus therefore will not only improve the possibility of having children for the native but the children will be good and they will do well in life. Venus is a powerful maraka for Aries ascendant which is the sign placed in the eleventh house. We thus see that the same two planets in a chart hold different indications for the native and a relative of his.

51. Each house represents some parts of the body. The degrees upto the cusp of that house from the beginning of the sign in that house will represent the left side of the parts of the body represented by the house, and the degrees from the cusp to the end of the sign will represent the right. For example let the cusp of the ascendant be at 10 degrees in Virgo. The left side of the limbs will be represented by the arc between 0 degrees and 10 degrees in Virgo. The right side will be represented by the arc between 10 degrees and 30 degrees in Virgo.

FIRST HOUSE

1. This house refers to the following:
(i)   Body, constitution, complexion, strength, appearance, and stature.
(ii)   Temperament, character, peace of mind, happiness and sorrow, inclination to work (If Saturn and Rahu are in the first house the native will be lazy. If Mars and Mercury are there the native on the other hand will be of active disposition), tendency to insult others, asceticism, sleep,

        dreams, knowledge, and attitude towards other's money.

(iii)   Success, fame, reputation, and victory over enemies.

(iv)   Infancy of the native.

(v)   Head. If the cusp (see NOTE at the end of Chapter Five) of the ascendant is in the first drekkan then also this house indicates the head, if in the second drekkan, throat, and if in the third drekkan, Basti, i. e. part of the body from genitals upwards half way to the nável.

(vi)   Longevity, health, and freedom from disease. Good aspect (meaning thereby that the aspect will be by a planet that is a beneficial planet for the ascendant) to the cuspal degree of the ascendant indicates good health; adverse aspect to it causes ill health during the major or sub-periods of the aspecting planet.

(vii)   Living in a hostel.

(viii)   Loss of money.

2. This house should generally be examined for all matters connected with the self. The owner of the first house in the sixth, eighth or the twelfth house with a malefic planet will impair health.

3. If this house is under adverse influence it means that the native had a difficult birth. In the alternative, in such a case, it can be the primary cause of ill-health throughout native's life.

4. If the first house, the house in which the Moon is placed and their owners are powerful, there can be no danger to the life of the native in his infancy. A powerful owner of the first house is indicative of long life.

5. If the Moon is in the first, fifth, seventh, eighth, ninth, or twelfth house and is afflicted, the native has short life.

6. The native is long lived and fortunate if the first house and the dispositor for its owner are aspected by beneficial planets. If this is not true even partially in a horoscope the native will not live long and will not prosper in life.

7. The association of the owners of the first and the second houses in the sixth, eighth, or the twelfth house can lead to impaired vision.

8. Good health is assured to the native if the owner of the first house is more powerful than the owner of the sixth.

9. Planet influencing the first and eighth houses and their owners determine the kind of death the native would have.

10. When the Moon in the birth chart is placed in the sign of a planet which is adverse for the ascendant, the native will not be at peace or happy with himself. The mental state will take after the nature of the adverse planet.

11. The native gets a bulky body when watery planets such as Jupiter, Moon, Venus or the owner of fourth, eighth, or the twelfth house influence the first house.

12. The stature of the native will be short, medium or tall according to the influence exerted on the ascendant, its owner and the nature of the sign in which the owner is located. If all the three ascendants (the first house, the house in which the Moon is located and the house occupied by the Sun) give the same finding it can be taken as confirmed.

13. If there is a "long" sign in the first house and the owner of that house is also in a "long" sign, the native will be tall. For finding out as to which signs are "long" or "short", see the Chapter on Signs. The same logic can be applied to find out the sizes of limbs.

14. The constitution is determined by the owner of the first house in the navansha chart or the most powerful planet in the horoscope whereas the complexion is determined by the dispositor of the Moon in the birth chart or the navansha chart. Each planet represents some shade of complexion. The Sun represents red or dark brown, the Moon very fair, Mars ruddy, Mercury light with greenish hue, and Jupiter fair but pale. Venus represents swarthily clear complexion and Saturn dark.

15. The Sun represents bones in the body. If the Sun is the owner of the first house and is afflicted, it will cause trouble in the bones in its major or sub-periods. Similarly the Moon represents blood and can cause problems relating to blood including hypertension if it is the owner of the first house and is afflicted. Mars represents muscles and would cause troubles relating to muscles, Mercury represents skin, Jupiter represents fat in the body, Venus represents reproductive fluids and Saturn represents nerves. If any of these is the owner of the first house and

is afflicted, it would cause disease relating to that component of the body that it represents.

16. If the owner of the first house is weak and afflicted, the part of the body which is represented by the sign in the first house will be afflicted. This will be particularly true if the sign in the first house is the mooltrikona sign of the planet. For example, if Aries is in the first house and Mars is weak and afflicted, then the native will have some trouble in his head.

17. If a planet situated in the first house is afflicted by malefic planets and does not have any redeeming beneficial influence, the body mass represented by the planet suffers. For example if this is so for Mars, muscles in the body would be diseased.

18. If the owner of the first house is debilitated and located in some house, the part of the body represented by the house in which the owner of the first house is located gets diseased. For example if the owner of the first house is Mars which is debilitated and it is located in the fourth house, the native would suffer from disease in the parts of body represented by the fourth house namely, chest, breasts, lungs etc. The nature of disease can be judged from the debilitated planet.

19. The planet that influences (i) the first house, (ii) the houses in which the Sun and Moon are placed and (iii) the owners of these houses, the most, should be determined. The planet that has the maximum influence on this planet should also be determined. These two planets together would decide the vocation that the native would adopt for his livelihood.

20. If the three ascendants(the first house and the houses in which the Sun and the Moon are placed) and the tenth house alongwith their owners and the Sun are powerful and have beneficial influence only, the man becomes famous in the world.

21. The native cannot accumulate wealth if the owner of the first house is weaker than the owner of the twelfth house.

22. When the owner of the first house is in the ninth or the tenth house, and the Moon is in the first house, it is indicative of a rajyoga (a combination which is likely to yield a high position and wealth to the native). The same conclusion can be drawn by taking the karakamsa as the first house.

23. The owner of the first house in an angular house aspected by a friendly planet is indicative of a rajyoga. The same conclusion can be drawn by taking the karakamsa as the first house.

24. If the Moon aspects an exalted owner of the first house it is indicative of a rajyoga. The same conclusion can be drawn by taking the karakamsa as the first house.

25. If the owner of the first house is powerful, not combust and is alone in an angular house it is indicative of a rajyoga. The same conclusion can be drawn by taking the karakamsa as the first house.

26. A sambandha between owners of the three ascendants is a rajyoga. It confers plenty of wealth. The same conclusion can be drawn by taking the karakamsa as the first house.

27. If the three ascendants are aspected by their respective owners it is a rajyoga. The native will wield power. The same conclusion can be drawn by taking the karakamsa as the first house.

28. The native will be popular or shall come in contact with the masses if the owner of the first house is related to the fourth house.

29. If Jupiter and Venus, particularly if they are beneficial planets for the chart, are located in the first house the man would have a pure mind. If Rahu and Moon are so situated the man lacks in brains, or, the mind may be constantly disturbed and apprehensive.

30. The native will be of a balanced nature if the first and the fourth houses and the Moon are influenced by a strong Jupiter.

31. The first house represents the self. If it is weak and is under the influence of planets that represent violence, the person represented by the house where the second sign of the owner of first house falls may be harmed by the native. Let us take Gemini in the first house. If the first house is weak and has Ketu in it aspected by Mars, the native will behave violently with his mother, since the second sign of Mercury will fall in the fourth house that represents mother.

32. The rules for determining the nature of relationship that the native will have with a relative of his are as follows:

(i)   A malefic planet, or owner of the sixth, eighth or the twelfth house, placed in the house representing the relative or aspecting it, or,

(ii)   the owner of the house of the relative placed in the sixth, eighth or the twelfth house from the ascendant, or,

(iii)   the owner of the house of the relative is placed in the sixth, eighth or twelfth house as counted from the owner of the first house, or,

(iv)   the owner of the first house in an inimical sign in the house of the relative, or,

(v)   the owner of the first house being inimical to owner of the house of relative, or,

(vi)   an afflicted or badly placed karaka for the relative, will indicate that the native will NOT HAVE GOOD RELATIONS with the concerned relative of his. The more the number of above conditions are satisfied with regard to a particular relative of the native, the worse and more bitter will the relations be between the native and the relative in question. On the contrary if these conditions do not exist and the two owners are placed in a mutually satisfactory position, the native will have cordial relations with the relative in question. It can easily be judged as to how cordial the relationship would be, depending upon the kind of placement that is present in the chart. The following are two rules of the thumb:

(a)   According to Hindu mythology, Saturn is the son of the Sun. The Sun is representative of father in the horoscope.

    (i)   If these planets are placed in adverse houses from each other (in the sixth, eighth or the twelfth), the native will not have good relations with his father.

    (ii) If Saturn is an adverse planet for an ascendant, and it aspects the Sun or is in sambandha with it in that horoscope, the relationship between the native and his father will not be cordial.

(b)   According to Hindu mythology, Mercury is the son of the Moon. The Moon represents mother in the horoscope.

    (i)   If these planets are placed in adverse houses from each other (in the sixth, eighth or the twelfth), the native will not have good relations with his mother.

    (ii) If Mercury is an adverse planet for an ascendant, and it aspects the Moon or is in sambandha with it in that horoscope, the relationship between the native and his mother will not be cordial.

33. In general a well placed and powerful owner of the first house is an asset to the native. For various good indications in the horoscope to fructify, it is absolutely essential to have a good first house and its owner.

34. The owner of the first house, if powerful and beneficial for the chart, located in any house promotes the affairs of that house.

35. A powerful owner of the first house associated with a strong owner of another house will promote the prospects of the houses, especially of the house having the mooltrikona sign of the planet, owned by the planet joining the owner of the first house.

36. If the owner of a house joins the owner of the first house in its own house, the promotion of that house where this association takes place is assured. Thus if the owner of the first house, for example, joins the owner of the second in the second house, the prospects of the second house will be much improved. Here the two adverse houses, viz., the sixth, and the twelfth have not been taken into consideration. If any of these adverse houses is involved, the affairs of that house will also prosper, which will mean that the evil results to be given by that house will be heightened. When the owner of the first house joins the owner of the eighth house in that house, the native lives long. The same may be said with regard to the third house.

37. If a strong and beneficial owner of the first house aspects or occupies a house or is located in a triangular house from a house, the houses thus occupied, aspected or located from will prosper. If the owner of any house is so influenced by the owner of the first house, i.e., it is joined, aspected, or has sambandha in any manner or is situated in a triangular house from the owner of the first house, the houses owned by the owner will prosper.

38. Effect of various SIGNS in the First House:

NOTE: (i)   The ownership and occupation of houses by a planet, sets up a relationship between these houses. When a sign is placed in a house, a relationship is generated between this house and another house due to ownership of the other house also by the owner of this house. This owner will therefore be inclined to act in a particular manner which is indicated in the descriptions recorded for different signs. This owner will be placed in some house. The inclination recorded will be modified due to the location of the planet and generally a connection will be set up between three houses-two owned by the owner of the sign and the third where it is placed. A sample analysis can be seen under Aries in the second house.

Thus if the Sun is the owner of the third house placed in the tenth house, the native will be a self made man but the Sun will be in eighth house from the house owned by it. It is, if powerful, likely to deny the native younger brother/sister, and his elder brother/sister may not have children. On the other hand let Jupiter be the owner of the third and the twelfth houses in a chart having Capricorn as the ascendant and let it be placed in the tenth house. It will, being the owner of the twelfth in the tenth house, separate the native from power and status that he holds and being also owner of the third house will make him undertake a short journey at the same time. Thus the result will be that the native will go away from his place of posting on a course or leave etc. or may be transferred to some other place bringing about a complete change in work environment during the major or sub-periods of Jupiter. Here Jupiter will not give results similar to the Sun as owner of the third house in the tenth house as it is also the owner of the twelfth house and its mooltrikona sign falls in the twelfth house. So the twelfth house result predominates and the third house becomes secondary to the twelfth house. But if we take Gemini in the twelfth house we will have Virgo in the third and since Virgo is the mooltrikona sign for Mercury, the planet will function more like the Sun own-

ing the third house for which results have been
recorded above, than like Jupiter.

(ii) The description of each sign given in the Chapter
on Signs ought to be referred to for more details
when the effect of each sign in the first house is
to be taken into account. Whenever the effect of
a sign rising in the first house is to be evaluated,
the drekkan rising should also be considered.
The first drekkan gives the pure effect of the sign
that exists in the house, for the owner of the sign
and the owner of the drekkan will be the same,
but the second and the third drekkans give
results somewhat changed from the first as the
second and the third drekkans have different
planets as their rulers and their influence will
also operate along with that of the owner of the
sign, modifying its effects. Whichever of the two
planets-the owner of the sign in the ascendant
and the owner of the drekkan-is more powerful,
that planet will show its influence predominantly. In the following remarks under each sign
the effects of various drekkans have not been
recorded for fear of repetition since these details
have been recorded in the Chapter on Signs in
paragraph (x) under each sign.:

Aries

The native will have ruddy complexion. He will have a quick
temper, will be determined, impulsive, quarrelsome, ungrateful
and will be prone to be deceived by women and servants. He will
be passionate, will be afraid of water, fond of female company
and will not be truthful. The stature will be middle and the
physique will be lean and muscular. The neck will be long and
the face oval. The head will taper to a narrow chin. The native
will enjoy good health. Mars here is the owner of the first as well
as the eighth house. It therefore represents the longevity of the
native and also death. The longevity of the native will be
proportional to the strength of Mars. The cause and the kind of
death the native will have, can also be judged from the influence

that Mars has on it. If Mars is bereft of beneficial influence, the native will lead a life of sin. The influence of Mars if transmitted to the fourth house and its owner will make the conduct of the native all the more suspect. The sign in each house in this case will correspond to the number of that house in the horoscope. For example the fifth house will have the fifth sign. If the fifth house and the Sun are afflicted, it can lead to troubles in the parts of the body signified by Leo, i.e., belly and heart. He will also have diseases indicated by Virgo in the sixth house. Details can be seen in paragraph (vii) under the relevant sign in the Chapter on Signs. The native will love sports and outdoors. He gets bored easily if the atmosphere is not according to his liking. Such a man lives away from water but there are dairies, farms, grain shops, or jewellery shops near his residence.

Taurus

The native can have mental illness. He will keep changing friends. He will be prone to injuries by weapons or fire, spend on account of these injuries and will face losses in life. Venus is the owner of the first and sixth houses. The native will therefore be liable to get involved in accidents. If the owner of the eleventh house-Jupiter, and Mars-the karaka for accidents, also influence Venus the possibility of having a number of accidents involving vehicles in life will considerably be strengthened. He will have relations with foreigners and outsiders to his faith and culture. A weak Venus will cause the native to suffer at the hands of female enemies. If Venus influences the first house and is afflicted, the native will suffer from illnesses during its major or sub-periods. He will also have diseases indicated by Libra in the sixth house. Details can be seen in paragraph (vii) under the relevant sign in the Chapter on Signs. His family will be separated from him often. He will be ill-tempered, angry, conceited, and lover of his own comforts. He will make a bad husband. The native will have a big face and moles there. The forehead and the neck will be thick, the eyes bright, hair dark and sometimes curly, and the complexion will be clear. The female under this sign will be comely. The native will have a well developed muscular system, heavy shoulders and will be stockily built. The stature will be middle. He will be happy in the latter part of his life and earn his livelihood from agriculture. He will have a weakness for women and will be of forgiving nature. The native will indulge in excesses-like overindulgence in eating, drinking and spending- and be the worse off for it. The native will be a plodder. He will be a tenacious and patient worker. He is capable of working very hard. He will talk little but will be a family man. He will be possessive and 'ealous. The temper will be placid till aroused when it will be like that of an angry bull. He will be firm in his views. Such a man also lives away from water but there will be shop of a goldsmith, an aviary or the residence of a widow near his house.

Gemini

The native will be clever, fair in complexion, fond of female company, happy, a pleasant talker, and humble. He will have dark eyes, a long and raised nose, and an active disposition. He will be tall and straight in build. He will have long arms and will walk smartly. He will be scientific, fond of reading, temperate and a good member of the society. Mercury owns the first and fourth houses for this ascendant. If it has separative influence on it of the Sun, Saturn, Rahu, the owner of the twelfth house or their dispositors, or at least of any two of these, the native will live away from his home land and will change his residence and the place of stay several times in life. The karakas for the mind, namely Mercury and the Moon alongwith owners of the first and the fifth houses show the status of mental health of the native. When Mercury is under some adverse influence it goes a long way in disturbing the mental equilibrium of the native since it is not only one of the significators as recorded above but is also the owner of the fourth house. If the Moon also has adverse influence, the fourth house and the karaka for the mother will have adverse influence leading to curtailment of mother's lon- gevity. A well placed Moon in the fourth house with Mercury there having no adverse influence will ensure success for the native in public life. Mars for this ascendant is an extremely violent planet as it is the owner of the sixth house and also of the eleventh. Located in the first house in association with or in aspect to Mercury, it makes the native prone to head injuries and influencing the Moon, it makes the mind of the native full of violence and anger. A connection is also established here between the sixth and the eleventh houses. The sixth house represents competition and the eleventh house indicates fulfilment of wish. If Mars is in good vargas or is under beneficial influence or if its malefic nature is subdued due to some reason, it will make the native succeed at competitions. He will be able to guess others' unspoken thoughts and make out implied meanings. He will be of a worrying nature which will effect his health. He may also worry over his children. He will have to ensure that he is relaxed and gets adequate rest to maintain good health. He will also have diseases indicated by Scorpio in the sixth house. Details can be seen in paragraph (vii) under the relevant sign in the Chapter on Signs. The native will live near a grove, garden or a well or other source of drinking water.

Cancer

The native will be of fair complexion, generous, fond of water sports, of sharp intellect, religious, loved by his subordinates and forgiving. He will be of a hasty, truthful, changeable, mild and gentle temperament. He may be troubled due to his wife. He will have a large circle of friends, property, and wealth. The number of children will be restricted. He will be of short stature, and slender in appearance. He may develop a large abdomen in later years. He must keep his weight under check by careful eating habits and regular exercises. He will also have diseases indicated by Sagittarius in the sixth house. Details can be seen in paragraph (vii) under the relevant sign in the Chapter on Signs. He will be moody, sensitive, timid and introverted. He will be moved to help others and like to keep his innermost thoughts to himself. He will express himself through creativity. The native will have a garden in his house or will stay near one. There will be a well or a source of drinking water near his house.

Leo

The native will be firm, arrogant, bold, fond of outdoors, magnanimous, clever, loyal and powerful. He will have a very short temper and cherish his independence. He likes flattery. He will be close to his mother. He will be majestic in appearance and dignified in demeanour. When the Sun is placed in the tenth house in Taurus, and Venus is unafflicted and powerful, the native will be famous and highly placed. He will be tall, large and muscularly built. He prefers non-vegetarian food and travelling. He will be handsome, broad shouldered and will have a well made bone structure. The constitution will be strong. He will also have diseases indicated by Capricorn in the sixth house. Details can be seen in paragraph (vii) under the relevant sign in the Chapter on Signs. The diseases are usually not long lasting and the recovery is quick. The native will live near a dairy, or a jewellery shop.

Virgo

The native will be truthful, rich, fond of learning, eloquent, easily influenced by women, sensual, kind and will look less than his age. He will be clever, will go into the details of the matter, analytical, self conscious and frank. He will be tall, slim, active and with a flat abdomen. He will have beautiful eyes. The native will practise moderation in all walks of life and therefore due to his careful and regulated life style he will maintain good health. He will also have diseases indicated by Aquarius in the sixth house. Details can be seen in paragraph (vii) under the relevant sign in the Chapter on Signs. Mercury is the owner of the first and tenth houses and shows a close linkage with the government and people in high places. If Mercury is weak and the tenth house, its owner and the Sun are also badly afflicted, the native will suffer at the hands of the government and he will be opposed to the ruler. The native will have a dairy, shop, well or a source of drinking water near the place he lives.

Libra

The native will be truthful, religious, and fond of female company. He will be attractive, loquacious, graceful and social. He will like to overeat and drink without moderation in company. His acceptance in society will be a matter of great concern to him. The social obligations will hardly leave any time for himself. He will be very well dressed. Females having this ascendant like to use good perfumes, jewellery, and beautiful clothes. Appearance is of importance to them. He sometimes does not have his own independent view on matters and prefers to echo those of the others to please them. Decision making is not an easy exercise for him. He can be a good teacher and also good at such jobs where he has to have contact on almost individual basis such as teachers, psychiatrists etc. He likes to please people. He will have good relations with the government. By habit he is easy going and does not like to exert himself. He will be tall and proportionately built. He suffers due to his excesses. He will also have diseases indicated by Pisces in the sixth house. Details can be seen in paragraph (vii) under the relevant sign in the Chapter on Signs. Venus is the owner of the first and also the eighth house. It therefore represents longevity and death. The analysis for Venus can be done in the same way as for Mars under Aries to determine the longevity and nature of death. There will be a grain shop or the establishment of a potter near his house.

Scorpio

The native will be violent, reserved, dauntless, brutish, ruthless, deceitful, irritable, inflexible, and heartless. Saturn for this horoscope is the owner of the third and fourth houses. Since its mooltrikona sign falls in the fourth house, Saturn will predominantly govern the mind. Being the owner of the third house, it will also indicate the self. If Saturn and Mars-the planet for cruelty-influence a house in the horoscope, the relative of the native represented by that house will suffer from cruelty and heartlessness of the native. As an illustration, if the fifth house is so effected, the native will be cruel to his children. If Jupiter is also influenced like wise the indication will be further confirmed. Here Mars is the owner of the first and the sixth houses. Therefore it will act in a manner similar to Venus for Taurus ascendant. The analysis given there may be seen. He may be in service. He will have more than usual determination, maturity and ambition. The native will have his friends among the personnel of armed and police forces. He is able to achieve his goal by sheer effort. As a result he will be highly strung. He will easily take to artificial stimulants like drugs and intoxicants. He will also have diseases indicated by Aries in the sixth house. Details can be seen in paragraph (vii) under the relevant sign in the Chapter on Signs. He will be of middle stature with a robust body. He will have plenty of curly hair. He will live near the house of a scholar or a famous man.

Sagittarius

The native will be liked by people in government, he will be good and clever at work and will be religious. He will be good at archery and can be a marksman. He will have vehicles and keep milch cattle. He will be eloquent, fair complexioned and graceful. He is fun loving and social. He is honest, and fair in his dealings. He keeps his worries to himself and in no circumstance would he like to put his true face to public gaze. He, in his fun sprees, commits indiscretion in eating and drinking and not only overloads his system but also puts on weight as a result. He lacks in self-disciple. He will also have diseases indicated by Taurus in the sixth house. Details can be seen in paragraph (vii) under the relevant sign in the Chapter on Signs. Here Jupiter is the owner of the first and fourth houses. He will be tall, well formed, handsome, and good hearted. The native will have a waterbody near his house or an advocate, or government servant will live near him.

Capricorn

The native will like to be near water. He will be cunning, clever, unscrupulous, ruthless, diffident, a backbiter and given to defrauding others. He will be lazy, and religious. The native will keep the company of people of the lower strata of society. He generally does not talk unless he has something important to say. He is ambitious, and sober, and hankers after success. He will be tall and slim and will be weak in the lower parts of his body. He will have deep set eyes and a pointed nose. He will also have diseases indicated by Gemini in the sixth house. Details can be seen in paragraph (vii) under the relevant sign in the Chapter on Signs. He will be long lived if Saturn is powerful and will not have bad qualities if the first house is aspected by at least a beneficial planet. Such a situation of planets will also make the native very wealthy with age. The native will have a garden, well or the house of a scribe or land surveyor near his house.

Aquarius

The native will be of stable temperament, fond of water sports and female company and liked by them, well behaved and popular. He will be secretive, greedy and fond of flowers and fragrances. He will be highly strung, irritable, stubborn, generous and active. He will be so involved in his work that he would not like to take up any other diversionary pursuit. A powerful Saturn improves the qualities of the personality and makes the native long lived. Saturn, being the owner of the first house and Mars the owner of the third house, are both indicative of the "self". If these two planets afflict factors representing a relative of the native, he will be treated very cruelly by the native. If these planets influence the eighth house, the native will commit suicide. He will love humanity but will tend to neglect his immediate family. His behaviour will appear eccentric and people will not understand him easily. He will be tall, oval faced and fair in complexion. He will be handsome and proportionately built. He will suffer from high blood pressure and diseases arising out of stress due to his constant preoccupation with his work and lack of relaxation. He will also have diseases indicated by Cancer in the sixth house. Details can be seen in paragraph (vii) under the relevant sign in the Chapter on Signs. The native will live near a house in ruins, pond, flower beds, or a temple. The owner of the first house here is also the owner of the twelfth house. The native will be fond of visiting unknown places and will spend well. He may be connected with hospitals, monasteries or asylums. He may live at a place distant from his place of birth.

Pisces

The native will be fond of living near water. He will be gentle, learned, talkative, anxious, impressive, reputed and will remember a good turn done to him. He will be fond of his wife. He will be romantic, spiritual, open, ingenuous, and imaginative. He can work well with children or in the field of dramatic or stage arts. He will have trouble with his weight which will have a tendency to increase with age. He will also have diseases indicated by Leo in the sixth house. Details can be seen in paragraph (vii) under the relevant sign in the Chapter on Signs. Here Jupiter is the owner of the first and the tenth houses. The native will live near a school, conference hall, or a dispensary.

39. Effect of the owner of the First House being in various houses has been given below. It is however dependent on certain

factors that have been recorded below. These factors have to be
studied very carefully. These are capable of altering the nature
of the effects to a very large extent. A weak planet may be
powerless to give results. The time when these results will
fructify has been dealt with in detail at the beginning of this
Chapter. It should be seen:

A.   (i) Whether the owner of any house, the effect of whose
placement in a house is being ascertained, is a malefic
planet for the ascendant.

      (ii) Whether the owner of the house is exalted, in
mooltrikona sign, in own or friend's sign, is well
aspected, well associated or generally well placed in
a house.

    (iii) Whether that planet is in a situation reverse to the
one above like debilitation etc. in a house.

B.   (i) The gender, element, quality and characteristic of the
sign in which the owner of the house is placed
should be taken into account.

     (ii) The location of the owner of the house in navansha
will also be relevant. If it is placed in the eighth
navansha in the sign, it will not give good results. For
example the Sun in Aries at 25 degrees will be in the
eighth navansha and will therefore not be well placed
to give good results.

    (iii) The owner of a house will not be able to yield good
results if it is placed in the sixth, eighth or the twelfth
house in the navansha chart from its dispositor. For
example, let the owner of the third house be the Sun.
Let it be in the tenth house, the owner of which is
Jupiter. Thus the dispositor of the Sun is Jupiter. If
the Sun is in the sixth, eighth or the twelfth house
from Jupiter in the navansha chart, it will not give
good results.

    (iv) When more than one result is given, we look for the
state of relevant karakas, to select the one that will
be the most appropriate. If the result of a placement
is recorded as loss of wealth or early death of the
mother, and if we find that the karaka for wealth is
in a good state but the karaka for the mother is
afflicted, the second alternative should be picked up.

C. A planet when placed in a house will aspect other houses from there. It should be checked whether the houses aspected are places of enemy's sign, place of mooltrikona, own, or friend's sign. The strength of the aspecting planet is of primary importance but even a debilitated planet will mildly tend to improve the affairs of a house that it aspects provided the aspected house contains a sign owned by the planet or a sign that is friendly, or a mooltrikona sign of the aspecting planet. If the planet aspects a sign owned by an enemy of the planet, it will tend to deteriorate the affairs of that particular house by aspect.

D. The karaka properties of the owner of a house have also to be taken into account when evaluating the effects of that planet in different houses.

E. Whenever the owner of a house by placement in a house indicates some result that is likely to happen in the life of the native, it must be corroborated by the karaka for that aspect. If the karaka is weak and incapable of giving good results, the indication will not materialise fully. For example if the owner of the second house placed in the ninth indicates that the native will be wealthy, but the karaka for wealth, Jupiter, is weak and badly placed, the indication for wealth will not fully materialise.

F. (i) If the owner of a house is well placed in any house, it will yield good results otherwise not.

(ii) Attention is specifically invited to paragraph 21 in the opening remarks above. Further, the owner of a house located in the eighth house from the house it owns will tend to deny matters covered by that house.

G. The owner of a house by being placed in a house, as seen above, will by occupation or aspect influence several houses. The result of such a placement for each house will be according to analysis carried out on the broad guidelines contained in paragraphs A, B, C, D, E and F above.

H. The effects that are indicated below for placement of the owner of any house in different houses from the first to the twelfth, are broadly on the basis of occupation of and

seventh house aspect by the planet on various houses.
The results recorded below are generally for the owner
of the house well placed in a sign. Modifications will
have to be considered in the light of what has been stated
above:

First

The native will be long lived, have good health, be physically
strong and successful in his efforts. He will be self made, will
occupy a high position and hold property. He will be popular
and wealthy. The younger brothers/sisters, neighbours and colleagues of the native will gain. The mother of the native will
command respect. The children of the native will travel abroad,
if the fourth house is connected with the first, for higher studies
and will make long journeys. They will be of good conduct. The
native may marry more than once, or have liaison with more than
one woman. If the owner of the first house is an enemy of the
owner of the seventh house, the native will not have a satisfactory
married life and will find difficulties in the way of partnerships.
The spouse or partner will face danger to his life or adversity.
The results will be satisfactory if the sign in the seventh house
is that of exaltation, mooltrikona or friend's sign for the owner
of the first. He may not get along well with his maternal uncle,
and his wife's family. He may not be very close to his own
relatives.

Second

The native will serve somebody but will have wealth with little
effort. He will be stoutly built and will be of good conduct. He
will be eminent in his clan and will be attached to his family in
case the owner of the first house is a friend of the owner of the
second, is exalted there or is in its mooltrikona sign. The owner
of the first, if well placed in the second house (due to reasons
recorded in the previous sentence), it will improve the longevity
of the native. The native will also earn in the name of his wife.
The native will beget children with difficulty. A powerful owner
of the first house well placed in the second house is an excellent
indication for very high status and wealth for the children of the
native especially the first child. This is also a sign that the native's

mother will gain due to her high position or eminence, or she may be a working lady earning independently. The native's maternal uncle will fare poorly in life. The native may not have good relations with his father and his wife. He may have relationship with more than one woman. He will do well in school and later will be well read. He may have a religious bent of mind. He will find it difficult to pull along in a partnership. He will be wealthy.

Third

He has good relatives and friends. He will marry more than once. He will be courageous and a self made man. He will be efficient in work. He will earn wealth through his own efforts but if there are indications in the horoscope for poverty, the native will have to work very hard to overcome these indications for even a reasonable modicum of wealth. His wife will prosper after her marriage. The native will be religious. He may be in service of somebody. He will be good at conveying his ideas and may travel frequently. He may do well as a mathematician or musician. He will be a skilled writer. He will earn through writing if the first and third houses which are related to each other here are also connected to the second, tenth or the eleventh house. The native's children will be prosperous and their ambitions will be fulfilled without much effort on their part. If the two planets-owners of the first and the third houses-are friendly, the native will be attached to his younger brothers/sisters, neighbours or the children of his elder brother/sister. He will be aloof from his kith and kin and his wife's family.

Fourth

He will be on cordial terms with his parents, and will receive patrimony, have support of the government, will be wealthy, and live in comfort. He will have property, learning, conveyances and will be mentally at peace. He will have better than average appetite. He will be of studious nature and may be interested in the occult. He may be popular with the masses and may do well in inter-personal relationships. The native's mother will have an independent profession at which she will excel herself. The elder brother or sister of the native may do well at speculation or in the field of fine arts. The native's first child will go abroad and the second will attain a high position in life after his marriage. The native will not be on close terms with his younger brothers/sisters and neighbours and may not like his father and elder brother/sister. He will have few friends.

Fifth

He will be highly intelligent, well placed and will keep good health. His mother will be rich from the earnings of her business. He will have good, well behaved children but there is danger to the life of his first child. The first child shall be fortunate if he survives and religious. The native will be attached to his children if the owners of the first and the fifth houses are friendly. He will be clever and will have interest in music, fine arts, speculation and sports. He will have good income and his ambitions will be fulfilled. He will be initiated in spiritual practice and will take to japa (repetition of spiritually energised words called mantras). If the owner of the first house is debilitated or otherwise badly placed without any beneficial influence on it in the fifth house, the native's maternal uncle will have a powerful station in life. The uncle may be short lived. This will be so since the owner of the first house, which will be the eighth house as counted from the sixth house, will be in the twelfth house from the sixth, and will thus form a Vipareet Rajayoga. The native will not be able to pull along with his mother-in-law.

Sixth

A powerful owner of the first house here makes the native have more than one wife. He will be healthy, rich, fond of his maternal uncle, successful at elections, competitions and litigation, fond of pets, prone to act against his own people, property owner, miserly, comfortable and reputed. If the owner of the first house is a beneficial planet, the native may face problems from his enemies. The native will spend much and will get fame and wealth from abroad. He may be in service but he may be doing a job that is not to his liking and the native may take it as drudgery. A weak and afflicted owner here makes the native sickly, indebted, dirty, and low in body vitality. The native takes to arms. He may become a robber, soldier, policeman or a surgeon, provided the second, tenth or the eleventh house is also connected here. The reason is simple. The first, third and the eleventh houses are indicative of acts done by the self. The sixth house is representative of weapons or sharp edged instruments. The second is the house of money, the tenth represents profession and the eleventh, gain and income. There is a danger that the native may be a complicated personality.

Seventh

The native's wife will be beautiful and well behaved. The native is likely to be attached to his spouse unless there are indications to the contrary. The married life will be to the fore. He will be handsome and sensual, and will like female company. He will travel extensively. The native prospers in partnerships or by the efforts of his wife. His wife may not live long and he may marry again after the death of his first wife. He will turn reclusive later in life. If the owner of the first house is a male planet and is located in the seventh house it indicates that the native will get married with difficulty and he will have extra marital relations. The affairs of the first house will prosper. He will not like his relatives. The native's mother may get comforts, house and conveyances from the government. His children may travel extensively and may author books or reportage on international affairs. His father will earn well from speculation, entertainment or through his children. The children will be fortunate.

Eighth

The native will be ailing, thievish, given to gambling, sensual, and have a peaceful death if the owner of the first house is a beneficial planet for the chart. Also the native may be a scholar, get legacies and recover long overdue money which can be in the form of arrears of pay, gratuity, long term deposits etc. If the owner of the first house is a malefic planet for the chart, the native will not live long and is likely to lose an eye. He may also get hooked on drugs. The native will not be good looking. He will be miserly, preoccupied with the thought of his wealth and may have to work hard to earn it. He may be learned and have an interest in the mystical side of life. The native will not have a happy married life. He may face dangers, see his family members pass away, will be involved in accidents or may get injured. He may not like his father and his younger brothers and sisters. He may not have neighbours or he may keep himself aloof from them. He may always be under a notion that he has certain imperfections in him and may therefore suffer from a complex. The native's mother will benefit through speculation or fine arts. His children will have property and conveyances. If the owner of the first house also owns the eighth house, this placement of the owner of the first house shall make it a highly beneficial planet.

Ninth

The native will like travelling over long distances and overseas. He will have a large clan. He will be learned, happy, and respected. He will be fortunate. He may study matters in detail and engage himself in research projects. He will gain through the younger brother/sister of his wife. He will be happy with his father, younger brothers/sisters, neighbours and colleagues. If the owner of the first house is a beneficial planet which is powerfully placed in the ninth house and is a beneficial planet for the chart, the native's father will be highly religious and rich. The native will enjoy good reputation and will be highly religious. He will inherit property and wealth. His mother may be in service that brings her in contact with foreigners and at which she may do well, but the native will not have good relations with her. The native's first child will make his fortune abroad. His elder brother or sister will be a self made person and may earn through his pen.

Tenth

The native will be highly placed. He will gain through the government and will be respected. The native will earn by the dint of his own efforts. If the owner of the first house is a naturally beneficial planet which is beneficial for the chart, the native will be known for his good conduct. The native's mother will enjoy pomp and high status which she will get after her marriage. He will be well behaved, a scholar, and will respect his parents and the preceptor. He will have the goodwill of the government and reach a high position in life. The native will have comforts and vehicles. He will be fortunate. This placement is not conducive to good relations with children, brothers and sisters. The affairs of the fourth house will prosper. The children will be in service abroad.

Eleventh

He will be reputed, will have good children, will be long lived, have good conveyances, be rich and happy. He may marry more than once. The native will gain and earn much during the major or sub-periods of the owner of the first house. The native will have highly placed benefactors and friends. He will always be successful and will have good health. His ambitions will be fulfilled. He will recover quickly from illnesses. The first child will be lucky after his marriage. The elder brothers/sisters will be well placed in life, and in case the owners of the first and eleventh houses are friendly to each other, the native will be very close to them and his friends. If the owner of the first house is debilitated or otherwise badly placed without any beneficial influence on it in this house, the native's maternal uncle or his enemies will be very highly placed.

Twelfth

He will commit bad deeds, be cruel-hearted, petty minded, may live abroad, be arrogant and a spendthrift. He will have a good number of enemies. He will face hindrances and will find it difficult to succeed in his endeavours. He will be slim in build. The native will prefer his own company, will be isolated, will visit lonely and deserted places, may be connected with jails, asylums and hospitals and he may have to live in them. He will be the cause of his failures. His bank balance will be poor. He may find interest in the occult and may work for his spiritual emancipation. He can be learned. This placement is good for the wealth of younger brothers/sisters. It also indicates that the mother will be fond of visiting religious places, going on pilgrimages and attending to religious duties sincerely. She can be wealthy and well placed in life. However, the native's children will have to work hard for success and face disappointments in life.

SECOND HOUSE

1. This house refers to the following:
(i)   Wealth, acquisition, purchase and sale of goods, jewels, clothes, perfumes, efforts for acquisition of wealth, miserliness, financial status, gains and losses from dependents, earning from right or wrong sources, and financial success in career.
(ii)   Law suits. Administration and governing. Status in life.
(iii)   Family, and relations with family members, persons close to the native and all those who are to be fed and maintained by the native.
(iv)   Death. This is a more powerful maraka house than the seventh.
(v)   Childhood, schooling and early educational matters.
(vi)   Face, cheek, chin, nose, tongue, nails, teeth, and lips. If the first drekkan is rising, this house indicates the right eye. If second drekkan is rising on the cusp of this house, it refers to the right shoulder. If the drekkan rising is the third, it refers to right side of genitals and anus.
(vii)   Oral knowledge and speech. Truthfulness.
(viii) Nature of education. Early or school education.
(ix)   Food and drink. Appetite. Taste both with respect to food and art.
(x)   Cheerfulness, and fixity of the mind. Imagination. Generosity.
(xi)   Second marriage. The time of marriage, description of second partner, and the state of such married life.
(xii)   Mother's elder brother/sister.
(xiii) Wife's longevity.

2. This house indicates accumulated wealth. Ketu represents a flag and therefore height. If a beneficial planet for the chart together with Ketu is located in its own sign in this house it shows that the native will have immense wealth. On the other hand owner of the sixth, eighth or the twelfth house in the second house can lead to dissipation of accumulated wealth.

3. Powerful owners of the second and the fifth houses connected with a powerful Venus indicate musical ability.

4. The owner of this house invests any matter that it influences

with worth. If such an owner happens to be Jupiter which is a karaka for worth, then it becomes doubly effective to do so.

5. The native is a drunkard if this house and the Moon are connected with Saturn and Rahu which are adverse for the chart.

6. The native becomes wealthy if this house or its owner is connected with owner of the eleventh house or Jupiter.

7. The native suffers from dogbite if:
(i)   an afflicted Saturn is in the second house, or,
(ii) the owner of the second house is associated with or aspected by an adverse Saturn for the chart, or,
(iii) a malefic planet is located at or near 80 degrees 13 minutes 6 seconds (this is not related to the second house. It can be anywhere in the chart.).

8. Affliction of this house by separative planets (The Sun, Rahu Saturn, owner of the twelfth house, and the dispositors of these planets) leads to separation of the native from his parents in childhood.

9. As recorded earlier, this house refers to the nature of education a native will receive. Saturn and Rahu are significators of disease. The Sun is the karaka for health and represents doctors and physicians. Therefore if at least two of these three planets influence this house, the native is likely to study the subject of disease and health. Also see paragraph 7 under SIXTH HOUSE below and paragraph 5 under TENTH HOUSE in Chapter Five.

10. When the owner of the second house is placed in a good house or the second house has relationship with a good house, and the significators of education namely Jupiter and Mercury have at least average strength, the native will do well at school and will excel himself at all examinations and tests in his early classes.

11. Effect of various SIGNS in the Second House (A careful study of NOTE in paragraph 38 under FIRST HOUSE will be of use.):

Aries

Mars, the owner of the second house will also be the owner

of the ninth house. It will be a very good planet for the native having Pisces ascendant. It will be the owner (counted from the seventh house) of the third and eighth houses for the wife of the native, and will by nature be adverse for her. It will be indicative of her·longevity, and if well placed will confer long life on her. It will be the owner of the first and sixth houses (counted from the ninth house) for the native's father and cannot be called wholly favourable for him. It will have its mooltrikona in the second house from the ascendant, which would be the sixth house from the ninth, and the malefic nature of Mars due to its ownership of the sixth house will be pronounced. It will own the fifth and tenth houses (counted from the fifth house), and will be an excellent planet for the native's children. It will be the owner of the sixth and eleventh houses (counted from the fourth house) and will be highly adverse for the native's mother, etc. The results for the relatives of the native (father, mother, wife, children etc.) should be counter checked with the use of the karakas in the manner given for the karakas in the Chapter on Planets before the results are taken as final. The native and his sons will earn their livelihood through fair means. If the owner is powerful he will be wealthy, truthful, learned and will possess vehicles. A powerful Mars will make the native gain without effort and the father to maintain good health. A weak Mars or afflicted by Ketu will not only cause problems in this direction but will also make the mother of the native very prone to serious accidents or operations. The younger brother of the wife may help the native earn money. The native will take starting new ventures as a challenge and in the event of failure of the first business will, without demur, move to the next. He will be impulsive in his investments. Mars placed in the first house will make the native religious, wealthy and fortunate. Mars in the second house is excellent for wealth. Mars in the third house may restrict the number of younger brothers/sisters, but they will prosper in life. The native will be good at his work and a successful person in life. Mars in the fourth house gives lot of wealth to the native in the form of immovable property, and higher studies in logic, or engineering. It does not appear to be adverse for married life of the native. Mars in the fifth house makes the native's father and children have uncertain fortune, since it will be debilitated here. If the Moon is waxing, well placed and powerful, or if the debilitation is cancelled, the native's children will have all the benefits in life. The native will have a sharp intellect. It will be adverse for the health of the mother. If Mars is powerful, his wife will be long lived. Mars in the sixth house will not be good for the native. If under adverse influence, it may indicate that the native may have some trouble in his mouth for which surgery may have to be done. He may have a defect in his speech. He may be put to loss by his enemies or maternal uncles. His mother may meet with an accident on a short journey. Mars placed in the seventh house makes the person happily married. It does not appear to be adverse for married life of the native. Mars in the eighth house will give results similar to its placement in the sixth house. It may not be good for the longevity of the native's wife. Mars in the ninth house is not good. It makes the native's father have bad temper and disputes with members of the longer family. The father will be unfortunate. The native may still be very wealthy. Mars in the tenth house will be excellent. The native will attain a high position in life. He will be of good conduct, wealthy and powerful. Mars when placed in the eleventh house is the surest indicator that the native will have great wealth. It will be exalted here, and being the owner of the second and ninth houses, it will be occupying the eleventh house and aspecting the fifth. Mars in the twelfth house is an indication that the native will spend on a journey abroad during the period of this planet. This is also not good for the welfare and comforts of the native's father. He may be ailing at the time of the close of his life. This location also takes away from the capability of the planet to do good to the children of the native.

Taurus

The native will earn his living from agriculture. He will acquire milch cattle, and precious metals. He will be constantly preoccupied with devising ways to conserve his wealth. He will be well off and will be fond of collecting works of art. His investments will be wise. Here the owner of the second house is Venus which is also the owner of the seventh house. Venus will be a powerful maraka for the native. If afflicted, it will cause severe trouble in its major-period and sub-period of an adverse planet or vice-versa. In such a case it may also be responsible for death of the native and will considerably reduce the longevity of the wife. When Venus is afflicted and influences a weak planet in the horoscope, it will annihilate the matters indicated by that planet as a karaka. Thus if Venus influences Jupiter, the native may not have children or may lose them. But if Jupiter is powerful and favourable, the native will earn from business or in partnership with the family of his wife. He may gain wealth after his marriage, may be as dowry or gifts from his wife's family. His mother will have property and conveyances and will be learned. His daughter will have her independent source of income if Venus is in the third or sixth house. In case the ninth house is also involved, she may earn by writing romantic novels. Venus badly placed especially in the fourth house and having connection with an adverse Mars or Ketu may involve the father of the native in a major accident.

Gemini

The native will gain wealth through females and his wealth will remain in the hands of women. The owner of the second house here is also the owner of the fifth house. The planet involved is Mercury. Both these houses are connected with eloquence and the karaka for eloquence, Mercury, is their owner. Thus Mercury fully represents eloquence. If Mercury is strong, the native will be a wonderful singer or speaker. He will gain financially by his speech and from his children. Mercury also represents money. If this planet is powerful, the native will earn well from speculation, clubs and games of chance. He will successfully complete his education. The children of the native will be attached to the family but the affection will not be steady as Mercury is not a steady planet. If Mercury and Venus are weak and afflicted by a planet having his mooltrikona sign in the sixth, eighth or twelfth house, or a Node, the wife of the native will not live long as the owner of eighth house counted from the seventh and the karaka for wife will be under adverse influence. The native will have wealth and cattle. He will have the opportunity to have the company of saints. The financial status will be changeable. The native is liable to make faulty investments or he may change jobs from time to time. If Mercury is placed in the eleventh house from the ascendant, the native will be wealthy, very intelligent but shall only have daughters.

Cancer

The native will face danger from water. He will earn well from timber, liquid related businesses, catering or hotel business. His finances may wax and wane. He may not show promise in his early years at school. He may be miserly and his wealth will be enjoyed by his children who may join professions related to hygiene, nursing or medicine. He will be fond of sweets. The wealth will be self earned. He will love his daughters. A powerful Moon will make the native like his family. This will also ensure a long lived wife. He will be good looking. His father may suffer from oedema, tuberculosis or lung troubles. His mother will be of friendly disposition and will have a large circle of female friends. When the Moon is placed in the first house with a natural malefic planet or one that is adverse for the chart, the native may experience shortage of funds during the periods of the planet.

Leo

The native will earn money through trade in forest produce and put his earnings to the good of all. He will strive to earn as much as possible through fair means which gives him a feeling of security. The speech of the native will be impressive. His family will be dignified. He will like to have non-vegetarian food. He will be forthright. If the Sun is powerful, the native will earn from the government or through highly placed persons. His mother's elder brother can be of high status or connected with the government. His children also will prefer government jobs. The Sun in the second house is indicative of the fact that the native's eldest child will be very highly placed. If the Sun is favourable and well placed in the house close to its cusp, the native will have high status.

Virgo

He will have good business acumen and will earn through it. The owner of the second house is Mercury which is also the owner of the eleventh house. It therefore is representative of wealth and value. A powerful Mercury will make the native earn well from an early age, as Mercury tends to give its results early in life. Which ever house is influenced by it will prosper as Mercury represents value here. To illustrate the point: if Mercury occupies or influences the fourth house, the native will be highly and well educated; if it influences the fifth house, he will be very intelligent, and will have very good, well behaved and highly qualified children who will do well in life, etc. However the status of finances will not be stable. When Mercury is powerful, his elder brother/sister will be learned and wealthy. If Mercury is placed in the twelfth house, his younger brother/sister will earn his livelihood by writing and will be self made. Such disposition of the planet is however likely to make the native suffer from slight speech defect. His mother may gain a legacy or recover money that had long been locked up. This can be further analysed in the manner similar to Gemini in the eleventh house in Chapter Five.

Libra

The native trades in clay, earth, stone or their products and grain. His partnership will be successful. Even his wife can be a successful business partner. The owner of the second is also the owner of the ninth house. Venus therefore is a powerful representative of wealth which will come to the native much beyond the effort that he will put in for it. The wealth will be earned with the help of or through wife or women. If Venus is weak it indicates loss of wealth in the same reverse manner both for the native and his father. The native's children can do well at speculation and also earn through professions connected with entertainment. A powerful and well placed Venus can be good for the status of the children especially the first born. The native will be generous and charitable. He will also be very learned. This can be further analysed in the manner similar to Scorpio in the ninth house described in Chapter Five.

Scorpio

He will be religious, humourous, fond of female company, and friendly. He will play truant from school in his early years since he could not feel interested in school work. He will be a good physical education teacher or an expert in callisthenics. He will not desist from making money through foul or unscrupulous means. The owner of the second is also the owner of the seventh house here. See observations that have been recorded for Venus as a maraka under Taurus above. His son will be a self made man who may join the military or a uniformed service and, if the planet is strong, he will rise high in his profession. Such a Mars will make the native's maternal uncle (his mother's younger brother) wealthy with substantial property. A weak and afflicted Mars will be very dangerous for the father of the native. He may face accidents or undergo major operations. This can be further analysed in the manner similar to Taurus above.

Sagittarius

The native earns through his ability, four legged animals, milk and juices. The earnings and expenses will keep pace. The owner of the second is also the owner of the fifth house. The analysis done for Mercury when Gemini is placed in the second house, may be seen above. His investments will be successful if Jupiter is in good state, other wise the native is likely to suffer losses from speculation. He will be well known. His father may serve a foreign law or educational concern or he may be associated with an international religious movement which will not be the one in which he is born. A strong and well placed Jupiter will make the native's mother very wealthy. His elder brother/sister will come by property and vehicles and will lead a comfortable life after marriage. His younger brother may go away and live at a short distance from his native place. His mother's younger brother will go abroad. A weak and badly placed Jupiter may cause the elder brother of his wife to have serious setback in his profession or face dishonour in its major or sub-periods.

Capricorn

The native will earn his bread abroad, through the government or agriculture. He will have to work hard for making his livelihood. He will take recourse to unfair means to earn his wealth. He will be a poor pupil in his early years. He will be thrifty and will have the ability to make sound investments. The owner of the second is also the owner of the third house. When Saturn is placed in the third house, the native will travel abroad during the periods of Saturn. The native will gain from his younger brothers/sisters, neighbours and colleagues if the owner is powerful. His elder sister/brother may be wealthy. His mother may not be able to save. His children will have very good income from their professions. Saturn in the eighth house is bad for the wealth of the native. Saturn in the ninth house indicates an irritable and sickly father.

Aquarius

The native will trade in flowers, fruits and produce of water. He will collect contributions for religious and charitable purposes. He will have to work hard for his wealth. He will be miserly. The owner of the first house is Saturn which is also the owner of the second house. If Saturn is placed in the second house, or is strong and well placed anywhere else in the horoscope, it will give the native wealth but after much effort and late in life. A powerful Saturn will indicate that the eldest child of the native would be a prosperous and well placed person in life. Such a Saturn will also be good for the mother. If Saturn is in the second house, the elder brother/sister may continue higher education through correspondence.

Pisces

Jupiter is the karaka for wealth and owns the second and eleventh houses. It will therefore indicate wealth and worth fully here. Its influence on any other house will imbue the matters represented by that house with worth and make them prosper. This can be analysed in the manner similar to Virgo above and Sagittarius in the eleventh house in Chapter Five. The native will have steady income and steady expenditure. He will earn through education, and by locating treasure troves. He will have wealth.

12. Effect of the owner of the Second House in various houses (A careful study of the opening notes from A to H in paragraph 39 under FIRST HOUSE will be of utmost use.):

First

The native will be selfish, miserly, attached to his wealth, engaged in service, known in the family for his wealth and sensual. He will be able to earn by his own efforts. He will live in comfort and will have good family life. He will not be fond of his relatives. His married life will be happy and he will have successful partnerships. His wife may not be long-lived and may predecease him. The native's children may be wealthy and may reach a high position in life. His elder brother/sister may gradually lose his property and may live away from his place of birth. His mother will have comforts and status in life and she will be a person who would be willing to help those in need. His father will not gain from speculation.

Second

The indications of this house will prosper. The native will earn well through his profession and live comfortably but his acts will be unpopular. He will be worried over earning money. He may marry more than once. The wives will be long lived. His children will be eminent in life. His mother will have very good income and useful friends. Depending upon the nature of the planet, his father may not have enemies or he may vanquish them completely. A naturally beneficial planet that is also a good planet for the chart here will make the native handsome and soft spoken. Reverse will be the result in case it is a malefic planet. In case the owner of the second house is Saturn, the native may suddenly gain property as a part of patrimony.

Third

The native will get along well with his younger brothers/sisters if the owner of the second house is a beneficial planet for the chart or a friend of the owner of the third; if it is not, it will not be so and he will also get into the bad books of the government. The native will be a religious speaker and will find that luck is favouring him. He will earn his wealth through his own efforts. He will gain through short tours, younger brother or sister, journalism, writing, publication and publicity. If there is malefic influence on the owner of the second house, the native is likely to earn his livelihood through prostitutes. The younger brothers/sisters, neighbours and colleagues of the native will be wealthy. His children will be well off in life. His mother will be extravagant and may not keep good health.

Fourth

The native will be a long lived person, truthful and likely to get patrimony if the owner of the second house is a beneficial planet for the chart. If otherwise, the owner of the second house in the fourth will hasten the death of the mother. The mother will be wealthy with a fat bank balance and the father will have lot of property. All the ambitions of the mother will be fulfilled. She will be attached to her elder brother/sister. The father of the native will prosper during the major or sub-periods of the owner of the second placed here, provided the planet is weak and afflicted and does not receive any beneficial influence here. The native will gain from father and government. He may be an agriculturist, a dealer in property or automobiles or an educationist. He will die abroad. The native will gain through property, estates and mines. There will be no change of residence.

Fifth

The native will gain through his children, entertainment, cinema, theatre, speculation or earn by dint of his learning. He will be wealthy. He will be miserly, and unhappy. A powerful owner of the second house in the fifth will make the mother wealthy. He will be reputed for his ability to handle difficult assignments well. He will show exceptional intelligence and ability in his early years of schooling. A powerful and beneficial owner of the second house placed here may make the native a good singer. The first born child will be wealthy. His maternal uncle will go abroad. His father may serve a foreigner. However, since the owner of the second is also a maraka, if there is malefic influence on the owner of the second house or if it is weak and afflicted, there is a possibility that the native may lose a child.

Sixth

The native will be able to suppress his enemies. He may accumulate wealth and own land but he will have to work hard for it and face obstacles. He will acquire plenty of property. He will never find it difficult to raise loans. The native will always gain in transactions. He will gain through competitions. The maternal uncle of the native will prosper. The native may get estranged from his family. The native may earn his wealth through black-marketing or other dubious means. He may create dissensions among his friends and relatives for his gain. He may get in serious legal trouble due to his activities. His father may be in government service. If the owner of the second house is weak and afflicted in the sixth house without any beneficial influence, the native's wife or his partner may be very wealthy and highly placed in life, but the native may suffer losses through thefts or servants.

Seventh

The wife of the native will be wise, rich, thrifty, and fond of comforts if the owner of the second house is a beneficial planet. She will be childless and ailing if the owner of the second house is a malefic planet and weak. He will get wealth, comforts and pleasures by and after his marriage, but there is a possibility that the native and his wife both may not be morally upright. He will get money through his partner or wife. He will be successful in litigation. He may earn well from abroad if the seventh house and its owner have strength. He may become a doctor. He will gain through women. His children will come up in life on their own. A strong owner of the second house will make his second child live long. His younger brother will be sensual and may lose heavily in speculation. The owner of the second house will be a powerful maraka for the native.

Eighth

The native will be inclined to commit suicide, be wasteful of his wealth, poor, given to bad deeds and a fatalist. Life will not be smooth. He will not be rich. The native will gain legacies, and recover seemingly irrecoverable money provided the eighth house and its owner are powerful. The native will be learned in spiritual and mystical matters. A weak and afflicted owner of the second in the eighth house with no beneficial influence will be conducive to much wealth and power for the father and younger sister/brother. The native's children will get conveyance, house and comforts through the government. The native may lose his wife or she may become part of a scandal. The native may face trouble from his elder brother/sister.

Ninth

A beneficial owner of the second house will make the native generous, wealthy and true to his word. A malefic planet on the other hand makes him poor and a hypocrite. The malefic owner will also reduce the brother of the native to penury. The wealth of the native will accrue through rightful means. He may earn through international trade or by dealing with foreigners. He will have good relations with his younger brothers/sisters. His children will attain high positions due to their intelligence and ability to give sound advice. They may be secretaries in government or even ministers. This house being the eighth from the second house signifies loss from and demise of the native's bank. Therefore a connection between the second and the ninth house, when adverse planets are involved, signifies loss due to the failure of bank. However this will not be so if the owner of the second house is also connected with the eleventh house. The connection of the second house with the ninth also means that the native will earn through research, international trade, religion or long journeys. The native will keep poor health in his early years which will improve with years.

Tenth

The native will get a high position, gain from and be respected by the government. An owner of the second house in its own or good vargas in this situation also makes the native look after his parents in their old age. A strong owner of the second house in this position makes the native earn a lot of money but if the owner of the second house is a malefic planet the means of earning can be questionable and the native may take bribes. This location of the owner of the second house means that the owner of the tenth house counted from the fifth will be connected with the sixth house similarly counted. This is a clear indication that the children of the native and especially the first child will be successful at competitive examinations, join service, or succeed at election or in litigation. The native's family will be a highly placed one. A weak and afflicted owner of the second house in the tenth house will make the father of the native indebted and suffer losses due to enemies, but make the younger sister/brother rise high in life. The native will come out at the top of successful examinees at examinations or tests in school.

Eleventh

The native will be sickly during his early years, will earn well and easily. He will spend well on the maintenance of a large number of dependents. He will be well known if the owner is a beneficial planet. A malefic and weak owner will make the native poor. The native will be a money lender and earn money from money. He could also earn by doing business in foodstuffs, running a boarding school or by giving lectures. He will have children in the major or sub-periods of the owner of the second house. His children will be intelligent and may join him in these ventures. His mother will be long lived if the owner of the second is powerful. His elder brother/sister will be popular and have comforts and conveyances.

Twelfth

Poor and miserly, the native will spend heavily and earn from abroad. School education of his children and family affairs will also be sources of expenditure. If the owner is a beneficial planet the native will have sufficient wealth to make the two ends meet. He may have to pay moneys to the government by way of penalties or fines. He will earn money by employing labour. His deals will be unscrupulous and he may take bribes. If the owner of the second house is weak and afflicted in this house without any beneficial influence, the native's wife or his partner may be very wealthy and highly placed in life. He may spend a good sum of money on food and his family. The native's eldest child may be a source of trouble to him through out his life. The native will suffer loss due to indiscreet or incautious speech. If there is malefic influence also on the Sun, Moon or Venus, the native may have trouble with his eyesight.

THIRD HOUSE

1. This house refers to the following:
(i) Self.
(ii) Physical and moral courage. Fights and causing distress to

others. Valour, courage, risk-taking, recognition for efforts, perseverance and patience.

(iii) Mental ability and inclination, intellectual hobbies, literary efforts and studiousness. Mental confusion and waking from sleep.

(iv) Meals.

(v) Hands, arms, ears, collar bone, neck, shoulder blade, upper chest, throat and the nervous system. Part of the hand between the root of the thumb and the root of the index finger. If the first drekkan is rising, this house indicates the right ear; if the cusp is in the second drekkan, the right arm; and if it is in the third, the right testicle.

(vi) Cousins, kindred, acquaintance, neighbours, younger brother or sister, female servants, colleagues, mediators, brokers, representatives and friends.

(vii) Longevity of the native as it is the eighth house from the eighth. Death of parents.

(viii) Adventurous or short journeys, walking, and sports.

(ix) Division of property, dire poverty (being the eighth house from the eighth), and removal from and change of residence.

(x) Religion (being seventh from the ninth house).

(xi) Correspondence, writing, accounting, mathematics, books, publication, news, information, library, bookstore, rumours, carrying tales, signing contracts, conveying messages, and public instructions.

(xii) Children of elder brother or sister.

(xiii) See paragraphs 5 under Chapter on Planets and 1(x)(a) under NINTH HOUSE in Chapter Five.

2. Well placed planets here or powerful owner of this house gives a capacity for profound interest and deep research.

3. Rahu or Ketu with Mars or with the owner of the sixth in the third can cause disease in the parts of the body signified by this house.

4. Rahu located here can cause death of father during its major or sub-period.

5. Powerful connection between the third and the fourth

houses means that the native would take part in politics, as the fourth house is a house indicating masses.

6. Similarly if the third and the eighth houses are so related with the second or seventh house, it shows that the native would commit suicide since the third house represents the self.

7. If the sixth or the tenth house has connection with the third house it may lead to a military career or the native may join a uniformed service. The job that the native takes up may involve regulatory functions.

8. The following combinations are for troubles in parts of the body indicated by this house:

(i)   Throat trouble is indicated if the owner of the third house is associated with Mercury and has malefic influence on it.

(ii) Throat trouble or loss of wealth is indicated if there is a planet in the third house where it is either debilitated, combust or is in an enemy sign and is aspected by a malefic planet for the chart.

(iii) A malefic planet for the chart located in the third house aspected by or in sambandha with another such planet can lead to throat or ear trouble.

9. A movable sign in the third house indicates that the native will love travelling and change, unlike a fixed sign here. It will also make the mind sharp and ambitious. The native will have close ties with his younger brothers/sisters, neighbours and colleagues. A common sign here makes the mind more receptive.

10. We have explained methods to determine the number of children and their gender in paragraph 11 under FIFTH HOUSE below. By applying these methods to the owner of the third house and its bhavamadhya (cusp) we can determine the NUMBER and GENDER of native's younger siblings.

11. The rules for determining relationship between the native and a relative of his are recorded in paragraph 32 under FIRST HOUSE in this Chapter. If we wish to determine the relations that are likely to exist between the native and his younger brother/ sister, we should apply these rules, mutatis mutandis, to the third house.

12. The following conditions incline the native to join service:
(i)   If the first and the third or the sixth house are connected, the native is likely to be in service.
(ii)   Planets placed in the third house make the native inclined to service.
(iii) If the third or the sixth house is connected with the tenth or the eleventh house, the native is likely to be in service.

13. Paragraph 7 under the Sixth House could also be usefully studied for determining the career the native is likely to take up if the third, or the eleventh house is connected with the sixth.

14. Effect of various SIGNS in the third house (A careful study of NOTE in paragraph 38 under FIRST HOUSE will be of use.):

Aries

The native will have knowledge of several branches of learning. He will be honoured by the government. He will have the ability to invent things but will be argumentative. He will have the ability to convey his ideas effectively through written or electronic media. He talks well but is not a good listener. He may not get along well with his younger brothers/sisters. The owner of the third is also the owner of the tenth house here. Mars is an adverse planet for the native. Since the third house represents the self and the tenth represents the State, if Mars is placed in the first, second, tenth or eleventh house, the native will be associated with the affairs of the State and earn from it. The native is likely to take up service in the military or a uniformed force. A weak and badly placed Mars will be the cause of death of younger brother/sister and the father. It can also cause severe accident to his first child. The native's younger brother/sister will be short lived. This can be further analysed in the manner similar to Taurus in the tenth house in Chapter Five. The third house is the house representing the younger brother/sister. If for these relatives of the native we take this house as the ascendant, the trouble in their limbs can be analysed in the manner similar to Aries in the first house above. If Mars is located in the third house there is a possibility that the native may suffer loss of younger brothers.

Taurus

The native will have very good relations with his colleagues and younger brothers/sisters. He can convince others of his point of view by talking to them. He cannot use his memory effectively and takes a lot of time learning things. The native will be on good terms with the government. A powerful Venus in the horoscope will make the native have a good number of younger sisters, or female neighbours and colleagues. The owner of the third house is Venus which is also the owner of the eighth house. It will be the significator of longevity of the native. If strong and well placed in the horoscope, it indicates that the native will live long. It also indicates that the native's children will have good vehicles and they will have a comfortable life. A weak Venus will make the native liable to face dishonour through younger brothers/sisters, neighbours and colleagues. The younger brother/sister may suffer from the machinations of female enemies or suffer from diseases of reproductive or urinary tract. A weak Venus will cause loss to the mother through speculation or investments. She may also have a strong libido. She may have secret affairs. The native's father may not be any better in morals. One of the children of the elder brother/sister of the native will rise high in life and will occupy an important position. The elder brother/sister will gain from speculation or entertainment.

Gemini

There will be frequent change of residence and also work environment. The native will have good vehicles, be respected by all especially by women and will be generous. He will always tell the truth. The owner of the third house is Mercury which is also the owner of the sixth house. A weak and badly placed Mercury will give diseases according to its karaka quality and if the third house is also badly afflicted the diseases so caused will be fatal to the native. The mother of the native will suffer losses through her younger brothers/sisters, neighbours and colleagues. A powerful Mercury will make the first born child of the native earn wealth by trade. Such a Mercury will also make the father of the native rise high in society. His wife will go abroad. His younger brother/sister will possess property and will be learned. Such a Mercury will make the native a successful author or publisher.

Cancer

The native will be popular, religious, and a musician or a painter. He will be a quiet person. Third is a house indicating the interests of the native. Since the Moon indicates the mind, its ownership of this house makes it a very powerful representative of the interests of the native. The influence of such a Moon on a house can let us decipher as to the field in which the native is interested. For example, when such a Moon influences the fourth house by aspect or location, the native will be interested in the common man and people at large. The native will keep changing his place of residence and also the people with whom he works. The income of his children will fluctuate. They will have good friends but the friends will not be long lasting. His father will have smooth relations with his partners. The native's elder brother/sister will have more female children than male. The Moon placed in the tenth house will not be good for the longevity of native's younger sister.

Leo

The native will be valorous but will keep bad company. He will be coveteous, violent, arrogant and will talk rudely. He will be intelligent. The younger brother/sister of the native will talk rudely but, if the Sun is strong and well placed, will have the goodwill of the government and people in high places. If the Sun in this case has connection with the first, second, fourth or tenth house, the native will be closely associated with the government and persons in power. The Sun placed in the tenth house will deny the native younger brother/sister. His father will associate with highly placed persons or persons in government. His children will be ambitious, have friends in high places and their earnings will be from lawful sources. The younger brother/sister of the native will be dignified in appearance. The children of elder brother/sister will join the government, and depending upon the strength and location of the Sun, are likely to have a high position in life.

Virgo

The native will excel himself in analysis, computation, in mathematics, computer science, and engineering. He will also be interested in writing and languages. He may even write books in a foreign language. He will be well behaved and will earn through the goodwill of friends. He will be critical of not only those who come in contact with him but of himself also and will be given to bouts of depression. The younger brother/sister of the native will be well behaved. Mercury, the owner of the third is also the owner of the twelfth house. The native will travel from time to time and live away from his home. He will be in a profession where he may have to communicate with persons abroad or those living in jails, hospitals or asylums. Mercury will not be a good planet for the native, or his children. It will be neutral for his father. It will be good for his mother and for his elder brother/sister. It will be excellent for his younger brother/sister. On this basis, when it is placed in a good house from the ascendant for any of these relatives or the native, the prospects will be damaged for the affairs of that house if it is adverse for that ascendant, and enhanced if it is good. For clarifications see Aries under the second house. This can be further analysed in the manner similar to Gemini in the twelfth house in Chapter Five.

Libra

The native will have good relations with his younger brothers/sisters. He will be interested in, and do well, in the field of fine arts, dramatics and poetry. Here Venus, the owner of the third is also the owner of the tenth house. However, since the mooltrikona sign is placed in the third house, the third house results will predominate. Therefore the native will excel in his profession. His younger brother/sister and the children of his elder brother/sister will be good looking and polished. The native can be a radio or television artist. His father may have close contact with females in his profession. His mother may be sensual. This can further be analysed in the manner similar to Aries above. He will be a good public speaker. He will be fickle minded. He will keep bad company and spend heavily on his comforts.

Scorpio

The native will be greedy, friendly with the poor, unreliable and will cause hurt to others. He will come in conflict with his brothers/sisters. He will be logical, intelligent and analytical. The owner of the third is Mars which is also the owner of the eighth house. Mars therefore becomes a significator for the longevity of the native. A powerful and well placed Mars will make the native live long but he will not have wealth since the houses for poverty, i.e., the third and eighth houses, will get strengthened. The kind of influence Mars and the eighth house will have will decide the nature of native's death. The native will be dependent on his wife who may have a golden touch, since her ninth and the second houses will be strong. If Mars is located in the third house there is a possibility that the native may suffer loss of younger brothers.

Sagittarius

The native will be popular among friends and neighbours and will be liked by his brothers/sisters. He will like travelling and will have interest in religion and philosophy. He may also work in association with his maternal uncle or may even be in his service. The owner of the third is Jupiter which is also the owner of the sixth house. The younger brothers/sisters will be learned and wealthy but may suffer from ill health in the major or sub-periods of Jupiter if it is weak and badly placed; the native may have to incur debts during this time. The wife of the native may travel abroad during the major or sub-periods of such a Jupiter. A strong Jupiter will be inclined to confer wealth on the children of the native during its major or sub-periods. He may talk in hyperbole or be very forthright. He will have good relations with the government.

Capricorn

The native will be happy, at peace and live in comforts, but these benefits will come to him later in life. A well placed and powerful Saturn will make the close of life comfortable for the native. He will be religious, learned and rich. He will have deep interest in geology, agriculture or birds. He will be aloof from his neighbours, brothers/sisters and colleagues as he will find it difficult to communicate with them. Saturn, the owner of the third is also the owner of the fourth house. He will like to work in a group. If Saturn has separative influence of at least two out of the owner of the twelfth house, Rahu, the Sun and their dispositors, the native will change his residence. The partner of the native will prosper in life if Saturn is powerful and located in the third or the fourth house. The native will live long. The native will have his friends from among the common people and will work in a profession which will involve his coming in contact with the masses. If Saturn is located in the third house there is a possibility that the native will suffer loss of younger brothers.

Aquarius

The native will have interest in music and dance, will be forgiving and truthful. He will have talent for writing. He cannot get along well with his brothers/sisters, neighbours or colleagues as he will consider himself superior to them. The owner of the second is also the owner of the third house. His younger brother will leave his native place and settle away from home where he will do well in life. The native will gain from younger brothers/sisters and neighbours and will be long lived in case Saturn is strong and well placed. Such a Saturn will also be conducive to wealthy children who will earn well from their profession. If Saturn is located in the third house there is a possibility that the native may suffer loss of younger brothers.

Pisces

The native will be born with a silver spoon in his mouth. His wife will love him. She will be well behaved. He will have children and friends. The owner of the third is Jupiter which is also the owner of the twelfth house. If Jupiter is powerful and placed in the third, or the ninth house the native will not only live long and have good younger brothers/sisters, neighbours and colleagues but will travel abroad during the major/sub-period of Jupiter. He will be interested in philosophy and religion and will have good relations with his brothers/sisters, neighbours and colleagues. An afflicted Jupiter will give losses to the native caused to him by his younger brother/sister. This can be further analysed in the manner similar to Virgo above.

15. Effect of the owner of the Third House in various houses (A careful study of the opening notes from A to H in paragraph 39 under FIRST HOUSE will be of utmost use.):

First

The native will be argumentative, will not have good relations with his relatives, keep bad company and serve others. He will defraud others and will be selfish. He will be hard working and his achievements will be of his own making. He will be courageous. His married life will be according to the nature of the aspect that the owner of the third will be throwing on the seventh house. The owner of the third house is not a good planet. If the other house that it owns is also adverse, it will be very bad for the chart and its influence on the seventh house will be disastrous. Such will be the case when the owner is Jupiter or Mercury, and the sign in the third house is Gemini or Sagittarius respectively. Such a Jupiter or Mercury casting its influence on the seventh house will cause major problems for the native. If it is associated with or in sambandha with Venus simultaneously, the native can expect no reprieve from a marriage that will be like a mill stone round his neck. If the other house that it owns is the second or twelfth, or an angle, the nature of the planet will be adverse but not very bad. It will still cause problems for the native in his married life. He may distinguish himself as a musician or artist. An owner of the third house that is friendly with the owner of the ascendant in the first house will make the younger brother/sister of the native like him; and the native may have good relations with his neighbours and colleagues. His mother, if she has an independent profession, will suffer losses at it. She may be involved with a hospital or asylum. A powerfully placed owner of the third house in the first house will make the children of the native rise high in life and be wealthy. His father will be sensual.

Second

A malefic owner of the third house here reduces the longevity of the native. He may be stout in built. He will be poor, unscrupulous and not cordial to his relatives. He will hanker for women and other's wealth. He may lose his younger brother/sister during the major or sub-periods of the owner of the third house. However, a beneficial owner of the third house here will make the native wealthy and powerful by his own efforts. His younger brother/sister will live away from his native place and will be wealthy there. His children are likely to be wealthy and well placed in life. His mother may be extravagant, or may not be of friendly nature and may like to be alone. His father will keep good health and may not suffer from enemies or thieves. The father will be happy with his servants.

Third

He will have good relatives, be religious and respected by the government. He will gain through the government. He will be bold and prepared to take risks. He will be a writer of big works on law, philosophy or religion. The native's younger brother/ sister will be inimical to his father if the owner of the third house is an enemy of the owner of the ninth house but they will be friendly with the native and he will gain from them. The wife of the native will be fortunate, well behaved and religious. This is a good position with regard to the fortune and wealth of his children. His elder brother/sister will be happy with his children, and he will have a good position in the society.

Fourth

The native will be happy with his father and family members but will not have good relations with his mother. She may be extravagant and introverted. She may join a secret society. He will squander away his family wealth. He will earn property and acquire vehicles by his own efforts and enterprise. He will have several hobbies and he may be a public figure. He will continue higher education by taking correspondence lessons. His younger sister/brother will be wealthy who will acquire wealth by his own efforts. His wife may be troublesome, but if the owner of the third house is powerfully and well placed in the fourth house, she will have wealth and status in life.

Fifth

The children of the native, his brothers and nephews will be looked after by him. His children will have their ambitions fulfilled and they will be wealthy in due course. He will be long lived and charitable. He will endeavour to gain knowledge all the time. His younger brother may attain the post of a secretary or minister. The native may act as a host or compere at functions or soirees. If a malefic planet influences the owner of the third house, his wife will be problematic and may make his life difficult.

Sixth

The native will have some ailment in the ear or a chronic disease. He will acquire property and be antagonistic to his younger brother/sister and maternal uncle. He will be dear to his maternal aunt during the major or sub-periods of the owner of the third house. Death of a younger brother/sister of the native can be predicted during the major/sub-period of the owner of the third house. He will face trouble from his enemies. This is an indication that the younger brother/sister of the native will join the army or become a doctor. Paragraph 7 under the Sixth House should also be usefully studied for determining the career the native is likely to take up if the third, or the eleventh house is connected with the sixth. A powerful owner of the third well placed in the sixth house will give wealth, property and learning to the younger brother/sister. The native's wife or his partner will visit abroad. An adverse but weak and afflicted owner of the third house here is likely to give favourable results to the native with respect to worldly affairs.

Seventh

The native will serve the government. He will keep indifferent health during his childhood. His wife will be beautiful. The wife may be a foreigner or the native may have foreign partners in business. A malefic owner of the third house here inclines the wife of the native to have illicit relations with the native's younger brother. The younger brother/sister will keep the welfare of the native in mind if the owners of the third house and the ascendant are friendly with each other. His mother will be from a distant place. His brother will go abroad. The well being of the brother abroad and the success of the visit will depend upon the navansha position of the owner of the third house (kindly refer to paragraph 39 B (ii), (iii) under FIRST HOUSE above).

Eighth

The native may not have brothers and sisters. If the owner of the third house is a weak and afflicted malefic planet for the chart, he will lose his arms or he will die in his childhood. A powerful owner of the third house in a favourable sign will enhance longevity. Such an owner will also be highly beneficial for the wife and children of the native. Death of a younger brother/sister of the native or serious illness to them can be predicted during the major or sub-periods of the owner of the third house. The mother will lose in the game of chance or speculation. If the owner is well placed the native will be in good health. The owner of the third house placed in the eighth house and having contact with the owner of the sixth house will give good financial returns in its major or sub-periods. The native may get involved in a criminal case or may face scandalous allegations against him. Troubles for him can also arise out of a legacy.

Ninth

The relations of the native with his younger brothers/sisters will depend upon the nature of the owner of the third house. If the owner is very malefic for the chart, the relations will be bad. Otherwise, not only the relations will be cordial, the native will also be a scholar. The younger brother/sister will be long lived and healthy. They will inherit property and be well off in life. The native will prosper after his marriage. His wife's younger brother may join him as a partner. If the owner of the third house is weak and afflicted and has no beneficial influence, the native's mother will have good standing in the society and will be wealthy. His children will earn well by their ability, entertainment or specu-lation. The native may do research and write learned theses. His father may not be a good person.

Tenth

The native will have the goodwill of the government. He will be affectionate towards his parents. He may not have younger brother/sister particularly if Mars is weak and unsatisfactorily placed in the horoscope. When with this placement of the owner of the third house, Jupiter is badly placed from the houses it owns or it is weak in the chart or it has adverse influence on it, his elder brother/sister may be childless. He may join service by self effort.

Writing may have a role to play in his getting the service. The native may change his residence due to transfer in service. He will be able to write best sellers which will earn him money and fame. He will be highly respected. His wife will go in for higher studies and will be learned. She will also be religious and spiritually inclined. She may lose her father during the major or sub-periods of the owner of the third house.

Eleventh

The native and his younger brother/sister will be wealthy, and hold a high position. He will earn through railways, telegraph, radio, television etc. and work hard to earn his wealth. His brothers will do well in life and they will be close to him and each other. The native's children may be under the influence of his younger brother/sister. He may be in service. His health may not be satisfactory. His elder brother/sister will be very attached to his/her children if the owner of the third house is friendly with the owner of the eleventh house. A powerful owner of the third house in the eleventh house will allow the native's father-in-law to earn well from speculation or entertainment and his wife to get a windfall. If the owner is a beneficial planet, she will be a religious person. She will have a much happier and prosperous time after the birth of children to her. If the owner of the third house is weak, afflicted and has no beneficial influence here, the mother of the native will be rich and rise high in life.

Twelfth

The native will oppose his younger brothers/sisters and friends. He will be lazy. He will be fortunate after his marriage. His younger brother/sister may suffer losses or may be related to a secret society or hospital. The younger brother/sister may be well placed in life and wealthy but will leave his/her native place and live elsewhere, perhaps abroad. His father-in-law may fall sick during the major or sub-periods of the owner of the third house in the twelfth house needing hospitalisation. The maternal uncle of native's wife may go on a long journey. The native may also have trouble in his ear. If the owner of the third house is a highly malefic planet for the chart and afflicted in the twelfth house, there is a possibility that one of native's children, perhaps the eldest, may meet with a serious accident and succumb to it.

FOURTH HOUSE

1. This house refers to the following:

(i)   Dwelling houses, tents, gardens, fields, immovable property, ancestral house in which one is born, wells and tanks, water, liquid, going away from the house or leaving the birth place, canopy, holes, caves, ground, entrance, subterranean places, ancient monuments and architecture.

(ii)   Patrimony, treasure, and cattle.

(iii) Conveyance, horses, and elephants.

(iv)   Close of life, end of any undertaking.

(v)   Public in general (to be distinguished from people with whom the native interacts which is covered by the seventh house). Native's popularity among the masses.

(vi)   Mother, and women as respectable for the native as his mother. Native's relationship with them.

(vii) Happiness, comfort, promotion and victory. Home and domestic environment. Capacity to relax.

(viii) Holy places, piety, moral virtues, trust, and righteous conduct. Beneficial planets here are good for meditation.

(ix)   Breasts. Chest. If the cusp of the house is in the first drekkan this house represents the right side of the nose. If there is second drekkan then it represents the right armpit and and if it is the third drekkan which contains the cusp then the right thigh and buttock are represented.

(x)   Erudition, mind, intellect, qualifications of a person, high school and collegiate education, and knowledge of religious texts and Vedas.

2. Affliction of this house leads to mental disorders. The first, fourth and fifth houses, their owners, the Moon and Mercury are representative of the intellectual and emotional side of man. If these are afflicted it can lead to lunacy.

3. The fourth house, its owner and the Moon under influence of Rahu give rise to phobias and fits.

4. If the Moon becomes the owner of the fourth house it doubly represents the mind and wherever such a Moon is located the native shows that kind of inclination. For example such a Moon in the fifth house would make the man keenly interested in fine

arts. Such a location in the sixth house will make a man fond of sports and pets.

5. The first and the fourth houses, their owners and the Moon if powerful, friendly to each other and linked together make a man a leader of the masses.

6. Riots play a part in the life of the native if this house, its owner and the Moon are linked with Rahu.

7. If Saturn and the owner of the first house influence a powerful fourth house and its owner the native would have lot of landed property and will earn well from it.

8. Separative influence of at least two of the Sun, Saturn, Rahu, owner of the twelfth house and their dispositors on the fourth house and its owner makes the native change his residence. If in this process the tenth house is also involved the change is due to one's profession i. e. transfer.

9. A weak owner of the fourth house under malefic influence brings about quarrel with members of public (i. e. unknown persons of general public).

10. The native is selfish if the fourth house, its owner and the Moon are exclusively under the influence of Saturn and Rahu. If this yoga does not have any beneficial influence it can also mean that the native would suffer from tuberculosis.

11. The native is dispassionate if the Moon, and this house are connected with Saturn.

12. The native would be popular if this house and its owner are connected with the Moon.

13. The rules for determining relationship between the native and a relative of his are recorded in paragraph 32 under FIRST HOUSE. If we wish to determine the relations that are likely to exist between the native and his mother, we should apply these rules to the fourth house.

14. The native takes to agriculture when the fourth house is connected with the second, ninth or the eleventh house.

15. When the owner of the fourth house is placed in a good house or the fourth house has relationship with a good house,

and the significators of education namely Jupiter and Mercury have at least average strength, the native will do well at college. If the fourth house is related to the tenth house, the native will come out at the top of successful candidates at college examinations.

16. Effect of various SIGNS in the Fourth House (A careful study of NOTE in paragraph 38 under FIRST HOUSE will be of use.):

Aries

The wealth of the native is self earned. He will have vehicles, property and cattle. The owner of the fourth house here is Mars which is also the owner of the eleventh house. The native is likely to be popular among his friends and have a number of female friends. The native's parents may not be able to pull along well with each other. One of the parents may pass away early. The cause of disharmony between the parents will be the mother who would be self opinionated and stubborn. A weak Mars will be bad for the longevity of the father, and make the elder brother/ sister or the spouse of native's first child sickly. It will also be instrumental in souring any partnerships that the native's children enter into. Mars placed in the tenth house will ensure great success at collegiate examinations, provided it is unafflicted and has no sambandha with any planet that is adverse for the chart. This can be further analysed in the manner similar to Scorpio in the eleventh house in Chapter Five.

Taurus

The native will have much comforts and luxuries. The mother will be affectionate but will have much say in the household. The home of the native will be a meeting place for groups of like minded people and there will be regular entertaining. The owner of the fourth house here is Venus, which is also the owner of the ninth house. He will be mentally well evolved and will be imaginative. He may study abroad. The native will be highly educated and may undertake to write a learned thesis on the basis of research that he would carry out, may be with the younger sister of his wife. He will get patrimony and vehicles, and earn wealth and property without much effort. A weak Venus will curtail the longevity of the father. His first born child will be sensual and if Venus is well placed and strong, will do well in the field of fine arts. The native will become religious at the close of his life. This can be further analysed in the manner similar to Libra in the ninth house in Chapter Five.

Gemini

The native will keep changing his residence. The home will be a place for exchange of ideas in which friends and acquaintances will participate. Many a time the activities that the native will undertake will not be usual. The owner of the fourth house here is Mercury, which is also the owner of the seventh house. He will travel regularly. Since both these houses represent female relatives of the native, Mercury will carry a strong feminine influence. Whichever factor in the horoscope is effected by this planet will get a feminine characteristic. Thus Mercury will give the native only sisters if it effects the third/eleventh house or daughters only if the fifth house is under its influence. The native will gain wealth, property and vehicles due to his marriage and his wife and mother will have a close bond. His mother will be fond of reading and be of literary bent of mind. He may have a female business partner. He will be happy to be close to water or beautiful gardens. This can be further analysed in the manner similar to Virgo in the seventh house in Chapter Five.

Cancer

The native will be guided by his wife. He will be soft-spoken, handsome, learned and well behaved. The mother will be loving but also overbearing. He will like to live close to water and may change his residence frequently. His wealth may fluctuate. The Moon, being the owner of this house and also the karaka for the mind, represents the mind fully and with whichever house it is associated the mind of the native will dwell on that subject constantly and the native will like that matter or person. For example if the Moon is in the fifth house the native will be attached to his children and like entertainment or speculation. The native will also like to closely watch his children and will monitor all their activities. He will be proud of his home where he would like to spend as much time as possible.

Leo

The native will have well developed hobbies. He will keep a close watch on his children. His house will be classy and will be well lit and ventilated. He will be high minded but will get annoyed at trifles and lose his temper. He will keep poor company. His mother will be from a high family and of majestic appearance. The native will live away from his place of birth. If the owners of the fourth and twelfth houses are in sambandha, or Rahu and Saturn influence this house, the native will change his residence from time to time. A strong Sun will be indicative of the fact that the native will attain a high position towards the end of his life.

Virgo

The native will come across thieves and backbiters in life even though he may not like to mix with them. He will prefer service to an independent vocation. He will not have much interaction with his father and will keep changing his residence. The owner of this house is Mercury, which is also the owner of the first house. He will be learned and an intellectual. He will enjoy differences of opinion and debates as it will give him an opportunity to argue out the matter. A weak Mercury will make the native loose tongued and one who promotes dissensions and enjoys quarrels. If Mercury is strong, the native will acquire property and vehicles by his own effort and will be comfortable in life. He will be popular and may make a place for himself in his chosen field of knowledge. Since Mercury indicates multiplicity, the native will pursue several lines of intellectual study. He will be an intellectual, a linguist, close to his mother and popular. Mercury will indicate the mind and whichever house is influenced by it will be the field in which the native will show particular interest. The mother will like pomp and high status. She will be critical of others, of literary taste and will definitely show some interest in the study of languages. She will live long. The native's children will go abroad.

Libra

The native will have an equable, and friendly temperament. He will be humourous, well educated and learned. He has a strong sense of family ties. His house will be well decorated. He will have a good collection of art objects. His mother will be good looking, will have elegant taste and will be fond of perfumes and jewellery. She will try to keep balance and harmony in the house and will be house proud. The owner of the fourth house, Venus, is also the owner of the eleventh house and will therefore be a significator for the longevity of the parents. A powerful and unafflicted Venus will make them live long. Venus, being the owner of the fourth house, will influence the mind. If afflicted it will make the native sensual. If Venus is connected with the fifth, seventh or the twelfth house, the native will be oversexed. This can be further analysed in the manner similar to Taurus in the eleventh house in Chapter Five.

Scorpio

The native cannot get along with his mother and may separate from his parents early in life. His mother may be sensual, hard working and of exacting nature. He will keep changing houses, sometimes due to differences with his landlords. The owner of the fourth, Mars, is also the owner of the ninth house. He will be learned in the field of engineering or military science and may pursue the study to a high level. He may formally do research and write a thesis. The native will acquire property, vehicles and comforts without much effort. Mars, if weak and afflicted will be a maraka for the younger brother or sister of the native. It will also cause ailments to the mother of the native and may make her undergo surgical operations etc. This can be further analysed in the manner similar to Aries in the ninth house in Chapter Five. He will have poor temper and keep bad company. His first born child will have a tendency to be sensual and if Mars influences Venus in an adverse manner this tendency will manifest itself fully.

Sagittarius

The native will have servants and large vehicles. He may live abroad and may even marry a foreigner. His job will entail contact with foreigners and he will obtain fluency in several languages. He may deal in purchase and sale of property. His parents will be in the academic field or they will be religious. He will have good houses to live in. His mother will always look at the brighter side of life. She will be truthful to the extent of being tactlessly frank. She may thus offend people by her outspokenness. Jupiter is the owner of the houses of mother and wife. It will therefore have feminine characteristics. If it has connection with the fifth house, being the significator for children, it will give the native a number of female children. A powerful Jupiter will make the mother of the native prosperous and own property, and his younger brothers/sisters and neighbours gain through their children. The wife of the native may have independent means of livelihood.

Capricorn

The native will be born in a domestic environment where discipline will be considered of much importance. He will be unhappy with his mother. She will be hard working, thrifty, prudent, practical and hard headed. His parents may not have cordial relations with each other. The native will like to stay at home and enjoy his surroundings which will be neat and pleasant. He will like to visit water bodies and green and sylvan places with his friends. A powerful Saturn will signify prosperity and gain for the native since it being the owner of the fourth and fifth houses, will be a superb beneficial planet for Libra ascendant. The native will have happiness from his children and will be very attached to them. He will have a bright intellect and sharp mind. He will lead a comfortable existence. The mind may easily get depressed and worried. The native may get a position of confidence and power as a result of his popularity with the masses.

Aquarius

The native will always have a good number of people visiting his house. His relations with his parents and the relations of the parents with each other will be the same as described for Capricorn above. His mother will be gregarious, friendly and social. She will always support her weakest child and shield the children from the wrath of the father and teachers. He will be intellectually active and participate in mind warming group discussions. A strong Saturn will make the native happy on account of younger brothers/sisters, neighbours and colleagues since the owner of the third house will also be the owner of the fourth house. He is likely to keep changing his residence. The native's children may find that their income is inadequate to meet their requirements.

Pisces

The native will have a peaceful and contented domestic life. He will be attached to his mother. She will be simple, easy going and free with her money. She will also be sentimental and impressionable. The parents would be religious and artistic. The native will have spent his early years abroad. He will have his house close to a lake or a waterbody. The owner of the fourth is also the owner of the first house. A powerful Jupiter will make the native highly educated and a mature personality. He will have conveyances, a large house and comforts. The mother of the native will be rich and highly connected. She may be working, perhaps with the government as a teacher or therapist and will have her independent source of income. The native will have a comfortable and contented existence. His father may show interest in the occult, may make a study of it and practice spiritualism. This can be further analysed in the manner similar to Virgo in the fourth house and Sagittarius in the first house.

17. Effect of the owner of the Fourth House in various houses (A careful study of the opening notes from A to H in paragraph 39 under FIRST HOUSE will be of utmost use.):

First

The native will be known because of his father. He will be close to his father but will not be happy with the family of his mother. He will have vehicles for his use. He will be wealthy. He will have to deal with masses and if owners of the first and the fourth houses are friendly to each other, the native will be very well known and popular. He may have good education and may be connected with educational institutions or the field as such. He will remain at his native piace. His first child may go abroad and settle there. His mother will be well educated who may earn her livelihood independently. She may be connected with the government. His father will be learned and may delve in matters mystical. His younger brother/sister will, depending upon the strength of the owner of the fourth house, be wealthy. His wife will be attached to her home and comforts.

Second

A malefic owner of the fourth house will make the native oppose his father. A beneficial owner will however ensure that the native looks after his father well. He will be an agriculturist. His younger brother/sister may spend heavily; may suffer losses due to a loose tongue and spend heavily on food. His children will work for hospitals, asylums or secret organisations. During the major or sub-periods of the owner of the fourth house in the second, the work environment for the first child will undergo a complete change. The mother will have her ambitions fulfilled. She will earn through her own efforts. A weak and afflicted owner of the fourth house with no redeeming beneficial influence on it will make the father rise very high in life during its major or sub-periods. The native's wife's career may face serious problems and she may have to face slanderous charges. She may face humiliation and dishonour.

Third

The native may generally be quarrelsome and may cause unhappiness to his parents. He may cause harm to the members of his father's family. However he may earn well and may have children. He may look after his parents in their old age and may also extend help to his brothers/sisters, neighbours and colleagues. His higher education may be conducted through correspondence. The native may change or leave his residence during the major or sub-periods of the owner of the fourth house. He may go away from the place of his birth and live elsewhere at the close of life. The native's mother may not like his younger brother/sister. The children of his elder brother/sister may have poor health during the major or sub-periods of the owner of the fourth house.

Fourth

This is a good location. The native may have vehicles, property, and comforts. He may bring happiness to his parents. He may be religious, and long-lived. He may be generally well liked. The father may also prosper in life and be long lived. The native will be honoured by the government. He will have good higher education and be learned. The native will have the quality of his mind according to the nature of the owner of the fourth. He will be wealthy and lead a comfortable life. His children will be rich.

Fifth

The native may be lucky with regard to his father, long-lived, well behaved and may have good children. He may be attached to his children. In any case they may be prominent in his life. He may have vehicles for his use. He may be an intellectual or he may be successful at speculation or game of chance and make money through either of these sources. He may do well at entertainment or fine arts. He may get power and position through the masses, i.e., he may have a successful political career. His mother may be wealthy and fond of good food. When the fourth house is powerful his father may get a legacy suddenly, but he may have to face disappointments and disputes and generally not be able to do well in life. The father will leave his birth place and settle elsewhere, and have to work hard for whatever success that he gets in life.

Sixth

If the owner of the fourth house is a malefic planet the native may find faults with his father, squander his wealth and property and create enemies for himself. His mind will constantly be troubled on account of enmity. He will like to meet and remain in the company of foreigners and persons of absolutely different religious beliefs and culture. He may not be able to succeed at public life and may suffer losses if he tries to dabble in it. In case the concerned owner is a beneficial planet the native will be able to save wealth. His mother may be close to his maternal uncle and his younger brother/sister. She may be sickly and a cause of worry and discomfort to the native. An afflicted owner of the fourth house in the sixth will curtail the longevity of the mother and cause her death in its major or sub-periods. If the owner of the fourth house is weak, afflicted and has no beneficial influence here, the elder brother/sister of the native may be rich and rise high in life, but the native may have to face litigations on account of property. His father may face humiliation, reverses and disappointments in his career. The father may have to go to jail for misappropriation of money kept in his trust. His children may not be wealthy. They may earn from hospitals or disease.

Seventh

If the owner of the fourth house is a malefic planet the native's wife will cause unhappiness to his father. It will not be so in case the owner is a beneficial planet, when the native will look after his father-in-law and his wife may be attached to his father. In case the owner is either Mars or Venus the wife will be very talented. The wife will be barren if the owner is Mars. If the owners of the fourth and the seventh houses are friendly to each other, the native's mother will like his wife. The native may go on long journey in connection with his higher education and earn his livelihood at a distant place in case the sign in the seventh house is a movable one. He may complete an educational degree and start studies on a higher degree. His children may live away at a short distance from the native.

Eighth

The native will be cruel, bad tempered, poor and ailing. He will be known for his bad deeds. His house, vehicle or mother will be the cause of his death. He will get involved in serious litigation and lose his property and wealth during the major or sub-periods of the owner of the fourth house if Saturn or Rahu is also involved in this placement. His education will be rudimentary. He will not have peace of mind and will not be happy. His father will be short lived, but if the owner of the fourth house is weak and afflicted in the eighth house and has no beneficial influence on it, the father will not only have average longevity but will also enjoy power and pelf. His mother may not have good longevity. She may enjoy life and be interested in music and fine arts. His children may go abroad for education but they are also likely to lead an average existence. An afflicted owner of the fourth house in the eighth house may curtail the longevity of the mother and cause her death in its major or sub-periods.

Ninth

The native will live away from his father. When Jupiter or Mercury is powerful in the chart, he will have extensive knowledge in several branches of learning and will always behave in a respectable fashion. He may carry on research in some branch of learning and publish papers. The native may take up teaching or law as his chosen vocation. His father will acquire property but may not have good relations with the native's mother. His mother may fall sick during the major or sub-periods of the owner of the fourth house. He may be an agriculturist. He may follow his father's profession. He will be contented, philosophical or religious. His younger brother/sister will get wealth from his/ her marriage. His wife's younger brother/sister may have a strong influence on him. His children may be sensual, not be morally strong and may waste their wealth on pandering to their senses and matters that morally cannot be approved of.

Tenth

A beneficial owner of the fourth house here makes the native charitable and gain from the government, but if the owner is a malefic planet it will make the father of the native desert his wife and live with another woman. The native will have property and conveyances. The results, if the owner of the fourth house is powerful, will be similar to some extent to the owner of the fourth house being in the fourth house. The native will come out at the top of successful examinees at examinations in college or university. He will get a job, most probably government job due to his educational qualifications. He will get house, and comforts, and vehicles from the government or employer and he may have his place of work in his residence. If the owner of the fourth house is weak and afflicted and has no beneficial influence here, the children, especially the first child, and the elder brother/ sister of the native will rise high in life.

Eleventh

The native will be devoted to his father, he will be religious, pious, in good health and long-lived. He may be an agriculturist. A malefic owner will keep the father of the native abroad, a beneficial owner will make him only visit abroad. The native will be popular and will have a number of friends. A weak and afflicted owner of the fourth house in the eleventh house will be bad for the health and longevity of native's mother. It may bring about a separation of native's first born child from his spouse.

Twelfth

The father of the native will either settle down abroad or die early. A malefic owner of the fourth house here also casts doubts over the parentage of the native. The native will lose his ancestral property. The native may not keep good health during the major or sub-periods of a weak or afflicted owner of the fourth house. He will rarely have comforts. If the owner of the fourth house is weak and badly placed in the twelfth house and the Moon or Mercury is under malefic influence, the native will suffer from a terrible inferiority complex. A powerful owner of the fourth house here will be excellent for the mother of the native, however if it is adverse or afflicted, the mother may die during the major or sub-periods of the owner of the fourth house. If the owner of the fourth house is weak, and afflicted, and has no beneficial influence here, the children of the native will be rich and rise high in life.

FIFTH HOUSE

1 This house refers to the following:
(i) Children.
(ii) Intelligence, affection, discretion, talent, memory, and good speech and counsel. Oral, qualifying or departmental examination (but not competitive examination).
(iii) Good behaviour, far sightedness, and sobriety.
(iv) Belly, stomach and heart. The right cheek, right side of the heart, or the right knee depending on the drekkan that contains the cusp.
(v) Good deeds in the past lives. Meditation. Spiritual practice. Mantras and Yantras (religious diagrams for vener-

ation and specific results), Ishta Devata (one's chosen deity), disciples, and invitation to religious ceremonies.

(vi) Fall from a high office (being eighth from the tenth house), ministership and royal insignia.

(vii) Authorship of epics.

(viii) Being social, society, banquets and parties, romance, love affair, cinema, entertainment, place of entertainment, theatrical performance, sports and pleasure. Aesthetic sense. Physical attraction between opposite sexes and licentiousness. Courtesan.

(ix) Speculation. Game of chance.

(x)   Ambassador.

(xi) Hospitalisation of pet animals (being twelfth from the sixth house).

(xii) Brother younger to the first younger brother (being third from the third house). Friends of the partner or wife. Father's father. Elder brother's/sister's spouse or his partner in business.

(xiii) See paragraphs 5 under Chapter on Planets and 1(x)(a) under NINTH HOUSE in Chapter Five.

2. A. The native is likely to have children as:

   (a) (i) A beneficial planet for the chart, in or aspecting the fifth house, or a benign Moon in this house makes the house fecund.

       (ii) The fifth house is not weak or afflicted.

   (b) An unafflicted owner of the fifth house powerfully and well placed in the chart will promise children.

   (c) Fruitful signs in the fifth or the eleventh house promise children.

   (d) Jupiter, the karaka for children, well placed, unafflicted and at least averagely powerful assures birth of children to the native.

   (e) The owners of the fifth and first houses have sambandha.

   (f) The owner of the fifth house in sambandha with the Moon, or placed in Moon's drekkan will give a number of daughters.

   B. The native is likely to be childless if:

   (a) barren signs tenant the fifth or the eleventh house,

   (b) owner of either of these houses is not in a fruitful sign,

(c)   the Moon is also not located in a fruitful sign,
(d)   the ascendant does not have a fruitful sign in it,
(e)   owner of the first house does not occupy a fruitful sign,
(f)   Jupiter, the karaka for children is afflicted by malefic planets, or by a powerful maraka for the ascendant, or
(g)   the fifth house or its owner is weak and badly afflicted.
(h)   If the owner of the fifth house is placed in the sixth, eighth or the twelfth house or in an inimical sign, there will be difficulty in having children.
(i)   When the first and fifth houses and Jupiter are weak the native may be childless.

It should not be predicted that the native will be childless merely because one condition from the above has been fulfilled in the horoscope. The issue should be examined in its totality.

3. The fifth house signifies the first pregnancy, the seventh the second, and the ninth the third and so on (the seventh house is third from the fifth house signifying younger brother to the first child etc.).

4. For women the fifth house from the Moon is more important for judging children than the fifth house from the ascendant.

5. Birth of a child to the native can be predicted when during transit Jupiter forms a link with the owners of the ascendant, and of the houses in which the Sun and the Moon are placed by association, aspect etc.

6. Being negation of the sixth house (being the twelfth house from the sixth), the fifth house indicates freedom from disease.

7. Naturally malefic planets like the Sun, Mars, and Saturn are considered weak in the fifth house. If these planets are owners of good houses but are located in this house, they must have aspects from beneficial planets without which they do not give good results with regard to the affairs of the houses they rule.

8. A planet in the fifth house operates as the karaka for marriage.

9. The Moon, afflicted by malefic planets in this house, causes early death of the father.

10. If the Moon is afflicted by Saturn and Mars here, the father

of the native will suffer seriously from disease in the very first major-period of a planet, in the life of the native, in the sub-period of the owner of the navansha in which the major-period planet is situated.

11. We should first verify whether the horoscope indicates any children for the native. If it does, it should broadly be analysed whether the number of children will be small or large. Thereafter, there are several methods to find out the number of children one will have. Four of these methods which are considered reliable to a reasonable degree are given below. Results should be worked out according to all the four. The majority of results may be taken. It will give a fairly accurate result:

(1). (i) NUMBER OF CHILDREN: The owner of the fifth house will be in some sign. We will calculate the exact position that it occupies. This can easily be worked out for the date and time of birth from any suitable ephemeris. Then we calculate the number of navanshas it has travelled in that sign. The number of navanshas fully traversed by the owner of the fifth house will be the number of children the native will have.

We take a concrete example to explain this simple method. Suppose the ascendant is Gemini. The owner of the fifth house will be Venus. Suppose at the time the native was born it was at 10 degrees 25 minutes in Aries. We know that navansha is the ninth part of a sign of thirty degrees. Therefore a navansha will extend over 3 degrees and 20 minutes of a sign. Hence the first navansha in Aries will be of Aries from 0 degree to 3 degrees 20 minutes, the second will be of Taurus and will extend from 3 degrees 20 minutes to 6 degrees 40 minutes in Aries, the third will be of Gemini and will begin at 6 degrees 40 minutes and continue upto 10 degrees in Aries, the fourth will be of Cancer and will begin at 10 degrees and last till 13 degrees 20 minutes in Aries etc. These can easily be found from the table of navanshas. Now as we notice, Venus here is at 10 degrees 25 minutes in Aries. Therefore it has completed three

navanshas in Aries (of Aries, Taurus and Gemini)
and is in the fourth. The number of children will be
equal to the number of navanshas fully traversed.
Therefore the native is likely to have at the most
three children.

(ii) GENDER OF CHILDREN BORN: The next question
to determine is the number of sons and daughters the
native is likely to have. For this we consider all the
navanshas that have been completely traversed. Out
of these navanshas that have been completely traversed we have to examine as to how many navanshas
have male planets as rulers and how many have
female rulers. The number of male and female
navansha rulers so determined will be the number of
boys and girls the native will respectively have. For
the purpose of this rule we categorise the male and
female planets as below:

Male planets—Sun, Mars, Mercury and Jupiter.
Female planets—Moon, Venus and Saturn.
We will again take up the illustration that we had
considered above. We know that Venus had traversed first three navanshas completely in Aries.
From the chart for rulers of navanshas it is seen that
the first navansha in Aries is ruled by Mars, the
second by Venus and the third by Mercury. Thus of
the three navanshas fully traversed, one is ruled by
a female planet and the other two by male planets.
The native can at the most have one female and two
male children.

(iii) As has been suggested at the beginning, we must
verify whether the horoscope shows large number of
children or otherwise. If the number seems to be
large, examine whether (a) the owner of the fifth
house is in vargottama navansha, or (b) it is aspected
by Jupiter or (c) by Venus in the birth chart. If one
such factor exists, the original number of children
arrived at should be multiplied by two. If another
such factor also exists, the original number should be
multiplied by four. If the third factor also exists, the
original number should be multiplied by six. The

proportion of gender will remain the same.

However, extreme care ought to be exercised when prediction is being made for a very large number of children. When there is Taurus, Leo, Virgo or Scorpio on the cusp of the fifth house; or, Jupiter or the owner of the fifth house is in one of these signs, the number of children will be restricted. If there is aspect of Jupiter or Venus on the owner of the fifth house, we must check whether (i) Jupiter or Venus, as the case may be, is a beneficial planet for the ascendant and (ii) it is powerful. If these two conditions are fulfilled and the sign factor, just described above, does not exist, only then the multiplication effect should be considered. The aspect or association of Jupiter or Venus with the owner of the fifth house should be within 4 degrees.

Thus in the example given above, if Venus were being aspected by Jupiter, we should have presumed that the native would have a maximum of six (three multiplied by two) children of which two would be daughters and four sons.

(iv) NUMBER OF PREGNANCIES DESTROYED: It is not necessary that the number of children indicated will all be born to the native. There is a possibility that some will be lost due to miscarriage etc. The natal chart should indicate such a loss. When there are such indications, the number of pregnancies that are likely to be destroyed can be determined in the following manner:

Examine if there are naturally malefic planets occupying the navanshas fully traversed by the owner of the fifth house. If yes, there will be loss of pregnancies in the manner referred to above. The number of malefic planets occupying navanshas fully traversed will be equal to the number of pregnancies lost.

Suppose Rahu is in Taurus in the navansha chart. Taurus has been traversed fully by Venus as we have seen above. Rahu is a naturaly malefic planet. Therefore the native is likely to lose one child before its birth. It must be clarified that in case we multiply the number of probable children due to aspect of Jupiter or Venus etc., we will not multiply the number of children that are going to be lost due to this malefic influence. To clarify matters, we revert to the example we had taken up earlier with Venus being the owner of the fifth house placed in Aries. Here if Venus were being aspected by Jupiter, we should have presumed that the native would have a maximum of six (three multiplied by two) children. One child will be lost due to placement of Rahu in Taurus. The native will therefore have five children.

(2). An analysis on the lines indicated above from (i) to (iv) can also be made on the bhavamadhya (middle point of the house) of the fifth house.

(3). The owner of the fifth house will occupy some sign in the navansha chart. The number that is arrived at by counting from the sign in the first house (in the birth chart) to this sign will be the number of children that the native is likely to have.

We will clarify this rule by the same illustration that has been adopted for rule 1 above. Venus is the owner of the fifth house and is in Cancer navansha. The sign in the first house of birth chart is Gemini. Counting from Gemini upto Cancer we get two: That will be the number of children the native is likely to have. It must be noted that this rule does not take into account the number of pregnancies that are destroyed as in rule 1 above. This will be the number of children born to the native.

(4). The number of planets aspecting the fifth house or occupying it will be the number of children the native is likely to have. The sex of the children can be determined from the sex of these planets as laid down above. Severely malefic planets, occupying or aspecting the house may force destruction of pregnancies. Number of such planets influencing the house will be the number of pregnancies destroyed.

(5). These rules are equally applicable in determining the number of siblings of the native. Applied to the third house and · its owner they yield the number of younger brothers and sisters and applied to the eleventh house and its owner they give the same information with regard to elder brothers and sisters.

12. The owner of the fifth house located near the owner of the first house in the horoscope indicates that the native will beget children early in life. The closer the location, the earlier the birth of children. If the Moon is powerful in the chart this should be predicted from the Moon ascendant (taking the house in which the Moon is located as the first house).

13. The rules for determining relationship between the native and a relative of his are recorded in paragraph 32 under FIRST HOUSE. If we wish to determine the relations that are likely to exist between the native and his children, we should apply these rules to the fifth house.

14. Effect of various SIGNS in the Fifth house (A careful study of NOTE in paragraph 38 under FIRST HOUSE will be of use.):

Aries

The native will have good children unless there are other malefic influences. He will have children later than normal in life. His children will be of independent mind and if subjected to controls will rebel. His mother will be rich and inherit wealth. She may talk of religion. His father will be very intelligent and learned and may be engaged in research. The father will inherit property. If Mars is afflicted or influences the fifth house it can cause miscarriages since it is also the owner of the twelfth house which is the house of separation. Mars will otherwise be auspicious for the native being owner of the fifth and also of the twelfth house. The native may have more than one liaison with females as Mars gets rulership of houses of love affairs and pleasures of the bed. If Mars in any manner also influences the seventh house or its owner, this tendency will be further accentuated. Mars in this role gives an insatiable sexual appetite and if it is weak and influences Venus, also gives perverted sexual urge. Since from the house of children, i.e., the fifth house, the number of signs falling in a house and the number of house as counted from this house are the same, any house afflicted will show ailment in that part of the body of the children, especially of the first born. For example the ninth house will have the fifth sign, Leo. If the ninth house and the Sun are afflicted, it can lead to troubles in the parts of the body signified by Leo, i.e., belly and heart of the child. This can be further analysed in the manner similar to Scorpio in the twelfth house in Chapter Five.

Taurus

The native will move from one passionate relationship to the next. He will not be able to discipline his children correctly since he will spoil them in their younger days. He will have an excellent daughter who will be beautiful and well behaved. The children will be hard working and will like to take up medicine, surgery, banking, mining or agriculture as their profession. The owner of the fifth, Venus, is also the owner of the tenth house. Venus will grant affluence, power and status to the native. The son of the native will be in service. If Venus is afflicted it can make the native's children suffer from female enemies or illnesses of the urinary system and kidneys. Such a Venus will be a maraka for the mother of the native. His father will be wealthy or may be able to talk well and in depth on religious or other subjects.

Gemini

The children will be handsome, intelligent, virtuous and capable but they will be born late as the native will take time to decide as to when he should have them. He may not be able to devote enough time to his children due to other preoccupations. The owner of the fifth, Mercury, is also the owner of the eighth house. The children of the native may be short lived and the elder sister may have a miserable married life, if Mercury is weak and afflicted, the fifth house has adverse influence and Jupiter is also not in a good condition. His mother will be a proficient musician. His younger brother/sister may suffer from diseases in ear, throat, or arms.

Cancer

The native will have more children than normal, most of them females, born to the native rather early in life and all of them will be handsome, able and reputed. His children will not be able to amass wealth but will in their second halves of life rise to prominent positions. The native will be attached to them. The native will have special talent in the field of fine arts or entertainment. A weak or waning Moon can see him lose money in speculation or game of chance. He will have good memory. A strong and waxing Moon connected with the ninth or tenth house can grant the native success in political field and in getting political power.

Leo

The children of the native will be irascible, intelligent, a source of pride to the native, and will be non-vegetarian. They will have impressive personalities and good appetite. A powerful Jupiter will ensure that they earn a lot of wealth abroad. They will do well in their first halves of life and their fortune will be on the wane in the second half. The native may not be able to devote enough time to them. The native will be passionate, sensual, and will enjoy drama, and other stage entertainments. A powerful and well placed Sun will make the native get a position of power.

Virgo

The native will have studious children who will display special ability in mathematics, science and languages. The love relationship of the native will be changeable and dogged by cynicism. The native may decide not to have children. There may be problems on account of the children being beyond the control of the native or he may have children late in life. The native may lose money through impulsive and unsound investments, games of chance and indiscreet spending. He will love his wife. The owner of the fifth, Mercury, is also the owner of the second house. This can be analysed in the manner similar to Gemini in the second house above.

Libra

The children of the native will be handsome, well behaved and able. They will have talent. The owner of the fifth house, Venus, is also the owner of the twelfth house. A weak and afflicted Venus will reduce the longevity of the children. It will bring about the death of the elder sister. It can pose danger and cause accidents to native's wife. The native's father will be learned and engaged in research when Venus is well placed. Venus will be a beneficial planet for the children of the native since it will own the first and eighth houses from the fifth house. Though it will be the owner of the twelfth house, its mooltrikona sign will be located in the fifth house. Therefore, a well placed Venus should bring benefits to the children. If it is in the fifth or twelfth house, the children will be long lived; if in the fourth house, they may travel abroad during the periods of Venus; if in the seventh house, they will go on journeys time and again, and if in the eighth house, the eldest child will have property and vehicles. This can be analysed in the manner similar to Aries above and Taurus in the twelfth house in Chapter Five.

Scorpio

The native will invest and spend his money without proper thought. He will be secretive and hide his feelings. He may not be liked by his children and his wife and his relationship with them may not be pleasant. His children will be hard working, exacting, introverted and determined. They will have little sentimentality in them. The native will enjoy sports and entertainment. The native will have to face unfounded and baseless charges in life. Mars is the owner of the fifth and tenth houses. This is an excellent planet for the native and if well placed and powerful, can do a lot of good to the native in its periods. However, if it does not have sambandha with a bad planet in the chart, the sub-period of any such bad planet in the major-period of Mars will be highly troublesome. This can be analysed in the manner similar to Taurus above where Venus has similar ownerships. However the diseases that Mars will give will not be the same as recorded for Venus.

Sagittarius

The native will have children who will be courageous, frank, will suppress enemies, and reach high positions in, or receive honours from the government. He will be prosperous and comfortable. He will be cheerful and optimistic but will not be able to have romantic liaisons. The owner of the fifth house is Jupiter, which is also the owner of the eighth house. His children will be learned, will have good houses and will lead a comfortable life. If Jupiter is afflicted, the native will have trouble from or on account of his children. When Jupiter is weak and afflicted, the danger to the children especially the first born, will be much more since Jupiter is also the karaka for the children. His elder

brother/sister will get married into a highly placed family or one
that is connected with the government. His father will travel
abroad or may be learned in secret or mystical knowledge. This
can be further analysed in the manner similar to Gemini above
or Pisces in the eighth house in Chapter Five.

Capricorn

The native will be a martinet with his children who may be
born late in life. He will reject many partners before settling
down in life. The children will not be good looking. They will be
hard working, down to earth and practical in life. Saturn will be
the owner of the fifth and also the sixth house. A powerful Saturn
in the fifth house will make the children of the native wealthy
and the mother of the native to get wealth through her younger
brothers/sisters, neighbours or colleagues. If Saturn is weak and
afflicted, his children will be sickly. If with such a Saturn, the
sixth house is under adverse influence and Mercury is also weak,
the first born child of the native will suffer from severe speech
defect. A powerful Saturn well placed will make the native's
father rise high in life. The rise will be slow but steady and may
come late in life.

Aquarius

The native will have a sober and dignified son. The native may
consciously decide to have children late in life due to his social
and other preoccupations. The owner of the fifth is also the owner
of the fourth house. The native will gain through his children if
Saturn is powerful. Also in such a situation Saturn will act as a
great beneficial planet and will confer prosperity, status and
comforts on the native if powerful. The native will have a good
chance of getting power and position through his popularity
among the masses. The mother of the native will also be wealthy
and will have a happy family life. A weak Saturn will reduce the
income of the younger brothers/sisters of the native. He will not
give much time to his children. The children will be few but
highly intelligent and creative.

Pisces

The owner of the sign being the karaka for children, if strong and well placed, will mean birth of children to the native during its major or sub-periods. The native will be fond of sports and arts. The owner of the fifth house is Jupiter. Jupiter is also the owner of the second house. A powerful Jupiter is a good indicator of native's success at speculation or games of chance. He can also be a powerful and intelligent orator. He may also show intellectual promise of a high standard in his school days. Jupiter, for the elder brother/sister of the native, has feminine characteristics, as it owns the fourth and the seventh houses from the eleventh house and if Jupiter influences the third house, the elder brother/sister will have mostly daughters. This can be further analysed in the manner similar to Gemini for the second house above.

15. The owner of the Fifth House in various houses (A careful study of the opening notes from A to H in paragraph 39 under FIRST HOUSE will be of utmost use):

First

The native will be well behaved, intelligent, reputed and learned. He will have but a few children. He will have good relations with his children provided no planet inimical to the owner of the fifth house aspects or joins it here. The native will have an equable temper and will be sentimental. He will talk well and pleasantly. He may get spiritual power if the owner of the fifth house, having beneficial aspect, is strongly disposed in the first house. The native's father will be highly placed and wealthy. He may also be learned and religious. A malefic owner of the fifth house, weak and badly placed, will cause loss of family property, during its major or sub-periods. The property may be confiscated or acquired by the government.

Second

A beneficial owner of the fifth house in the second makes the native rich and comfortable. Such an owner of the fifth house, if well placed in the second house will make the native famous. Reverse would be the result if it is a malefic planet. The owner of the fifth in the second house makes the native eloquent, good at or interested in music. A child may be born to him in the major or sub-periods of the owner of the fifth house. He will have a beautiful wife and his children will be well behaved. The native may get back old and held up payments from the government. His father may have contact or dealings with foreigners. The mother will have wealth and she will earn in a joint enterprise with her daughter-in-law. The native's children will be highly placed in government or command a distinct status in society. His younger brother/sister will settle at a place away from their place of birth.

Third

The children of the native will be attached to him . The native will be wise and will talk pleasantly. He will look after his brothers, his own children and the children of his brothers. He would be a capable man. His mother will talk badly and may suffer loss due to it. She will be extravagant. A powerful and well placed owner of the fifth house will make the native's children lucky. Their wishes will be fulfilled. They will be independent and efficient. His father will be lucky in marriage and will be attached to his grandchildren. The native's wife will be rich. This is also a good location for the native to have musical talent. The native may develop hobbies in the field of other fine arts too.

Fourth

The native will be attached to his mother but a malefic owner of the fifth house makes the native antagonistic to his parents. His mother will be long lived, but sentimental. The number of children will be restricted and a child may pass away during the major or sub-periods of a malefic owner of the fifth house in the fourth house. He will pursue his family trade. He may get close to powerful personalities due to his learning and ability to give good advice. This location of the owner of the fifth house is conducive to bring power and authority to the native due to his eminence in learning, intellect or popularity. His father will be in average circumstances or may be learned in occult matters. His father may get legacies or moneys that had appeared irrecoverable.

Fifth

The native will be virtuous, learned and reputed. He will have good children who will do well in life. The native will rise high in life and may reach a position of trust in his organisation or government. The native may have more than average number of children. The children will be long lived. There is a possibility that the native may achieve success in spiritual practices. He will be wealthy and will be able to get what he would like to have in life. Children may be born to him in the major or sub-periods of the owner of the fifth house. The owner of the fifth house shall be a highly maraka planet for the mother of the native. The native's father will be very fortunate and if the owner of the fifth house is a naturally beneficial planet, he will also be highly religious. However, a naturally beneficial planet being the owner of the fifth house in the fifth shall be a great maraka planet for the elder brother/sister of the native.

Sixth

He will suffer at the hands of his enemies. His wife will be ailing, sharp tongued and poor. If the owner is a malefic planet he will be in bad health and poor. The evil results are reduced to some extent if the owner is a beneficial planet. The native is likely to benefit from his maternal uncle. The maternal uncle will be prosperous. During the major or sub-periods of the owner of the fifth house, if it is a malefic planet, the native's maternal uncle may have to be admitted to a hospital or asylum, or he may go away from his home. The native's children may behave like his enemies or suffer from illnesses. This is not a good position for the health of native's children though they will be hard working and work their way to much wealth. A powerful owner of the fifth house in the sixth is an indicator of father's wealth and high position. This location is not good for the longevity of the native's elder brother/sister.

Seventh

The native will have well behaved and successful children who will live abroad and attain an eminent position there. If the owner of the fifth house is a malefic planet, one of the children will die abroad. The number of children will be more than average. The native will have an attractive personality but he will be a Casanova. The native may get married during the sub-periods of the owner of the fifth house in the seventh house and have a devoted wife. If the owner of the first, third or the eleventh house also influences the owner of the fifth house in the seventh, the native will marry the person with whom he was in love. Thus this is a combination for, what is commonly known as, love marriage. His mother will be well educated or may have wealth. A powerful owner of the fifth house in the seventh is an indicator of father's wealth and high position. The native's elder brother/sister is likely to be happily married and will get wealth, comforts and prosperity from marriage. There is every possibility that if the native enters into a business partnership, comparatively the partner would benefit more from it.

Eighth

The native may not marry. If married, the wife of the native will be disobedient, his children, if born, devoid of good qualities and the native will himself be cruel and uncouth. He may not have even an average intellectual calibre. He will lose at speculation or games of chance unlike his mother who is likely to do well at them. He will not have finer instincts. His daughter will be ailing. A younger brother/sister may be born to the native during the major or sub-periods of the owner of the fifth house in the eighth. His younger brother/sister may join the army or become a surgeon or may suffer from an eye ailment during the major or sub-periods of the owner of the fifth house in the eighth.

Ninth

The native will be a highly creative person. He will be proficient in music, poetry and learning. He will attain a high position in life. He will be well thought of by the government. He will be wealthy and will be a person well placed in life. He is likely to have sudden gains in speculation or games of chance, if a beneficial owner of the ninth, Rahu or Mercury also influences this placement. He will be an intellectual or a sincerely religious person. He is likely to write books. His affairs may take a turn for the better after the birth of his first child. His son may have an exceptionally good command over his speech. His younger brother/sister may get married through advertisement in the newspapers. His elder brother/sister may get married during the major or sub-periods of the owner of the fifth house in the ninth house. The native's wife may earn through writing, means of communication or publishing. She can also gain through her younger brother/sister. She will have a wide circle of friends and acquaintances.

Tenth

This is a very good location for the owner of the fifth house as this in itself is equal to a powerful rajyoga. The closer will the owner of the fifth house be to the cusp of the tenth house, the more powerful will the result be. The native will be a gentleman holding a high position under the government successfully. His mother will be happy and feel proud to see him succeed in life. She will get wealth after her marriage. An owner of the fifth house in the tenth house will act as a powerful significator of death for her. Such an owner will also be bad for the health of his children. His children will have troubles caused by their enemies who will be highly placed and powerful people. His wife will be owner of property and will gain through it. She may also get patrimony. Her income can also be from matters related to education. If the owner of the fifth house is adverse in the tenth house, it may indicate death of native's mother-in-law during its major or sub-periods. Such an owner can cause stress in the marriage of native's elder brother/sister. He may become a counsellor, adviser or minister.

Eleventh

The native will be respected by the government and lead a happy and contented life. He will be truthful, and helpful and will have good children. The native may write large books from which he is likely to earn substantially. His father could also be a writer. A child may be born to him in the major or sub-periods of the owner of the fifth house in the eleventh house. He may gain through speculation, entertainment or his ability to advise well. He may, if the nature of the sign in the eleventh house is correct, become a professional counsellor. His children may join him in his business and due to their ability may improve the status of the venture considerably, bringing in gains. For such a location of the owner of the fifth house, whatever has been written for the native will be true for his wife as well.

Twelfth

A beneficial owner of the fifth house here makes the native live abroad. This location indicates that the native will not be happy with regard to his children. The native is liable to have heart or stomach trouble or mental disorder. He may suffer loss of a son if the owner of the fifth house here is afflicted or is a malefic planet for the chart. Such an owner of the fifth house will be inclined to involve the native's wife or partner in serious accidents and cause heavy expenditure for them on illnesses, debt repayments or hospitalisations. He will spend a lot on entertainment and on his children. This is a position which is indicative of dispassion and a spirit of non-attachment in the native. He may be a seeker of the divine and may at the close of life succeed in his quest. This position may make the native ruthless.

SIXTH HOUSE

1. This house refers to the following:
   (i)   Worries, fear of calamities, vices, cruel acts, misunderstanding with elder brother/sister, sin, and humiliation.
   (ii)   Open enemies, danger, thieves, and obstructions.
   (iii) Wounds (caused whether by assault or by fall), disease, food and dietary habits, dysentery, swelling of any part of the body, boils, eye trouble, urinary or venereal disease, colic, gout, exertion, weariness, fall from a boat, death at the hands of an enemy, and fighting in a battle.
   (iv)   Arms and weapons. Sharp edged instruments. Surgery.
   (v)   Step mother. Maternal uncle. Kinsmen and native's relations with them.
   (vi)   Foreigners and people of different faith and culture.
   (vii) Kidneys and intestines. Right part of the chin, right part of the stomach, and right calf depending on the first, second or the third drekkan that contains the cusp of this house.
   (viii) Debt, and receiving charity. Pet animals.

(ix) Competition. Competitive examination.

(x) Untimely meals.

(xi) Poison.

(xii) Service, daily jobs, work, subordinates and servants. Also those acts the native has to do against his wishes.

(xiii) Tenants on native's agricultural land or in his house.

(xiv) Prison.

(xv) Industries, public health, sanitation, and working class.

(xvi) Trance.

2. If the sixth and tenth houses are connected, or their owners are friendly and related to each other in some manner and the owner of the sixth house is powerful, the native follows his father's profession.

3. This house represents the vocation of the native that he adopts to meet his needs, or by the force of circumstances. It is not what he would like to do or a vocation that is ideally suited to his taste.

4. Naturally malefic planets here are strong and give the ability to defeat enemies but are bad for health and make the native struggle in life.

5. The owners of the sixth, eighth and eleventh houses, Mars and Ketu, and their dispositors are planets that are responsible for accidents and injuries.

6. The owner of the sixth house, Saturn and Rahu are significators for illness. The influence of these planets on any house causes disease relating to parts of the body represented by that house. If Saturn becomes the owner of the sixth house it becomes more representative of disease. If Rahu occupies the sixth house of which the Saturn is the owner, such a Saturn is an extremely potent significator of illness.

7. As discussed in the previous paragraph, Saturn and Rahu are significators of disease. The Sun is the karaka for health and represents doctors and physicians. The sixth house is not only representative of disease but also represents weapons (including sharp edged instruments) and surgery. The third and eleventh houses are representative of the arms of the man. The third house represents the right hand, the eleventh the left. Incidentally, if the

third house is more powerful than the eleventh, the man will be right-handed, otherwise left-handed. Now, if a powerful owner of either of the two houses representing arms is related to the sixth house, it shall be indicative of the fact that the native will wield weapons (including sharp edged instruments). Weapons can be used by criminals, uniformed forces, doctors etc. How to distinguish whether the native will be a doctor, criminal or a member of uniformed force etc.? It may be considered in the following manner:

   (a)   If the eighth or the twelfth house is also involved alongwith the above two houses in the relationship, and there is no beneficial influence, the native is likely to be a person who uses weapons to cause death or loss to others. He is therefore likely to be a robber or a murderer.

   (b)   If the relationship of the two houses does not involve the eighth or the twelfth house or if one of these two houses is involved, the relationship has powerful beneficial influence, the native is likely to wield weapons for a good cause and may be in a uniformed service.

   (c)   When the combination mentioned in (b) above also involves the Sun, Saturn and Rahu or at least two of the three, the native will wield weapons for a good cause connected with health and disease. He will be a doctor or a surgeon.

   (d)   When the owner of the sixth house or Mars is more powerful than the planets out of the three listed above which are involved in the combination, the native will be a surgeon, otherwise a physician.

   (e)   Needless to say that a person can only be a doctor or a surgeon if he has had a good education. Therefore, the significators for education and learning, viz., Jupiter and Mercury, should not be weak in the horoscope.

   (f)   If they are weak, the native shall be a rural quack.
         Also see paragraph 9 under SECOND HOUSE above and paragraph 5 under TENTH HOUSE in Chapter Five.

   8. Planets is the sixth, eighth and twelfth houses and planets having sambandha with the owner of the sixth house will also be the significators of diseases.

9. When the first, second, and the eleventh houses have adverse influence and the owner of the sixth house is related to the second house the native incurs heavy expenditure and gets indebted.

10. Mars for Gemini ascendant is a powerful representative of this house as it is also the owner of the eleventh house. If it is located in the fifth house it makes the native suffer from thefts.

11. A powerful and beneficial planet in this house together with Ketu makes the man have mighty enemies. A naturally beneficial planet which is a favourable planet for the chart placed here will tend to increase the number of enemies.

12. Beneficial planets here make a native gain through subordinates, malefic planets indicate losses due to and through them and expenses incurred on them.

13. If the owner of this house is located in the eighth house, and is weak it causes serious physical trouble in its sub-period in the major-period of the weak owner of the second, seventh, eighth, or the twelfth house. Therefore we must be careful when we pronounce good results on the basis of Vipareet Rajyogas involving the owner of the sixth house. See paragraph 26 under the opening remarks.

14. This house refers to disease, the twelfth house to hospitalisation and the eleventh house being twelfth from the twelfth house and sixth from the sixth house refers to recovery from disease.

15. Disease is likely to trouble the native during the period of the planet in this house or the planet in sambandha with the owner of this house.

16. Mercury in this house indicates that the native has fads regarding food, Mars indicates a tendency to overeat, Jupiter here is good for health, Moon shows fondness for liquids and spirits especially if the sign in this house is also a watery one, Venus here shows liking for good food and drink and danger from excesses, and Saturn here leads to malnutrition.

17. For foreign influence eleventh house and Rahu should also be examined. The influence of owners of this and the eleventh

house and Rahu on any house makes the concerned aspect of life have a foreign element in it.

18. Successful raising of loans in favour of the native can only be possible if beneficial planets are connected with the sixth house and its owner.

19.   (a) The affairs of the house, the owner of which joins the owner of the sixth house in the eighth house, will suffer a serious set back in the sub-period of the owner of the concerned house in the major-period of the owner of the sixth house. For example if the owner of the second house joins the owner of the sixth house in the eighth house, then in the sub-period of the owner of the second house and in the major-period of the owner of the sixth house, the native will have serious setback in his affairs pertaining to the second house.

      (b) Similar results can be expected in the sub-period of the owner of a house in the major-period of the owner of the sixth house, in case the owner of the house is located in the sixth house and the owner of the sixth house is placed in the eighth.

20. Following are some combinations for specific ailments:

      (a) (i)   If the owner of sixth house is situated in the first or the eighth house with malefic planets it causes boils.

           (ii) Boils, wounds etc. are also caused by placement of Mars or Ketu in the sixth or the eighth house.

      (b) (i)   If the owner of sixth house is associated with the owner of the first house and the Sun anywhere in the horoscope it causes fever.

           (ii) Fever is also caused if the Sun is placed in the sixth or the eighth house.

      (c) If the owner of sixth house joins the owner of the first and Jupiter it ensures good health for the native, but for a married female native it will indicate illness to her husband.

      (d) If the owners of the first and sixth houses join Venus it signifies illness to wife.

      (e) Conjunction of owners of the first and sixth houses

with Rahu or Ketu causes the native to suffer losses through thefts and he would be prone to danger from snakes.

(f) If the conjunction referred to in (e) above takes place in an angular house it indicates serious throat trouble.

(g) If the owner of the sixth house joins Mars and does not have any beneficial aspect it indicates disease in male genitals.

(h) If the owner of the seventh house joins Venus in the sixth house the wife of the native would be frigid.

(i) If the combination mentioned in (h) above occurs in an angular house it indicates that the native would be imprisoned.

(j) If the owner of the sixth house aspects the first house and Mars is located in the badhakasthan (see details under SEVENTH HOUSE, NINTH HOUSE and ELEVENTH HOUSE in Chapter Five) for that ascendant, it means the native will suffer from occult practices performed against him by his enemies.

(k) If the Sun and the Moon are in the second or the twelfth house and are aspected by Mars and Saturn, the native will suffer from eye trouble. Any of the luminaries in one of these houses aspected by at least one of the two malefic planets referred to above will be able to cause trouble in the concerned eye which is indicated by the location of the luminary. Powerful affliction by these malefic planets may result in loss of sight in the eye. The second house indicates the right eye and the twelfth the left.

(l) Malefic planets occupying or aspecting the houses of sight will cause eye trouble.

(m) The third (right ear) and eleventh houses (left ear) and Jupiter when afflicted by Mars and Saturn will cause troubles in the ears or with hearing.

(n) Mars in, or any malefic influence on, the fifth house will cause trouble in the stomach.

(o) Venus in the sixth, seventh or eighth house will be responsible for troubles in the reproductive or urinary system.

(p) The owner of the sixth house in the seventh or the eighth house; or, the owner of the eighth house in the seventh will cause troubles in the rectum or excretory system.

21. A house aspected or occupied by a naturally malefic planet which is also a malefic planet for the horoscope will cause damage or trouble in that part of the body which is indicated by the concerned house.

22. The rules for determining relationship between the native and a relative of his are recorded in paragraph 32 under FIRST HOUSE. If we wish to determine the relations that are likely to exist between the native and his maternal uncle, or if we wish to know whether the native will like to have pets, we should apply these rules to the sixth house.

23. When the owners of the first and the sixth houses are associated with or have sambandha with Saturn in an angular or triangular house, the native is likely to be imprisoned. Also see paragraph 20 under TWELFTH HOUSE in Chapter Five.

24. Effect of various SIGNS in the Sixth house (A careful study of NOTE in paragraph 38 under FIRST HOUSE will be of use.):

Aries

The native will be susceptible to cold, cough, headache and fever and is liable to get hurt from time to time. He will also have ulcers and boils. The head and forehead will be the vulnerable parts of the body. He should be careful of fire, weapons and poison. He will have violent, combative and rash enemies. His maternal uncle will be indiscreet and a man of quick temper. The native is likely to suffer losses or theft of his material wealth and cattle. Mars, the owner of the sixth is also the owner of the first house. The native will constantly face trouble from enemies and thieves. His children will be wealthy. His wife may face separation from him due to violent and bad behaviour of the native towards her. His father will have a high position which can be with the armed or uniformed forces. This can be further analysed in the manner similar to Scorpio in the first house. He will gain from milch cattle and foreigners or people of other religions, especially Muslims. They will always assist him in his endeavours.

Taurus

The native is best suited to be a surgeon. He will have tenacious enemies. They will become inimical to him because of constant provocation by him. He will be a victim of highway robbers. He will have a strong constitution and will rarely fall ill. The parts of body that are likely to get diseased are gums, throat, eyes, face and the neck. The diseases may become chronic and he will take a long time recovering from them. His maternal uncle will be a well and stockily built person engaged in banking, agriculture or medicine. He will be slow and steady in his job. The owner of the sixth house is Venus, which is also the owner of the eleventh house. The eleventh house is sixth house from the sixth. Therefore eleventh house will also represent those matters that the sixth house represents. Thus Venus is a strong significator for accidents, disease and injuries. Venus will cause injuries, accidents, and diseases in its major or sub-periods. The injuries will be sustained by part of the body or by the relative indicated by the house which is influenced by such a Venus. If Venus is joined by Mars or Ketu, the karaka for injuries, the results will be more pronounced. If Venus is joined by Saturn, the karaka for diseases, the results again will be pronounced in respect of disease. This can be further analysed in the manner similar to Gemini in the first house, and Scorpio in the sixth house. He will be given to overeating and heavy drinking. He is likely to get diseases due to over-indulgent habits of his. He will not be on good terms with his children and relatives.

Gemini

The native will have trouble in his arms and lungs and with his nerves. He will have more than average number of enemies or opponents mostly among females, educated persons or traders. He will keep low company. His maternal uncle will be an intellectual person who will be impractical in worldly affairs and will dissipate his energy in fruitless pursuits. Here Mercury is the owner of the sixth and the ninth houses. This makes Mercury have a strong foreign influence in it. If such a Mercury is closely connected with the seventh house, the native may marry a foreigner or a person who does not belong to his faith, region or caste. The native will travel long distances in connection with his service. If Mercury is powerful the native will do well in service and will have good relations with his subordinates. The wife of the native will have to suffer losses due to her younger brothers/ sisters. She may travel frequently over short distances and stay away from home. A strong Mercury is also conducive to success-ful academic career of native's children. His children will be attached to their family. Mercury under malefic influence will make the native prone to losses due to failure of banks. This can be further analysed in the manner similar to Sagittarius in the sixth house below and Pisces in the ninth house in Chapter Five. If Mercury influences the seventh house with Venus or the Moon, the younger brother or sister of the native will have a female child as the first born. An afflicted Mercury will cause losses to the native through his enemies.

Cancer

His son will be the cause for his enmity with government, politicians, scholars and highly placed persons. The enemies will not be able to harm him physically because they will be timid but they will try to harm him clandestinely. His maternal uncle will be demagogic and may be in a job involving people at large. The son will be handsome and dignified. A weak and badly placed Moon will make the mind of the native sinful and he will contract enmity with females. The native will suffer from digestive dis-turbances and troubles in his chest. A female native may suffer from cysts, tumours and cancer in the breast. There will be imbalance of fluid in the body.

Leo

The native will be prone to heart, stomach and spinal disor-ders, largely due to his hearty and immoderate ways of living. He may also have to suffer from bone trouble. The native will have highly placed enemies. His uncle will be generous and dignified and have impressive appearance who may be partic-ular on family honour. The native will be antagonistic to his maternal uncle and may be instrumental in the death of his brother's daughter. He will have to suffer loss of wealth due to women. He will be antagonistic to his relatives, people in gov-ernment or highly placed individuals.

Virgo

The native will have no enemies worth the name but he will squander his wealth over women of easy virtue or prostitutes. He will not be steady in his job, will change it from time to time and strive to be self employed. Due to his sense of independence he cannot work for anybody and will come into conflict with his superior. The native will be highly strung. He will suffer from ulcers, and stomach disorders. He will prefer to stay away from home. His maternal uncle will be slim and of fault finding nature who will show interest and ability in study of languages. The owner of the sixth here is also the owner of the third house. The native will be reserved with his younger brother/sister. This can be further analysed in the manner similar to Gemini in the third house.

Libra

The native will be involved in disputes with his brothers over division of wealth. He will try to have good relations with his subordinates and colleagues. He will prefer a job like marketing, that puts him in touch with a large number of people. His stomach and eyes will be liable to have troubles due to his excessive life style. He may also have troubles in his genitals and part of his lower abdomen below the navel. He may have enemies among people in the field of fine arts or entertainment. He may have some female enemies. His maternal uncle will be handsome and fond of good living, he may keep a good and luxurious house and he will prefer a peaceful and harmonious existence. The owner of the sixth is Venus here which is also the owner of the first house. This can be analysed in the manner similar to Taurus in the first house.

Scorpio

The native will suffer from diseases in the excretory, and reproductive systems. He will work much harder than usual and come in conflict with his subordinates due to his exacting nature and over insistence on discipline. There will be partition of property and discord over it. His enemies will be violent persons given to extremism, immoderate living, alcohol and other vices. His maternal uncle will be hard hearted, hard working person who will set high goals for himself and then set about achieving them. The uncle may therefore be a tough task master. The native will be in danger from poisonous reptiles and insects, persons who carry tales, wild animals and thieves. The owner of the sixth is Mars here which is also the owner of the eleventh house. This can be analysed in the manner similar to Taurus above and Gemini in the first house.

Sagittarius

The native will trap animals. He may suffer from diseases of the liver and pancreas. He can also have troubles in his thighs and hips and parts of the body in that region. He will be forthright with his subordinates and persons who come in contact with him. His way of talking without mincing words sometimes offends people. He may take up a profession concerned with teaching, the legal field or the stage. He may travel in connection with his job but would be the happiest at home. His maternal uncle will be a truthful and just person who will be very frank in his opinions which many a time people may not like. Jupiter is the owner of the sixth and the ninth houses. His wife may travel over short distances frequently and stay away from home. She may work in a hospital or asylum. His children will do well in their schools and at examinations and will be wealthy in life. This can be further analysed in the manner similar to Gemini above.

Capricorn

The native will have differences with his well wishers over money. He will have problems with his bones, knees, skin, gums and teeth. He will have to work hard at his job to attain success. His enemies will be men of wealth. His maternal uncle will be a prudent, hard working and thrifty man who will have an urge to do well in life. The uncle will be reserved who will give an impression that he does not care for his relatives. The owner of the sixth house is Saturn which is here also the owner of the seventh house. This will make the wife the of the native shun company and live in seclusion. Saturn is the karaka for illness. It is also the owner of the house of illness. It thus becomes a very powerful factor for causing illness. If it is badly located in the second or eighth house it is certain to cause physical troubles in its major or sub-periods.

Aquarius

The native will spend money over wells, matters relating to water, flowers etc. He will suffer from hypertension, heart trouble, and troubles in shins and joints. His enemies will be highly placed persons. He will face danger from water and creatures that live in water. His maternal uncle will be handsome and involved in group and social affairs. The owner of the sixth here is also the owner of the fifth house. A powerful owner of the sixth house well placed in the chart will raise his father to a high position late in life. His mother will be extravagant. The first child will keep indifferent health and will be quiet. The children of the native will earn well if Saturn is located in the sixth house.

Pisces

The native will be highly self centred and this will lead to disharmony with wife, children and other relatives and friends. Such discord is also likely over women. He will have trouble with his back, and feet. He may have oedema. At work the native will prefer to be his own master in the form of a partnership where he can express his creativity. His maternal uncle will be a mild hearted, impractical and visionary sort of a person. Jupiter being the owner of the sixth is also the owner of the third house. His father will have a powerful position in service. His elder brother/sister may not have any children or may lose a child. This can be further analysed in the manner similar to Sagittarius in the third house.

25. Effect of the owner of the Sixth House in various houses (A careful study of the opening notes from A to H in paragraph 39 under FIRST HOUSE will be of utmost use.):

First

The native may join a uniformed service or a gang of thieves. He will be talkative. His maternal uncle will be prominent in his life. If the owner of the sixth house is friendly with the owner of the first, the relations between the native and his maternal uncle will be cordial. He will be healthy and rich but will cause trouble to his family members and expect favours from others. This may make the native's wife separate from him, may be because of her sensual nature and infidelity. An afflicted owner of the sixth house here makes the native get hurt by explosives, weapons, suffer from piles or boils or from enemies. The owner of the sixth in the first house causes a lot of trouble to the native, loss of wealth occurs and even friends turn into enemies in its major or sub-periods. A powerful owner of the sixth house, in the first house will be good for the native's father who will either do religious, pious and devotional deeds or may get a high position in life and wealth through writing or speculation.

Second

The native will study at good institutions, and be rich, and clever but he will not keep good health and will be of bad mentality. He will suffer from troubles in his eyes, especially in the right eye, particularly so if the Sun or the Moon is also either weak or afflicted;and, from diseases of the face, mouth or throat. The native will have to spend on his treatment, his family will face troubles and his enemies will increase and try to harm him. His father will be in service who will try to rise in his career and increase his wealth by adopting unscrupulous methods. His elder brother/sister may lose his wealth during the major or sub-periods of the owner of the sixth in the second house. The native too during this period will face an eroding bank balance and indebtedness. This location is bad for the longevity of native's wife. If the owner of the sixth house is weak, afflicted and has no beneficial influence here, the wife of the native will be rich and rise high in life. The native may keep pets.

Third

It will cause, in its major or sub-periods a lot of trouble to his younger brothers and sisters and the father of the native may die during this period. It will detract from the status and power of the native. Differences of opinion and quarrels will go against him and cause loss. He will be of bad conduct. His elder brother/sister may not have any children or may lose a child or more during the major or sub-periods of owner of the sixth house in the third. The native's wife can travel abroad during this period

or she may join a religious institution and live in seclusion there.
Paragraphs 6 and 7 under the Sixth House should also be usefully
studied for determining the career the native is likely to take up
if the third, or the eleventh house is connected with the sixth.

Fourth

The native will not have college education or it may have
several breaks in it. He and his father will always be at loggerheads. The father will also keep bad health. The native will get
patrimony but he may waste it and his debtors may claim that
property. Most of these results will be felt during the major or
sub-periods of the owner of the sixth house. He will also keep
pets. His mind will be disturbed and he will be attracted to a way
of life which will not have the approval of the society. His mother
will be close to his maternal uncle provided the owner of the sixth
house is friendly with the owner of the fourth. The maternal
uncle will be an agriculturist. The native may not like to meet
with all and sundry. His reserved nature may harm him in his
career. The domestic life will not be comfortable and his servants
will be a bothersome lot. If the owner of the sixth house is weak,
afflicted and has no beneficial influence here, the elder brother/
sister of the native will be rich and rise high in life.

Fifth

A malefic owner of the sixth house here causes discord
between the native and his children or father to the extent that
they may be the cause of death of the native. If the owner is a
beneficial planet, it will cause loss of wealth and make the native
unreliable and of bad conduct. The native will not hesitate to take
loans to gamble. His spouse will be extravagant. His children will
be sickly though they will earn well through their own efforts.
His younger brother/sister will keep changing his residence. A
powerful owner of the sixth house will ensure that the native's
father becomes a wealthy and powerful person.

Sixth

An afflicted owner of the sixth house here makes the native
get hurt by explosives or weapons or suffer from piles or boils

but the native will be wealthy and have a good position in society. The native will create a number of enemies for himself and he will reside at an unpleasant place. He will be of strong constitution, will remain generally healthy, happy and will be miserly. The maternal uncle of the native and his enemies will be long-lived. A powerful owner of the sixth house in the sixth will make the father of the native hold a good position in life.

Seventh

The native is likely to marry within his mother's or father's family. A malefic owner of the sixth house here makes the wife of the native cruel hearted and of bad conduct. She will always oppose the native and cause discord in the family. If the seventh house has a common sign, the marriage will be a failure, the native will separate from his wife and remarry. If the owner is a naturally beneficial planet the wife will be barren or she will repeatedly miscarry. The wife will be ailing and not be long-lived. The native may have extra-marital affairs. The owner of the sixth house here may cause disease in the genitals or rectum of the native.

Eighth

The planet, which is the owner of the sixth house, placed here will be the principal cause of death. The owner of the sixth house here may cause disease in the genitals or the rectum. If it is the Sun, the native will be killed by a tiger or a wild animal; if it is the Moon, he will have an early death; if it is Mars, by poison or by the bite of a poisonous creature; if it is Mercury, by poison; if it is Jupiter, due to his own perverse thinking; if it is Venus, the native will suffer from eye disease; and, if it is Saturn, due to dysentery or digestive disorders. If the owner of the sixth house is strong and well placed here, the native will have good longevity, if not, he may be morally degraded and unhelpful. If the owner of the sixth house is weak, afflicted and has no beneficial influence here, the native will be rich and rise high in life but will face serious setback to his health during the major or sub-periods of owner of the second, sixth, seventh, eighth or the twelfth house.

Ninth

The native will be lame, and on bad terms with his relatives and younger brother/sister if the owner of the sixth house is a malefic planet. He will not have faith in God. If it is a beneficial planet the native will escape the above fate but will be poor. His affairs will be harmed by his enemies. A powerful owner of the sixth house in the ninth house will make the native's father obtain a high position in judicial or administrative service. It will also make his maternal uncle prosperous and affluent. The native will be helped by his maternal uncle in case the owner of the sixth is a friend of the owner of the ninth house, if not, the maternal uncle will cause harm to his interests. The native is not likely to be on good terms with his father.

Tenth

An afflicted or malefic owner of the sixth house here makes the native get hurt by explosives or weapons or suffer from piles or boils. He may be in service. He will be cruel hearted and given to committing crimes. He may incur the wrath of the government. He will not have good relations with his mother. She might have had more than one marriage. He is not likely to have wealth and property and if he does have it, it will gradually be destroyed, or get involved in litigation. If the owner is a beneficial planet for the chart, he will be kindly inclined to his father but will be inimical to others. His children will be poorly off and may be burdened with debts. They will also be in service. If the owner of the sixth house is weak, afflicted and has no beneficial influence here, the elder brother/sister of the native will be rich and rise high in life. A favourable owner of the sixth house will ensure success to the native in competitions or elections.

Eleventh

The native may be in service. If the owner is a malefic planet for the chart, the native will be killed by his enemy and will suffer losses through thefts. If the owner is a beneficial planet for the chart he will be able to overcome his enemies, and earn through cattle. A favourable owner of the sixth house will ensure success to the native in competitions or elections. He will not be on good terms with his elder brother/sister. The elder brother/sister may keep poor health. He may gain through his maternal uncle. He may be in a uniformed service, employed in a factory, engaged in a garage or may earn his livelihood as a surgeon or doctor. The owner of the sixth house strongly placed in the eleventh house will ensure the prosperity of the younger brother/sister and make them learned. Such an owner is also good for the longevity of his mother. The native may have some trouble from his children who may also suffer from bad health.

Twelfth

The native will spend on cattle or he may suffer losses due to cattle. He is likely to meet his end on the way on a journey. He may earn abroad. He may not have a high moral standard. The native will not have much trouble from enemies and in raising loans. His maternal uncle will prosper. A weak and afflicted owner of the sixth in the twelfth house without any beneficial inf uence is likely to raise the native high in life. His mother may be a good writer or highly religious. She may travel a lot. His chil ren will accumulate wealth and may come about legacies. His ather may have property, houses and vehicles from the governm nt and his residence may contain his place of work.

Chapter Five

HOUSES
(Seventh to Twelfth)

The rules that generally apply to all the houses have been recorded exhaustively in the opening remarks in Chapter Four. Reference may be made to them whenever required. Matters pertaining to the seventh to twelfth houses have been dealt with exclusively in this Chapter.

SEVENTH HOUSE

1. This house refers to the following:
    - (i) Marriage. Partner. This house stands for long term relationships unlike the fifth house which indicates passing fancies and infatuations.
    - (ii) Legal ties.
    - (iii) Sexual intercourse. Success in love affairs.
    - (iv) Reproductive fluid. Genitals. Urine. Also the face, navel or feet according to the drekkan in which the cusp of the house lies.
    - (v) Journeys. Losing ones way on a journey. Break in journey, visit to several places during the same journey and places abroad.
    - (vi) Honour and reputation abroad. Generosity. Respect.
    - (vii) Danger to longevity.

(viii) Loss of memory.

(ix)   Trade. International trade. Contract, and agreement.

(x)   Partnership. People with whom the native deals with. Opponents, rivals, adversaries, and the opposite party in a law suit.

(xi)   Eating delicious food. Sweet drink.

(xii) Gift. Giving in charity.

(xiii) Adopted child. Second child (this house being the third from the fifth house, indicates younger brother/sister to the eldest child of the native).

(xiv) Third younger brother/sister to the native (first younger brother/sister to the native being indicated by the third house, the second by the fifth house being third from the third).

(xv)   Honour and credit of the Government (being the tenth from the tenth house).

(xvi) Badhakasthan for the ascendants having common signs.

2. In Horary Astrology the seventh house should be examined for a query relating to lost property. This house describes the thief. The first house of Prasna (query) chart represents the owner of lost property, the fourth the place of property, and the seventh the thief. If the owner of the seventh house or its occupier is weak or combust, it can be predicted that the thief would be apprehended.

3. Rahu or Ketu here makes the native psychically sensitive. This location of these shadowy planets can cause abnormalities in native's relationships.

4. As a general rule planets, except Jupiter or a well placed Moon, in this house are not conducive to smooth personal relationship. Mercury causes the relationship to be quick or superficial; Venus makes the nature sensual; Mars causes conflict but gives power; Saturn also tends to give power though it causes separation, selfishness and detachment, and the Sun gives a tendency to dominate.

5. Any relationship of Mars with Venus, the seventh house and its owner makes the native oversexed. The same result can be expected if there is an exchange or close relationship between the

seventh house and the twelfth. Participation of the fifth house in these relationships aggravates matters further.

6. It should be seen as to which planet is the most powerful among the owners of the second, seventh and the eleventh houses. Such a planet is likely to not only describe the spouse but also in its major or sub-periods give marriage.

7. If the Sun is the owner of this house one gets married at the age of 25 years. For the Moon it is 21, Mars, Mercury and Venus tend to make the native set married by the age of 20 years. Jupiter 24, and Saturn 29 years. This is true for male nativities. For a female horoscope each of these values should be reduced by 3 years. These are subject to the following amendments:

  (a) Whenever a malefic planet for the chart occupies the house, or gets in sambandha with the owner of the seventh house or the karaka for the spouse (Venus for the male and Jupiter for female nativities), marriage is delayed by two years. For every such malefic influence, two years should be added to the probable age of marriage.

  (b) If beneficial planets for the chart are associated or they aspect the above factors, marriage is hastened by the same number of years as are indicated above.

  (c) It is repeated that for each factor so influenced the number of years mentioned above have to be added or substracted as the case may be.
  This is a rough method. The age worked out in this manner should then be verified by the Vimshottari Dasa system.

8. The time of marriage can be determined through transit by the use of following rules, once the major, sub and inter-periods have been determined in which marriage is likely to take place:

  (i) Add the longitudes of owners of the first and the seventh houses. Marriage is likely when Jupiter transits the point so obtained.

  (ii) Marriage is likely when Jupiter transits the point obtained by adding the longitudes of the owners of the house in which the Moon is located and the seventh house.

  (iii) Marriage is likely during the major or sub-period of a powerful owner of the seventh house when Jupiter transits the sign in which the owner is situated or through the houses which are triangular to it.

(iv) Marriage is likely during the major or sub-period of a powerful owner of the navansha in which the owner of the seventh house is located when Jupiter transits the sign in which the owner of the navansha is situated in the birth chart or through the houses which are triangular to it.

(v) Marriage is likely during the major or sub-period of the Moon or Venus, whichever is more powerful, when Jupiter transits the sign in which the owner of the seventh house is situated or through the houses which are triangular to it.

(vi) Marriage is likely during the major or sub-period of the owner of the seventh house which is associated with Venus or if the two planets are in sambandha with each other in any other manner.

(vii) Marriage is likely during the major or sub-period of a planet in the seventh house which is associated with the owner of that house.

(viii) Marriage is likely when Jupiter and the Moon transit the sign next to the one in which the dispositor in navansha chart of the owner of the first house is located. For example let Mercury be the owner of the first house in a nativity. Let it be placed in Leo in the navansha chart. Let the Sun be in Pisces in the birth chart. Marriage can take place when Jupiter transits Aries alongwith the Moon.

(ix) Marriage is likely when Jupiter transits the sign in which the owner of the seventh house or Venus is situated.

(x) Marriage is likely when in transit Jupiter is in an angular house and the Moon joins it there.

9. (a) Early marriage is indicated if the owners of the first and seventh houses are linked.

(b) If the owner of the seventh house is placed in a sign owned by Venus or Saturn and is aspectd by a naturally beneficial planet which is also favourable for the chart, the native will have liaison with many women or will have more than one wife. The same result may be expected if the owner of the seventh house is exalted.

(c)　The native will have several wives if the owner of the seventh house is powerful and Venus is placed in Gemini, Sagittarius or Pisces.

(d)　The native may marry more than once due to some wish of his remaining unfulfilled, such as not having a child or a male issue, if:

(i)　the owner of the seventh house is placed in the sign of a naturally malefic planet which is also an adverse planet for the chart, is associated with a planet that is adverse for the chart, and the seventh house in the birth or navansha chart has a sign owned by Mercury or Saturn; or,

(ii)　the owner of the seventh house is debilitated, and the seventh house in the birth or navansha chart has a sign owned by Mercury or Saturn.

10. A naturally malefic planet which is also an adverse planet for the chart, in the first, second, fourth, seventh, eighth or the twelfth house will disturb the married life and may make the wife short lived. This will be neutralised if the spouse's horoscope also has a similar malefic planet in one of these houses.

11. If the owner of the seventh house in a male chart is a planet that denotes aristocracy, e. g. the Sun or Moon, and is influenced by a beneficial planet for the chart, which is indicative of worth, e. g. Jupiter, or the owner of the second or eleventh house, the man marries into a high class family.

12. If the seventh house, its owner and the karaka (Jupiter for the husband and Venus for the wife) are influenced by separative planets it indicates a divorce.

13. The native will gain financially from his wife if the owner of the seventh house and Venus in a male chart are in sambandha in the fifth, seventh or the eleventh house.

14. When the second, seventh, and the eleventh houses are connected with beneficial planets for the chart, it would mean that not only the partner would be from a respectable family but that the married life would be happy and the partner would be virtuous.

15. The wife will be long lived if the owner of the seventh house and Venus are strong in a male chart.

16. If Jupiter is the owner of the seventh and tenth houses and is powerful, it means that the native will enjoy ruling powers and will be in the good books of the government (the seventh house is tenth from the tenth house).

17. This house is the badhakasthan for ascendants having common signs. During the major or sub-period of a planet owning the badhakasthan, or of a planet occupying the badhakasthan, the native may suffer from bad health or there may be anxiety about his health. Badhakadhipati (the owner of the house that is a badhakasthan for the ascendant) is not bad for other aspects of life.

18. Good aspect to the occupier or the cusp of this house indicates good relations with persons indicated by this house. So this house is also to be referred to if it is to be examined whether a person can mix freely in company.

19. If the cusp of the seventh house is in the first drekkan of a sign alongwith malefic planets, the native is to have deformed and bad teeth. The rule of the thumb would therefore be that if a person has bad teeth it is likely that his spouse would be sickly, troublesome or short lived.

20. A movable sign in the seventh house will let the native earn through his reputation.

21. The rules for determining relationship between the native and a relative of his are recorded in paragraph 32 under FIRST HOUSE in Chapter Four. If we wish to determine the relations that are likely to exist between the native and his wife, we should apply these rules to the seventh house.

22. The owner of the seventh house from the ascendant or from the Moon when placed in the vargas of a naturally beneficial planet and aspected also by naturally beneficial planets is indicative of the fact that the native will have a beautiful wife.

23. Effect of various SIGNS in the Seventh House (A careful study of NOTE in paragraph 38 under FIRST HOUSE in Chapter Four will be of use.):

Aries

This sign in the seventh house makes the native commit bad deeds if Mars is weak or afflicted. He may be impotent. His wife may be badly behaved, ill tempered and greedy. She would not be the right match for the native. He may marry more than once. He will be miserly and fickle minded. The first house for the wife of the native also has the first sign. Therefore if a sign is afflicted that part of the wife's body represented by that house will either have trouble or defect. Mars, the owner of the seventh house, is also the owner of the second house. If it is powerful the wife will be long lived. Mars will be the significator of death for the native. If it is placed in an adverse house, i. e., the sixth, eighth or the twelfth house, it will cause much physical trouble to the native. This can be further analysed in the manner similar to Scorpio and Taurus in the second house as given in Chapter Four.

Taurus

The wife of the native will be house-proud, well behaved and will earn independently. She will be good looking. She will handle money wisely. The native and his wife will enjoy socialising. The owner of the seventh house is Venus here, which is also the owner of the twelfth house. This sets up a link between the first and the sixth house for the spouse of the native and will therefore cause illnesses or trouble from enemies to the spouse in its major or sub-periods especially if the owner is afflicted or badly placed. A powerful Venus is excellent for the longevity of the children and wife. This can be further analysed, with regard to wife, in the manner similar to Taurus in the first house in Chapter Four. The native will be sensual. His second child may be sickly. The native is prone to suffer losses in a partnership.

Gemini

The native will have a fair, learned, good tempered and wealthy wife. She will be engaged in intellectual pursuits and will be of independent nature. If there is inadequate communication between the two married partners it may lead to an early break down of married life. Influence of separative planets on the seventh house, its owner and significator of spouse (Jupiter or

Venus as the case may be) will cause an early separation between the two. The spouse will leave the native and live elsewhere. The owner of the seventh house is also the owner of the tenth house. An afflicted Mercury will make the spouse mentally disturbed. A powerful Mercury will confer authority and respect on the native and property on the wife. She will be close to her mother. His maternal uncle may be an eloquent person. His second child may get associated with the government due to his intellectual attainments. The native's father will be wealthy if Mercury is strong and well placed.

Cancer

The spouse will be kind hearted, sentimental, sensual, handsome and changeable. The native will marry more than once or will have serious liaisons. The Moon if powerful and away from the Sun will ensure a long living spouse. The Moon, if related to the sixth or the eleventh house will make the spouse much interested in sex. Such a Moon related to the fifth house will make the native have love affairs. If the owner of the first, third or the eleventh house is also involved, out of these love affairs his marriage will emerge. The native will be attracted to mother figure and will seek maternal traits in his wife. His mother will have serious mental troubles if the Moon is badly placed and weak. His father will have varying income and may have more elder sisters than brothers.

Leo

The spouse will be impressive to look at and if the Sun is powerful she will be from a family higher than the native's. She will be hard hearted and hard working. The spouse will be dominating, career oriented, tough but generous. The native will have to be careful in dealing with his spouse otherwise there may be tension in domestic life. The native's father will gain from the government if the Sun is strong and well placed. His maternal uncle will not be rich. The native will try to enter into partnership with highly placed persons.

Virgo

The spouse will be soft spoken, kind hearted and learned but she will be finicky and critical of others. The second child of the native will have proficiency or interest in languages. The native will be changeable in his affections and he may have more than one marriage. The owner of the seventh here is also the owner of the fourth house. The spouse will therefore be connected with the government. His younger brother/sister may benefit from speculation or games of chance or may have eloquence or musical talent. A strong and well placed Mercury will make the maternal uncle of the native very wealthy. This can be further analysed in the manner similar to Gemini in the fourth house in Chapter Four.

Libra

The spouse of the native will be cultured, elegant and handsome. She will like to collect expensive but artistic items. She will be fond of jewellery, perfumes and good things of life. The spouse will be passionate, generous and loyal and will work for domestic peace. Venus, the owner of the seventh house here is also the owner of the second house. Venus is, therefore, a powerful significator of death for the native. The nature of death of the native will depend on the influence Venus receives in the chart. In a male chart a powerful Venus will ensure long and healthy life for the wife of the native since Venus is the owner of the first and the eighth houses for the wife of the native as counted from the seventh house and also the significator for wife. The native may earn his wealth through partnership. He will have good meals. This can be further analysed in the manner similar to Taurus in the second house in Chapter Four.

Scorpio

The spouse of the native will be argumentative, jealous and of quick temper. He will also have weakness for women. The native will have to be careful in communicating with him otherwise there is likelihood of separation. The owner of the seventh here is also the owner of the twelfth house. If Mars is weak the native will have to spend substantially on his spouse and the spouse would be sickly. If Mars is connected with the fourth house the spouse may be a surgeon in a hospital, since the fourth house is the tenth as counted from the seventh house indicating profession or service. Here Mars is significator of two houses namely the seventh and the twelfth houses, which are representative of sex urge and pleasures. If Mars influences the fourth house and the Moon, sex will be uppermost in the mind of the native. If Mars influences the fifth house and Venus, the native will be oversexed, he will have love affairs and he will get married to one of his beloveds. If Mars is powerful the children of the native especially the first born, will be long lived and healthy. This can be further analysed in the manner similar to Aries in the twelfth house.

Sagittarius

The spouse will be courageous but not very intelligent. She will be loving, accommodating and good natured. She will be talented and will have good self control. The owner of the seventh house is Jupiter here which is also the owner of the tenth house. The native will gain from the government, and if Jupiter has relationship with the first house through aspect or occupation, the native will occupy a high government position. Jupiter, being the karaka for husband, will in a female chart be a prominent significator of husband. If Jupiter is powerful, the husband will be long lived and healthy. He will be a teacher, lawyer or a religious preacher. If Jupiter has connection with the fourth house, the spouse will be in government service. A powerful Jupiter is a clear indication that the father of the native will be wealthy and will earn without much effort since Jupiter is the significator for wealth and is the owner of the second and eleventh houses here as counted from the ninth. This can be further analysed in the manner similar to Pisces in the tenth house.

Capricorn

The spouse of the native will be greedy, hard hearted and unreliable, but he will be hard working and a person of the world. The native will marry late in life. The spouse will be taciturn and will avoid company. The difference in age between the native and his spouse will be big. The spouse will be from an ordinary family and will look up to the native for guidance. However the family of the spouse will continue to have a prominent place in the life of the spouse. The owner of the seventh house is Saturn which also owns the eighth house. If Saturn is powerful the native's spouse will be long lived, rich and hard working. The elder brothers/sisters of the native will gain in property matters through him and undertake short journeys for educational purposes. The spouse will talk little but rudely. A weak Saturn will make the native sickly.

Aquarius

The spouse will be highly religious, forthright, attached to the native and known for her good behaviour. Also, the spouse will be handsome and involved in community or group activities. If Saturn is weak the spouse will be sickly since the owner of the sixth here is also the owner of the seventh house and may be hospitalised for chronic ailments. The relationship with the opposite sex can also be Platonic for intellectual and companionship reasons. The spouse can be from a family lower in status than the native's and much senior to him in age. The native's maternal uncle may be rich. The native will not be successful in partnership and may fall sick or face other troubles in journeys.

Pisces

The native will be the happiest if the spouse looks up to him for guidance and support. He will be talented and will have good self control. The spouse can be a foreigner who would be an artist or an intellectual. She may not be worldly wise and will be sentimental. The spouse will be indiscreet. The children of the native will not be well behaved, and they will cause unhappiness to him. Jupiter being the significator for husband in a female nativity is also the owner of the seventh house. It therefore represents husband doubly. Influence of separating planets on Jupiter will work for separation of the native from him, and if Ketu or a planet having its mooltrikona sign in the sixth eighth or twelfth house aspects or is associated with it the husband will be short lived. If these planets also influence the seventh house in addition to Jupiter the indications recorded above will be further confirmed. The owner of the seventh house here is also the owner of the fourth house. The mother of the native will be close to the spouse of the native and the spouse may have an independent profession. There will be serious hindrances in the undertakings of the father of the native and his ambitions will be fulfilled with great difficulty. The native's children will live at a short distance from him in a different town. The younger brothers/sisters of the native will gain through their children.

24. Effect of the owner of the seventh house in various HOUSES (A careful study of the opening notes from A to H in paragraph 39 under FIRST HOUSE in Chapter Four will be of utmost use.):

First

The native will have liaison with other women besides his wife or he may marry more than once. He will be sensual and love his wife dearly. He may marry someone whom he knew since childhood. The wife will have all comforts and will be of good conduct. He will have successful partnerships and goodwill of the government. If the owner of the seventh house is friendly with the owner of the first, the native's spouse will be very attached to him and helpful in his progress. When the owner of the seventh house is placed in the first house, one of native's brother will settle down abroad and will help him. The native's second child and the children of his younger brother/sister will be long lived and will prosper well in life. His maternal uncle will be wealthy. His mother may have property and may lead a comfortable and peaceful life.

Second

A malefic owner of the seventh house in the second house is indicative of the fact that the wife of the native will be bad tempered and will waste native's money. A beneficial or friendly owner of the seventh in the second house will ensure that the native gets wealth through his wife or marriage. She will either not have children or have only daughters inspite of her desire for a son. She will be rich. If the owner of the seventh house is a friend of the owner of the second house, the native's wife will get along well with the family of the native, and she will cook according to the native's taste. There will be separation from wife for long periods. The native may marry more than once. He will get wealth through partnership. The owner of the seventh house when powerfully placed in the second house, will make the second child of the native or his wife, depending upon the strength of the karakas, live long. The native's mother will have vehicles and comforts and she may have income from property. His children will be self made and will be in a profession that involves writing.

Third

The native will be friendly with and kind to his brothers/sisters, neighbours and colleagues. He may get married through advertising in the newspapers. His wife will be beautiful and from a good and wealthy family but if the owner of the seventh house is a malefic planet, she will not like him and may even have liaison with his brother, neighbour, friend or his colleague. The native may marry more than once. His wife will be a major influence on his religious beliefs. If the owner of the seventh house is friendly to the owner of the ninth house, the native's spouse will like his father and will be a help to the native in his progress in life. The spouse will prosper after marriage. A naturally beneficial planet owning the seventh house which is also a beneficial planet for the chart, when placed in the third house may make the spouse religious. There is danger of loss of a child. His children, particularly the first child, will earn their livelihood by writing. His elder brother/sister will have good and fortunate children, and if other indications support, the elder brother/sister may have wealth earned through entertainment or speculation.

Fourth

The native may study abroad. He may do well at collegiate studies. If the owner of the seventh house is a male planet and is located in the fourth house it indicates that the native will get married with difficulty and he will have extra marital relations. An owner of the seventh house that is friendly with the owner of the fourth house will ensure that the wife of the native will have cordial relations with his mother. The native will speak harshly, he will not like his father but the wife of the native will look after his father well. The wife may leave the native from time to time and live at her father's house. There will be a marked improvement in comforts in native's life after his marriage and he may get vehicles and property from it. This location of the owner of the seventh house also indicates that the native will serve under a female boss and will do well in his profession. He may travel during the major or sub-periods of the owner of the seventh house. His father will be wealthy and will be well liked due to his soft and dignified speech. His first child will travel a lot in connection with his job. His mother may have mental trouble if the owner of the seventh house is afflicted and weak. The native may so in for partnership in business in property or vehicles.

Fifth

The native may marry late and may have difficulty in having children. The wife of the native will love her children dearly but may not like him. She will advise the native on important matters. She will predecease him. She will have her independent source of income and her ambitions will be fulfilled. The native is likely to marry his beloved if the owner of the first, third or the eleventh house is also involved, or may have several long standing love affairs. His children will like to write and will be good at it. They will also be self made. The native will be courageous, tough minded and fortunate. He will have good business acumen and will have comforts and vehicle through partnership and business. He may have successful business partnership with a female or his mother. He may be close to powerful people. Women at high positions will be kind to him. His father will find sources of income without much effort and his income will be only through rightful means. His elder sister/brother will find that his status in life improves considerably after his marriage.

Sixth

The native may not get married, if married his wife may be ailing or there may be unhappy married life. He may marry a cousin, a foreigner or someone who is from an entirely different region or cultural background. The native may, if the owner of the seventh house is weak and badly placed in the sixth house, suffer from disease in the genitals and may not be able to have sexual intercourse. There may be separation from wife due to interference in affairs by the maternal uncle of the native. The maternal uncle may be wealthy but the owner of the seventh house is a significator of death and will therefore, during its major or sub-periods, will pose danger to his longevity. During this period the native may have to face law suits causing debts to him. If the owner is a naturally beneficial planet, it becomes a maraka for the native and the cause of death could be women. The native may contract tuberculosis from a woman. His children will accumulate wealth by their own efforts or may earn by writing. His younger brother/sister may be very intelligent. His elder brother/sister may find life difficult.

Seventh

The native and his wife will have all the happiness and comforts of married life and will have excellent children. He will be long lived. His partnership will prosper and he may occupy a high position in government. He will be known for his good conduct. The native will have an attractive personality for the opposite sex. His brother/sister will be intelligent, god-fearing, well placed in life and happy with their children. His mother will be happy and comfortable. The native's children will be capable of writing learned and large works on travel, law or philosophical subjects. They will be religious. A powerful owner of the seventh house influenced favourably by beneficial planets will, in its major or sub-periods, give the native riches from abroad and status. A weak and afflicted owner on the other hand will be dangerous to the native's social standing, health and well being.

Eighth

The native may not get married and prefer the company of loose women. If he does get married, he is likely to get monetary benefit from it. He will be unhappy, and worried. Long journeys will not be happy and beneficial to him. His partner, second child or his wife will earn well. If the owner is a beneficial planet he will look after his wife well. The native's mother will be happy and pleased with life. A weak or afflicted owner of the seventh house in the eighth will cause the spouse of the native to meet with an accident, fall fatally sick or may be dishonoured. It may also cause mental illness to the mother of the native. His first child may change his residence. His younger sister/brother will lose at speculation or may fail or do badly at qualifying or departmental examinations at which he had appeared.

Ninth

The native and his wife will be well behaved and good persons. The native will prosper after his marriage. The wife of the native will be attached to her brothers/sisters, and neighbours. If the owner is a malefic planet she will be ugly and badly behaved or he will be impotent. The spouse may indulge in unnatural sex practices. The native may form partnership with younger sister/brother of his wife. If the owner of the seventh house is a friend of the owner of the ninth house, the native's spouse will be affectionate towards his father. The native may, if the twelfth house is also involved, travel overseas and benefit by these visits. He will also undertake journeys for religious purposes. His wife will be responsible for good or adverse relations of the native with his younger sister/brother. If the owner of the seventh house is a malefic planet for the ascendant or is weak and afflicted, the native's father may pass away in its major or sub-periods. A well placed and powerful owner of the seventh house will be conducive to progress and prosperity of the father.

Tenth

If the owner of the seventh house is a malefic planet, the native will be punished and persecuted by the government; the father-in-law of the native will not be a gentleman and will misbehave with him, and his partners will bother him. The owner of the seventh house that is a naturally beneficial planet, or a beneficial planet for the ascendant and powerfully placed in the tenth house will give the native honour and repute, and benefits from abroad. His profession will involve much travelling. The native is likely to get house and conveyances due to his profession and standing with powers that be. The spouse will be learned and on the basis of his accomplishments may establish his independent source of income. The native's eldest child may develop disease in his ear during the major or sub-periods of the owner of the seventh house in the tenth. His wife may be self-willed.

Eleventh

The wife of the native will be beautiful and devoted to him. The native will gain through his wife and partnership. He is likely to have good children but will have more female children than male. There can be loss of children. There will be a touch of sensuality in the native. His first child will have a dominant spouse. The native's spouse will be good at matters pertaining to entertainment and fine arts and may earn through these matters. If the owner of the seventh house is friendly to the owner of the fifth, the spouse will be very attached to her children. A strong owner of the seventh house in the eleventh is indicative of the fact that the native's sisters/brothers will be fortunate and will prosper well in life.

Twelfth

This is not a good location for marital life of the native. If the karaka for the spouse is weak and afflicted and the owner of the seventh house is afflicted and badly placed in the twelfth house, the native's spouse is likely to either pass away early (if maraka planets or an adverse Planet having its mooltrikona sign in the sixth, eighth or twelfth house or Ketu is involved), or there might be a separation. With this location of the owner of the seventh house but a strong karaka for the spouse, the spouse is still likely to predecease the native but the death will take place after a long and full life. The spouse will be extravagant and the cause of discord in domestic life. The spouse will be bad tempered, sickly, sensual, is likely to have extra marital relations, and will leave the native to live separately. The native will be sensual and is likely to have liaisons with members of opposite sex secretly or abroad. If the owner of the seventh house is powerful and well placed in the twelfth house, the native's eldest child will be long lived but he may settle down abroad. The native will form partnership with foreigners and the business may have international connections.

EIGHTH HOUSE

1. This house refers to the following:

(i)   Scrotum and anus. Excretory organs. Bladder. Left part of the chin, or stomach or left calf depending on the drekkan rising.

(ii)   Piles, fistula and other diseases of the rectum. Urinary disorder. Facial disease.

(iii)   Butchers, slaughter houses, coroners, and health inspectors.

(iv)   Incurring debts and giving of loans.

(v)   Hidden meaning. Occult. Tantra. Marital bond.

(vi)   Boat. Accident. Adhi (mental distress) and vyadhi (physical distress and pain), calamity, death-its place, cause, and nature. Mutilation, amputation, defeat, insult, sorrow, punishment given by the government, severe difficulties, obstruction, fear of enemies, arrest, detention, ill repute, criminal and violent attitude of the mind. Weapons. Morbid sexuality.

(vii)   Ability to manipulate others.

(viii) Drugs.

(ix)   Split between friends or partners, diplomatic defeat.

(x)   Going across waterbodies including the sea. Strange adventures of body and mind. Path through rough mountainous regions or wild and dense forests. Losing one's way.

(xi)   Matters relating to wealth etc., must be examined from this house also. (This house is seventh from the second house. It is therefore complimentary to the second house.). Unearned wealth. Acquiring and constructing religious property. Business matters and investments.

(xii)   Financial matters relating to death, viz., legacy, insurance, will, gratuity, and inheritance.

2. In Hindu Astrology the danger to life upto the age of 8 years is called BALARISTA. Reference is also invited to paragraph 19 under MOON in Chapter on Planets.

(a)   A child may not survive this period if the Moon has no beneficial influence on it and is waning, weak, debilitated, and badly afflicted. If the ascendant also has similar drawbacks, the conclusion will be further confirmed.

(b)   If the birth is during the day, the Moon, with malefic influence is waxing and placed in the eighth house, it forms Balarista; if the birth is during the night, the Moon, with malefic influence is waning and placed in the eighth house, Balarista is formed.

3. If a child is born when the last degree or the first degree of a sign is rising in the ascendant, and the ascendant is occupied or aspected by malefic planets, the native will not live long.

4. A child born with the last degree of Cancer or the first degree of Leo rising, or the last degree of Scorpio or the first degree of Sagittarius rising, or the last degree of Pisces or the first degree of Aries rising in the ascendant, and malefic planets aspecting the first house, will usually have a short life. If the native lives, he will have a prosperous life with high status.

5. When Balarista is indicated since the Moon has the disabilities mentioned above or otherwise but:

(i) the Moon also has beneficial influence, is powerful or is placed in the drekkan of Jupiter, Venus or Mercury, or

(ii) the ascendant is powerful or its owner is very powerful having aspects of beneficial planets from angles and has no malefic influence, or

(iii) an angle is occupied by a strong naturally beneficial planet or by the dispositor of the Moon, or

(iv) a powerful Jupiter is placed in the first house, or

(v) the Sun for a day birth or the Moon for the night birth is in the eleventh house, or

(vi) Rahu occupies the third, sixth or the eleventh house aspected by at least one powerful beneficial planet, the Balarista will not be fatal but the child may have severe ailments in its infancy.

6. Generally, if there is severe Balarista, and there are no redeeming features, the time of death of the infant can be fixed in the following manner:

(A) First determine whether the child is going to live for a few years or death is likely to take place within the course of months of birth. For this consider as follows:

(i) If the owner of the first house or the dispositor of the Moon, is weak and placed in the sixth, eighth or the twelfth house, the native will live for as many number of years as the serial number of the sign in which the above owner or dispositor is placed. For example if the owner is placed in Libra, the native will survive for 7 years (the serial number of Libra being seven).

(ii) If the owner of the drekkan in which the cusp of the ascendant is placed, or the owner of the drekkan in which the Moon is placed, is in the condition and placement mentioned in (i) above, the serial number of the sign so arrived at will indicate the number of months the native is going to live.

(B) The day of death can be determined to be the one when the Moon transits (a) the house where the most powerful planet causing the Balarista is located at birth, or (b) the house that it occupied at birth, or (c) the ascendant; is powerful there, and is aspected by powerful malefic planets there.

7. The span of life has been categorised as short, medium or long. Short is upto the age of 32 years, medium from 32 upto 80 years and long from 80 upto 120 years. See paragraph 19 below. There are several complicated mathematical methods to compute the longevity of a native but in practice it has been observed that these methods many a time do not work. There are some simpler methods that are recorded in the following paragraphs (8 to 18). They have been found to be quite accurate.

8. (a) For the purposes of longevity, the owner of the tenth house should be considered in the same manner as Saturn.

(b) The first, third and the eighth houses, their owners and Saturn should be examined for strength. If all these factors are strong, the native has a long life. If 75% out of these factors are strong medium life and if only half are strong then short life should be predicted. It is also advised that the owner of the eighth house should be powerful but not as strong as the owner of the first house.

9. If the:

(i) The owners of the first and the eighth houses, in the birth and navansha charts, are friends; and,

(ii) the dispositor of the Moon and the owner of the eighth house counted from the Moon, in the birth and the navansha charts, are friends; the native will live long. If they are neutral to each other, the native will have a medium term of life, and if they are enemies, the native will be short lived.

10. If:
(i) the owner of the first house is more powerful than the owner of the eighth house;
(ii) dispositor of the Moon is more powerful than the owner of the eighth house counted from the Moon;
(iii) the owner of the first house is more powerful than the owner of the eighth house in the navansha chart; and,
(iv) dispositor of the Moon is more powerful than the owner of the eighth house counted from the Moon in the navansha chart; the native will be long lived. If they are equal in strength, he will have medium term of life. Otherwise, the native will be short lived.

11. We should find out which of the two owners is more powerful-the owner of the eighth house or the owner of the second. Then see whether the stronger of the two is in an angular, cadent or succedent house. If it is in an angle, the native will live long. If in cadent house, the duration of life will be medium and if in succedent, short.

12. The analysis laid down in the preceding paragraph should be carried out for the stronger of the two planets- the owner of the eighth house from the Atmakaraka and the owner of the eighth from the seventh house from the Atmakaraka, i. e., the owner of the second house from Atmakaraka and result drawn with regard to the length of life accordingly.

13. If beneficial planets for the chart and the owner of the first house are in:
(a) the angles, it indicates that the native will live long;
(b) the cadent houses (the second, fifth, eighth and the eleventh houses), it indicates that the native will have medium term of life; and,
(c) the succedent houses, short life.

14. If malefic planets for the chart and the owner of the eighth house occupy the:
(a) succedent houses, long life;
(b) cadent houses, medium life; and,
(c) angles, short life.

15. (i)   A very powerful owner of the first house in an angle,
          aspected by beneficial planets but having no aspect
          or association with malefic planets is indicative of
          long life and prosperity.
    (ii) The owners of the first and the eighth houses togeth-
          er in a good house and aspected by at least a
          powerful beneficial planet promise long life.

16. Jupiter and the owner of the first house in angles, and
malefic planets not placed in the angles, triangular houses and
the eighth house will ensure long life.

17. We should find out:
(i)   the signs ruling the drekkans in which the cusp of the
      ascendant and the Moon are placed,
(ii) the signs in which the owner of the ascendant and the
      dispositor of the Moon are placed in the navansha chart,
      and
(iii) the signs in which the owners of the first and the eighth
      houses are placed in the dwadwasansa chart.
      Then it must be determined for (i) above whether:
      (a)   both the signs are movable, or one is fixed and the
            other common, or
      (b)   both the signs are common, or one is movable and
            the other fixed, or
      (c)   both the signs are fixed, or one is movable and the
            other common.
      If (a) is true for (i) above, it is indicative of long life.
      If (b) is true for (i) above, it is indicative of medium life.
      If (c) is true for (i) above, it is indicative of short life.
      Similarly, results should be drawn for (ii) and (iii) by
      applying (a) to (c) above.
      If all the three results, or majority of them, indicate
      the same length of life, it should be taken as con-
      firmed. If the result is different in each case, we
      apply the rule given in the next paragraph.

18. We should find out:
(i)   the signs in which the owners of the first and the eighth
      houses are placed,
(ii) the signs in which the Moon and Saturn are placed, and

(iii) the signs in the first house and in the hora-lagna. For the method to calculate hora-lagna see the NOTE at the end of this Chapter. Then it must be determined for (i) above whether:

    (a) both the signs are movable, or one is fixed and the other common, or

    (b) both the signs are common, or one is movable and the other fixed, or

    (c) both the signs are fixed, or one is movable and the other common.

    If (a) is true for (i) above, it is indicative of long life. If (b) is true for (i) above, it is indicative of medium life. If (c) is true for (i) above, it is indicative of short life. Similarly results should be drawn for (ii) and (iii) by applying (a) to (c) above.

    If all the three results or majority of them, indicate the same length of life, it should be taken as confirmed. If the result is different in each case, we take the result that has been obtained by considering (iii). However, in case the Moon is in the ascendant or the seventh house and the three results obtained by analysing (i), (ii) and (iii) differ, then take the result given by (ii).

    When life span is determined by one, two or three results according to the previous paragraphs, the maximum number of years for each span of life are as follows:

Life Span	one result	two results	three results
Long	96 years	108 years	120 years
Medium	64 years	72 years	80 years
Short	40 years	36 years	32 years

However, the native will have a long life notwithstanding the span of life indicated by any other combination if:

    (i)   the owner of the first house or the Atmakaraka is in association with, in sambandha or aspected by a powerful naturally beneficial planet and another strong naturally beneficial planet is in an angular house, or

    (ii) the owner of the first house, the Atmakaraka or Saturn is associated with any exalted planet, or

    (iii) the owner of the first house or the Atmakaraka is placed in an angle associated with or aspected by Jupiter and Venus, or

(iv) the first house has a common sign (Gemini, Virgo, Sagittarius or Pisces) and its owner is in an angle or a triangular house or is exalted anywhere in the chart, or

(v) the first house has a common sign (Gemini, Virgo, Sagittarius or Pisces) and there are two malefic planets in an angle as counted from the powerful owner of the first house, or

(vi) the owner of the tenth house is exalted and a malefic planet occupies the eighth house, or

(vii) the Atmakaraka is the strongest planet in the horoscope. For the purpose of determination of longevity the strength of the Atmakaraka should be assessed on the following two principles:

(a) Whether there is another planet that has degrees in a sign very close to the degrees held by the Atmakaraka in any sign, and the Atmakaraka is weak due to debilitation etc? Thus if the Atmakaraka is at 25 degrees in a sign and the other planet is at 24 degrees in some sign, it can be a competitor for being the most powerful planet in the horoscope. The degrees held by any other planet in the horoscope cannot be more than the degrees held by the Atmakaraka by virtue of the definition of Atmakaraka, as given earlier.

(b) Whether a planet is located in its sign of exaltation, mooltrikona, sign owned by it, or friendly to it. When the Atmakaraka is weak, and the planet that is close in degrees to the Atmakaraka is powerful due to its being exalted etc., it is possible that the Atmakaraka will not be the most powerful planet.

19. We will now study a method by which we can arrive at the exact number of years the native is likely to live.

Let us presume that the longevity is medium in a horoscope determined on the basis of two out of three results. Let us presume that the results for (i) and (ii) above contribute to the finding that the native is likely to live for a medium span of life.

To clarify matters, if the life span comes out to be short or medium and subsequently we raise it to long due to the exceptions (i) to (vii) recorded in the preceding paragraph, the maximum number of years to be taken for the purpose of following calculations will be taken as before according to the number of results on the basis of which the life span has been determined to be long, medium, or short. Thus, if the span of life on the basis of two results comes out to be medium and due to some of the above seven exceptions, it is raised to long life, the maximum number of years that the long life is expected to last will be, on the basis of two results, i. e., 108 years.

If the ascendant is Leo, the planets involved in (i) shall be the Sun and Jupiter. The planets involved in the (ii) are the Moon and Saturn. Thus the Sun, the Moon, Jupiter and Saturn shall contribute to the determination of number of years that the native is likely to live.

Let us presume that the Sun, the owner of the first house is at 10 degrees 20 minutes 28 seconds (=10. 34 degrees) in Leo, Jupiter, the owner of the eighth is at 20 degrees in Pisces. Further let the Moon be at 12 degrees in a sign and Saturn at 16 degrees in some sign.

Any planet shall contribute its maximum mite when it is at the beginning of the sign and shall contribute zero years when it is at the end of the sign.

The native is likely to live for a medium span of life. Therefore he will complete the maximum span for short life and live some more number of years after that. The maximum number of years for short life on the basis of two results is 36 years and for medium it is 72 years. The difference in years in the two spans is 36 years.

Each of the four planets can travel for 30 degrees from one end to the other in a sign. Therefore for each degree travelled by the planet in a sign the number of years to be reduced from the above difference of 36 years will be 36/30=1. 2 years. Thus when the planet is at 0 degree in a sign it will contribute 36-0*1. 2=36 years. When it is at 1 degree, it will contribute 36-1*1. 2=36-1. 2=34. 8 years, etc. We can therefore calculate the contribution made by each of the four planets to life as below:

Planet	Degrees in sign	Contribution in years
Sun	10. 34	36-10. 34*1. 2=23. 592
Jupiter	20	36-20*1. 2=12
Moon	12	36-12*1. 2=21. 6
Saturn	16	36-16*1. 2=16. 8

The first set on an average contributes (23. 592+12)/2=17. 796 years. The second set on an average contributes (21. 6+16. 8)/ 2=19. 2 years.

Average contribution, taking into account both the sets, is (17. 796+19. 2)/2=18. 498 years. These are the extra years that the native will live over and above the short span of life of 36 years. Therefore the age for the native works out to be 36+18. 498=54. 498 years.

20. The methods to determine the cause of death of the native:
(a) The most powerful planet that occupies or aspects the eighth house will be the cause of death of the native.
(b) If there is no planet that occupies or aspects the eighth house, then the sign placed in this house will rule the cause of native's death.
(c) The sign in which the owner of the eighth house is placed in the navansha chart also gives the cause of native's death.
(d) The owner of the 22nd drekkan as counted from the drekkan in which cusp of the first house is placed is also indicative of the cause of death.

21. When the owner of the eighth house is a malefic planet and the house is occupied by at least another malefic planet, the native will be killed by reptile bite, by being mauled by a wild animal, by burning or by use of a sharp edged weapon.

22. When two malefic planets, placed in angles, aspect each other fully, the native is done to death by the order of the government, or by the use of fire, weapons or poison.

23. The native's end will be peaceful:
(a) If the owner of the twelfth house is:
    (i)   A naturally beneficial planet, or
    (ii) placed in the sign of a naturally beneficial planet, or
    (iii) placed in the navansha of a naturally beneficial planet, or
    (iv) placed anywhere in the horoscope, is joined or aspected by a naturally beneficial planet.
(b) The twelfth house is occupied by a naturally beneficial planet.
(c) An analysis carried out on the lines similar to the above on the fourth house will also be conducive to reaching the correct conclusion.

24. Following are the marakas in descending order of strength and will kill during their major or sub-periods if the life span determined earlier is coming to an end:

(a) A malefic planet for the horoscope determined in accordance with the rules laid down by Parashar, in sambandha with the owner of the second house in the second or seventh house.

(b) A malefic planet as determined above, in sambandha with the maraka owner of the seventh house in the second or seventh house.

(c) The owner of the second house.

(d) The owner of the seventh house.

(e) A malefic planet determined as above, situated in the second house.

(f) A malefic planet determined as above, situated in the seventh house.

(g) A naturally beneficial planet owning two angular houses in sambandha with a maraka planet.

(h) (i)   A node of the Moon placed in the second, or seventh house in sambandha with a maraka planet; or,

(ii)   placed in the seventh house from a significator of death, or placed with it.

(i) The owner of the twelfth house.

(j) A malefic planet as determined above, which is in sambandha with the owner of the twelfth house, or placed in the twelfth house.

(k) The owner of the third or eighth house weak and badly placed in the chart.

(l) The owner of the sixth or eleventh house.

(m) Any malefic planet as determined above.

25. The owner of the eighth house in sambandha with a malefic planet, with Saturn or with the owner of the tenth house becomes a maraka provided it is not placed in the eighth house. If it is the owner of the first and eighth houses, it should not occupy its own house, to remain a maraka.

26. If Saturn is a malefic planet for an ascendant, and has sambandha with a maraka planet, it becomes the most powerful maraka. When Saturn is a maraka it will supersede all other marakas and end the life of the native during its major or sub-period.

27. Add the longitudes of the owners of the sixth, eighth and the twelfth houses. Whenever Saturn transits the point in a sign so obtained, or signs triangular to it there is danger to life.

28. For day births add the longitudes of the Sun and Saturn. This point would be in some constellation. The major or sub-period of the planet that rules the constellation can be fatal. For night births add the longitudes of the Moon and Rahu and proceed as above.

29. Add the longitudes of the Sun, the Moon, Jupiter and Saturn. We will get a point the longitude of which will be the result of the addition. If the life span has been determined to be short, the native will pass away when Saturn transits over this point the first time in the life of the native. If the life span is of medium length, the death of the native will occur when Saturn transits over it the second time, and if the life span is long, the third time. However, since the well known rule is that the transit results will be subservient to the results indicated by major or sub-periods, therefore, the results indicated by the transit of Saturn must conform to the major or sub-periods results.

30. The influence received by the first and the eighth houses and their owners determine the nature of death. For example if the owner of the sixth, or eleventh house, Mars or Ketu is influencing these factors, or even the eighth house and its owner only, the man would die due to injury or violence.

31. If there is a movable sign on the cusp of the eighth house in the birth or navansha chart, the native will die in a foreign country; if it is a fixed sign, death will take place at home, and if it is a common sign, on way to home.

32. If the third house is connected with the eighth house, death is likely to occur during a short journey.

33. If the third and the twelfth houses are both connected with the eighth house, death will be caused by native's younger brother/sister.

34. If only the twelfth house is connected with the eighth house, death will take place in a hospital, nursing home etc. or at an unknown place away from home.

35. If the eleventh house is connected with the eighth house, death will occur at a friend's or elder brother's house.

36. If the ninth house is connected with the eighth house, the native will die while on a long journey, abroad or at a far off place.

37. The owner of the first or third house in the eighth house, or occupier or owner of the eighth house in the constellation of the owner of the first or third house, or the owner of the eighth house in conjunction with owner of the first or third house is indicative of suicidal tendencies in the native.

38. When the owner of the first, third or the eleventh house (these are indicators of the self) influences the eighth house, and Saturn, the person commits suicide.

39. If the Sun is located in the eighth house, is weak in an inimical sign and has the aspect of Mars and Rahu (Rahu aspects the fifth, seventh and the ninth signs from the sign occupied by it) it destroys the eye of native's father. It can also cause bone troubles to the native.

40. This is a watery house. If this house and its owner are connected with the twelfth house and are under the influence of malefic planets it indicates that the native would go on sea voyages.

41. If the eighth house has adverse influence, the native will go to sea in search of livelihood. If the ninth house is more powerful than the eighth, he will do well abroad and will be prosperous. If the tenth house is also more powerful than the eighth house, the native will make a mark for himself and will have a high position there.

42. The Sun and Moon do not become malefic planets by their ownership of this house.

43. If there are three or more malefic planets in this house there is likelihood of the native suffering from disease in the genitals.

44. If Mars or Ketu occupies this house and is aspected by a malefic planet, it causes boils.

45. The owner of the first house does not become a malefic planet if it is also the owner of the eighth house and is placed in a house owned by it.

46. Rules for getting a legacy:
(A) The eighth house and its owner are powerful, and,
(B) (i)   the owner of the eighth house is closely connected
            with, or placed in the second, ninth, tenth or the
            eleventh house, or
    (ii)   a powerful owner of the second, ninth, tenth or the
            eleventh house is placed in or is closely connected
            with the eighth house.

47. Effect of various SIGNS in the Eighth House (A careful
study of NOTE in paragraph 38 under FIRST HOUSE in Chapter
Four will be of use.):

Aries

The wife or the partner of the native will not be thrifty. The
investments made by the native will not be done after due
thought and may cause losses to him later. The wife or business
partner will partly be responsible for these decisions. The native
will be physically strong and if he takes to athletics or callisthenics
he will excel at it. He will suffer setbacks in litigation. The native
may live abroad and die there. The owner of the eighth house here
is also the owner of the third house. If Mars is powerful and well
placed, the native will be long lived and will enjoy good health. A
weak and badly placed Mars will be bad for the health of native's
younger sister/brother who may pass away during the major or
sub-periods of Mars. This can be further analysed in the manner
similar to Scorpio in the third house in Chapter Four.

Taurus

This is quite opposite of Aries in the eighth house. The wife
of the native will be thrifty and will be careful with money. She
will have some independent source of earning. The owner of the
eighth house here is also the owner of the first house. If Venus
is weak, the native will suffer from reproductive or urinary
system disorders and may have worries on account of females.
Venus may cause illness to the younger sister/brother of the
native. His first child may go in for higher studies and may have
good vehicles. His father may be sensual. Venus will be the
significator of death for native's spouse. The native may travel

over water. This can be further analysed in the manner similar to Libra in the first house. The native will die at home of excesses like overeating at night or of injuries inflicted by cattle.

Gemini

The owner of the eighth house here is Mercury, which is also the owner of the eleventh house. Mercury is significator of speech and is connected with the house of speech and entertainment as counted from the seventh house. Therefore a powerful and well placed Mercury will make the wife of the native a good singer, a compere, an opera artist or a person who takes part in radio plays, an entertaining speaker etc. She will gain through her children, entertainment and speculation. Such a Mercury will also be good for the elder sister/brother of the native. He will rise high in life by the dint of his scholarship. If Mercury influences the third house, the native's younger sister/brother will serve abroad; if it influences the ninth house, the first child of the native is likely to have mainly female children. The native's father will travel a lot over short distances in life involving crossing of waterbodies and may change his residence several times. If Mercury is weak and afflicted the native will have a short life. The native will die of disease in the spleen or rectum or due to taking some liquid. The native will be manipulative in nature. He will have good business acumen and will start several innovative but profitable ventures. If Mercury is powerful it will give the native big profits from his investments. This can be further analysed in the manner similar to Virgo in the eleventh house below.

Cancer

The Moon is the owner of the eighth house. A weak and afflicted Moon will make the native liable to sudden death in early childhood. The principles of balarishata have been clearly enunciated above. The wife of the native will be involved with family affairs and money matters. A powerful Moon will make the wife wealthy but her wealth will wax and wane. Such a Moon will also make the elder sister/brother of the native highly placed. His father may spend heavily from time to time. The native may be killed abroad, die abroad by drowning, or of bite by poisonous insects or reptiles. He may also have imbalance of watery element in the body. His younger sisters/brothers may suffer from troubles from female enemies. They may have troubles in the chest or breasts. The native's first child will have worries and mental trouble if the Moon is ill disposed. An afflicted Moon in the chart with connection with the twelfth house will take the native to seas.

Leo

The native will have making money as primary goal in life. The wife will also be equally ambitious. If the Sun is powerful the wife will be wealthy and, it will also make the elder sister/brother of the native highly placed. Such a Sun will be indicative of the fact that the native's children will be mentally very bright. His mother will have the ability to be a good adviser. The native's father will spend on charities and will have the ability to go deep into spiritual and occult matters. The native may be killed by wild animals or in a fight with thieves.

Virgo

The owner of the eighth house here is also the owner of the fifth house. This is not good for the longevity of the children especially the first born. If Mercury and Jupiter are weak and afflicted there will be loss of children. A powerful and well placed Mercury will make the wife of the native gain enormously, but according to the nature of this planet the gains in volume and frequency will fluctuate. Such a Mercury will be good for making the mother of the native a good musician. She may earn well from games of chance or speculation. If Mercury is weak, the native's younger brother is likely to be a lowly paid clerk in a business establishment. The native may contract debts. This can be further analysed in the manner similar to Gemini in the fifth house in Chapter Four. The native will die in his native place. He will be mourned by his kith and kin and will be accorded all the due funerary rites. The cause of death can be his excessive way of living, a woman or indigestible food.

Libra

The native's wife will spend lavishly and will not be good at handling money. The owner of the eighth house here is Venus which is also the owner of the third house. If Venus is afflicted it will cause diseases in reproductive or urinary system of younger brother or sister. A good Venus will make the wife earn easily or give discourses on religion, aesthetics, law or history and may undertake short journeys in the process. The native's children will have conveyances and will gain through immovable property. His father will travel abroad in connection with his business of perfumes, fine clothes, or other luxury items. He will like the company of females and may have clandestine affairs with several women. This can be further analysed in the manner similar to Taurus in the third house in Chapter Four. The native will die at night of stomach trouble, hunger or grief. He may be killed by his enemy.

Scorpio

The native will be indiscreet in his investments and will suffer losses therefrom. The wife of the native will also be impetuous in her handling of finances. The native will be argumentative and of quick temper. The owner of the eighth house is also the owner of the first house. Such a Mars, if powerful and well placed will make the wife of the native wealthy, and the father of the native to travel abroad and gain from it. The native will be long lived. But a weak, badly associated or badly placed Mars will make the wife liable to be involved in a fatal accident and younger brother or sister of the native to undergo serious surgery. The native will die at his place of residence of bite by poisonous insects. The cause of death can also be disease in the mouth or face. A powerful Mars will make the children of the native acquire property and vehicles with minimum efforts. This can be further analysed in the manner similar to Aries in the first house in Chapter Four.

Sagittarius

The eighth house is the house of legacies and money belonging to wife, partners and others. The owner of the eighth house, Jupiter, here is also the owner of the eleventh house. Jupiter is the significator of wealth . Therefore Jupiter, if powerful in the horoscope of the native, will make him come by legacies and moneys of others in his life, especially when the major or sub-period of Jupiter operates. A powerful Jupiter will make the wife of the native an intelligent and eloquent speaker. She can be proficient in religious matters or law and will earn by her speech. If Jupiter influences the ninth house, native's children will have mostly female offsprings. This can be further analysed in the manner similar to Gemini in the eighth house above. He will also live long. The native may succumb abroad to injuries inflicted by a projectile, or animals or to disease in the rectum or genitals.

Capricorn

The wife of the native will be financially productive affording a sense of security to the native. The native will become more and more fortunate as he advances in age. He will have distinct interest in the occult at which he will become learned and proficient. He will be close to his father but will not be demonstrative in his affection. The investments made by the native will take long in bearing fruits. The native's father will be in financially unsatisfactory state and may have to face dishonour if Saturn is not powerful. If Saturn is powerful, not only the native is long lived as the owner of the eighth house and the significator for longevity is the same planet, i. e., Saturn, but also the father of the native will leave his birth place at an advanced age in life and live away from it. The father will shun company and prefer seclusion. The wife may talk rudely unless Saturn has beneficial influence on it. His elder brother/sister will be wealthy. His maternal uncles will build houses by the dint of their own efforts. The cause of native's death will be a marine or riverine animal. He will be meritorious, learned and generous.

Aquarius

The nature and productivity of the investments made by the native will be similar to those under Capricorn above. A powerful Saturn will make the wife of the native come by money and may be legacies. The native's children will keep changing their residences. The owner of the eighth house and the significator of longevity being the same, if it is powerful, will make the native long lived. The owner of the eighth house, being Saturn is also the owner of the seventh house. An adverse Saturn will make the wife of the native behave dishonourably with the native. The native will suffer from boils etc. and succumb to it in somebody else's house. He will suffer loss due to fire and will have to work very hard which may also be the cause of his death.

Pisces

The owner of the eighth house here is also the owner of the fifth house. This owner is Jupiter. It is also the significator for children. If Jupiter is weak and afflicted, the native is likely to lose some of his children during the major or sub-periods of Jupiter or be dishonoured by them. A powerful Jupiter will make the wife of the native wealthy. The native will be wounded by weapon and die of it or succumb to fever or he may drown. This can be further analysed in the manner similar to Sagittarius in the fifth house in Chapter Four.

48. Effect of the owner of the eighth house in various houses (A careful study of the opening notes from A to H in paragraph 39 under FIRST HOUSE in Chapter Four will be of utmost use):

First

If the owner of the eighth house is Saturn and is located in the first house, it makes the native long lived. Any planet that owns the eighth house and is well placed in the first will tend to give a long span of life to the native. The owner of the eighth in the first house will also give rise to illness and worries. The native will be argumentative and will face obstacles in his endeavours. He may also get hooked on drugs. He will earn his livelihood by being in government service. This location makes the owner of the eighth house a powerful significator of death of the wife. The native's mother will enjoy high status in life. She may be an ardent practitioner of religious rites. The native's children will be learned and will have the facility of good conveyances and comforts in life. The owner of the eighth house here will be dangerous for the welfare of native's younger sister/brother. His elder brother may have a brother, younger than him but elder to the native, connected with the government. His father will not be wealthy and his success in speculation and investments is doubtful. The native's father will have a strong libido.

Second

The native and his wife will be short lived in case the owner of the eighth house is debilitated or afflicted. He will have troubles with his family and may not get wholesome food. He is likely to have eye and teeth troubles. He will be engaged in bad deeds and will not be rich if the owner is a malefic. If the owner is a beneficial planet it will yield good results but government will be the cause of death of the native. The mother of the native will gain from her children. His first child will attain position of high status and will have conveyance and residence by virtue of his position. He will have his place of work also at home. The native's father and younger sister/brother are likely to rise to a high position if the owner of the eighth house does not have any beneficial influence. The native will be secretive or harsh in his speech.

Third

If the owner of the eighth house is Saturn and is located in the third house, it makes the native long lived. Any planet that owns the eighth house and is well placed in the third will tend to give a long span of life to the native. The same will be the result if the owner of the eighth house is strong and placed in a friend's house in the third. He will speak harshly if the owner of the eighth is in the third house and will be either without younger brothers/sisters or will be opposed to younger brothers/sisters, neighbours and colleagues. The wife will gain without much effort. She will also talk of religious matters. His elder sister/brother will do well in life. The native will find it difficult to communicate with his father. The owner of the eighth house placed in the third, in an afflicted condition is likely to lead from one death to the next in its major or sub-period causing the native extreme grief.

Fourth

The native will not have comforts and peace of mind. In fact, the mind will have sinful tendencies. He may be divested of his property by circumstances beyond his control. His vehicle may cause trouble to him. His mother may fall seriously sick. The parents of the native will face troubles. His younger sister/brother may be indebted or lose his wealth due to the machinations of his enemies. If the owner of the eighth house is a beneficial planet and the owner of the fourth house is friendly to the owner of the eighth, the younger sister/brother may earn with the help of his maternal uncle. The native's mother will be a pleasant and likable person. She may be religious and god fearing. His eldest child may go abroad for studies. The children are likely to suffer loss of property. In an extreme case and if other indications support, one of native's children may suffer from mental trouble and may have to be admitted to an asylum. His wife is likely to be a working lady having independent income. She may come from a highly placed family connected with the government. A weak and afflicted owner of the eighth house having no beneficial influence here is indicative that during the major or sub-period of the owner of the eighth house, the father of the native may reach a high position. The elder sister/brother of the native is likely to be badly behaved and may suffer reverses in his profession in the major or sub-periods of the owner of the eighth house. The native will get the accumulated wealth of his father. The native's father may be ailing.

Fifth

A malefic owner of the eighth house in the fifth will be dangerous to the longevity and health of native's children. The native's father will frequently undertake long journeys and may go abroad, or he may give up worldly concerns for a secluded religious life. The native may not be intelligent or may have mental disorder and have no interest in culture or religion. He is likely to suffer losses in speculation. He may gamble away whatever wealth he has. His wife will earn to maintain the family on her meagre income. His younger sister/brother may be in a uniformed service. The native will not keep good health either. The evils will be lessened to a large extent if the owner of the eighth house is placed in the eighth navansha. The native may die of stomach or heart trouble.

Sixth

If the owner of the eighth house is afflicted and placed in the sixth without any beneficial influence, it will confer on the native power and wealth. However the native may have bouts of ill health and his maternal uncle may face a critical time during the major or sub-periods of the owner of the eighth house. His father may lose his job or may have to go away on official duties in these major or sub-periods. This location is good for the wealth of native's children. If the Sun is the owner of the eighth so placed, it will make the native opposed to the government; if it is the Moon or Jupiter he will be ailing; if it is Mars he will have a quick temper; if it is Mercury he will be timid and will have diseases in his mouth, and if it is Saturn he will face all kinds of troubles. The wife of the native will spend heavily and may also earn from abroad or through institutions like hospitals or asylums. The native will be able to keep his enemies in check and may even win them over. He will be successful in litigation. He may face danger from water and reptiles in his childhood. His health may not be good but he will be long lived. The major or sub-periods of the owner of the eighth house may be adverse for the profession and status of the elder brother of the native who may face severe reverses in these fields during this time.

Seventh

This location is not good for the physical welfare of native's wife. She will earn well. She will be ill behaved. The native will suffer from stomach troubles, will be ill tempered and not of good conduct. If the owner of the eighth house is a malefic planet, the native will not like his wife and she will be the cause of his death. His father will have limited income and may be dependent on his friends and acquaintances. The native may travel abroad on secret assignments. The native's mother will be intelligent and well read. She will be interested in spiritual matters and the occult. His children may change their residences several times. They will be courageous. His younger sister/brother may remain worried on account of the health of his children. A powerful owner of the eighth house in the seventh is a very good indication of the prosperity and high status of native's elder brother or sister.

Eighth

If the owner of the eighth house is not afflicted, the native will keep very good health and will be long lived. He will be prosperous and travel over water for enjoyment. He will be hard working but will not be reliable. His father will be religious and may spend on religious matters and he will have good eyesight. The father will always be bothered by heavy expenditure. The younger sister/brother will lead a healthy life and the elder sister/brother may have good status in life. The native's children will be mentally healthy and will have physical comforts, property and conveyances. His wife will be earning and may help him financially in maintaining the family but the marital life may not be particularly cordial due to her fidelity being questionable. His mother will have talent in fine arts and music. The owner of the eighth in the same house will act as a powerful significator of death for the spouse of the native. If the owner of the eighth house is weak, afflicted and has no beneficial influence here, the native will be rich and rise high in life but his longevity may be reduced.

Ninth

The native will be cruel, keep the company of persons given to misdeeds and will not be friendly. He will neither be interested in higher studies nor can he be successful at it. Religion will not attract him and he will not be a person to respect either his elders or his preceptor. He may write scandalous and libelous articles which may not be based on facts and may have the motive of black mail behind them. His father may find partnerships unsuitable. He will either not have younger brothers or sisters or may fall out with them. His opponents will fear him. He may have a disfigured face. Both the native and his spouse will be of suspect moral fibre. The native's father may settle down abroad. The native may not have good relations with his father. The spouse of younger sister/brother may be sickly. The elder sister/ brother may earn well from his profession and his children may do well in life. If the Sun is badly placed in the eighth house, and the owner of the eighth house being in the ninth, the native's father is likely to pass away within a year of his birth.

Tenth

The native will not have a smooth career. The career will have obstacles and failures. The native may have to undergo humiliating situations. He may also face charges of misappropriations and other irregularities. He may be punished by the government. The native is not likely to be rich. If the owner of the eighth house is powerfully disposed in the tenth house, the native is likely to gain a legacy. In such a situation the native is expected to live long. This location of the owner of the eighth house is not good for the native's mother. She may keep poor health, her conduct may not be above board and she may face problems from one of her daughters-in-law. The native's father may have to incur heavy expenditure and he may find it difficult to save money. The native will be an employee of the government. He will be lazy. His children will not do well at college level studies and at examinations. They may not have a comfortable life and are not likely to be happy. If the owner of the eighth house is weak, afflicted and has no beneficial influence here, the younger sister/ brother of the native will be rich and rise high in life.

Eleventh

The native will have a difficult childhood but he will prosper and be happy later in life. Unless the owner of the eighth house is a naturally beneficial planet which is also beneficial for the chart, the native will be short lived and keep bad health. The owner of the eighth house in the eleventh with a naturally beneficial planet which is also beneficial for the chart will make the native long lived. His friends are likely to be friends of fair weather. The friendships will not last long. The native's sister/ brother will have a difficult life and the native may not pull along well with him. The native's children will be given to deceit and bad conduct. They may not be long living. The native will be of average intelligence. He will not gain in his ventures, and gambling and speculation are not likely to be beneficial to him. His maternal uncle is likely to be in a uniformed service. The bad results will be considerably improved if the owner of the eighth house is placed in the eighth navansha.

Twelfth

The native will be deformed, ill behaved, may be a criminal and poor. He will have to face heavy expenditure. He may be short lived and meet his death in unfamiliar circumstances and may not be given due after-death treatment, or he may die in a hospital or asylum. His children can also not hope to do well in life. Their education will also not be successfully completed. The native's father may hold property abroad. His mother may be god fearing and religious. If the owner of the eighth house is weak and afflicted and placed in the twelfth house with no beneficial influence, the native may prosper in life. If the owner of the eighth house is a beneficial planet for the chart, it is likely that the mother is well placed in life. His younger sister/brother will face difficulties in his career and may not be successful in his undertakings due to the machinations of his enemies. His elder sister/brother may earn well from his profession but will be forced to spend heavily on family obligations.

NINTH HOUSE

1. This house refers to the following:
   (i) Guru.
   (ii) Father.
   (iii) Auspicious occasions, good deeds, dips in holy rivers, and visits to shrines. Charity. Worship, dharma, religion, intuition, Prarabdha (part of accumulated karmas of the past lives the good or bad results of which have to be experienced in this life), penance, spiritual initiation, dream, next world, providential help, and past births.
   (iv) Badhakasthan for ascendants having fixed signs.
   (v) Fortune. General prosperity. Sudden and unexpected gains. Rewards for one's efforts. Favours from the govt.
   (vi) Hips, groin, lower vertebrae and upper legs. Left cheek, left part of the heart and left knee according to the drekkan rising.
   (vii) Efforts for acquisition of learning, highest levels of knowledge, research, invention, discovery, law, judges, philosophy, medicine, publications of works of substantial and of more lasting nature than those covered by the third house which are of ephemeral nature like news.
   (viii) Long journeys and communications to far off places, foreigners, emigration and immigration.
   (ix) Mother's servant. Younger brother's/sister's spouse. Friends of elder brother /sister.

(x) (a) Predictions can be made with regard to the father of the native by taking the ninth house as the first house in the horoscope of the native. The house second from the ninth (i. e., the tenth house) will tell about the wealth of the father, the third about his brothers, the fourth about his mother and comforts, and so on.

(b) A similar analysis can be attempted by taking the house where the Sun or the Pitrukaraka (see paragraph 3 in opening remarks of Chapter Two) is located, as the first house for the father.

(c) See paragraph 5 of opening remarks of Chapter on Planets also.

2. Being seventh from the third house it is complimentary to the third house and therefore should also be examined for younger brothers/sisters.

3. If there is a link between the first and the ninth houses the native becomes fortunate and religious. Take the house in which the Moon is situated as the first house. We call this house the Moon ascendant. We define the Sun ascendant similarly. If the yoga is true simultaneously for the Sun and the Moon ascendants also, the above result can be taken as confirmed. The element of spiritualism in this yoga gets a boost if Saturn simultaneously influences the fourth house, its owner and the Moon as it will make the native dispassionate.

4. The fifth house represents devotion and the ninth religiousness. Jupiter is the karaka for religion. A person will be religious if:

(i) The fifth and the ninth houses and Jupiter are strong, or

(ii) (a) Jupiter is strongly placed in the first, third, fifth or the ninth house, or

(b) Jupiter is in the same sign as the Moon, or

(c) Jupiter aspects the fifth or the ninth house or both as counted from the sign occupied by the Moon.

(d) Jupiter is not an adverse planet for the chart and influences the fourth house or the Moon.

(iii) Saturn is not an adverse planet for the chart and influences the fourth house or the Moon.

5. If the owner of this house is powerful it indicates divine assistance and sudden gain. The form that this assistance will take will depend upon the house in which the owner is located. For example if the owner is in the tenth house the native will get ruling powers or help from the government and its employees through chance, coincidence or luck. If it is in the fourth house he will so get conveyances etc. or assistance from the mother.

6. If there is a debilitated planet in this house or if its owner is debilitated or combust, it makes the native a hypocrite in religious matters.

7. If this house is strong there is a possibility of sudden and pleasant gains. If Mercury is the owner of such a strong ninth house, the possibility of such gains becomes very strong as this planet has a similar effect. If a strong ninth house owned by Mercury is tenanted by Rahu or Ketu this result is bound to occur because in such a situation all the elements that govern sudden gains will be influencing this house. Similar will be the result if Mercury joins or is aspected by a lunar node here.

8. A person would like to keep exalted and spiritual company if the owners of the first and the third houses are connected with this house.

9. This house is fifth from the fifth house. Therefore when considering matters pertaining to children this house has also to be examined.

10. The probable years in the life of a native can be fixed from the owner of this house in which the native may gain well and fortune may smile on him. Following is the tentative age which may prove fortunate for the native, to be deduced from the owner of the sign in which the owner of the ninth is located. The owner of the sign should be powerful and free from affliction:

The owner of the Sign	Years of age
(i) The Sun	22
(ii) The Moon	24
(iii) Mars	28
(iv) Mercury	32
(v) Jupiter	16, 32, 42, 50
(vi) Venus	25
(vii) Saturn	26, 36, 42

11. (i) The rules for determining the relationship between the native and a relative of his are recorded in paragraph 32 under FIRST HOUSE in Chapter Four. If we wish to determine the relations that are likely to exist between the native and his father, we should apply these rules to the ninth house.

(ii) (a) If the sign placed in the sixth, eighth or the twelfth house in the horoscope of the native becomes the ascendant sign in the horoscope of his son/daughter, the relations between the two will not be cordial.

(b) On the other hand if the sign in the ascendant of the son/daughter of the native is one that is placed in the second, third, fifth, ninth or the eleventh house of the native, the relations between the two will be good.

(c) If the sign in the tenth house of the native is placed in the ascendant of the native's son/daughter, the latter shall be abler and more talented than the native. In fact this principle could be applied to any two charts provided the sign involved is strong in the chart when placed in the first house.

12. Effect of various SIGNS in the Ninth House (A careful study of NOTE in paragraph 38 under FIRST HOUSE in Chapter Four may be of use.):

Aries

The native holds that his views are always correct and this may lead to arguments with others. The native may rear animals. He will be generous. The number of houses counted from the ninth house and the number of sign in that house will be the same. This can be analysed with regard to disease and disability in a part of the body of the father of the native in the manner similar to Aries in the First House in Chapter Four. The father will be of quick temper and restless. He will be impetuous and will be of athletic build. The owner of the ninth house here is Mars which is also the owner of the fourth house. If Mars is powerful it will, in its major or sub-periods give the native property, vehicle and comforts without much effort. The native shall be learned in engineering or warfare. His parents will be happy with each other. Such a Mars will be helpful to the native in excelling in the field of law, logic or research. If it is weak and afflicted, it is not only dangerous to the longevity of younger brothers and sisters but will make the father short lived. There is a chance that the native's wife either takes on a white collar job or her younger sister/brother attains a high position in life. This can be further analysed in the manner similar to Scorpio in the fourth house in Chapter Four.

Taurus

The native's father will be handsome and stockily built. He will have good business acumen. He is likely to be connected with agriculture, mining or medicine. The native will earn wealth from horticulture, mining or agriculture. He will acquire higher education only with hard work and continuous application. He may have foreign collaboration in business or it may extend beyond the borders of the country. Such business, in case Venus is powerful, will earn the native much wealth, since the owner of the ninth house here is also the owner of the second house. The native's wife may gain from abroad. Such a Venus will be very good for native's children as they will not only be well behaved but will benefit from the government and attain high positions in life. A weak Venus will make the father of the native fall sick and will curtail the longevity of native's wife. A weak Venus having bad influence over it will make the native's younger sister/brother sensual. This can be further analysed in the manner similar to Libra in the second house in Chapter Four.

Gemini

The native will study current and international affairs extensively. His father will be a learned man whom the native will like to emulate. The father will have an aptitude for mathematics or science. The native will be good at teaching, advertising and publicity and since the owner of the ninth house here is also the owner of the twelfth house, he may go abroad in this connection. The mother of the native may be taken over a long distance or abroad for treatment of a disease and may be admitted to a hospital there. If Mercury has connection with the first house or the Moon, the native will be spiritually inclined and interested in the occult. The native will be engaged in religious practices and will visit religious places. When Mercury is weak and afflicted, the native's first child is likely to lose one of his children. This child is also likely to practise secret Tantric rites. A powerful Mercury is a clear indication that native's elder sister/brother will be wealthy. This can be further analysed in the manner similar to Virgo in the twelfth house below.

Cancer

The father of the native will be shy, and home loving; he may be very warm at times and may become moody and quiet at the other, and he will have love and ability for music. This is a house for journey abroad. A watery sign here indicates that the native will travel abroad and may stay there for long periods. Since the Moon is considered a queen, and the ninth house is connected with favours from the government, if the Moon is well placed and powerful, the native is likely to gain from the government and may hold a high position in government. He may earn from religious occupations. His first child will be prone to beget more female children than male. A powerful Moon is a sure indication that the native will not only have a placid mind but also that he will be fortunate.

Leo

The native will have good vehicles and will be religious and rich. The native's father will be independent minded, ambitious, a good organiser and will like being praised; he will be authoritarian in outlook and will be the dominant personality at home though generous and a good host. The native will like to excel in scholarship, teaching, law etc. The ruler of the ninth house being the Sun, the native will be closely linked with highly placed persons and will, if the Sun is powerful, gain from them. The native will be pious, have interest in Yoga and may work for self realisation. A weak or afflicted Sun will cause stomach or heart trouble to his mother.

Virgo

The native's father will like clean surroundings, and be health conscious, given to regular exercises and wholesome food. He will be slim, self conscious, shy, a linguist, learned and reserved. He will however be critical of others and difficult to please. The native will also follow the footsteps of his father by learning languages and studying subjects like chemistry, psychology and law. He may be good at journalism. Since the owner of the ninth house here is also the owner of the sixth house, a weak Mercury will make the father ailing. A powerful Mercury will make the father be highly placed, gain property and conveyances and lead a happy and comfortable life. The native will do well at competitions without much effort if Mercury is powerful and well placed. The native will come in contact with foreigners in connection with higher studies. Mercury powerful and connected with the first house and Rahu or Ketu in the ninth house will give the native sudden gains. The native may be a hypocrite in religious matters. He may talk a lot but will not be sincere in what he says. He may be in service.

Libra

The native's father will be mild mannered, loving and a friendly person who would like luxuries and comforts. The owner of the first house is Saturn which is a friend of the owner of the ninth house here. Therefore unless there are adverse indications the native will have good relations with his father. The native will be known for his knowledge and intellectual bent of mind. The owner of the ninth house here is also the owner of the fourth house. A powerful Venus will therefore be an asset since it will be the owner of a triangular house and an angular house and will confer on the native wealth, status and comforts. The mother of the native will be house proud, good looking and fond of a good life. She and the native's father will be long lived, loving towards each other and healthy. A weak Venus will make the mother ailing, the father short lived and the native mentally disturbed due to losses. A strong Venus will also be conducive to high status for the brother/sister of native's wife. Ninth house with no other influence will tend to give only younger sisters to native's wife. This can be further analysed in the manner similar to Taurus in the fourth house and Aries in the ninth house.

Scorpio

The native's father would be a determined person who would set high standards and work very hard to achieve them. He would be addicted to stimulants and intoxicants. He would be ruthless and will have a relentless drive to achieve his goals. The father will love the native but will not be able to express it and may therefore appear cold and insensitive. The relations between the father and the native will be average. The native will be argumentative and will not be able to stand upto harsher aspects of life. The native will be irreligious and an atheist. The owner of the ninth house here is Mars which is also the owner of the second house. A powerful Mars will make the native gain without effort and the father to maintain good health. A weak Mars will not only cause problems in this direction but will also make the mother of the native very prone to serious accidents or operations. This can be further analysed in the manner similar to Aries in the second house.

Sagittarius

The father of the native will be generous, sober, balanced and learned. He will however be known for his outspokenness and frank behaviour. The owner of the ninth house here is Jupiter which is also the owner of the twelfth house. If there is no influence to the contrary, the native will be very religious and famous for his upright behaviour. The native will travel abroad. The native's father will have conveyances and will lead a comfortable life. He may be wealthy and may have property. A powerful Jupiter connected with the first house or the Moon may also make the native religious. This can be further analysed in the manner similar to Gemini above and Pisces in the twelfth house.

Capricorn

The native will strive to convert people to his own faith. He will have theological knowledge and will be religious in fanatical and ritualistic senses of the word. The native's father will be ruthless, reserved, a man of strong determination, having great organisational skills and ability to achieve what he sets as his goal. The father will also be frugal, loyal and cautious. Saturn owns the ninth and the tenth houses. It therefore becomes an excellent planet since it owns a triangular house and an angular house. If Saturn is powerful in the horoscope, it will give not only wealth but also power, and will make the native to rise to dizzy heights, but the progress will be slow though steady. It will be excellent for the welfare and prosperity of native's maternal uncle. If it powerfully influences the third house, the maternal uncle may become a high political personality. If Saturn is powerful and connected with the first or the fourth house, or the Moon, it will make the native very religious and dispassionate. Saturn in its major or sub-periods will show exceptionally good results. Normally the native will be born in an average family and will rise beyond his level of birth.

Aquarius

The native's father will be fond of gardens. The father will be handsome and of gregarious temperament. There will be constant stream of visitors to his father's house and he might even be working at a job which involves group activity; he may leave his place of birth and settle down elsewhere; he will face disappointments, and may have to deal with hospitals etc., and he may not have enough time for his children. The native will be independent minded and will be many a time considered unusual by even persons close to him. Saturn here owns the eighth and the ninth houses. Its mooltrikona sign falls in the ninth house, therefore it will on the whole not show bad results. If it is powerful, it will bring fortune to the native from abroad; if weak disappointments and danger.

Pisces

The native will be pious and a linguist. He may like travelling and may visit abroad. His father would have influence on him due to his honesty, religiousness and artistic abilities. The younger brothers and sisters of the native's wife will go away and settle elsewhere, may be abroad. They will also cause some expenses to her and may later get estranged from her. The native will have trouble in his business and with regard to his wealth from his enemies if Jupiter is weak. This can be further analysed in the manner similar to Gemini or Sagittarius in the sixth house in Chapter Four. The owner of the ninth house is Jupiter here which is also the owner of the sixth house. If such a Jupiter is associated with a planet that is malefic for the chart, the native is likely to have very adverse relations with his father.

13. Effect of owner of the ninth house in various houses (A careful study of the opening notes from A to H in paragraph 39 under FIRST HOUSE in Chapter Four will be of utmost use.):

First

The native will be respectful to his preceptor and will be god fearing. The native will be religious. The nature of his religious propensities will be determined by the owner of the ninth house. He will be well behaved and keep away from sinful conduct. He will be given to thinking deeply on matters. He may be knowledgeable in legal matters or philosophy. He may have close interaction with foreigners or may have links abroad. He will be in the service of the government. He will be rich but miserly. If the owner of the ninth house is a friend of the owner of the first, the father and the younger sister/brother of the wife of the native will be attached to him. His marriage will bring luck to him and he will have beneficial partnerships. He will have very good, well behaved, learned and successful children. His mother may also be employed and earning independently. His younger sister/ brother may gain from writing or taking up a job in the field of publishing, transport or communication. His elder sister/brother will be very happily married.

Second

The native will be truthful and well behaved, but will face troubles caused by animals. The native will earn easily and will be wealthy. Higher learning or research could be a source of earning. If the owner of the ninth is well placed in the second house, i. e., the owner is in its own, friend's, exaltation or mooltrikona sign and is powerful there, the native's wife will be long lived. For fixed sign ascendants this placement becomes dangerous since the badhakasthan owner will be in a maraka place. A badly placed owner of the ninth house in the second will make the father ailing. The father will be wealthy. The younger sister/brother of the native can be sensual. They may settle abroad or travel abroad frequently. Their spouses may find trouble from enemies or may fall ill frequently. Their sex life may be inadequate. The native's elder brother/sister will do well at the university in studies and will earn well later in life, may be through property or vehicles. His children will reach high positions in life.

Third

The native will be fortunate, wealthy and successful in life. He will travel a lot. He may do well in writing or communication field. His success may be related to his younger sister/brother. His children or elder brother/sister may earn through speculation, drama, music or entertainment. His first child will have very good, long lived and successful children. The father of the native will be long lived. If the native takes up a profession where he has to deal with foreigners he will flourish. He will be fond of his younger brothers/sisters, neighbours and colleagues. A younger brother or sister will do well in life. The native will also be fortunate and will gain from long journeys. His mother will prosper if the owner of the ninth house does not have any beneficial influence. These indications will also apply, mutatis mutandis, to the native's wife.

Fourth

A weak owner of the ninth house will be detrimental to the longevity of the father. If the two owners are friendly and the owner of the ninth house has beneficial influence on it, the parents will have good relations between them. The wife of the native will find employment through her own efforts. Her younger sister/brother may hold a high position. The native may be an agriculturist. He will be reputed. He will be attached to his father and will assist his father in various matters. The native will be learned, may carry out research in some branch of human knowledge and may write theses. He will have all comforts in life, be happy and may own vast landed property as well as vehicles. He is likely to get a high position and ruling powers in life through the masses. His children are likely to suffer losses if they gamble or speculate. The eldest child may have a clandestine love affair.

Fifth

This is a very favourable location. It sets up contact between the two triangular houses. The children of the native and his father will be lucky, prosperous and reputed. The native will start doing well in life after the birth of his first child. His children will help him in furthering his interests. The native will dress expensively. He will be religious and will honour the learned and intellectuals. His wife's younger brother/sister may benefit through television, radio, journalism etc. and may be wealthy. His mother may suffer from eye trouble or her family members may turn against her. The elder sister/brother of the native may gain through his partner or spouse. The gain may also accrue from long journeys. One of the younger sister/brother may marry through advertising in the newspapers.

Sixth

The native will not be fortunate. He will suffer losses through his servants. His enemies will prosper. He will face criticism and physical troubles. It is possible that during the major or sub-periods of the owner of the ninth house in the sixth, the native may get involved in disputes that may drain away his wealth and the root of these disputes may be traced to his father. The native's father will reach a high position in life and may have power and prestige from the government but is likely to have frequent illnesses or trouble from his enemies. The native's maternal uncle will be wealthy and will do well in life. The native will also be bothered and put to loss by the younger sister/brother of his wife. The spouse may travel frequently and stay away from the native for a while. His elder sister/brother will be financially in a difficult situation.

Seventh

The native will have a beautiful, loving and wealthy wife. She will be from a far off place. She may be attached to her younger sister/brother or may like to write or perform on the radio or television. The native will do well in life after his marriage. He will get full satiation of senses. He will succeed in international trade or prosper abroad. He may be sent on diplomatic assignments. The native's father will be attached to friends if the owner of the seventh and the ninth houses are friendly. The father will have his ambitions fulfilled. The native's elder sister/brother will be very rich and well placed in life. His second child will be fortunate. His children will take to the field of entertainment on screen or write stories or novels.

Eighth

The native's father may pass away early; he may be living abroad, in a secluded place; he may have things to do with hospitals or asylums; or he may be a member of secret societies or conspiracies. The family of the native will not be known for learning. The native will also not enjoy a good reputation. The native will face obstacles in his profession. If the eighth house is powerful and the owner of the ninth house has beneficial influence in this house, the native is likely to get ancestral property and wealth. A weak owner of the ninth house is bad for the fortune of the native. There is a chance of the native undertaking long sea voyages. His children will be learned and intelligent. The eldest child may be elected to the post of a minister.

Ninth

The native will be highly religious. He will be fond of his younger brothers/sisters, neighbours and colleagues if the owner of the ninth house is a friend of the owner of the third house. This location makes the native very fortunate and his father long lived and prosperous. The younger brothers and sisters of native's wife and the native's children will also prosper. His children will maintain good health. The native will be of good conduct, learned, may be religious and contented. He may be raised by · his maternal grand parents. He will travel abroad and gain by it. He will be in the good books of the government in power. He will be obedient to his parents and will look after them in their old age. This position of the owner of the ninth house generally

Predictive Astrology, an insight

accords a high position on the native. If there are other planets involved, they will indicate the support to the native's rise to power and the area in which he is likely to excel. For example if Mercury influences the owner of the ninth here, the native is likely to rise to the position of an eminent editor or writer or he may rise to greatness on the basis of his learning or power of speech. It must however be clearly understood that if the planet influencing the owner of the ninth house is an enemy of the owner, the results will not be satisfactory. When there is adverse influence on the owner of the ninth house and the Moon is also weak and afflicted, the maternal uncle of the native may be mentally imbalanced.

Tenth

A powerful owner of the ninth house in the tenth is a rajyoga. The native will be connected with the government and will gain from matters related to it. This position of the owner of the ninth house generally accords a high position on the native. He will have a high status. He will be attached to his parents. If the owner of the ninth house is friendly with the owner of the fourth house, the native's mother will love and regard his father. Such an owner of the ninth house will also give the native a good house, vehicles and comforts through the government or his employer. The native will be reputed for his competence and learning. His record in his association with the government will be spotless and he will be considered as an upright and straightforward person. If the owner of the ninth house is not friendly with the owner of the tenth or is debilitated there, the native will find that the government/his employer has turned against him and he will suffer losses due to the government/employer. His wife will be well known through her writings or appearance on television or radio. His elder sister/brother may find his financial condition unsatisfactory.

Eleventh

If the owner of the ninth house is well placed in the eleventh the native will be immensely rich. His income will be from right sources if the planet owning the ninth house is a naturally beneficial one. If the planet owning the ninth house is a malefic one, the income will be from sources which may not be termed fully legal. Further distinction can be made. If the owner of the ninth house is a naturally beneficial planet, but it is adverse for the chart, the income will appear to be from legal sources, but a part will be from such sources which have shades of illegality in them. This position of the owner of the ninth house generally accords a high position on the native. He will have high status and will enjoy conveyances. His children will be fortunate and do well in life. He will be long lived. His friends will also be highly placed and his elder sister/brother will benefit from the government. His younger sister/brother will have a happy marriage and he will do well in life after his marriage. The eldest child may marry for love. If the owner of the ninth house is weak, afflicted and has no beneficial influence here, the mother of the native will be rich and rise high in life.

Twelfth

The owner of the ninth house, if a malefic planet will make the individual lack in intelligence and be badly behaved; a beneficial planet will give diametrically opposite results. The native will go abroad. He may have to face obstacles and bottlenecks in his career and may have to work hard for success. When the owner of the ninth house is powerfully placed in the twelfth house, it will make the native religious and spiritually inclined. He will be generous to a fault and may spend lavishly on entertaining people. He will be learned in the matters of religion and the occult. He may travel abroad. Some of his grandchildren may not live long or do well in life. There may be loss of father or father may be the cause of losses to the native, depending upon the state of the karakas. There may be separation from father. Parashar has made a statement which is being recorded for whatever it is worth. According to him the native will lose his father in his 44th year of life if there is an exchange between the ninth and twelfth houses.

TENTH HOUSE

1. This house refers to the following:
   (i) Livelihood, work, employer, master in business, boss, appointment, promotion, occupation, vocation, kingdom,

government, aristocracy, rank, status, position of authority, public esteem, ruling powers, respect, honour, command.

(ii) Living abroad. Commerce, trade, business, doctor. Wealth.
Success.

(iii) Good conduct, Karmas (deeds) in this life, integrity, pil-
grimage, sacrifice, shraddha (last and annual funerary
rites), wisdom, credit, renunciation of worldly life and
taking to asceticism.

(iv) Quality, clothes, sky.

(v) Backbone. Knees. Left part of the nose, left armpit, and left
thigh depending on the drekkan.

(vi) Mother's partners in business.

2. When we wish to determine the VOCATION of the native:

A. The tenth houses as counted from (a) the first house, (b)
the house where the Moon is located, and (c) the house
where the Sun is placed, should be determined and their
strength should be assessed.

B. (i)   The most powerful of the above three tenth houses
should be examined to see whether it contains a
planet. If it does, that planet will be indicative of the
vocation the native will follow.

(ii) If there is no planet in the most powerful tenth
house, the next two in order of strength should be
examined in the manner described in (i) above. A
planet located there will indicate the vocation.

C. If of the three tenth houses determined above, all or two
are of similar strength and contain planets, the combination of all the indications will be the vocation, or the native
will change his vocation to the ones indicated by each
planet in the major or sub-periods of the planets that are
located in these tenth houses.

D. In case there are no planets in any of the three houses, the
most powerful of the three houses should be determined.
The owner of the navansha sign in which the owner of this
tenth house is placed, will indicate the vocation.

3. Other methods to determine vocation:

(i)   When several planets are placed in a sign anywhere
in the horoscope, the vocation indicated by the sign
or the house may be pursued.

(ii) Similarly the most powerful planet may also force the native to pursue vocation indicated by it, at least during its major or sub-periods.

(iii) The most powerful among planets that are placed close to the Sun, but not combust, or those that aspect the Sun can also indicate the vocation that the native is likely to take up.

4. The planet determined in the manner laid down above will indicate several vocations. The vocation that the native is likely to follow will depend upon the wealth that the horoscope promises to the native. Suppose the planet that determines the vocation of the native is the Sun. It can, among other things, make the native follow medical profession. If the horoscope shows plenty of wealth, the native will be a doctor. If wealth is going to be limited, the native can be a compounder assisting a physician.

5. If the first, second, tenth and the eleventh houses are influenced by the Sun, Rahu and Saturn, or at least two out of these three, the native will become a physician.

Also see paragraph 9 under SECOND HOUSE and paragraph 7 under SIXTH HOUSE in Chapter Four.

6. Venus in the tenth house is weak. It will not be good for affairs governed by its lordship or for which it is the karaka, if it is placed here.

7. If the first and the tenth houses, their owners and the Sun are powerful the native is a highly respected person.

8. If the tenth house, its owner, and the Sun are under the influence of separative planets, a person holding even a high position will have to give it up.

9. The native will be insulted time and again if the Sun and an adverse Saturn join each other in this house with no beneficial influence.

10. For the purposes of longevity, the owner of the tenth house should be considered in the same manner as Saturn.

11. Effect of various SIGNS in the Tenth House (A careful study of NOTE in paragraph 38 under FIRST HOUSE in Chapter Four will be of use):

Aries

The native will prefer to go in for a military, police, athletic, or surgical career or will be engaged in physical activity. He will aspire to reach the top of his profession and if Mars or the Sun is powerful and well placed, the native will attain his ambition. The native will be inclined to commit bad deeds, and criticise others at their back. The native's father will be rash with his wealth and may go in for wrong investments. The owner of the tenth house here is Mars which is also the owner of the fifth house. Mars is thus the owner of a triangular house and an angular house. Mars is an excellent planet for this ascendant and if Mars is powerful and well placed in the horoscope it will confer power, status and wealth on the native. The native's children will succeed at qualifying examinations. This can be further analysed in the manner similar to Taurus in the fifth house in Chapter Four.

Taurus

The owner of the tenth house is Venus here which is also the owner of the third house. If Venus is powerful the native will show great prowess in his job and will be known for his competence. He will get the job on his own merit and will reach a high position on the basis of hard work and good results shown by him. He will be a self made man. The native's job can be related to writing, publishing, publicity, or journalism related to entertainment, music, cinema, theatre etc. The native may also be holding a job which will be related to stock market or banking. If Venus is also related to the ninth house, the native will visit developed countries in connection with his job. If the planet has connection with the twelfth house the native will live away from his birth place in a region, which will be a more advanced area than his native place, in connection with his job. A weak and afflicted Venus will be detrimental to the career prospects of the native and will reduce the longevity of the younger brothers and sisters. It will be a powerful significator of death for the father. This can be further analysed in the manner similar to Aries in the third house in Chapter Four.

Gemini

The native will be prominent in his clan, respected by the government and reputed. The native's job can be related to writing, publishing, publicity, or journalism. He will also do well as a businessman, editor, commission agent or marketing manager. The owner of the tenth house here is Mercury which is also the owner of the first house. Since Mercury is also the owner of the first house, it will not have the disability of being ruler of the two angular houses. It will be an excellent planet for the chart. If Mercury is powerful and placed close to the cusp of the house, it will make the native reach great heights in his career, earn wealth, have status and excel himself in communication of ideas, either in writing or spoken. The native's father will gain from his children. The native's mother will also enjoy a good status. This can be further analysed in the manner similar to Virgo in the first house in Chapter Four.

Cancer

The native will delight in constructing tanks, or gardens. He will also like running a hotel or an antique shop, studying history, teaching, interior decoration or architecture, professions that involve helping others or coming in contact with a large number of people such as nursing or social service, as he will have inherent sympathy with the suffering people. The native's father will have hotel or timber business and his finances will fluctuate. The father will be soft spoken and may have a large number of female relatives. The father will have danger from water, but he will have a very congenial family life. The native may be an employee of a woman. Here the Moon is the owner of the most powerful angle. If the Moon is powerful and well placed, it will make the native respected and prominent in his field.

Leo

The Sun is the owner of the most powerful angle. If the Sun is strong and well placed, the native will have power and a high position in life. He will have respect also. He will be ambitious and independent minded and will like to be self employed. The native's father will not have much wealth unless the Sun is very powerful but he will be attached to his family. The native will talk harshly, will commit bad deeds and will be ruthless. The native's children will have to serve a powerful personality against their wish or may be troubled by powerful and highly placed enemies. His younger sister/brother may face danger from wild animals or the Sun.

Virgo

Here Mercury is the owner of two angles and it is inherently a beneficial planet. Therefore it will not be able to give good results. If it is badly placed in the second, sixth, eighth or the twelfth house it will, during its major or sub-periods, cause ill health to the native and his wife. Since Mercury is not only the owner of the tenth house but also of the tenth house from the tenth, a powerful Mercury will bring much respect to the native early in life and also an early marriage. The native will have mathematical talent and will excel in computing or astrology. He will also be successful in the field of communication of ideas, writing, editing and research. He will be an intellectual. A female member of the family will be dominant. The native will lack in courage and will have to face scandals. This can be further analysed in the manner similar to Gemini in the seventh house above.

Libra

The native will be humble. He will earn well from business and will be generous and compassionate. The native will be engaged in a job in which he will get in touch with history and antiquity, or a number of people or where he has the opportunity to show his talent for the beautiful or creative. Venus, the owner of the tenth house here is also the owner of the fifth house. It is an excellent planet for the chart for Capricorn ascendant and if it is powerful, is capable of giving the native not only power and status but also plenty of wealth through his children, entertainment or speculation. The native may gain through women. This can be further analysed in the manner similar to Taurus in the fifth house in Chapter Four.

Scorpio

The fields of surgery, psychology, investigation and chemistry will attract the native. The native will be hard hearted and arrogant. The owner of the tenth house here is also the owner of the third house. The native will be a self made man and if Mars is powerful the native will show excellent work in his chosen field. This can be further analysed in the manner similar to Aries in the third house in Chapter Four and Taurus in the tenth house above.

Sagittarius

The native may be an officer in the government and is likely to discharge his duties well. He will be well known. The native, however, will have a tendency to be inattentive to his responsibilities. He is likely to be a banker, teacher, legal practitioner, or a doctor. The owner of the tenth house here is Jupiter which is also the owner of the first house. Jupiter thus owns two angular houses but the first house is also of the nature of a triangular house. Therefore Jupiter is extremely beneficial for Pisces ascendant. This is a fortunate ownership with regard to affairs of the tenth house since Jupiter is also the significator for favours from the government. If Jupiter is powerful, the native will have a successful career and will not only attain an eminent position in his field but will also have good income. The father of the native will also earn well from speculation and he will gain through his children. He may earn his wealth through entertainment, cinema, theatre or music. This can be analysed further as for Gemini in the tenth house above, or Virgo or Pisces in the first house in Chapter Four.

Capricorn

He will be ruthless and his acts will be reprehensible. The owner of the tenth house here is Saturn which is also the owner of the eleventh house. Further the mooltrikona sign of Saturn falls in the eleventh house. Therefore results given by Saturn will be predominantly those of the eleventh house. A powerful Saturn will ensure that the native has a good income from his vocation. However, Saturn for this chart will be an adverse planet. The native will have the ability for organisation and determination to take any endeavour that he takes up to its logical conclusion. Therefore he will be successful as a manager, administrator, or leader of men. A powerful and well placed Saturn with no adverse influence on it, will be good for the longevity of the mother. The wife of native's first child will be sickly. His elder sister/brother will suffer losses. His wife may gain a powerful position through the masses.

Aquarius

If Saturn is weak and poorly placed, the native's wife will have liaisons with other men and the native will also be untruthful, greedy and irreligious. The native will take up such professions where he comes in contact with a large number of people, be involved in group activities, can express himself freely and is able to satisfy his urge to be of service to others. The owner of the tenth house here is Saturn which is also the owner of the ninth house. Saturn is thus the owner of an angular and a triangular house. It is an excellent planet for the chart and if powerful will not only give the native wealth, status, success and power with little or no effort on his part but will also make the native's father and younger brothers/sisters of the native's wife very wealthy. The native's father will be very attached to his family.

Pisces

The native will be intelligent, learned and obedient to his father. He will be prominent in his clan. He will have several hobbies and interests and may find it difficult to decide which to pursue as a vocation. However the sources of income will be several through many of these hobbies that the native will pursue. The owner of the tenth house is Jupiter which is also the owner of the seventh house. Jupiter being a naturally beneficial planet, is the owner of two angular houses. It will therefore be unable to give good results for Gemini ascendant and if badly placed in the second, sixth, eighth or the twelfth house, it will in its major or sub-periods cause ill health to the native and his wife. This can be further analysed in the manner similar to Sagittarius in the seventh house above.

12. Effect of the owner of the Tenth House in various HOUSES (A careful study of the opening notes from A to H in paragraph 39 under FIRST HOUSE in Chapter Four will be of utmost use):

First

A lot of power, public esteem and prestige is indicated if the owner of the tenth is well located in the first house and the Sun is powerful in the horoscope. The income will be good. The native will like to be his own master and may try to be self employed. He may be learned and live abroad. He will be of good conduct and may even be inclined to asceticism if there are other suitable factors present in the horoscope. The native will not have good relations with his mother but will be attached to his father. If the owner of the tenth house is a malefic planet, the native will also be antagonistic to his father and his mother will be masculine. He may keep indifferent health in his early years. His children will be in international concerns or may come in close contact with foreigners in their work environment. The native is likely to largely have female children if a powerful owner of the tenth house is connected with Venus or the Moon and the eleventh house in any manner.

Second

The native will be highly placed, gain from the government and will be wealthy. He will come from a well known family. The native will do well at school and may come out at the top of successful children at the school examinations. He will be truthful and will honour his word. There is a possibility that the native may join his family business or that his job may involve talking. When the second house is powerful and the owner of the tenth house is well disposed in the second, the native will get a legacy or gain through death of a family member. His mother will gain through her partner but will be greedy. If the owner of the tenth house is weak, afflicted and has no beneficial influence here, the younger sister/brother of the native will be rich and rise high in life.

Third

The native will not like his mother and younger brothers/sisters, neighbours and colleagues. The native may not have younger sister/brother, or may have a very limited number, if Mars is a beneficial planet for the chart and is powerfully placed. However his younger sister/brother is likely to reach a high position in life. Whatever position and rank the native attains will be entirely on his own effort. He will be in government service. The native is likely to earn from writing or journalism. He will have to travel over short distances regularly in connection with his job. If the owner of the tenth house is a beneficial planet, he will look after his younger brothers and sisters. The native's father will earn through partnerships. When the owner of the tenth house is inimical to the owner of the ninth, the native's father will not like the profession the native takes up. His children will also be in service.

Fourth

The native will be learned and attached to his parents and will look after them well. He will be respected and will have status in society. He will do well in life and will have house, comforts and vehicles from the government or his profession may have to do with property or vehicles. It is likely that the native's mother had known his father since childhood and married him, may be for love. However the marital fidelity of the mother will be in doubt. If the owner of the tenth house is weak and afflicted here and does not have beneficial influence, the native's first child is likely to do well in life abroad and his elder brother/sister will also be well placed. When the owner of the ninth house is related to the owner of the tenth house, the likelihood of the native reaching a very high position in life cannot be discounted. The native's home will also be his place of work.

Fifth

The native will have riches, and children. He may have something to do with the management of programmes of music and fine arts or may earn his wealth through speculation. His job could be related to gambling or games of chance. The owner of the tenth house in the fifth having beneficial influence will make the native religious and given to a simple devotional life. In the alternative, the native could hold the position of a confidante and adviser to a powerful personality. He will be very learned. The native's children will have high status in society. A powerful owner of the tenth house will be indicative of younger sister/ brother being long lived. The owner of the tenth house, if weak and afflicted will act as a powerful significator of death for native's mother. In any case, the major or sub-periods of the owner of the tenth house will see the native's mother falling sick repeatedly. Such an owner of the tenth house does not augur well for the health and well being of the spouse of the elder sister/ brother.

Sixth

The native will be in a job where he will have to do sinful acts against his wish. The job may involve doing cruel and violent deeds. He may develop enmity in discharge of his duties. He may change his job frequently. He may deal with foreigners or people from distant parts of the country, diseases, hospitals, health matters or pet animals. He may also deal with arms, weapons, explosives etc. He will keep good health. He will be lazy, miserly and will face troubles from his enemies. The enemies will be highly placed and powerful. If the owner of the tenth house is powerful, the native will do well at competitive examinations, and will make his source of income through success at them. A weak and afflicted owner of the tenth house will impair the prospects of the native of rising high in his profession. This is not a good location for the affairs of the tenth house. He will be intelligent. The native's father will earn well through the government and the father will belong to a high family. If the owner of the tenth house is weak, afflicted and has no beneficial influence here, the elder brother/sister of the native will be rich and rise high in life. His maternal uncle will be a man of high status.

Seventh

The placement of the owner of the tenth house in the seventh indicates that the native will have partners in his business and if the owner of the tenth is powerful and well placed, he will gain from such partnership. He may be in the foreign service of the country and hold diplomatic assignments. The native's wife will be good looking, loving, well behaved and good tempered. She will have wealth and property and will be well read. She may assist the native in his business affairs. When the owner of the tenth house here has malefic influence, the native's job may involve managing females for the purpose of gratification of senses. He could thus be a pimp or procurer and he may himself be morally degraded. Such an owner of the tenth house is also bad for the longevity of the first child of the native's younger sister/brother. His elder sister/brother will go abroad and may live there.

Eighth

The native will be ailing and will have troubles in his right side of the body. He may be a criminal or a cruel person. A weak and afflicted owner of the tenth house in the eighth will mar native's career and make him short lived (see paragraph 10 above). When the owner of the tenth house is placed in the eighth alongwith a malefic planet that is adverse for the chart, the longevity of the native will be severely curtailed. Such an owner of the tenth house will bring humiliations and dishonour to the native through his career. He may be imprisoned for irregularities committed in discharge of his official duties for making illegal wealth. He may be an undertaker, coroner or a butcher, if malefic influence, especially of Saturn is there on the owner of the tenth house. He is likely to be long lived. It will also make the native's father a spendthrift and financially weak. This placement of the tenth owner makes the native's mother oversexed which may cause difficulties for the native. If a powerful Jupiter influences the owner of the tenth house here, the native will have a well developed spiritual personality. He may be an advanced tantric. If the owner of the tenth house is weak, afflicted and has no beneficial influence here, the younger sister/brother of the native will rise high in life.

Ninth

This is a happy position. If the owner of the tenth house is well placed in the ninth and is powerful there, the native will be attached to his parents, wealthy and truthful. The native may travel long distances in connection with his job and may earn from abroad. His conduct will be unblemished and his deeds fit to be emulated. He may be spiritually advanced and be a religious preceptor. If Mercury is powerful and well placed in the horoscope, the native will be a known scientist or mathematician. When Jupiter influences the owner of the tenth house here with a strong Saturn or Mercury well placed in the horoscope, the native may be a legal luminary. His father will be self made, wealthy but miserly.

Tenth

This is a happy location and, if there is no adverse influence on this house, will make the native to rise to a very high position. He will have a successful career and will be respected. He will have house, vehicle and comforts accruing out of his job. He will have wealth and will be handsome. The good results are further accentuated if the owner of the tenth house is a beneficial planet. The native's father will be wealthy and eloquent. His mother will be long lived and happily married. His children will not have trouble from enemies and will lead a healthy life.

Eleventh

This is also a happy position. If the owner of the tenth house is well placed in the eleventh and is powerful there, the native will have plenty of profits and will be in a position of power. He will have highly placed friends. He will gain by employing others. His elder brother/sister is likely to stay away from him. If the owner of the first house is weak and under malefic influence with the owner of the fourth or sixth house involved in this placement, the elder brother/sister is likely to be short lived and prone to hospitalisation. His children may not have successful partnerships and the spouse of the eldest child may be sickly.

Twelfth

This indicates that the native will squander away his father's wealth. He will have liaisons with other women. The native may derive his income from hospitals, nursing homes or asylums. He may go to a far away place in connection with his vocation. Unless the owner of the tenth house is powerful and has beneficial influence on it, the native's career will not be smooth and successful. If there is beneficial influence on the owner of the tenth house, and the Sun or Jupiter is strong and well placed in the chart, the native will be interested in spiritual upliftment and will seek self-realisation. The native's father is likely to have landed property. If the owner of the tenth house is weak, afflicted and has no beneficial influence here, the first child of the native will be rich and rise high in life.

ELEVENTH HOUSE

1. This house refers to the following:
    (i)   Gains, receipts.
    (ii) Ambitions and aspirations. Hope, realisation of ambition.
    (iii) Shins and lower legs. Left ear, left arm, or left testicle according to the drekkan rising.
    (iv) Elder brother/sister. Daughter-in-law /son-in-law.
    (v)   Success in undertakings, efforts bearing fruit, absence of misery.
    (vi) Badhakasthan for ascendants having movable signs.
    (vii) Friends, close associates (the third house refers to casual associates), lover, lasting friendship, community concerns, fondness for society and, compromise.
    (viii) Victory over enemies.
    (ix) Termination of a will or legacy (this house being the fourth from the eighth house). See FOURTH HOUSE 1/(iv) in Chapter Four.
    (x)   Discharge from hospital, release from jail or returning home (this house is twelfth from the twelfth house).
    (xi) See paragraphs 5 under Chapter on Planets and 1(x)(a) under NINTH HOUSE above.

2. A planet situated in this house confers gains. The source of these gains will be according to the karaka qualities and lordship of the planet.

3. Matters pertaining to any house will be gained in the following transit positions:
    (a) The owner of the first house reaches a position in transit which is triangular to the sign occupied by the owner of the concerned house, in the birth chart or in the navansha chart. For example, suppose we wish to consider the likely time when the native can get married. Let the owner of the seventh house, having Scorpio, be Mars. Let Mars be in

Virgo. The owner of the first house is Venus. The native may get married when Venus in transit comes to Capricorn or Taurus. Similarly if Mars is in Leo navansha then if Venus in transit comes to Sagittarius or Aries the native may get married.

(b) The owner of the concerned house, during transit, reaches positions similar to (a) with respect to the owner of the first house.

(c) The owner of the concerned house transits the same sign that is occupied by the owner of the first house in the birth chart or in the navansha chart.

(d) Owners of the first house and the concerned house aspect each other during transit.

(e) When during transit the karaka for the concerned house comes to the sign in which the owner of the first house or the owner of the Moon ascendant is situated.

(f) When during transit the owner of the first house comes to the concerned house as counted from the first house or to the concerned house as counted from the Moon ascendant in the birth chart.

(g) When during transit Jupiter comes to a triangular sign from the sign occupied by the owner of the concerned house in the birth chart or from the sign occupied by it in the navansha chart.

(h) If the owner of the first house and the owner of the concerned house are each other's temporary and natural enemies or are adverse to each other because they occupy signs which are sixth/eighth to each other, whenever these two planets would join each other in transit, the native will develop enmity with the person indicated by that concerned house or will have unpleasant results pertaining to that house. If on the other hand these two planets are friendly to each other naturally and also temporarily and occupy good positions from each other, in the above transit situation the native will feel good results concerning that house.

(i) The results pertaining to a particular house will materialise in the above given circumstances only if the owner of that house is powerful and the relevant major or sub-period is current.

(j) The major or sub-periods of a planet will be pleasant if during the currency of its major or sub-periods the planet transits through the first, third, sixth, seventh, tenth or the eleventh house. If a friend of the major or sub-period planet or a beneficial planet for the horoscope transits through the first house at that time, the major or sub-period is pleasant.

(k) Good results in a major or sub-periods of a planet would be experienced when the Sun or Jupiter passes through the sign of exaltation or mooltrikona for that planet, or its own sign. Similarly adverse results of the major or sub-periods would be felt when the Sun transits its sign of debilitation, or sign inimical to it.

(l) When the Moon passes through a house owned by a friend of the major or sub-period planet or its sign of exaltation, the house occupied by this owner, or through the third, fifth, sixth, seventh, ninth, tenth or the eleventh house counted from the major or sub-period planet, it will then show good results pertaining to the house being transited by it.

(m) If the major or sub-period planet is powerful (is retrograde, or exalted, or in own house, mooltrikona sign, friend's house etc. at birth) then it yields good results of any house that it transits through. If it is weak in the chart and also in transit then it harms matters covered by the house it passes through. Reference is invited to paragraphs 38 to 43 in opening remarks under Chapter Four for additional information on the subject.

4. Since the third, seventh and the eleventh are airy houses, if any two are related to each other, the native travels by air.

5. If the owners of the first and the eleventh houses are naturally beneficial planets and are related to any house and its owner, the native gets very attached to the relative indicated by that house and is always helpful to that person. If in place of naturally beneficial planets the combination is formed with naturally malefic planets, the results would be just the opposite. The reason is that these two houses act as the self and the eleventh house also represents friendship.

6. When the first and eleventh houses are related to each other, the native earns money through his own efforts. If the second

house is also involved in this combination and there is an aspect of a beneficial planet on it, the native gets very wealthy.

7. If the owner of the eleventh house is a beneficial planet and is also the owner of the second, it enhances the worth, status etc. of matters which it influences.

8. This house, being second from the tenth house, refers to the finances of the govt.

9. If Jupiter occupies this house under malefic influence the daughter of the native becomes a widow early in life.

10. A very weak owner of this house shortens the life of the mother of the native.

11. All planets generally give good results if they are placed in this house.

12. The owner of the eleventh house placed in any house will make the native gain those matters that are indicated by that house or the gain will be through them. Similar will be the result if the owner is in sambandha with the owner of a particular house. For illustration if the owner of the eleventh house is placed in the second house, the native will gain wealth. If it is in sambandha with the owner of the fourth, the native will gain vehicles and property.

13. (i)   A common sign in this house and the owner of the eleventh house in a common sign will make the native acquire friends of doubtful nature.

(ii)   A planet placed here indicates the class of persons that the native will befriend. For example Saturn in the eleventh house will make the friends of the native come from common strata of society. The Sun here will make the native befriend the highest. Venus here is indicative of the fact that the native will either have female friends or those who are associated with theatre or fine arts, etc.

(iii)   He may befriend persons whose ascendant is owned by the planet that is placed in the eleventh house in the native's chart.

(iv)   If the planet placed in the house is adverse for the ascendant, the friendship will later cause trouble.

(v)   If there is no planet in this house, these conclusions may be derived from the owner of the sign in this house.

14. We have explained methods to determine the number of children and their gender in paragraph 11 under FIFTH HOUSE in Chapter Four. By applying these methods to the owner of the eleventh house and its bhavamadhya we can determine the NUMBER and GENDER of native's elder siblings.

15. The rules for determining relationship between the native and a relative of his are recorded in paragraph 32 under FIRST HOUSE in Chapter Four. If we wish to determine the relations that are likely to exist between the native and his elder brother/ sister, we should apply these rules to the eleventh house.

16. Effect of various SIGNS in the Eleventh House (A careful study of NOTE in paragraph 38 under FIRST HOUSE in Chapter Four will be of use.):

Aries

The female native will be prone to have difficult child births. She may have to undergo surgical operations to deliver her of child. The native will gain from trading in cattle, from the government and from abroad. He will own vehicles. He will be independent minded and will not hesitate in expressing himself fearlessly. He may thus alienate his friends and colleagues. He may find it easier to work independently and not in a group. Mars, the owner of the eleventh house here is also the owner of the sixth house. If Mars is powerful and well placed the native will be successful at competitions and elections but since the eleventh house is sixth from the sixth house, it also indicates accidents and injuries. Mars by nature is a planet that governs accidents and injuries. Therefore Mars here is a planet that totally represents violence and injury. If it is in any manner connected with the first house and is ill placed and weak, it will make the native a victim of misadventures leading to injury. If such a Mars influences the first or fourth house and the Moon, the native will have a violent nature. Any house that comes under the influence of Mars will cause the relative indicated by that house to face the brunt of native's violent nature, and the limb of the native indicated by that house will also be prone to wounds and damage.

Taurus

The native will mostly have female friends. He will generally not have a large circle of friends; only a handful will be close to him but friendship with them will last for the life time. The native will gain through women, and by lending money and earning interest on it. He will be rich and a proficient agriculturist. Venus, the owner of the eleventh house here is also the owner of the fourth house. The native will get admission to the educational institution he aspired to join. He will profit by dealing in immovable property or vehicles. He will gain property and vehicles. The elder brother, sister or a close friend of the native will suffer from enemies or urinary, eye or kidney trouble if Venus is weak and badly placed. Such a Venus will also be a strong significator of death for the father of the native. The native's elder brothers/ sisters will have their maternal uncles and female enemies prominent in their lives.

Gemini

There will be gain in matters that the native takes up. He will be a scholar, will be liked by women and will enjoy good meals. He will have vehicles. He will have friends who have literary or varied interests and with whom the native can have open discussions. The owner of the eleventh house here is Mercury which is also the owner of the second house. Since both these houses indicate wealth and since Mercury is also related to vocation and business, if it is powerful it will make the native prosper in his business, give long life to mother, give vehicles and property to the elder brother/sister and make their minds sharp and agile; if it is not so, and afflicted, it will make the native undergo anguish over his declining fortunes and cause distress and loss of longevity to the mother. Kindly also refer to Virgo in the second house in Chapter Four.

Cancer

Agriculture, water related trades and service will be especially beneficial to the native. He will also profit by dealing in books. He will be happy to be near water. Gains will fluctuate and if there is no influence on this house and its owner, the native will only have elder sisters. The native's friends will be generally females, there will be long lasting friendships but doubts and suspicions will dog them. A weak and afflicted Moon will shorten the life of native's mother. Since the Moon indicates the mind, .its ownership of this house makes it a very powerful representative of the areas in which his father is interested. The influence of such a Moon on a house can let us decipher as to the field in which he is interested. For example, when such a Moon influences the fourth house by aspect or location, the native's father will be interested in the common man and people at large.

Leo

The native will be fond of hunting, travelling and physical fitness. He will be engaged in business in timber, forest, or horticultural produce. He will be highly ambitious and if the Sun is powerful and the house has beneficial influence, his ambitions will be fulfilled. A powerful Sun will also be helpful in making the elder brother of the native rise high in life. If there is no other influence on this house, the native will only have elder brothers. His friendship will be among highly born or highly placed persons, he will be very loyal to them and expect the same from them. The native will have limited number of children. If the Sun is afflicted and the house also has adverse influence, the native's spouse will suffer from heart or stomach ailments. He will be able to get his work done through show of anger. His conduct will not be commendable.

Virgo

The intellect and knowledge of the native will be well known. He will gain through undertakings that he takes up. He will be happy and generous. He will own vehicles. Mercury, the owner of the eleventh house here is also the owner of the eighth house. The native's father will travel a lot and live away from home. The native's spouse will earn through entertainment or speculation. A strong Mercury and a powerful eighth house will make the native gain legacies, held up money or old invested money will mature and come the native's way. If Mercury is in any manner connected with the ninth house, the first born child of the native will have largely female children. If Mercury is weak and has adverse influence, the native will suffer losses and disappointments. He will mix with people who share similar intellectual and artistic interests. He will have very few true friends and he may keep changing his friends. He cannot bear weaknesses and flaws in others. This can be further analysed in the manner similar to Gemini in the eighth house above.

Libra

The native will be well behaved and humble. He will talk well and gain. The native will have a large circle of friends who will either be women, people interested in theatre and arts or who are engaged in pursuits of fine arts. These friendships will be long lasting. If there are no influences on this house to the contrary, the native will have a number of elder sisters and they will be good looking and artistically inclined. The owner of the eleventh house is Venus here, which is also the owner of the sixth house. The native may gain from his maternal uncle. He may be successful at competitions. Association with foreigners will be beneficial. This can be further analysed in the manner similar to Aries in the eleventh house above. The propensity of Venus to cause injury to the native will be further accentuated if it, in any manner, is connected with an adverse Mars or Ketu. If it is connected with an adverse Saturn or Rahu it will cause illnesses that it represents.

Scorpio

The native will adopt unscrupulous methods to earn profits. He will not be truthful. He will be knowledgeable about Mantras and the science of Tantras and will earn through this esoteric knowledge. The native will be impatient with his friends and elder brothers/sisters and there will be disagreements with them. The owner of the eleventh house here is also the owner of the fourth house. The native will gain property and since Mars is also the significator for property, this result will be prominent in the life of the native if Mars is powerful. A powerful Mars will ensure that the native gets admission to the desired engineering or defence college. Such a Mars will afford wealth through children, entertainment or speculation to the spouse of the native. The eleventh house represents arm of the native. Therefore it is symbolically representative of premeditated action on the part of the native. Mars is cruel. Therefore if Mars influences the significator for a relative, the native will be intentionally cruel to him. A weak Mars will be a powerful significator of death of the mother. This can be further analysed in the manner similar to Aries in the fourth house in Chapter Four.

Sagittarius

He will be a companion of the highly placed persons and will earn by his own efforts. He will be clever and rich. He will have a large number of friends and companions and will have the ability to work with them easily. Jupiter is the owner of the eleventh and the second houses here. The native will earn well through teaching or legal practice. Jupiter will also have the ability to improve the prospects of matters that it influences through their significators or houses. For example if Jupiter is connected with the Sun and the tenth house, the native will rise to a high position. The elder brothers of the native will be scholarly, will have property and live in comfort. If Jupiter is powerful, the native's mother will be long lived. This can be further analysed in the manner similar to Virgo and Pisces in the second house in Chapter Four.

Capricorn

The native will earn well from boats and other sea faring vehicles, matters related to water, construction of canals and ponds, from government and by journeys overseas, but will also spend the earnings quickly. The native will find it difficult to make friends but he will be loyal to them and the friendship will be long lasting. The native will not be able to work in a group. He will have elder sisters. The owner of the eleventh house here is also the owner of the twelfth house. The mooltrikona sign of Saturn is in the twelfth house. The native's income will not be commensurate with the effort that he will put in for it. A weak Saturn will lead to losses through elder brother/sister or friends. This can be further analysed in the manner similar to Aquarius in the twelfth house below.

Aquarius

He is likely to take to crime to earn his livelihood. If Saturn is powerful, education and learning will be the means of earning the livelihood and the native will be sober and rich. The native will have a small circle of close friends. They will be like members of the family and will share with him the same interests. The native will prefer to form groups through which he will champion the cause of the weak and disabled. He will be sociable. These activities will become so onerous that the native may start neglecting his family. Saturn, the owner of the eleventh house here is also the owner of the tenth house. If Saturn is powerful, the native will have very good income from his vocation and will be wealthy. He may work with or for his elder brother/sister, or in an enterprise owned by his friend.

Pisces

The native will meet his friends at social gatherings. The number of friends will continue to grow. He will gain through his friends and the government. The owner of the eleventh house, Jupiter here is also the owner of the eighth house. If the eighth house is powerful and Jupiter is well placed, the native is likely to get a legacy. Jupiter will tend to give the native's eldest child only female children and the native's father much touring if it influences the ninth house. When one of the lunar nodes influences Jupiter, which is weak and has bad influence on it, the native may meet with a serious accident. This can be further analysed in the manner similar to Virgo above.

17. Effect of the owner of the eleventh house in various houses (A careful study of the opening notes from A to H in paragraph 39 under FIRST HOUSE in Chapter Four will be of utmost use.):

First

The native will be wealthy, genuine and will possess vehicles. His efforts will yield good results. He will like to have good people as his friends and will shun evil company. He will be short lived and thirst may be the cause of his death. If the owners of the two houses are friendly, the native will have good relations with his elder brothers/sisters and will have good and long lasting friends. They will in any case be prominent in his life. His wishes will be realised. The native's paternal uncles/aunts may be connected with theatre or arts. Unless the owner of the eleventh house has beneficial influence, his mother will suffer from worries and ill-health. The native's children will go abroad and may serve in the foreign service of the country. The first child will be well married and he will do well in life after his marriage.

Second

The native will be wealthy, miserly and will possess vehicles. He will successfully complete his school education and he will love his family. His family will own property, wealth and vehicles. His paternal uncles/aunts will be sickly and suffer from thieves, fire, poison, weapons or enemies. The native may suffer loss of his first born child. A powerful owner of the eleventh house here will let the native earn profits from his business investments. He will gain through banks or financial institutions. The second house indicates the residence of elder sister/brother. The eleventh house is the native's self. Thus there is a relationship set up between the self and the residence of elder brother. Therefore it is likely that the native may help to build or set up the house of his elder brother.

Third

The native will have servants and his younger brothers/sisters, neighbours and colleagues will gain. His efforts will be successful. He will have the courage to take up matters single handedly and complete them on his own. The native will like to travel and will gain from these travels. This location is very lucky for the native's wife. She is likely to gain sudden benefits and will, due to good luck, have good children and wealth. The children will also be lucky and religious. If the owner of the eleventh house is weak and afflicted here and does not have any beneficial influence on it, it will prove very beneficial to the mother of the native but the native's younger brother will be a source of trouble to him and he will suffer losses due to him, particularly if Mars is weak in the horoscope and badly placed. The native will make friends with persons who have similar hobbies.

Fourth

The native will get patrimony and will be attached to his parents. His parents will be long lived in case the owner of the eleventh house is strong and free from affliction. He may be an agriculturist. The native's wife will gain from speculation. Her children will be connected well with the government. When a powerful Venus either influences the combination or it is well placed in the horoscope, the native will acquire wealth and vehicles. If a favourably disposed and powerful Mars is involved in place of Venus in this combination, the native will acquire plenty of property. A weak and afflicted owner of the eleventh house will cause illnesses to the elder brothers/sisters and trouble to them from their enemies. The native's aspiration for acquiring power, fame and status will be fulfilled if the owner of the eleventh house is friendly with the owner of the tenth house, or the tenth house is owned by the owner of the eleventh house.

Fifth

The native's children will gain. He will be scholarly, capable and knower of mantras and tantras. All the wishes of the native will be fulfilled. He will have good, well behaved and long-lived children and will have big profits from his ventures. A powerful owner of the eleventh house will get the mother of the native wealth from a legacy. If the owners of the two houses are friendly, the native's first born child will be attached to his paternal uncles/aunts. The native's elder brother will marry more than once and may be sensual. His father may travel extensively.

Sixth

The native's maternal uncle will gain. The native will suffer losses from thefts or fire. A powerful owner of the eleventh house will make the mother long-lived. This position is not good for the life of native's children, especially the first born child. It will be particularly so if the owner of the eleventh house is weak and afflicted in the sixth house. It will also be bad for the health of the elder brothers/sisters. Paragraph 7 under the Sixth House should be usefully studied for determining the career the native is likely to take up if the third, or the eleventh house is connected with the sixth. The native will not keep good health. He may live away from his home town and may be hard hearted and selfish. He is likely to have trouble in his left ear, or if Jupiter is weak and under adverse influence in the horoscope, he may have hearing defect.

Seventh

The native's wife will be wealthy and will gain. She will be well behaved and attached to the native. The native will get help and assistance from the relatives of his wife. He will however not be worldly wise and will be a poor manager of his finances. He may try to woo other females. If the owners of the two houses are friendly, the native's wife will be attached to her children. The children will in any case be prominent in her life. The native's business partner will be speculative in nature and in case the owners of the two houses are inimical to each other, he will lose in speculation. The native's father will be a self made man.

Eighth

If the owner of the eleventh house is a malefic planet, it is likely to bring death to the native in its major or sub-periods. If it is a beneficial planet the native will keep good health and will gain from legacies or will regain moneys which had long been held back from him. He will not be rich and will earn with lot of hard work. The native's father will travel regularly and live away from home from time to time. The native's spouse will have proficiency in music and fine arts. The spouse will predecease the native. The elder brother/sister of the native is likely to lead a difficult life in service unless the owner of the eleventh house is powerful and well placed in the eighth house. The eldest child of the native is likely to have loose morals.

Ninth

If the owner of the eleventh house is in the ninth, the native will be fortunate. He will be rich and hold a high position. He will be attached to his younger brother/sister. If the owners of the two houses are friendly, the native's father will have good relations with his younger brothers/sisters, neighbours and colleagues. They will in any case be prominent in his life. The native may earn profits in international trade or generally from abroad. He may have to undertake long journeys in the process. The native will gain from his father. If Saturn or the owner of the eighth house influences the owner of the eleventh house, the native will gain from father after his death. Unless there is malefic influence, the gains to the native will be from right sources.

Tenth

The native will be rich and will gain through the government. His father's younger sister/brother will be rich. The spouse of the first born child of the native will be sickly if the owner of the eleventh house is weak and afflicted. If the owner of the fourth house is not inimical to the owner of the eleventh house, the desires of the native with regard to property, vehicles and general comforts in life will be fulfilled; and the native's parents will have close and loving relationship with each other. The younger brother/sister of the native will not be fortunate. Such a disposition of the owner of the eleventh house will make the native philanthropic and ready for genuine service of the people.

Eleventh

The native will be very rich, will own vehicles and will have servants. He will have very good and obedient children who will do well in life. The native will be able to generally attain his ambitions in life. The native's wife will be elegant and if Venus is connected with the eleventh house, will be interested in fine arts, music and drama. She may also be attracted to speculation. She will be well read. If the owners of the fifth and eleventh houses are inimical to each other, the native's first born child will not have good relations with his spouse. The native's brothers/sisters will be long lived and fortunate.

Twelfth

The native will have to work hard to earn money in small

measures but he will spend heavily. If the owner of the eleventh house is a beneficial planet and has good influence on it, the expenditure will be for charitable and religious purposes. The native's father will change his residence several times. The native may earn from hospitals etc. or from abroad. His friends may actually be his secret enemies and may work against his interests silently. The native will observe that his friends not only do not actually help him but also try to take away any advantage that comes his way. His mother may not be fortunate and may have to face several obstacles and disappointments in life. She will however be religious and interested in the occult and spiritual matters. A powerful owner of the eleventh house, well placed in the twelfth house will make the younger brothers/sisters of the native wealthy and powerful. The native may live near the house of a person of high status. If the owner of the eleventh house has malefic influence including that of Rahu in the twelfth house, the native's elder brother may be imprisoned.

TWELFTH HOUSE

1. This house refers to the following:
    (i)   Expenditure, extravagance, loss.
    (ii)   Unforeseen troubles, sorrow, worries, misfortune.
    (iii)   Punishment, seclusion, imprisonment, restriction on freedom, isolation, and confinement.
    (iv)   Bad deeds. Fall both physical and figurative.
    (v)   Secret enemy. Conspiracy and underground movements. Secret and occult societies. Secret plots and spies.
    (vi)   Deceit and persecution.
    (vii)   Kidnapping, looting, crime, arson, rape, poisoning, bootlegging, smuggling, and blackmailing etc.
    (viii) End, spiritual practices, moksha (emancipation from the cycle of births and death), sin, hell, heaven, occult. Past karmas (deeds done in previous lives).
    (ix)   Feet and toes. Infirmity in a limb. Left eye, left shoulder, and left side of the genitals and anus depending on the drekkan rising.
    (x)   Going away from home, exile, extradition, travels, and going abroad.
    (xi)   Sexual pleasure. Sound sleep.

- (xii) Inferiority complex.
- (xiii) Suffering in secret.
- (xiv) Selfless and profound service to the society, and acts arising out of pricking of one's conscience.
- (xv) Repayment of loan by the native (for repayment the eighth house also has to operate since on repayment the creditor will earn which is indicated by the second house from the seventh).
- (xvi) Father's wealth and property devolving on the native.
- (xvii) Elephants and horses. Large cattle and beasts (sixth house refers to pet animals).
- (xviii) Loss due to marriage or wife. Loss of wife.
- (xix) Termination of appointment.
- (xx) Hospitals, jails, asylums, monasteries, and places of seclusion.
- (xxi) Institutionalised religion.

2. The nature of the planet and the nature of influence on that planet will decide whether the results accruing out of this house will be to the liking of the native or not. For example whether expenditure will be to native's liking can be determined in this manner.

3. The Moon in this house in a movable sign or aspected by Saturn makes a person wander.

4. When the twelfth house is influenced by malefic planets and the owner of the twelfth house is also similarly influenced by such planets, the native will wander from one country to the other.

5. A planet connected with the second, seventh (or ninth) and the twelfth houses makes the native go away from his family on a long journey to a far away place.

6. If this house is connected with the second, sixth, and the tenth houses it indicates service in a hospital. If this house is connected only with the sixth house then it shows that the native would be hospitalised.

7. If the fourth and the twelfth houses are connected it indicates a change in residence.

8. If the ninth and this house are related a long journey and life abroad are indicated.

9. If the Sun or the Moon is located in this house and is afflicted by malefic planets, the native is likely to lose his eye-sight. The same principle can be used for predictions regarding native's relatives. For example if there is the Sun in the eighth house with such affliction it would mean loss of sight to the father.

10. All planets barring Venus are considered badly placed in this house. Venus is good both in the sixth (though not for married life) and the twelfth houses.

11. Venus benefits the house or planet from which it is in the twelfth house.

12. If the owners of the fourth and the twelfth houses (watery houses) influence the eighth house and its owner, death by drowning is indicated. However if the twelfth house is occupied by a planet it will then act according to the nature of the occupying planet. In the above combination the owner of the fourth house only reinforces the watery effect of the owner of the twelfth house. The combination basically depends upon the connection between the eighth and the twelfth houses.

13. If the weak and afflicted owner of the twelfth house is placed in the third, sixth or the eighth house and has malefic influence without any redeeming beneficial effect, it gives rise to Vipareet Raj Yoga and confers immense riches.

14. This house also indicates wastage. So if the Sun is located here it would mean complete expenditure of the self. The man would therefore be selfless. Moon here would mean irritability and emotional imbalance. Mars here means the native makes efforts for others. Mars here can also lead to muscular atrophy. Mercury here would make a man extremely talkative. Jupiter here would make the man keep giving unsolicited advice. Venus in this house can make a man lustful. Saturn here can make the native nervous in nature.

15. If the three ascendants, the twelfth house, and their owners are influenced by satvik planets, and the fourth house, its owner and the Moon are under the influence of Saturn the native attains moksha (liberation from the cycle of births and deaths).

16. The nature of expenditure and also whether it would be pleasant or otherwise will depend on the nature of the planet connected with this house whose period is current causing the expenditure.

17. If Venus is in the twelfth house and is connected with Saturn and Rahu the native will have insatiable sexual appetite. His relations with his wife will not be cordial but the wife will be long lived.

18. The native will suffer from insomnia if the twelfth house, its owner, Venus and the Moon all have malefic influence.

19. The owner of a house situated in the twelfth house, or the owner of the twelfth house in any house, or a sambandha between the owner of the twelfth house and the owner of any house, will cause loss to the native of matters that are signified by that house.

20. (i) When the first and twelfth houses, their owners and Rahu are related, the native is likely to be imprisoned.

   (ii) If the second and the twelfth; or, the third and the eleventh; or, the fourth and the tenth; or, the fifth and the ninth houses have equal number of planets, the native is likely to be jailed. If beneficial planets are also involved in this combination in any manner, the native may be released from jail early, or if only beneficial planets form this combination, he may be placed under some restriction for his own benefit. See paragraph 23 under SIXTH HOUSE in Chapter Four also.

21. Effect of various SIGNS in the Twelfth House (A careful study of NOTE in paragraph 38 under FIRST HOUSE in Chapter Four will be of use.):

Aries

The native will rear cattle and spend on them. He would spend heavily on beautiful things but at the same time realising the necessity of thrift will try to curb his extravagance. Mars, the owner of the twelfth house here is also the owner of the seventh house.

The native will be sensual and if Mars or Ketu influences Venus he may even indulge in perverse sexual practices. A weak and adverse Mars will necessitate surgical operations and hospitalisation of native's spouse. She may also, due to her bad temper, get annoyed with her husband and leave him on an impulse. Without any other influence, these separations may not be permanent. A powerful Mars will give long life and vitality to the first born child of the native. Such a Mars will grant erudition to native's mother and prosperity to his father in the form of property. This can be further analysed in the manner similar to Scorpio in the seventh house above.

Taurus

The native will keep animals and will have relationship with several women. He will be thrifty but would like to buy beautiful and elegant items. His wife will spend money on things of good taste and good living. The owner of the twelfth house, Venus here is also the owner of the fifth house. Venus will be a good planet for the chart for Gemini ascendant. It will however separate the native from his children from time to time if it influences the fifth house by aspect or occupation. He will spend on and invest in shares, bonds and securities. If Venus is weak, the native will lose through investments and speculation. He will also spend on or lose through his children. The native will have strong sex urge. This can be further analysed in the manner similar to Aries or Libra in the fifth house in Chapter Four.

Gemini

The native's enemies will be under check, he will spend a lot on marriages and will always try to speak the truth. The owner of the twelfth house here is Mercury, which is also the owner of the third house. The native will be capable of detailed planning and research. He will travel inland extensively and will live away from home from time to time. If Mercury influences the fourth house, the native will keep changing his residence regularly. He may not have younger brothers or sisters or he may not be social with his neighbours. This can be further analysed in the manner similar to Virgo or Pisces in the third house in Chapter Four.

Cancer

Water sports will be the favourite past time for the native. He will spend money on tanks, wells and waterbodies. He will like to remain secluded for long periods of time when he would like to reflect. He will be extravagant from time to time. The Moon represents the left eye. Since the twelfth house also stands for the left eye, if the Moon is weak and afflicted, the native is bound to lose his left eye or have defective sight. His elder brother/sister will have fluctuating wealth. If the Moon is under bad influence and weak, the native may not be rich. His younger sister/brother will be connected with the government and if the Moon is powerful, he may occupy a high position. His mother is likely to travel abroad. His children may suffer from imbalance of watery element in the body, or if the Moon is adverse, may die by drowning.

Leo

The Sun stands for eyesight. The twelfth house is also representative of the left eye. If the Sun is weak and afflicted, the native is likely to lose his eyesight. The native will be fond of visiting gardens and forests. He will be extravagant and many a time, out of his desire to do good to others, will act in a manner prejudicial to his own interests. He will however have the capacity to delve deep and successfully in spiritual and metaphysical matters. The younger brothers and sisters of the native's father will be highly placed with imposing personalities. The native may live in the neighbourhood of a high dignitary. His elder brother/sister is not likely to be rich.

Virgo

The native will be at peace with himself. He will spend his wealth on charitable and good works like marriages, construction of temples, pilgrimages etc. The native will have immense capacity for work or meditation in solitude for long periods. Mercury, the owner of the twelfth house here is also the owner of the ninth house. Mercury will be beneficial to the native if strong; if weak, the native will suffer losses through his father or wife's younger brother/sister. This can be further analysed in the manner similar to Gemini in the ninth house above.

Libra

Some of the younger brothers/sisters, neighbours and colleagues of the native will be at loggerheads with him. He will be
miserly. The native will get into indebtedness or financial crises
due to his expensive habits. The owner of the twelfth house here
is Venus, which is also the owner of the seventh house. The
native will have to spend heavily over his wife, if Venus is weak.
An afflicted Venus may cause loss of wife to the native. Such a
Venus will also make the native have strong sex urge. This can
be further analysed in the manner similar to Taurus in the
seventh house above.

Scorpio

The native will be truthful though of bad temper and given to
ruthlessness. He will be extravagant and will resent intrusion in his
private life even if it is by his closest friends and in his interest. Mars
owns the twelfth and the fifth houses here and if powerful will be
beneficial to the native. Mars will cause the native to spend over
his children and speculation. A weak Mars will make the native lose
money by speculation and gambling. An afflicted Mars may cause
loss of children. This can be further analysed in the manner similar
to Aries in the fifth house in Chapter Four.

Sagittarius

He will be good at archery, be able to suppress his enemies
and will get wealth from the government. The native will have
spiritual experiences. He will have to face heavy expenses. He
will have an urge to prefer solitude. Jupiter is the owner of the
twelfth as well as the third house. It is also the significator of
wealth. Since the third house is the eighth house from the eighth,
Jupiter cannot give much wealth to the native in its major or sub-
periods. Due to this ownership, unless Jupiter is very powerful,
the native cannot expect to get rich in the major or sub-periods
of this planet. If it is weak, it will restrict the number of younger
brothers or sisters and cause losses and heavy expenditure to
them. Such a Jupiter will also make them travel a lot and stay
away from home. A strong Jupiter will make them comfortable,
prosperous and happy and will make the native undertake

successful journeys in connection with legal, philosophical or hospital work. This can be further analysed in the manner similar to Pisces in the third house in Chapter Four.

Capricorn

Water sports will be the favourite past time for the native. He will spend money on tanks, wells and waterbodies. The native will be fond of going away on pleasure trips abroad or to distant places for a break. He will be alternately extravagant and careful with his money. The owner of the twelfth house is also the owner of the first. A powerful and well placed Saturn may assist the native in showing good academic results at college. The native may gain from agriculture. This can be further analysed in the manner similar to Aquarius in the first house in Chapter Four.

Aquarius

The native will be knowledgeable, and good at doing various things. He will be wealthy. The native will spend on humanitarian and charitable works. The expenditure will tend to be heavy, though if Saturn is strong, the income will also be substantial from abroad or nursing homes. Saturn as owner of the twelfth house will have powerful separating influence. When such Saturn influences a house, its owner and its karaka, the native will be separated from the matter indicated by these factors. This can be further analysed in the manner similar to Capricorn in the eleventh house above.

Pisces

His relations with the government will be good. He will be of a likable personality, and will talk well. Jupiter, the owner of the twelfth house here is also the owner of the ninth house. The native is likely to go abroad on intellectual work. It will have its mooltrikona sign in the ninth house. Jupiter will represent the feet of the the native fully. Since the twelfth house is taken to be neutral when the nature of the planets for any ascendant is judged, Jupiter here will predominantly give the results of the ninth house. If it is powerful, it will make the native religious, philosophical or having good knowledge of law. Such a Jupiter connected with the first house will make the native highly spiritual. This can be further analysed in the manner similar to Gemini or Sagittarius in the ninth house above.

22. Effect of owner of the Twelfth House in various HOUSES (A careful study of the opening notes from A to H in paragraph 39 under FIRST HOUSE in Chapter Four will be of utmost use.):

First

The native will be generous and extravagant. He will like to be elegantly dressed. He may not have good health and may suffer from such ailments that necessitate his hospitalisation. The native will leave his place of birth and live away from it. He will suffer from enemies. He may face persecution and punishment for his membership of secret societies. A powerful owner of the twelfth house well placed in the first house will ensure that the native's younger sister/brother earns well from his profession. His younger sister/brother will have highly placed friends who will help his interests. Such an owner of the twelfth house will also be beneficial for the mother of the native since it will make her wealthy, inclined to be of noble character and good behaviour. It will make the native's father learned and wealthy. This placement is not good for native's children even if the owner of the twelfth house is of normal strength. They will not be fortunate and though tending to live long, if the owner of the twelfth house is aspected by Saturn, will face serious reverses in their lives. The native's maternal aunt will be short lived if the owner of the twelfth house is weak and afflicted.

Second

The native will find it difficult to accumulate wealth. If the owner of the twelfth house is weak and afflicted and does not have beneficial influence here, the native's wife will have high status and wealth. Such an owner will also be instrumental in native's father losing his property and wealth for the repayment of loans. A powerful owner of the twelfth house indicates a highly religious and spiritual nature of native's mother. The native will earn wealth by his efforts. He will stay in his native land for a short while and will thereafter go abroad where he will be successful. A weak and badly placed owner of the twelfth house with malefic influence and a poor Mercury in the chart will cause defective speech in the native. It may also bring about losses to the native due to his loose tongue. If instead of Mercury, the Sun, the Moon or Venus is involved in this combination, the native is likely to have defective eye sight. A badly placed owner of the twelfth house here will make it difficult for the native to have his meals honourably. His younger sister/brother or his eldest child is likely to lose his jobs. His elder sister/brother will earn from property or vehicles.

Third

This location of the twelfth owner is indicative of the fact that the native will travel a lot and will stay away from home for long periods. He will also travel abroad during the major or sub-periods of the owner of the twelfth house. He will be selfish. He may develop ear ailments if the owner of the twelfth house and Jupiter are afflicted and weak. There may be loss of younger sister/brother. The younger brother of the native will have to spend heavily and will be introverted. The native's mother will travel abroad. His partner in business will have successful association with foreign concerns. The native will feel drained of vitality during the major or sub-periods of the owner of the twelfth house. If the owner of this house is powerful and well placed in the house, the native's children are likely to get a legacy. The native's father may go on long journey in connection with his higher education and earn his livelihood at a distant place in case the sign in the seventh house is a movable one.

Fourth

The native's mother will be beset with troubles. The native will not have happiness and comforts during the major or sub-periods of the owner of the twelfth house. The native will lose wealth and property and he will have an introverted mind. He is likely to change his residence more than once. The native's spouse will be successful at a competitive examination and will get a job as a result. His son may cause his death. If the owner of the twelfth house is weak, afflicted and has no beneficial influence here, the children of the native will be rich and may rise high in life. The native will lack mental peace and will be worried over trifles.

Immovable property, if an adverse Mars or Saturn influences the placement, whether owned by him or rented by him for his use will be a source of constant harassment. When Venus is afflicted in the chart, the native will find that vehicles are the cause of his trouble.

Fifth

The owner of the twelfth house in the fifth is indicative of troubles and losses to and due to the children. The native may not have children. He may go to holy places to pray for a son. However if the owner of the fifth house is in the fifth with the owner of the twelfth house, the native is likely to get a child in the major or sub-periods of the owner of the twelfth house. It also indicates that the native will have a sensual mind and will spend on entertainment, speculation, or his children. There may be separation from children at some time in life. The native is likely to alienate a powerful person. The native's mother will get a windfall of wealth. If the owner of the twelfth house is placed powerfully in the fifth house and Mercury or Jupiter is strong in the horoscope, the native's father will be a scholar. The father will have wealth and vehicles if Jupiter or Venus is strong in the chart.

Sixth

If the owner of the twelfth house is weak and afflicted and does not have any beneficial aspect, the native will hold a high position and will be wealthy but he will not have marital happiness. He may also be involved in protracted litigation which may finally end in his favour. The native will spend on good causes. He will have satisfactory sex life. In some cases the native may be over sexed and may have liaison with several women. His enemies and maternal uncle will have troubles. His mother will travel extensively and will also go abroad. She may, if there is a strong Mercury in the chart, take to writing. The longevity of the native will be affected and he may suffer from eye trouble or may be blind, if there are other indications in the nativity to this effect. His children will have to face heavy expenses and losses.

Seventh

This location of the owner of the twelfth house is not conducive to the welfare of native's spouse. The spouse will be indebted or ailing, and will be separated from the native from time
to time. She will have to face troubles from her enemies or
through litigation. The native will therefore have constant worries, expenses and sorrow. The native will try to grab of others
property and wealth through litigation. He will travel extensively
and visit abroad. His morals may not be satisfactory and the
native may have relations with other women. If the owner of the
twelfth house is powerful, it will give the native's mother comforts, wealth and vehicles. Such an owner will also be good for
the longevity of native's children. His wife could be the cause of
his death, if the owner is a malefic planet; if it is a beneficial
planet, the cause of death will be a woman of loose morals.

Eighth

If the owner of the twelfth house is weak and does not have
any beneficial aspect, the native will be fortunate, hold a high
position and will be wealthy, but he will not have a happy
married life. He may have heavy outgo of money during the
major or sub-periods of the owner of the twelfth house. This
location is also indicative of the fact that the native will have
medium span of life and will die in an asylum, nursing home or
hospital, or away from home. The native is likely to be estranged
from his family. The major or sub-periods of the owner of the
twelfth house will be pleasant and happy if the eighth house is
strong. A strong owner of the twelfth house here is excellent for
the welfare, fortune and wealth of native's mother. The native's
father will have to live away from home in discomfort. His
children will be without comforts, happiness or property.

Ninth

The native will go abroad and on long journeys and stay there
for some time. The owner of the twelfth house here will also
cause troubles to the native and his younger sister/brother. Their
affairs will take a downward plunge in its major or sub-periods.

This location is not good unless the owner of the twelfth house is a friend of the owner of the ninth house and a beneficial planet, or the owner of the ninth house is powerful and placed in the ninth. If the two owners are friendly, the native's parents will be attached to each other and his mother will have dominating influence over his father. The native's younger brothers/sisters, neighbours and colleagues will be few and he will not be close to them. He will show scant respect to his father, elders or preceptor. He may get alienated from most of his friends. His children will face troubles on account of their children. There is a possibility of loss of some grand children.

Tenth

The native will be a servant of the government. He will travel on government duty and will be posted away from his birth place. His career may have ups and downs and he may be subjected to worries and sorrows due to it. He may be divested of his position and power during the major or sub-periods of the owner of the twelfth house. The native, during this period, will also have to change his residence with the change in his status. If the tenth house and its owner are also subjected to the influence of adverse Sun, Saturn or Rahu, the loss of position and power could be more lasting. He may also have to incur expenditure on account of the government. His profession may be related to medicine, hospitals or jails. His parents will not stay with him, may be because his mother will have an acid tongue. The native's father will have wealth in the form of property but he may lose most of it in an attempt to repay the sums owed by the native to the government. The native's mother-in-law will be of poor health which will always be a source of worry to him. If the owner of the twelfth house is weak, afflicted and has no beneficial influence here, the native's children will be rich and may rise high in life.

Eleventh

The native's income and outgo of wealth will almost be balanced. The native will be worried over the future of his children. His friends will work against his interests and will actually be secretly inimical to him. A malefic owner of the twelfth house will cause trouble to the children and separation from them. He will not have many friends but the number of secret enemies will be large. There may be misunderstanding with his elder sister/brother. The wife of his eldest child may predecease him. His elder brother/sister will be wealthy and extravagant. If the owner of the twelfth house is placed powerfully in the eleventh house, the native's younger sister/brother will be prosperous and very highly placed in life. The younger sister/brother will also be known for his good deeds and upright behaviour. The native will be well known and truthful.

Twelfth

If the owner of the twelfth house is weak and does not have any beneficial aspect, the native will hold a high position and will be wealthy. If it is not so, the native will face heavy expenditure and will be troubled by his enemies. However a powerful owner of the twelfth house having benign influence, in the twelfth will make the native prosperous abroad, religious and interested in spiritualism. If the owner is weak, he will be mentally disturbed and irritable. A movable sign in this house, or the Moon or Mercury here will make the native travel incessantly. The maternal uncle of native's wife will be well off. A powerful owner of the twelfth house will make the native's children long lived, his elder brother/sister wealthy and his mother fortunate. The twelfth house is the tenth from the third house. It is therefore the house of respect, honour, vocation etc. for the younger sister/brother of the native. If it is powerful, it is obvious that the native's younger sister/brother will have these measures to the full in their lives.

NOTE

    (a) When reference is made to good or bad aspects, it is meant that they are aspects by planets that are beneficial planets or otherwise for a particular ascendant. In Western Astrology the aspects are catagorised as good aspects or bad aspects, irrespective of the nature of the planets. These aspects in Western Astrology are being given for information of the reader. They are as follows:

(i)   Conjunction (when two planets or astrological points are 0 degrees apart, or very near to each other)- this is good if naturally beneficial planets conjoin, otherwise not.

(ii) Semi-sextile (approximately 30 degrees apart)-good.

(iii) Semi-square (approximately 45 degrees apart)-bad.

(iv) Sextile (approximately 60 degrees apart)-good.

(v)   Square (approximately 90 degrees apart)-bad.

(vi) Trine (approximately 120 degrees apart)-good.

(vii) Opposition (approximately 180 degrees apart)-bad but may become beneficial if naturally beneficial planets are involved.

(b) When reference is made to the cusp of a house, such Nirayan cusp should be determined by first calculating the cusp according to the tables given in Raphael's Tables of Houses and then reducing the value so obtained by an appropriate value of the Ayanamsha. In Hindu astrology, this will be the middle (Bhavamadhya) of the house, whereas in western system the Sayan cusp is taken as the beginning of the house.

(c) HORA-LAGNA can be calculated in the following manner: Suppose we wish to find the hora-lagna at the time of birth of a native. Take the time of sunrise from any ephemeris. Find the difference in time between the time of birth and the time of sunrise. Take the number of hours, ignoring the minutes and seconds if any in this time difference. Let this be H. Add one to the number of hours. It will be H+1. If the sign in the ascendant is odd, count H+1 signs from the sign (taking it as the first sign) in which the Sun is placed. That will be the sign in the hora-lagna. If the sign in the ascendant is an even sign, count from the ascendant. For example, if Taurus is in the ascendant and the value of H is 3, counting 3+1=4 signs from Taurus, the sign in the hora-lagna will be Leo.

(d) Generally by referring to any navansha table we can find the navansha sign in which any heavenly body would fall. However a simple method is available to find the navansha sign without referring to a table. The navansha sign in which a planet is placed can be calculated in the following manner:

Convert the longitude of the planet into signs, degrees, minutes and seconds. See in which ninth part of a sign of 30 degrees will the degrees, minutes and seconds of the planet will lie. Multiply the signs by 9 and add the serial number of the ninth part found above to it. Divide the result by 12. The remainder will be the serial number of the sign in which the planet will be located in the navansha chart.

This can be better understood through an illustration. Let the planet have the longitude of 122 degrees 25 minutes. This is equal to 4 signs 2 degrees 25 minutes. Since each ninth part of a sign is equal to 3 degrees 20 minutes, we can readily say that 2 degrees 25 minutes will be in the first ninth part.

We multiply 4 by 9 and add 1 to it. The result is 37. We divide 37 by 12. The remainder is 1. Therefore the planet will be in Aries navansha.

Chapter Six

A New Look at the Vimshottari Dasa System

We have studied the signs, planets, lunar nodes and houses in some detail in the preceding chapters. We are in a position to determine the results that each planet is expected to give when its influence operates. The determination of the nature of these results and the moment when they are expected to occur will be the theme of this chapter. Some rules to fix the time for the happening of an event on the basis of transit of planets have already been given in the preceding pages. However, timing of events is a detailed subject which has been dealt with in another independent book by me.

2. The method to determine the strength of a planet is given in paragraph 14 in the opening remarks of Chapter Two. We are aware of the fact that a powerful and beneficial planet will confer beneficial results and a weak malefic planet will cause trouble. It is also well known that a weak beneficial planet will not be capable of conferring good results, and a powerful malefic planet will desist from giving adverse results. However to judge the nature of a planet in a more precise manner, we ought to take recourse to the determination of Vinshopaka strength of each planet.

3. There is permanent natural relationships between the planets. The relationship of each planet with other planets is given under each planet in Chapter Two. The permanaent relationship that the Nodes have with other planets is given in Chapter Three. There is temporary relationship also between the planets depending upon their location in the birth chart with respect to each other. A planet will be temporarily friendly with those planets in the chart that are placed in the second, third, fourth, twelfth, eleventh or the tenth sign from the sign in which that planet is located. All other planets, not so located, will be inimical to that planet. Thus a planet will either be:

(i) an intimate friend of another planet if it is friendly with that planet on both the counts, i.e., on account of permanent as well as temporary relationship, or

(ii) will simply be friendly to it, if it is neutral to the planet in permanent relationship but friendly in temporary relationship, or

(iii) neutral to the planet if it is friendly on one count and inimical on the other, or

(iv) inimical to the planet if it is neutral to the planet in permanent relationship but inimical in temporary relationship, or

(v) a great enemy of the planet if it is inimical to that planet on both the counts.

4. For determining the Vinshopaka strength of a planet, we first check the location of the planet in six vargas (sub divisions) of Rasi, Hora, Drekkan, Navansha, Dwadsansha and Trinshansha. If the planet is placed in its:

Own varga	it will get full 20 marks
Intimate friend's varga	it will get 18 marks
Friend's varga	it will get 15 marks
Neutral varga	it will get 10 marks
Enemy's varga	it will get 7 marks
Great enemy's varga	it will get 5 marks

5. The following are the fixed digits for vargas for the calculation of Vinshopaka strength as given by Maharshi Parashar:

Rasi	6
Hora	2
Drekkan	4

Navansha	5
Dwadsansha	2
Trinsansha	1

These digits are incidentally indicative of the importance of various divisional charts. After the Rasi it is the navansha which is the most important, and thereafter it is the drekkan.

6. To calculate the Vinshopaka strength of a planet in a varga, we multiply the marks got by the planet due to its location in that varga with the respective fixed digit and divide it by 20. This can be expressed in the form of a formula as below:

Vinshopaka strength in a varga=F * M/20,

where F is the fixed digit given above and M are the marks obtained by the planet due to its location in that varga.

For illustration, let us calculate the Vinshopaka strength of a planet in Rasi and Dwadsansha. Let us presume that the planet is in its own varga in Rasi and in a neutral varga in the Dwadsansha. It therefore gets 20 marks in Rasi and 10 in Dwadsansha. The fixed digit for Rasi is 6 and for Dwadsansha it is 2.

Therefore, the Vinshopaka strength for Rasi varga=6 * 20/20=6.

The Vinshopaka strength for Dwadsansha varga=2 * 10/20=1. The Vinshopaka strength for each varga for a planet should be worked out in the above manner. The sum of six such Vinshopaka strengths (for six vargas) will be the resultant Vinshopaka strength of the planet. These resultant strengths should be worked out for each of the seven planets from the Sun to Saturn. Based on the permanent relationship (given in the Chapter on Lunar Nodes separately under Rahu and Ketu) that the Nodes have with the other seven planets, resultant Vinshopaka strength can be worked out for the two Nodes also.

7. (i) A planet getting at least 10 points in the resultant Vinshopaka strength will be inclined to do good. The planet will be more and more disposed to do good as the strength progresses from 10 points to the maximum 20.

If the planet gets less than 10 points in the resultant Vinshopaka strength, it will be inclined to cause harm. If the strength is less than 5, the planet will, by nature, be malignant.

(ii) For more accuracy, the strength of a planet calculated mathematically according to paragraph 14 of Chapter Two should be taken alongwith its resultant Vinshopaka strength. This can be done in the following manner:

Let the resultant Vinshopaka strength of a planet be 11. 4 out of 20.

Let the strength of the planet as calculated under paragraph 14 of Chapter Two be 71 % .

In terms of percentage the resultant Vinshopaka strength will be 11. 4 * 100/20=57 % .

The net strength of the planet will therefore be (57+71)/2=64 %. This net strength will reflect the nature and the ability of the planet to give results fairly accurately. The stronger the planet, the more inclined and capable will it be to give favourable results, or desist from giving adverse results. We are already aware of the fact that a powerful and beneficial planet will confer beneficial results and a weak malefic planet will cause trouble. It is also well known that a weak beneficial planet will not be capable of conferring good results, and a powerful malefic planet will desist from giving adverse results.

8. Another point that has to be borne in mind when assessing the nature of a planet is its debilitation. The debilitation of a planet should be examined carefully and it should be seen whether the debilitation has been annulled in the chart. This is called Neecha-Bhanga. The debilitation of a planet gets annulled in the following manner:

(i) The dispositor of the debilitated planet is powerfully placed in an angular house from the ascendant or the Moon; or,

(ii) The owner of the sign in which this debilitated planet would have got exalted is powerfully placed in an angular house from the ascendant or the Moon; or

(iii) The owner of the navansha sign in which the debilitated planet is placed is in an angular or triangular house in the birth chart that has a movable sign in the ascendant;or,

(iv) The owner of the navansha sign in which the debilitated planet is placed is in an angular or triangular house in the birth chart that has a common or fixed sign in the ascendant, and the ascendant in the navansha chart has a movable sign; or,

(v) The debilitated planet is retrograde but not combust.

When there is an annulment of debilitation the debilitated planet gains in strength and becomes inclined to confer material benefits and status in its period on the native.

9. We shall now take the calculation of Vimshottari dasa time frame. This will tell us as to when the influence of a planet will operate. Each constellation is owned by a planet. Maharshi Parashar has assigned a certain number of years to each planet and also the order in which the major-periods will follow each other. A constellation extends over 13 degrees 20 minutes which represents the full number of years assigned to the owner of the constellation. According to the situation of the Moon within the constellation the balance of the major-period of the owner of the constellation can be worked out. Let us take an illustration. Suppose the Moon is at 8 deg in Libra at the time of birth. It shall be in a constellation owned by Rahu which begins at 6 deg 40 minutes in Libra and ends at 20 deg in the sign. Rahu has 18 * 360 = 6480 days in its full major-period. Thus 13 degrees 20 min are equal to 6480 days. Since the Moon has already travelled over 1 deg 20 min in the constellation, the balance of the major-period of Rahu will be 5832 days or 16 years (of 360 days) 2 months (of 30 days each) and 12 days.

10. We take the year to consist of 12 months of 30 days each in the calculations under the Vimshottari dasa system. Thus the year in the calculation of this time frame has 360 days. When we say that the major-period of the Sun extends over 6 years, we mean that the major-period runs for 6 * 360 =2160 days. We know that average current calendar year has approximately 365. 25 days, three consecutive years having 365 days and the fourth year having 366 days. The major-period of the Sun therefore will at least have one leap year and the balance five normal years. If we count the number of days in six years of the major-period of Sun, it will at least have 365 * 5 + 366 = 2191 days. We notice that there will be an error of 31 days if we take the length of the

calendar year to be the same as the year in the Vimshottari dasa time frame. Since the major-period of the Sun is the shortest, the error will be larger when we deal with the major-periods of other planets. For example, error in built in the major-period of Mars or Ketu will be at least 36 days. If we consider the major-period of Venus the error will be to the tune of at least 105 days. Thus without converting the 360 day year into calendar year, inspite of our best efforts mistake in the fixation of time of happening of an event through the use of Vimshottari dasa system is bound to take place.

11. Reason therefore directs that duration of each major-period or sub-period in the Vimshottari dasa system ought to be adapted to the current calendar and applied only then for fixing the time for an event.

12. We have seen that problem arises when we try to super-impose the definition of an year in the Vimshottari dasa system over the the definition of an year of the current calendar. This can easily be handled. If average calendar year is taken to be of 365. 25 days the major-period of the Sun will have 2160/365. 25 years or 5 calendar years and 334 days. Since number of days in a month in the current calendar varies from 28 to 31, the use of months in calculation of Vimshottari time frame is best avoided.

13. Once lengths of major, sub and inter-periods are adapted to the calendar, they can directly be applied to the calendar in timing of events. To save the reader unnecessary mathematical exercise we have altered the lengths of the major, sub and inter-periods of planets on above lines and these have been appended to the book in the form of ready to use tables. Tables to facilitate counting of days have also been appended.

14. The frame of time fixed according to rules laid down above will be found to be appropriate and in consonance with general trends in the life of the native, and it shall be obvious to him that the planets were yielding the expected results.

15. the tables for major, sub and inter-periods need some clarification.
    (1) Each table is to be read vertically.
    (2) The length of the major-period is given at the top. The length of the year is 365. 25 days.

(3) The sub-periods in the major-period of a planet are recorded from left to right vertically in the order in which they occur. The length of each sub-period is given at the bottom of the column relating to the sub-period.

(4) The inter-periods of planets in each sub-period in the major-period of a planet are given horizontally. The first inter-peiod in a sub-period is marked with an asterisk. Thereafter inter-periods will occur downwards in the column till the bottom most entry is reached, and then they start from the top till the last entry before the asterisk is reached, with which the sub-period will come to an end.

(5) The year is represented by 'y'.

16. The tables for counting the number of days are simple to use. The entries should be read horizontally. The entries are relevant for the first of each month.

Major period of Sun-total duration 5 years 334 days.								
	Sun	**Moon**	**Mars**	**Rahu**	**Jup**	**Sat**	**Merc**	**Ket**	**Ven**
Sun	6*.	9	6	16	14	17	15	6	18
Mo	9	15*	11	27	24	29	26	11	30
Mar	6	10	7*	19	17	20	18	7	21
Rah	16	27	19	49*	43	51	46	19	54
Jup	15	24	17	43	38*	46	41	17	48
Sat	17	29	20	51	46	54*	48	20	57
Merc	15	26	18	46	41	48	43*	18	51
Ket	6	10	7	19	17	20	18	7*	21
Ven	18	30	21	54	48	57	51	21	60*
Sub-per.	0 y 108 days	0 y 180 days	0 y 126 days	0 y 324 days	0 y 288 days	0 y 342 days	0 y 306 days	0 y 126 days	0 y 360 days

An year is equal to 365.25 days.

Table 415

	Moon	Mars	Rahu	Jup	Sat	Merc	Ket	Ven	Sun
Major period of the Moon-total duration 9 years 313 days.									
Mo	25*	18	45	40	48	42	18	50	15
Mar	17	12*	31	28	33	30	12	35	10
Rah	45	31	81*	72	86	76	31	90	27
Jup	40	28	72	64*	76	68	28	80	24
Sat	48	33	86	76	90*	81	33	95	29
Mer	43	30	77	68	81	72*	30	85	26
Ket	17	12	31	28	33	30	12*	35	10
Ven	50	35	90	80	95	85	35	100*	30
Sun	15	11	27	24	28	26	11	30	9*
Sub-per.	0 y 300 days	0 y 210 days	1 y 174 days	1 y 115 days	1 y 205 days	1 y 145 days	0 y 210 days	1 y 235 days	0 y 180 days

An year is equal to 365.25 days.

Major period of the Mars-total duration 6 years 328 days.								
	Mars	**Rahu**	**Jup**	**Sat**	**Merc**	**Ket**	**Ven**	**Sun**	**Moon**
Mar	8*	22	20	23	21	8	25	7	12
Rah	22	57*	50	60	53	22	63	19	32
Jup	20	50	45*	53	48	20	56	17	28
Sat	23	60	53	63*	56	23	66	20	33
Merc	21	53	47	57	51*	21	59	18	30
Ket	8	22	20	23	21	8*	25	7	12
Ven	25	63	56	67	59	25	70*	21	35
Sun	8	19	17	20	18	7	21	6*	11
Mo	12	32	28	33	30	12	35	11	17*
Sub-per.	0 y 147 days	1 y 13 days	0 y 336 days	1 y 34 days	0 y 357 days	0 y 147 days	1 y 54 days	0 y 126 days	0 y 210 days

An year is equal to 365.25 days.

Table 417

	Rahu	Jup	Sat	Merc	Ket	Ven	Sun	Moon	Mar
Major period of the Rahu-total duration 17 years 271 days.									
Rah	146*	130	154	138	57	162	49	81	57
Jup	130	115*	137	122	50	144	43	72	50
Sat	154	137	162*	145	60	171	51	86	60
Merc	138	123	145	130*	54	153	46	77	54
Ket	56	50	60	54	22*	63	19	31	22
Ven	162	144	171	153	63	180*	54	90	63
Sun	49	43	51	46	19	54	16*	27	19
Mo	81	72	86	77	31	90	27	45*	31
Mar	56	50	60	54	22	63	19	31	22*
Sub-per.	2 y 241 days	2 y 134 days	2 y 295 days	2 y 188 days	1 y 13 days	2 y 349 days	0 y 324 days	1 y 175 days	1 y 13 days

An year is equal to 365.25 days.

Major period of Jupiter-total duration 15 years 281 days.								
	Jup	**Sat**	**Merc**	**Ket**	**Ven**	**Sun**	**Moon**	**Mars**	**Rah**
Jup	102*	122	109	45	128	38	64	45	115
Sat	122	144*	129	53	152	46	76	53	137
Mer	109	129	116*	47	136	41	68	47	122
Ket	45	53	48	20*	56	17	28	20	51
Ven	129	152	136	56	160*	48	80	56	144
Sun	38	46	41	17	48	14*	24	17	43
Mo	64	76	68	28	80	24	40*	28	72
Mar	45	53	48	20	56	17	28	20*	51
Rah	115	137	122	50	144	43	·72	50	129*
Sub-per.	2 y 38 days	2 y 181 days	2 y 86 days	0 y 336 days	2 y 229 days	0 y 288 days	1 y 115 days	0 y 336 days	2 y 133 days

An year is equal to 365.25 days.

Table 419

Major period of Saturn-total duration 18 years 265 days.									
	Sat	Merc	Ket	Ven	Sun	Moon	Mars	Rah	Jup
Sat	172*	153	63	181	54	90	63	162	144
Mer	153	137*	57	162	48	81	57	145	129
Ket	63	57	23*	66	20	33	23	60	53
Ven	181	162	67	190*	57	95	67	171	152
Sun	54	49	20	57	17*	29	20	51	46
Moon	90	81	33	95	29	48*	33	86	76
Mars	63	57	23	66	20	33	23*	60	53
Rah	163	145	60	171	51	85	60	154*	137
Jup	144	129	53	152	46	76	53	137	122*
Sub-per.	2 y 352 days	2 y 239 days	1 y 34 days	3 y 44 days	0 y 342 days	1 y 205 days	1 y 34 days	2 y 295 days	2 y 181 days

An year is equal to 365.25 days.

	Merc	Ket	Ven	Sun	Mo	Mars	Rah	Jup	Sat
Merc	123*	50	145	43	72	50	130	116	137
Ket	51	21*	59	18	30	21	54	48	57
Ven	145	59	170*	51	85	59	153	136	162
Sun	43	18	51	15*	26	18	46	41	49
Mo	72	30	85	26	42*	30	77	68	80
Mars	51	21	59	18	30	21*	54	48	57
Rah	130	53	153	46	76	53	138*	122	145
Jup	116	48	136	41	68	48	122	109*	129
Sat	137	57	162	48	81	57	144	129	153*
Sub-per.	2 y 137 days	0 y 357 days	2 y 289 days	0 y 306 days	1 y 145 days	0 y 357 days	2 y 187 days	2 y 86 days	2 y 238 days

Major period of Mercury-total duration 16 years 276 days.

An year is equal to 365.25 days.

Table   421

Major period of Ketu-total duration 6 years 328 days.								
	Ket	Ven	Sun	Moon	Mars	Rah	Jup	Sat	Merc
Ket	9*	24	7	12	9	22	20	23	21
Ven	24	70*	21	35	24	63	56	67	60
Sun	7	21	6*	11	7	19	17	20	18
Moon	12	35	11	17*	12	31	28	33	30
Mars	9	24	7	12	9*	22	20	23	21
Rah	22	63	19	32	22	57*	50	60	53
Jup	20	56	17	28	20	50	45*	53	48
Sat	23	67	20	33	23	60	53	63*	56
Merc	21	59	18	30	21	54	47	57	50*
Sub-per.	0 y 147 days	1 y 54 days	0 y 126 days	0 y 210 days	0 y 147 days	1 y 13 days	0 y 336 days	1 y 34 days	0 y 357 days

An year is equal to 365.25 days.

Major period of Venus-total duration 19 years 260 days.								
	Ven	**Sun**	**Mo**	**Mars**	**Rah**	**Jup**	**Sat**	**Merc**	**Ketu**
Ven	200*	60	100	70	180	160	190	170	70
Sun	60	18*	30	21	54	48	57	51	21
Mo	100	30	50*	35	90	80	95	85	35
Mars	70	21	35	25*	63	56	66	60	25
Rah	180	54	90	63	162*	144	171	153	63
Jup	160	48	80	56	144	128*	152	136	56
Sat	190	57	95	66	171	152	180*	161	66
Merc	170	51	85	59	153	136	161	144*	59
Ketu	70	21	35	25	63	56	66	60	25*
Sub-per.	3 y 104 days	0 y 360 days	1 y 235 days	1 y 55 days	2 y 349 days	2 y 230 days	3 y 44 days	2 y 289 days	1 y 55 days

An year is equal to 365.25 days.

Table 423

Table for counting number of days when the year is a normal year and is followed by another normal year.

	Jan	Feb	Mar	Apr	May	Jun	Jul	Aug	Sep	Oct	Nov	Dec
Jan	0	31	59	90	120	151	181	212	243	273	304	334
Feb	334	365	28	59	89	120	150	181	212	242	273	303
Mar	306	337	365	31	61	92	122	153	184	214	245	275
Apr	275	306	334	365	30	61	91	122	153	183	214	244
May	245	276	304	335	365	31	61	92	123	153	184	214
Jun	214	245	273	304	334	365	30	61	92	122	153	183
Jul	184	215	243	274	304	335	365	31	62	92	123	153
Aug	153	184	212	243	273	304	334	365	31	61	92	122
Sep	122	153	181	212	242	273	303	334	365	30	61	91
Oct	92	123	151	182	212	243	273	304	335	365	31	61
Nov	61	92	120	151	181	212	242	273	304	334	365	30
Dec	31	62	90	121	151	182	212	243	274	304	335	365

The table is to be read horizontally for each month. The entry under each month is for the beginning of the month. Thus on the first of January the number of days passed in January is zero. On the first of February the number of days passed from the first of January is 31. On the first of October the number of days passed from the first of January is 273. On the first of September, the number of days passed from the first of previous January shall be 122. On the first of September, the number of days passed from the first of previous August shall be 334.

Care should be taken when the preceding or succeeding year is a leap year. For such calculations see tables ahead.

Table for counting number of days when the year is a normal year but is followed by a leap year.

	Jan	Feb	Mar	Apr	May	Jun	Jul	Aug	Sep	Oct	Nov	Dec
Jan	0	31	59	90	120	151	181	212	243	273	304	334
Feb	334	365	28	59	89	120	150	181	212	242	273	303
Mar	306	337	366	31	61	92	122	153	184	214	245	275
Apr	275	306	335	366	30	61	91	122	153	183	214	244
May	245	276	305	336	366	31	61	92	123	153	184	214
Jun	214	245	274	305	335	366	30	61	92	122	153	183
Jul	184	215	244	275	305	336	366	31	62	92	123	153
Aug	153	184	213	244	274	305	335	366	31	61	92	122
Sep	122	153	182	213	243	274	304	335	366	30	61	91
Oct	92	123	152	183	213	244	274	305	336	366	31	61
Nov	61	92	121	152	182	213	243	274	305	335	366	30
Dec	31	62	91	122	152	183	213	244	275	305	336	366

To be read as instructed in the box at page No. 424

Table 425

Table for counting number of days when the year is a leap year and is followed by a normal year.

	Jan	Feb	Mar	Apr	May	Jun	Jul	Aug	Sep	Oct	Nov	Dec
Jan	0	31	59	90	120	151	181	212	243	273	304	334
Feb	335	366	29	60	90	121	151	182	213	243	274	304
Mar	306	337	365	31	61	92	122	153	184	214	245	275
Apr	275	306	334	365	30	61	91	122	153	183	214	244
May	245	276	304	335	365	31	61	92	123	153	184	214
Jun	214	245	273	304	334	365	30	61	92	122	153	183
Jul	184	215	243	274	304	335	365	31	62	92	123	153
Aug	153	184	212	243	273	304	334	365	31	61	92	122
Sep	122	153	181	212	242	273	303	334	365	30	61	91
Oct	92	123	151	182	212	243	273	304	335	365	31	61
Nov	61	92	120	151	181	212	242	273	304	334	365	30
Dec	31	62	90	121	151	182	212	243	274	304	335	365

To be read as instructed in the box at page No. 425

Tables for divisions of signs.

Table I

Hora or 1/2 division of a sign		
Sign	15	30
1	5	4
2	4	5
3	5	4
4	4	5
5	5	4
6	4	5
7	5	4
8	4	5
9	5	4
10	4	5
11	5	4
12	4	5

The digits represent signs. The first column has signs. The entry in each column thereafter in the second row shows the extent of the division. Thus, the first division extends from zero to 15 degrees. Each row thereafter deals with a sign serially. It shows the signs the division has in each sign. Thus, the second division of Leo has Cancer as shown in column three of row seven.

Table 427

Table II

Drekkan or 1/3 division of a sign			
Sign	10	20	30
1	1	5	9
2	2	6	10
3	3	7	11
4	4	8	12
5	5	9	1
6	6	10	2
7	7	11	3
8	8	12	4
9	9	1	5
10	10	2	6
11	11	3	7
12	12	4	8

The digits represent signs. The first column has signs. The entry in each column thereafter in the second row shows the extent of the division. Thus, the first division extends from zero to 10 degrees. Each row thereafter deals with a sign serially. It shows the signs the division has in each sign. Thus, the second division of Leo has Sagittarius as shown in column three of row seven.

Table III

Sign	Navansha or 1/9 division of a sign								
	3/20	6/40	10	13/20	16/40	20	23/20	26/40	30
1	1	2	3	4	5	6	7	8	9
2	10	11	12	1	2	3	4	5	6
3	7	8	9	10	11	12	1	2	3
4	4	5	6	7	8	9	10	11	12
5	1	2	3	4	5	6	7	8	9
6	10	11	12	1	2	3	4	5	6
7	7	8	9	10	11	12	1	2	3
8	4	5	6	7	8	9	10	11	12
9	1	2	3	4	5	6	7	8	9
10	10	11	12	1	2	3	4	5	6
11	7	8	9	10	11	12	1	2	3
12	4	5	6	7	8	9	10	11	12

The digits represent signs. The first column has signs. The entry in each column thereafter in the second row shows the extent of the division. Thus, the first division extends from zero to 3 degrees 20 minutes. Each row thereafter deals with a sign serially. It shows the signs the division has in each sign. Thus, the second division of Leo has Taurus as shown in column three of row seven.

Table   429

Table IV

Dwadasamsa or 1/12 division of a sign

Sign	2/30	5	7/30	10	12/30	15	17/30	20	22/30	25	27/30	30
1	1	2	3	4	5	6	7	8	9	10	11	12
2	2	3	4	5	6	7	8	9	10	11	12	1
3	3	4	5	6	7	8	9	10	11	12	1	2
4	4	5	6	7	8	9	10	11	12	1	2	3
5	5	6	7	8	9	10	11	12	1	2	3	4
6	6	7	8	9	10	11	12	1	2	3	4	5
7	7	8	9	10	11	12	1	2	3	4	5	6
8	8	9	10	11	12	1	2	3	4	5	6	7
9	9	10	11	12	1	2	3	4	5	6	7	8
10	10	11	12	1	2	3	4	5	6	7	8	9
11	11	12	1	2	3	4	5	6	7	8	9	10
12	12	1	2	3	4	5	6	7	8	9	10	11

The digits represent signs. The first column has signs. The entry in each column thereafter in the second row shows the extent of the division. Thus, the first division extends from zero to 2 degrees 30 minutes. Each row thereafter deals with a sign serially. It shows the signs the division has in each sign. Thus, the second division of Leo has Virgo as shown in column three of row seven.

Table V

Part One: For odd signs
Trinsamsa or 1/30 division of a sign

Sign	5°	10°	18°	25°	30°
1	1	11	9	3	7
3	1	11	9	3	7
5	1	11	9	3	7
7	1	11	9	3	7
9	1	11	9	3	7
11	1	11	9	3	7

Part Two: For even signs
Trinsamsa or 1/30 division of a sign

Sign	5°	12°	20°	25°	30°
2	2	6	12	10	8
4	2	6	12	10	8
6	2	6	12	10	8
8	2	6	12	10	8
10	2	6	12	10	8
12	2	6	12	10	8

INDEX